The Invincible Company

Published by John Wiley & Sons, Inc., Hoboken, New Jersey.
Published simultaneously in Canada.

ISBN 978-1119523963 (Paperback)
ISBN 978-1119523987 (ePDF)
ISBN 978-1119523932 (ePub)

Cover image: Alan Smith
Cover design: Alan Smith

Printed in the United States of America
V10016957_022820

You're holding a guide to the world's best business models.
Use it to inspire your own portfolio of new ideas and reinventions.
Design a culture of innovation and transformation to become...

The Invincible Company

strategyzer.com/invincible

Written by
Alex Osterwalder
Yves Pigneur
Fred Etiemble
Alan Smith

Designed by
Chris White
Trish Papadakos

WILEY

The Invincible Company

An organization that constantly reinvents itself before it becomes obsolete. The Invincible Company explores the future, while excelling at exploiting the present. It cultivates an innovation and execution culture that lives in harmony under the same roof. It competes on superior business models and transcends traditional industry boundaries.

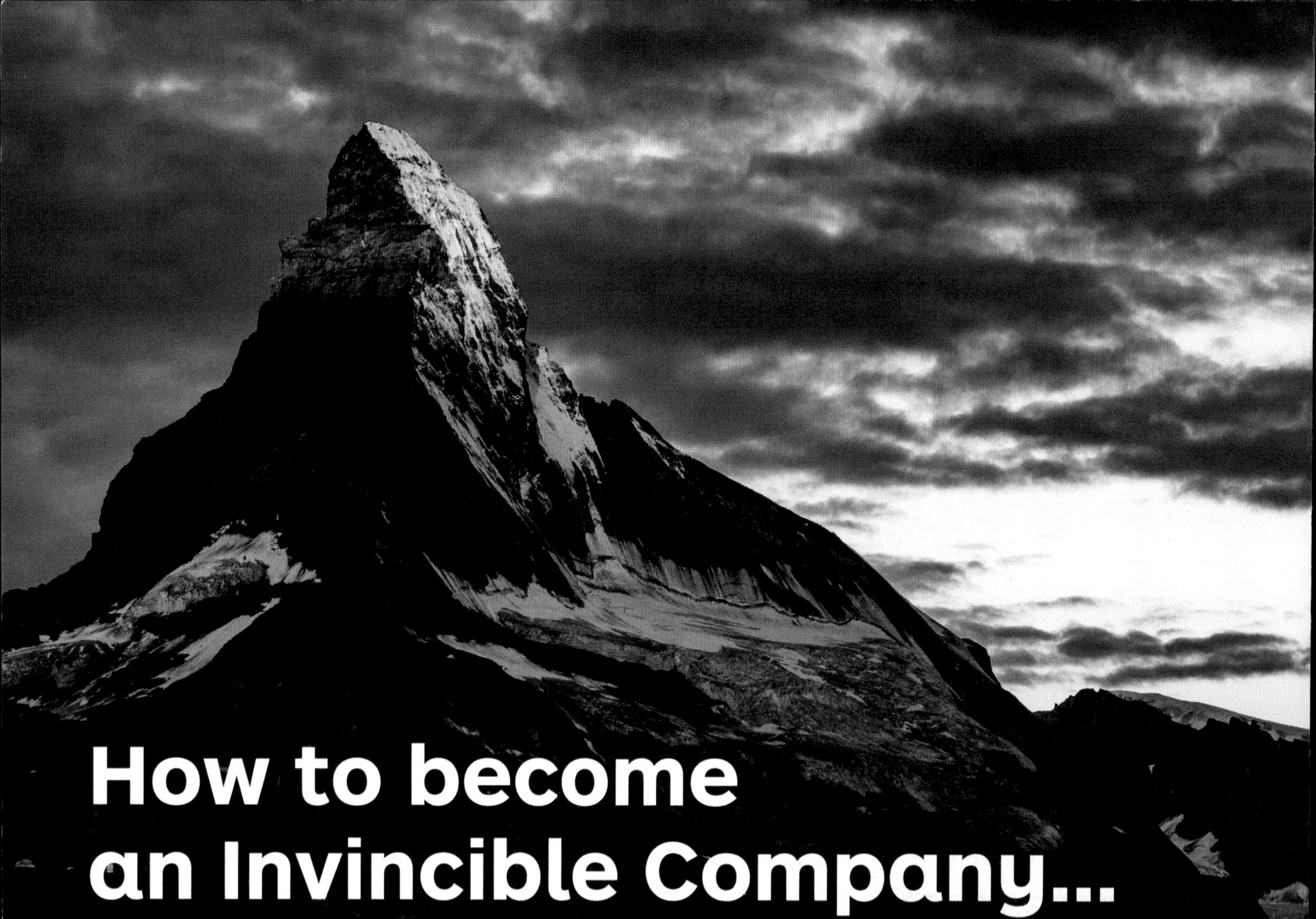
How to become
an Invincible Company...

Constantly Reinvent Yourself

To stay ahead of everybody else and beat disruption you need to constantly reinvent yourself. Business Models expire faster than ever before and you don't want to become obsolete alongside their decline. Competition increasingly comes from unexpected places like insurgent startups in addition to traditional incumbent rivals. Invincible Companies constantly reinvent who they are and where and how they compete in order to stay relevant and ahead.

Discover how to manage and improve what you have and simultaneously explore the future with business model portfolios.

Design, implement, and manage an innovation culture to constantly feed your innovation funnel and stay relevant.

Compete on Superior Business Models

It is increasingly a rat race to compete on new products, services, price, and technologies alone. Leave competitors behind and maximize market opportunities, new customer needs, and emerging technologies by embedding them in superior business models. Design, test, and build superior business models that disrupt others and are hard to disrupt.

Discover how to design, test, and manage superior business models.

Apply business model patterns to make the best out of market opportunities, new technologies, and product and service innovations.

Transcend Industry Boundaries

The most successful organizations aren't confined by industry boundaries or industry forces. In fact, they often crush industry boundaries and disrupt others. Their business model or portfolio of businesses is not the result of the area they work in; it comes from an organization that constantly explores new ways to create value around market opportunities.

Discover how to create and manage an ambidextrous organization that is capable of improving your core business and exploring completely new opportunities beyond traditional industry boundaries.

Learn how the Chinese company Ping An evolved from a traditional banking and insurance conglomerate to a technology group that competes in five distinct arenas and became one of the world's largest companies.

...and create more value

For Society

Small and large companies that constantly reinvent themselves have an enormously positive impact on society. They provide economic growth and potentially game-changing innovations. The best of them put environmental and societal impacts at the center of their endeavors to change the world for the better. On the other hand, the decline or death of companies can be devastating for cities and entire regions that will suffer from economic decline.

For Customers

Companies that constantly innovate and explore new business models, constantly create new and better value propositions at more attractive prices. Some innovations may be banal and just lead to more consumption. Yet, many will create substantial value for customers in the form of convenience, entertainment, well-being, and fulfillment.

For the Team

Invincible Companies thrive over centuries and provide long-term job security, while others that fail to reinvent themselves have to let go of thousands of employees. Invincible Companies provide a home for execution and innovation talent alike and they feature world-class organizational structures and processes that are fit for the challenges of the 21st century.

For Owners

Owners of Invincible Companies benefit from long-term growth, reduced disruption risk, and the attraction of world class execution and innovation talent. Invincible Companies thrive over the long term, because they harvest the fruits of managing the present, while already sowing the seeds for tomorrow's business. Their ability to exploit and explore simultaneously substantially reduces the risk of disruption and obsolescence and attracts the best talent.

From Business Model Generation to Invincible Company

The Invincible Company is the fourth in the series of Strategyzer books. It complements the previous books and addresses a number of jobs-to-be-done for innovation teams, entrepreneurs, and senior leaders who manage entire organizations. The new content is based on what we've learned from working with leading organizations around the world and from studying the world's few Invincible Companies.

strategyzer.com/books

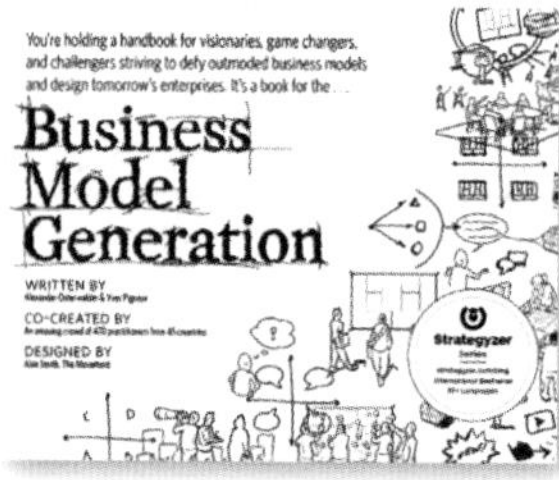

	Job-to-be-Done	Key Question	Key Tool and Process	Books
Innovate and Design *Invent and Improve*	Map your business, idea, or innovation	How do you create sustainable profits and value for your organization?	Business Model Canvas (BMC) or Mission Model Canvas (MMC)	*Business Model Generation* (2009)
	Map your product and service	How do you create value for your customers?	Value Proposition Canvas (VPC)	*Value Proposition Design* (2014)
	Maximize opportunities and compete on business models	How do I maximize opportunities and improve my business with the best business model design?	Business Model Patterns (invent patterns and shift patterns)	*The Invincible Company* (2020), *Business Model Generation* (2009)
Test and De-Risk	Test and de-risk your idea	How do you reduce the risk of pursuing a business idea that won't work?	Customer Development (Steve Blank) and Agile Engineering/ Lean Startup (Eric Ries), Test Card, Learning Card	*The Startup Owner's Manual* (Steve Blank, 2012), *Lean Startup* (Eric Ries, 2011), *Value Proposition Design* (2014)
	Pick the right experiments to test your idea	What are the most appropriate experiments to test and de-risk your ideas?	Experiment Library	*Testing Business Ideas* (2019)
	Measure the reduction of risk and uncertainty	Am I making progress from idea to realistic business model?	Strategyzer Innovation Metrics	*The Invincible Company* (2020)
Design Innovation Culture and Manage Portfolio	Stay ahead of competition and become invincible	How do you prevent disruption and constantly reinvent yourself?	Portfolio Map, Portfolio Actions	*The Invincible Company* (2020)
	Create an (innovation) culture	How do you design, test, and manage an innovation culture?	Culture Map (CM), Innovation Culture Assessment	*The Invincible Company* (2020)
	Invest in the best ideas	Which ideas and teams should I invest in?	Strategyzer Growth Funnel (SGF), Innovation Project Scorecard (IPS)	*The Invincible Company* (2020)
	Align (innovation) teams	How do you pull through execution and keep teams aligned?	Team Alignment Map (TAM)	*The Team Alignment Map* (2020)

How to Read This Book

Senior Leader

Innovation Leader and Teams

Entrepreneurs

As a business leader you establish the conditions to keep your organization humming and growing. You need transparency to understand which parts of your business have further potential to grow, which parts need renovation, and which parts are at substantial risk of disruption. You need to understand which initiatives have the potential to define tomorrow's business. You aim to make sound investments in the future, while consciously managing risk.

Use the **PORTFOLIO MAP (p. 10)**, *to design, test, and* **MANAGE (p. 49)** *your business portfolio. Create GUIDANCE to lead your teams in the right direction and transparency for everybody to manage the present and invest in the future.*

Create the conditions for success to establish an **INNOVATION CULTURE (p. 306)**. *Complement your core execution culture with a world class innovation culture.*

Ask the right **QUESTIONS FOR LEADERS (p. 212)** *to help your teams explore new opportunities and compete on superior business models.*

As an innovation leader and team you help your organization de-risk ideas that keep it growing and improving. You put the tools, processes, and metrics in place that help manage innovation. You understand how to enhance innovation opportunities by embedding them in sound business models in order to disrupt entire arenas or renovate your company's declining business models.

Use the **PATTERN LIBRARY (p. 130)** *to enhance market opportunities, new technologies, and other innovations. Apply Business Model Patterns to design superior business models.*

Use the **PORTFOLIO MAP (p. 42)** *to create the transparency your senior leaders need to make sound investment decisions. Show where the opportunities are. Learn how to* **MANAGE (p. 49)** *your business portfolio.*

Help your senior leaders implement an **INNOVATION CULTURE (p. 296)**. *Understand the key enablers that foster innovation and blockers that prevent innovation.*

As an entrepreneur your only goal is to de-risk your idea and turn it into a real business. You understand that the hard part of entrepreneurship is to constantly test and adapt your idea based on input from the real world. You know that superior business models—rather than technology or product innovation alone—will allow you to disrupt entire industries and build a more sustainable business.

Use the **EXPLORE MAP (p. 18)** *to visualize which one of your ideas has the most potential and is least risky. Use* **TESTING and INNOVATION METRICS (p. 88)** *to measure your progress from idea to business.*

Use the **PATTERN LIBRARY (p. 130)** *to enhance market opportunities, new technologies, and other innovations. Apply Business Model Patterns to design superior business models.*

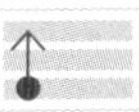

Establish the kind of **ENTREPRENEURIAL LEADERSHIP & TEAM (p. 310)** *that will help you succeed. Understand the key characteristics of winning teams.*

Contents

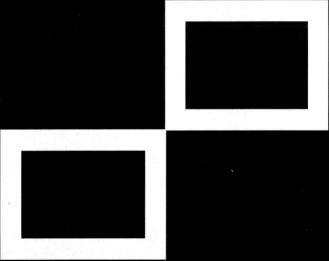

Business Model Portfolio

The collection of existing business models a company exploits and the new business models it explores in order to avoid disruption and ensure longevity.

Chasing Invincibility

No company is invincible. Those that come closest are the ones that constantly reinvent themselves in the face of disruption. These companies manage a portfolio of existing business models that they exploit and continuously improve. Simultaneously, they manage a portfolio of new business models that they explore to systematically produce new growth engines.

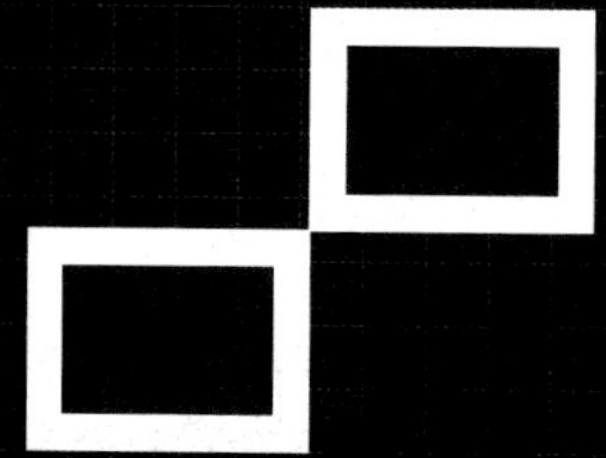

PORTFOLIO MAP

A strategic management tool to simultaneously visualize, analyze, and manage the business models you are improving and growing and the future business models you are searching for and testing.

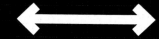

PORTFOLIO DICHOTOMY

We believe great business model portfolios are actually composed of two distinct portfolios with a completely different logic: the Exploit portfolio and the Explore portfolio. The former includes existing businesses, value propositions, products, and services that you are managing and growing. The latter includes all your innovation projects, new business models, new value propositions, new products, and services that you are testing.

Portfolio Management

Designing and maintaining a strong business model portfolio requires three main activities: visualize, analyze, manage.

VISUALIZE

The starting point for any good discussion, meeting, or workshop about your business model portfolio is a shared language to visualize it. You need a shared understanding of which business models you have and which ones you are exploring.

ANALYZE

A shared understanding of your business model portfolio allows you to identify if you are at risk of disruption and if you are doing enough against it. This includes analyzing which of your business models are most profitable, which ones are most at risk, and which ones you are exploring to ensure your future growth.

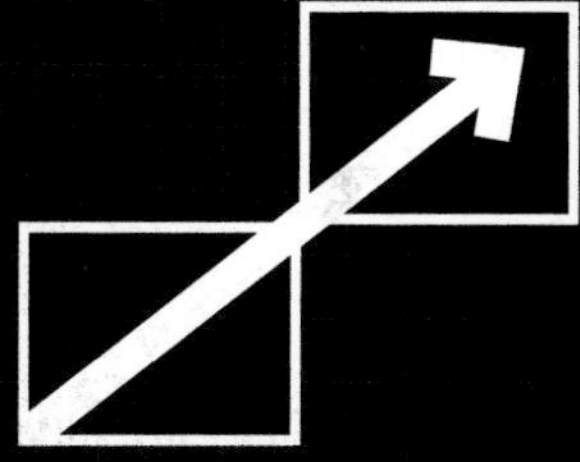

MANAGE

Good portfolio management includes taking action to design and maintain a balanced portfolio that protects you from disruption. This includes continuously growing and improving existing business models by shifting outdated ones to new business models and protecting those that are established. It also includes exploring completely new business models of which many will fail, but some will produce outsized returns and ensure your future.

Explore

Exploit

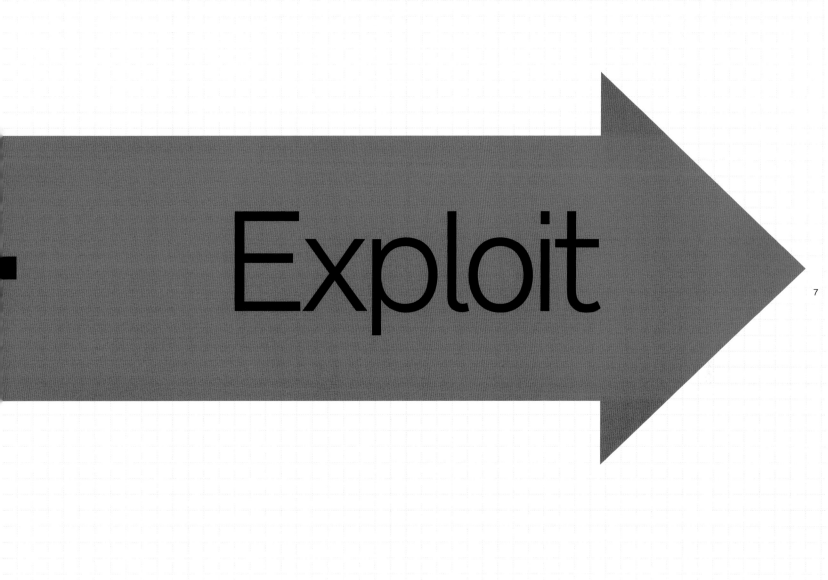

The Explore/ Exploit Continuum

Invincible Companies do *not* prioritize exploitation over exploration. They are world class at simultaneously managing the entire continuum from exploring new businesses to exploiting existing ones. They keep a culture of "day one," maintaining a start-up spirit, while managing thousands or even hundreds of thousands of people and multibillion-dollar businesses. Increasingly, this ability to manage exploration and exploitation is not just limited to large established companies. It is also a matter of survival for SMEs and start-ups with the shortening lifespan of business models across industries.

Explore	⟷	Exploit
Search and breakthrough	**Focus**	Efficiency and growth
High	**Uncertainty**	Low
Venture-capital style risk-taking, expecting few outsized winners	**Financial Philosophy**	Safe haven with steady returns and dividends
Iterative experimentation, embracing speed, failure, learning, and rapid adaptation	**Culture & Processes**	Linear execution, embracing planning, predictability, and minimal failure
Explorers who excel in uncertainty, are strong at pattern recognition, and can navigate between big picture and details	**People & Skills**	Managers who are strong at organizing and planning and can design efficient processes to deliver on time and budget

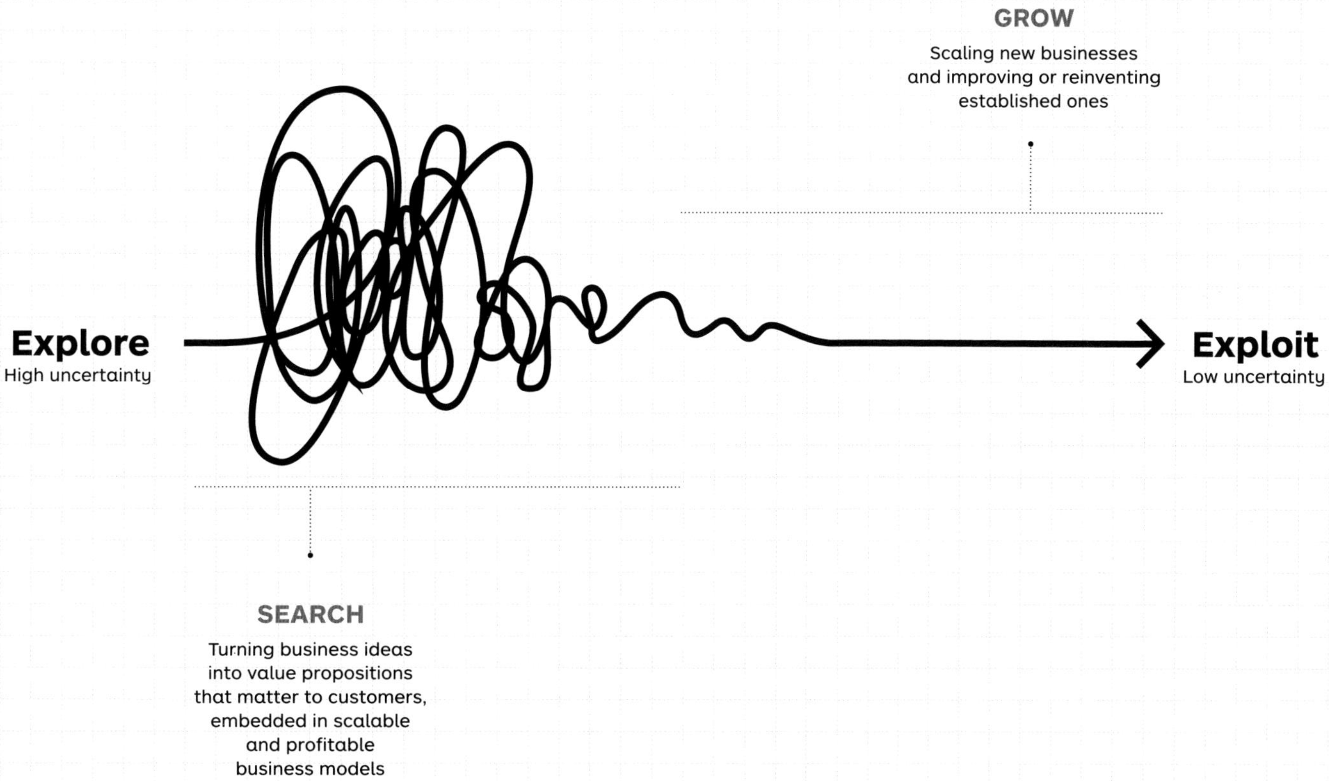

GROW

Scaling new businesses and improving or reinventing established ones

Explore
High uncertainty

Exploit
Low uncertainty

SEARCH

Turning business ideas into value propositions that matter to customers, embedded in scalable and profitable business models

DEFINITION

The Portfolio Map

A strategic management tool to simultaneously visualize, analyze, and manage the business models you are improving and growing and the future business models you are searching for and testing.

Explore Portfolio

Your portfolio of innovation projects, new business models, new value propositions, and new products and services, all mapped out in terms of **Expected Return** and **Innovation Risk**.

Exploit Portfolio

Your portfolio of existing businesses, value propositions, products, and services, all mapped out in terms of **Return** and **Death and Disruption Risk**.

Return
How lucrative a business area is for the company.

Expected Return
How lucrative a business idea could be for the company if it turned out to be successful.

Death & Disruption Risk
The risk that a business is going to die or get disrupted. Risk is high when a business is either emerging and still vulnerable, or when a business is under threat of disruption from technology, competition, regulatory changes, or other trends. Risk decreases with the moats protecting your business.

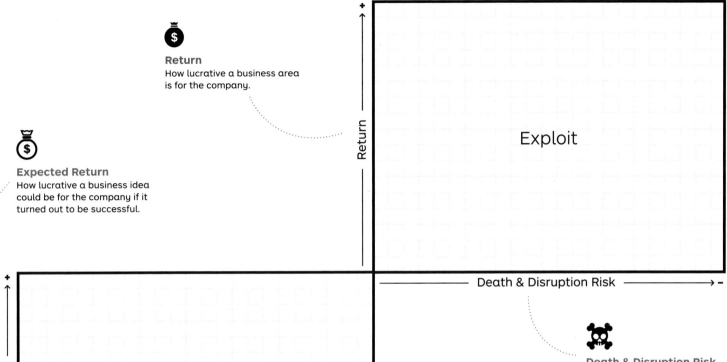

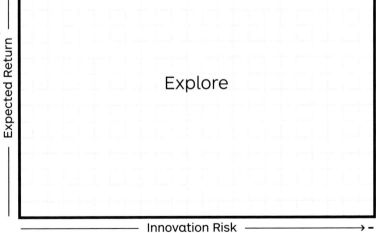

Innovation Risk
The risk that a (convincing) business idea is going to fail. Risk is high when there is little evidence beyond slides and spreadsheets to support the success chances of an idea. Risk decreases with the amount of evidence that supports the desirability, feasibility, viability, and adaptability of a business idea.

Portfolio Management

Explore: search

The Explore portfolio is all about the search for new ideas, value propositions, and business models to ensure the future of your company. Search involves maximizing expected returns and minimizing innovation risk. You improve the expected return by working on your business model design. You decrease the risk of working on an idea that might fail by testing and adapting it.

Exploit: grow

The Exploit portfolio is all about keeping your existing business models on a growth trajectory. This includes scaling emerging business models, renovating declining ones, and protecting successful ones. You ensure growth by improving returns and minimizing disruption risk. This is best achieved by shifting all of your business models from outdated ones to stronger ones.

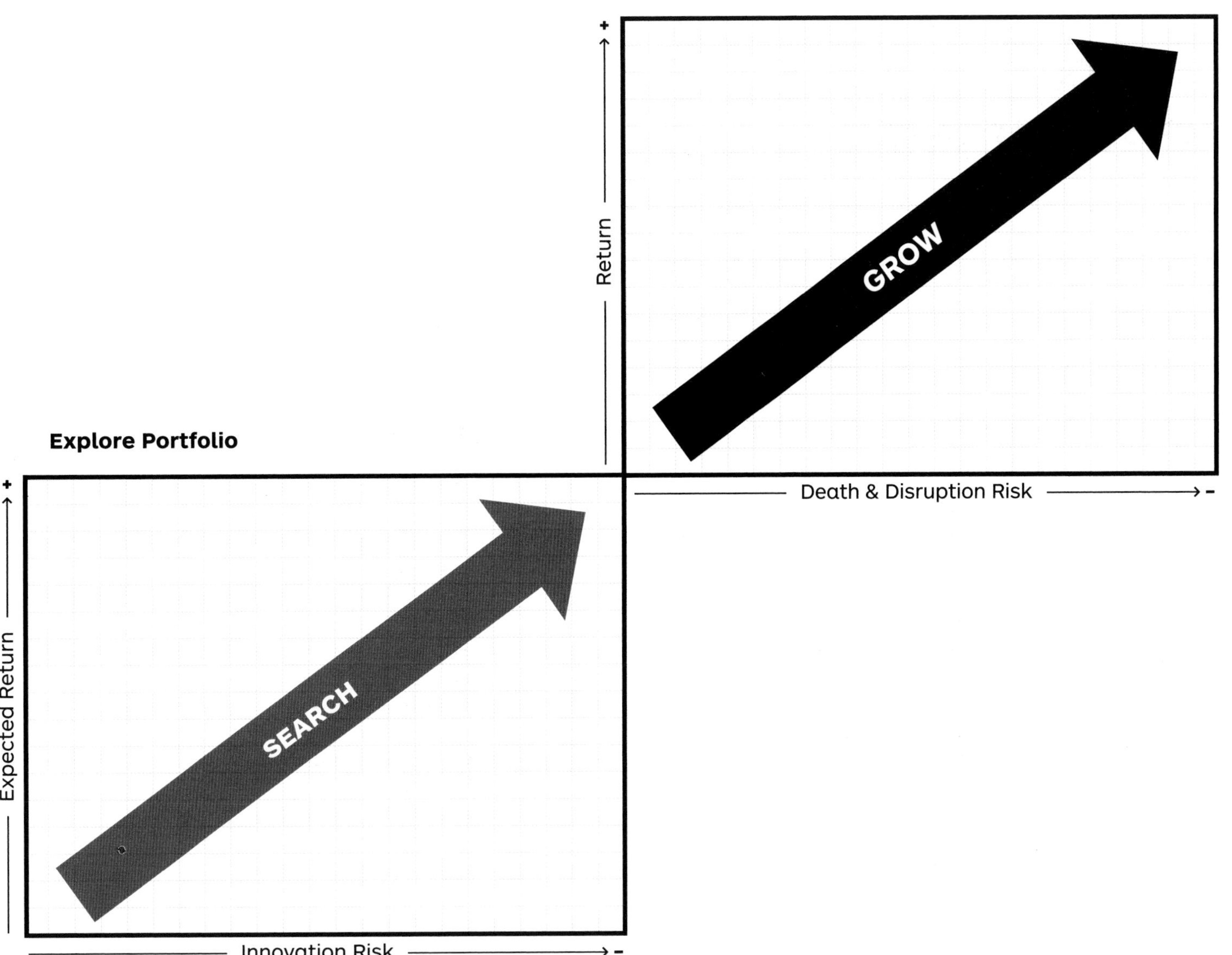
Exploit Portfolio
+
Return
GROW
Death & Disruption Risk
-
Explore Portfolio
+
Expected Return
SEARCH
Innovation Risk
-

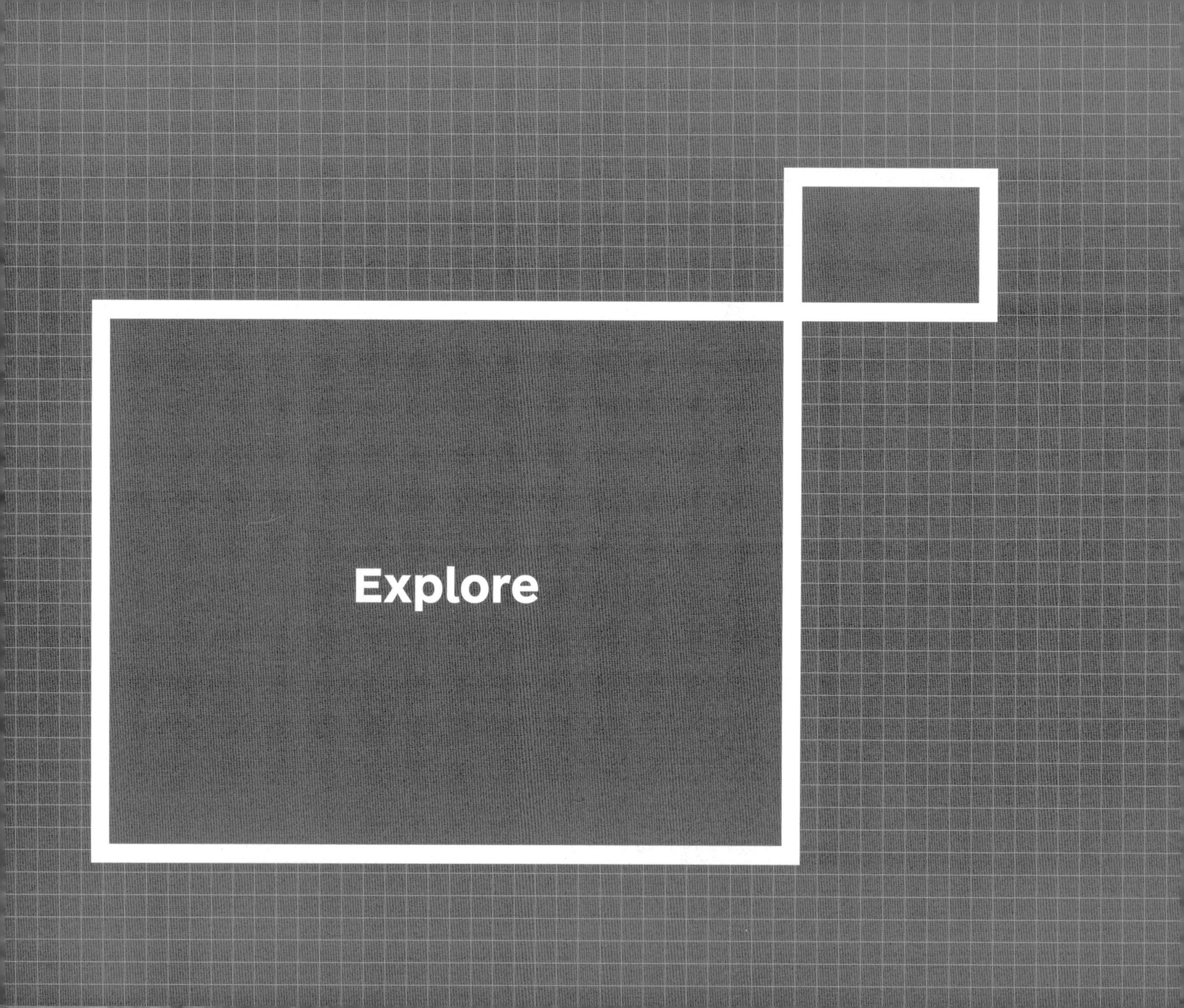
Explore

The Innovation Journey

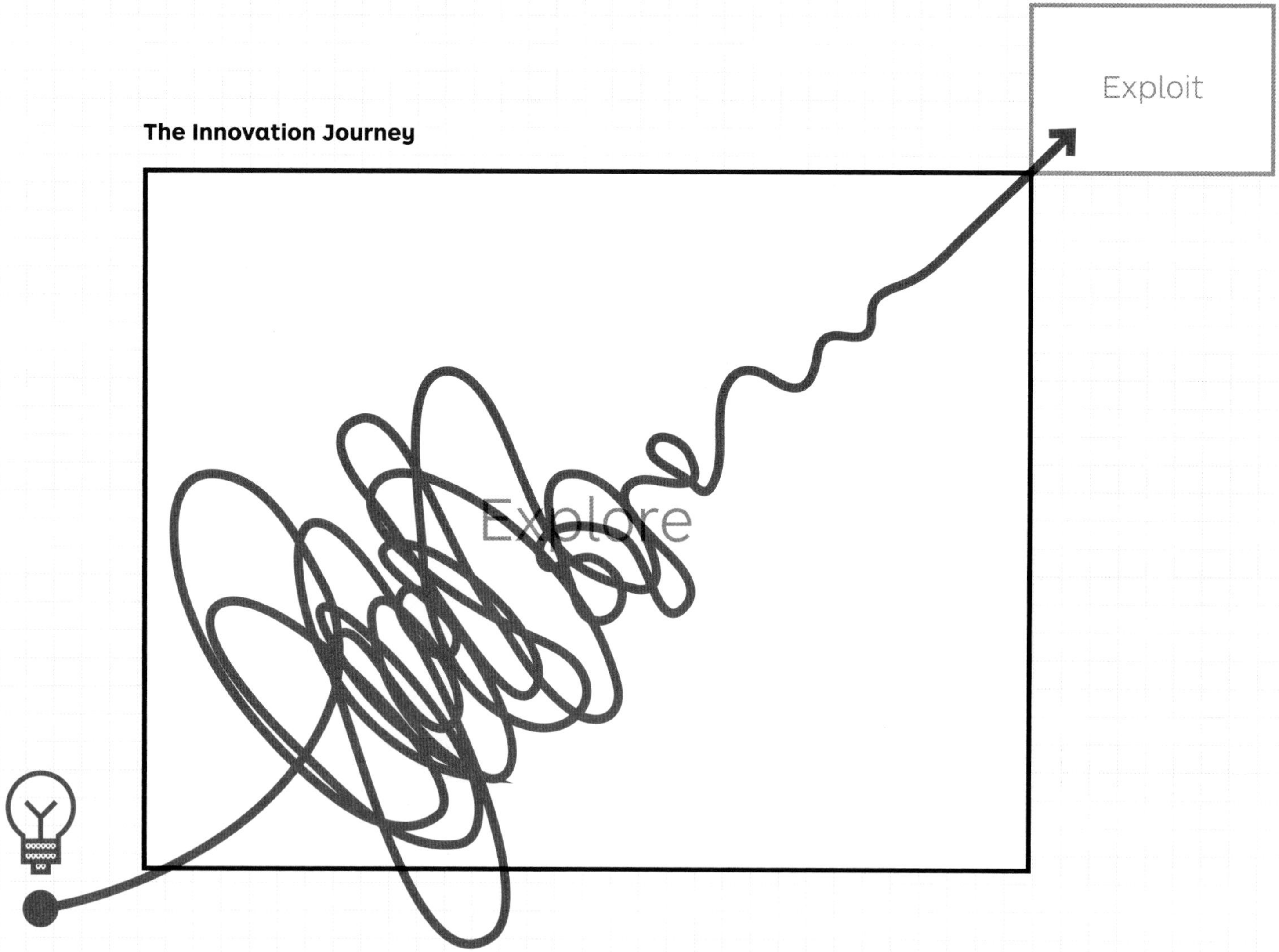

Explore

Exploit

Five Innovation Journey Myths

The journey of exploring new business ideas is not a linear one and differs radically from managing an existing business. We outline five myths regarding the innovation and entrepreneurship journey that may prevent you from turning an idea into a real business.

Myth #1: **The most important part of the innovation and entrepreneurship journey is to find and execute the perfect idea.**
Reality: **The innovation and entrepreneurship journey is about turning ideas into value propositions that customers care about and business models that can scale.**
Ideas are easy but they are just a starting point. The hard part is to constantly test and adapt ideas that look great in theory until you have sufficient evidence that they will work in reality. The exploration journey is all about adapting ideas iteratively until you find a value proposition that customers really want and a business model that can scale profitably.

Myth #2: **The evidence will show you a clear path forward when you systematically test ideas. The solution will magically emerge if you just test and adapt your idea often enough.**
Reality: **Innovation and entrepreneurship is about making informed decisions based on incomplete and potentially contradictory evidence. And sometimes killing an idea is the healthy thing to do.**
Turning an idea into a real business will always remain an art, even with the most rigorous testing process. It is rare that the evidence shows you an obvious path forward. Evidence allows you to detect patterns and make informed decisions that are less risky than opinion-based bets. Also, make sure you don't get stuck in testing or evidence analysis. Decide to persevere, pivot, or abandon an idea based on the evidence at hand.

Myth #3: **A small number of big bets will lead to a large return.**
Reality: **Exploration requires making a large number of small bets that you gradually reduce over time, based on evidence.**
In the early stages of innovation, it's impossible to know which ideas will work and which ones won't. Start out by investing small amounts of money and time in a large number of ideas and projects. Give ideas and projects that can provide real evidence follow-up investments. The best ideas and teams with the most promising returns will emerge if you do this systematically over several rounds.

Myth #4: **The skills required to explore a new business and to manage an existing one are pretty similar. Business is business.**
Reality: **Exploration and exploitation are two radically different professions that require a different skill set and different experience.**
Testing and adapting a business idea until it works requires a radically different skill set than managing a business. In innovation and entrepreneurship you deal with high uncertainty. You need to detect patterns in the data you gather from testing and transform that into something that can scale profitably. You get better at exploration the more experience you have, just like you get better at management over time.

Myth #5: **Innovation teams are renegades or pirates that are out to disrupt the old business. They need to operate in stealth mode to survive inside a company.**
Reality: **Innovators need to be seen as partners who are essential for the future of the company. Otherwise, any meaningful innovation is unlikely to emerge on a large scale.**
Innovation teams that are seen as renegades have a hard time accessing company resources like access to clients, brand, prototyping, and so on. They need to be seen as partners who have the mandate to create a company's future in order to operate successfully.

Exploit

Potential Steps in the Exploration Journey

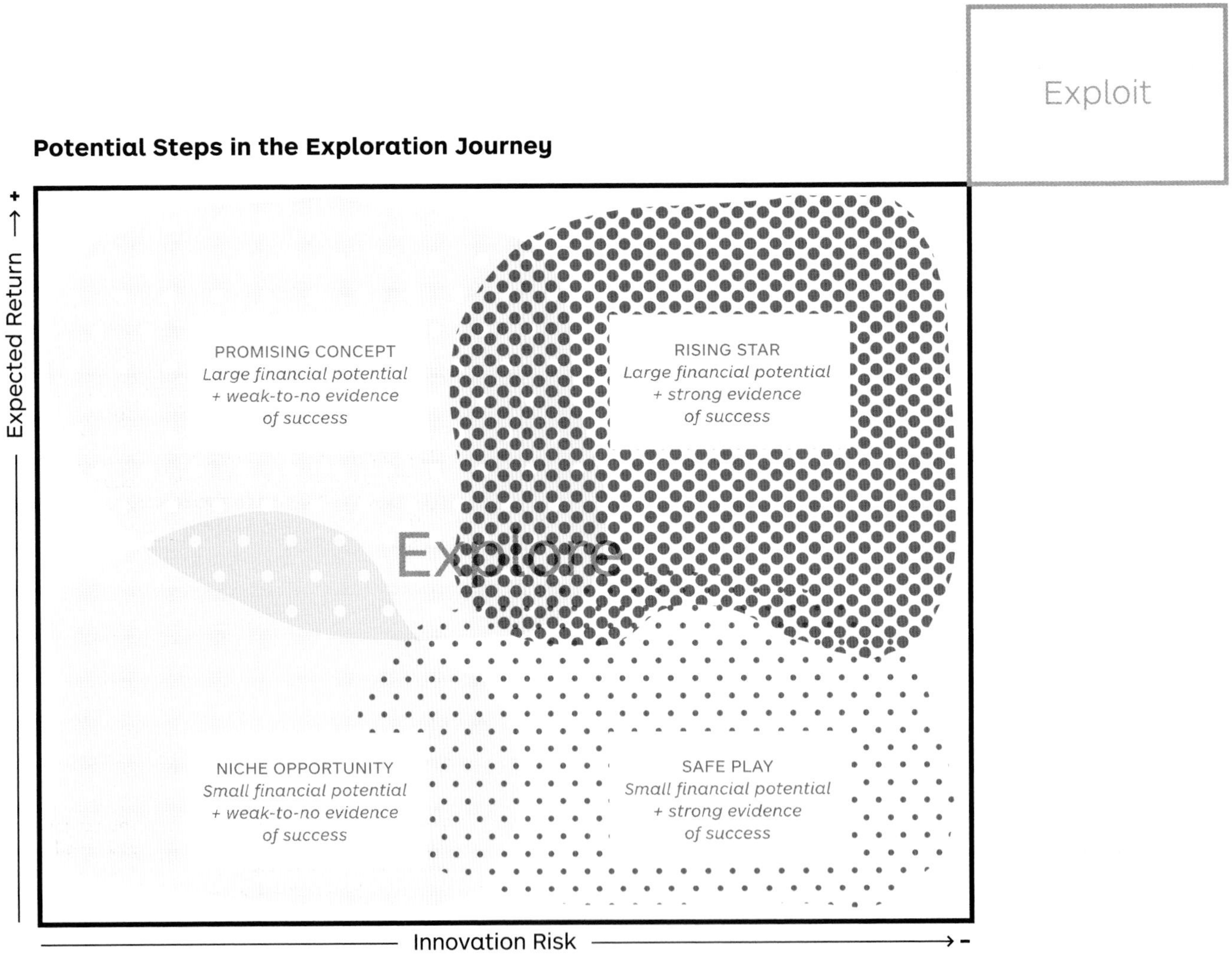

Expected Return and Innovation Risk

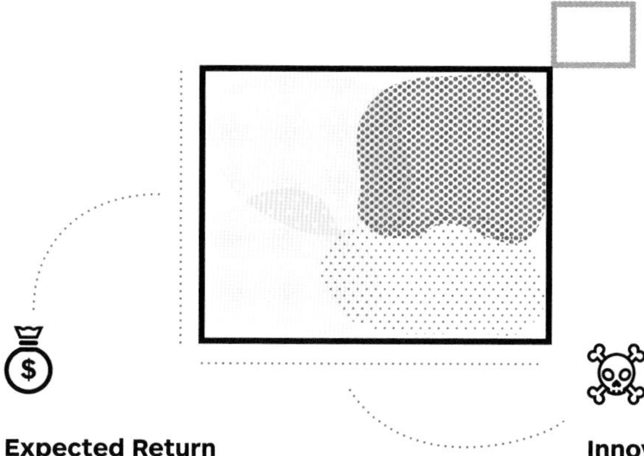

Expected Return
The financial potential (or impact) of a business idea if it is successful. You can pick how you define expected return according to your preferences. This may be profitability, revenue potential, growth potential, margins, or any other financial metric that allows you to evaluate the financial potential of an idea. Alternatively, you may focus on the social or environmental return, rather than the financial return.

Innovation Risk
There are four types of innovation risks that might kill a business idea: Desirability Risk, Viability Risk, Feasibility Risk, and Adaptability Risk.

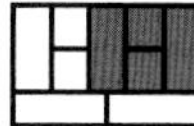

Desirability Risk
Customers aren't interested.

The risk that the market a business is targeting is too small, that too few customers want the value proposition, or that the company can't reach, acquire, and retain targeted customers.

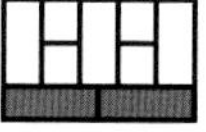

Viability Risk
We can't earn enough money.

The risk that a business can't generate successful revenue streams, that customers are unwilling to pay (enough), or that the costs are too high to make a sustainable profit.

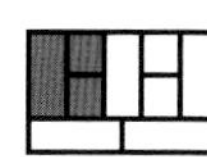

Feasibility Risk
We can't build and deliver.

The risk that a business can't manage, scale, or get access to key resources (technology, IP, brand, etc.), key activities, or key partners.

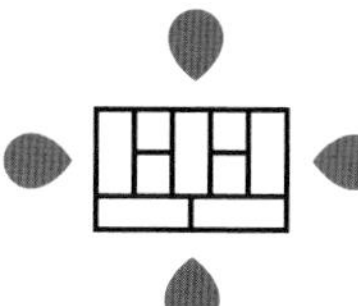

Adaptability Risk
External factors are unfavorable.

The risk that a business won't be able to adapt to the competitive environment, technology, regulatory, social, or market trends, or that the macro environment is not favorable (lacking infrastructure, recession, etc.).

This icon is the Business Model Canvas; *see p. 78 for an introduction.*

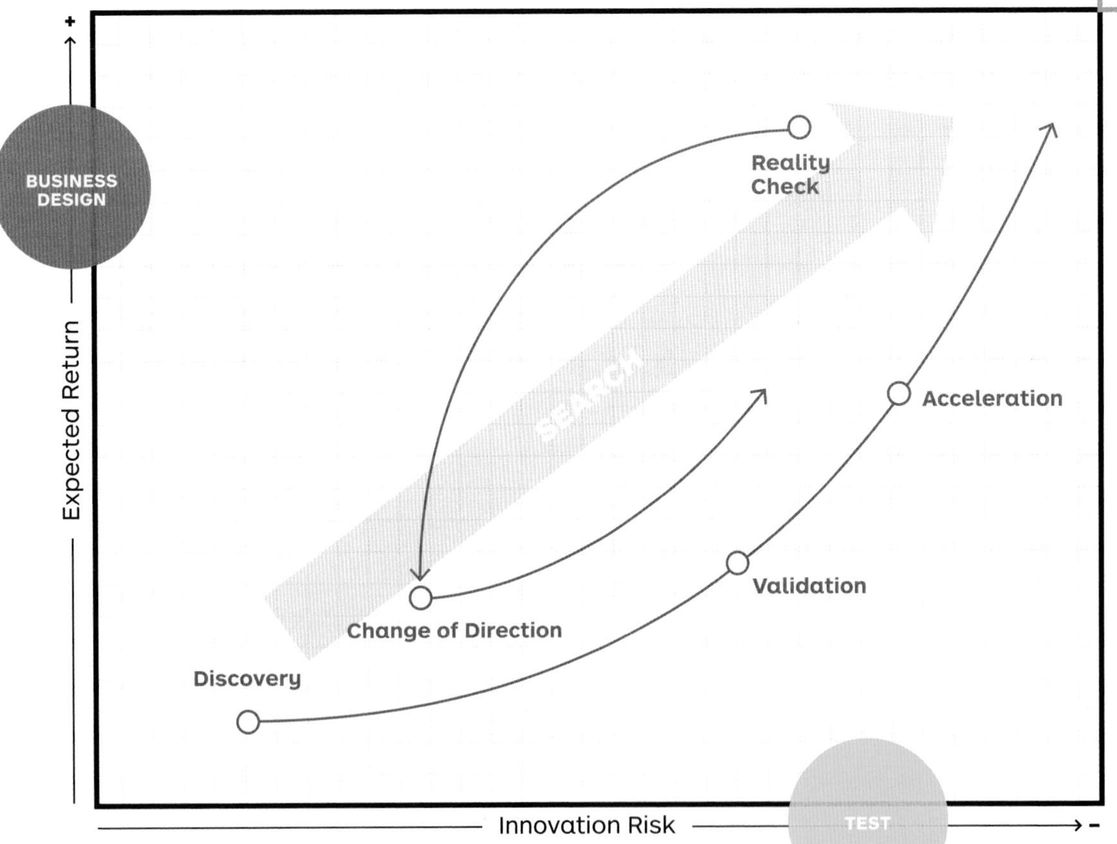
Exploit
Explore Journey
+
BUSINESS DESIGN
Expected Return
Reality Check
SEARCH
Acceleration
Validation
Change of Direction
Discovery
Innovation Risk
TEST
-

Search and Pivot

The journey in the Explore portfolio is one of search and pivot until you have enough evidence that a new business idea will work. The search for ideas, value propositions, and business models that will work consists of two main activities that continuously nourish each other:

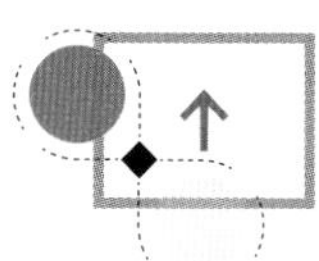

Business Design

Design is the activity of turning vague ideas, market insights, and evidence from testing into concrete value propositions and solid business models. Good design involves the use of strong business model patterns to maximize returns and compete beyond product, price, and technology.

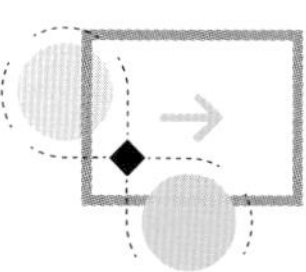

Test

Testing is the activity of reducing the risk of pursuing ideas that look good in theory, but won't work in reality. You test ideas by defining critical hypotheses, conducting rapid experiments, and learning from the evidence. The evidence may support or refute the value propositions and business models you are exploring.

Search Trajectory

Discovery
Customer understanding, context, and willingness to pay

This is where you begin to reduce risk through testing. Initial evidence indicates that customers care about what you intend to address (desirability). Further evidence typically indicates customer willingness to pay (viability). Discovery prototypes at this stage do not need technical skills. Examples are storyboards, videos, and mock brochures.

Validation
Proven interest and indications of profitability

At this stage you search for more solid evidence that shows interest for your products and services (desirability). First mock sales or letters of intent signal how much customers will pay (viability). First evidence of the required cost structure indicates expected profitability (viability). Technical prototypes suggest that you can manage activities and resources (feasibility).

Acceleration
Proven model at limited scale

At this stage you aim for a working prototype or first products and services to test your value proposition in a limited market. You search for evidence that shows that you can create and deliver customer value at a limited scale and with a profit. You search for evidence to justify larger investments to scale customer acquisition and retention, and test profitability at scale.

Pivot Trajectory

Reality Check
Failure of initial trajectory

A reality check is needed when new evidence indicates that the idea you've been testing is unlikely to work despite earlier promising evidence. It might lead you to question your entire business model or certain aspects of it. It requires rethinking which parts of your initial idea and business model you will keep and which ones you will abandon.

Change of Direction
Testing a new direction

At this stage you've pivoted from an initial trajectory to a new one. You have made significant changes to one or more elements of your business model. This means you need to reconsider the hypotheses underlying your new direction. You need to analyze which evidence is still relevant and which evidence isn't. A change of direction usually requires re-testing elements of your business model that you've already tested.

See p. 76 in Manage for more on the design-test loop.

See p. 128 in Invent Patterns for more on designing powerful business models.

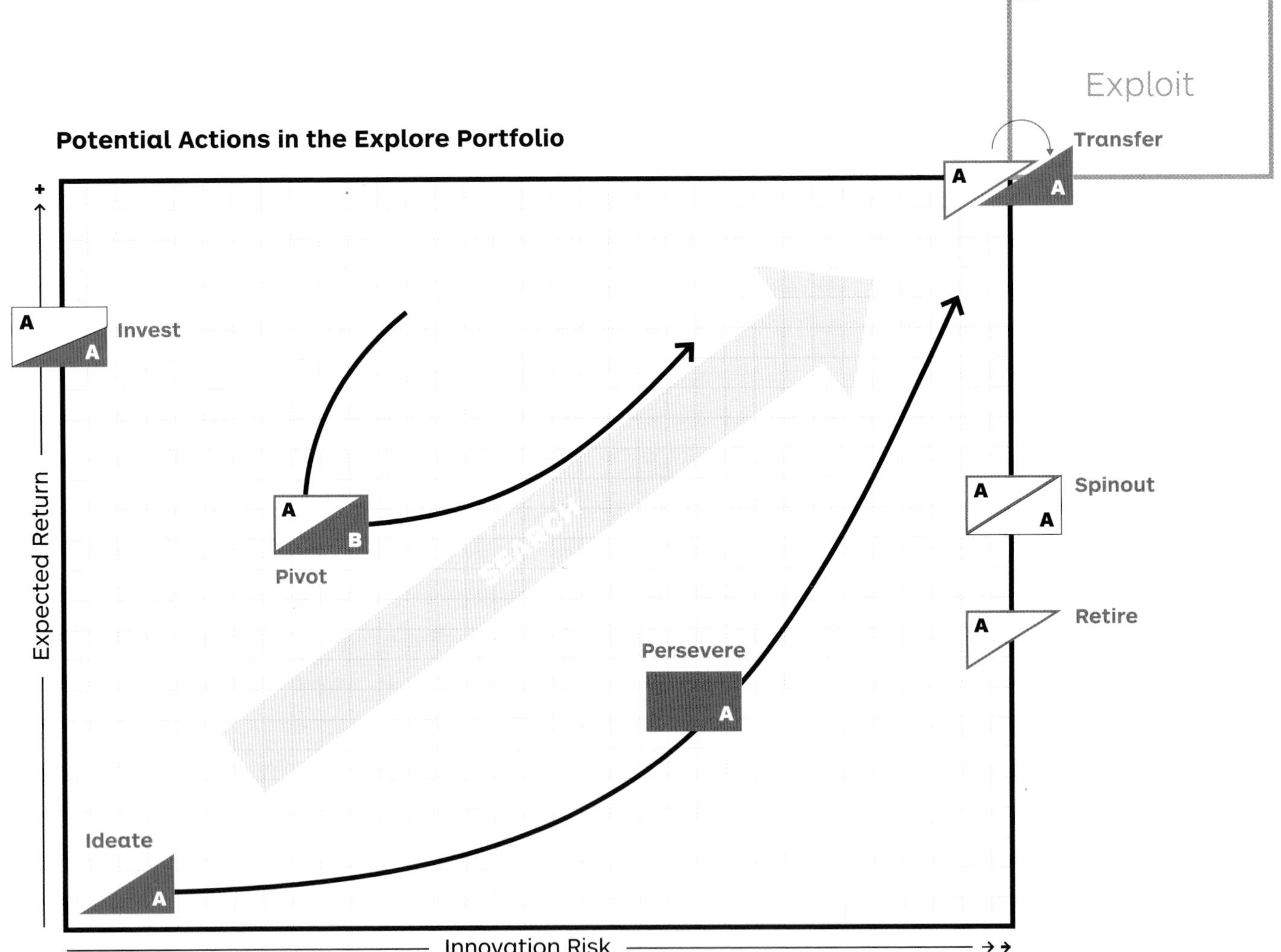
Potential Actions in the Explore Portfolio
Exploit
Transfer
Invest
Pivot
Spinout
Retire
Persevere
Ideate
SEARCH
Expected Return
Innovation Risk

Explore Actions

There are seven actions you perform in your Explore portfolio. All of them are related to shaping and testing new business ideas in order to improve their return and reduce their innovation risk. The exploration of new ideas may include everything from radically new business models all the way to testing incremental improvements of existing business models in the Exploit portfolio.

The idea to visualize actions with a triangle emerged after a discussion with Luis Felipe Cisneros. See p. 96 in Manage for more on Explore portfolio actions.

Ideate

A still exists but outside the portfolio
↓
A belongs to the portfolio

The activity of turning market opportunities, technologies, products, or services into first business model and value proposition prototypes. This typically happens in a workshop setting. At this stage, there is no real evidence that significantly reduces innovation risk, only assumptions that you plan to test. You capture results in slides and spreadsheets.

Invest

A exists, outside the portfolio
↓
A partly belongs to the portfolio

The decision to invest fully or partially in an outside start-up or exploration project to bolster your portfolio of internal projects.

Persevere

A belongs to the portfolio
↓
A is unchanged, inside the portfolio

The decision to continue testing an idea based on evidence. This typically happens after gaining insights you feel confident about from the analysis of the evidence. You persevere by further testing the same hypothesis with a stronger experiment or by moving on to your next important hypothesis.

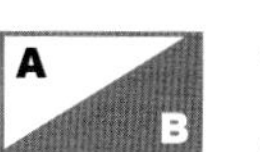

Pivot

A belongs to the portfolio
↓
A is changed into **B**, inside the portfolio

The decision to make a significant change to one or more elements of your business model. This typically happens after learning that the idea you've been testing won't work in reality without major modifications. A pivot often means that some of your earlier evidence may be irrelevant to your new trajectory. It usually requires re-testing elements of your business model that you've already tested.

Retire

A belongs to the portfolio
↓
A is killed

The decision to kill a search project based on evidence or lack of strategic fit. The evidence might show that an idea won't work in reality or that the profit potential is insufficient.

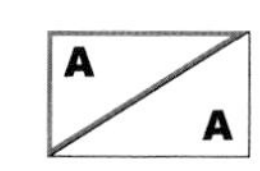

Spinout

A belongs to the portfolio
↓
A still exists but outside the portfolio

The decision to spin out rather than to kill a promising idea. This can either be in the form of selling it to another company, to investors, or to the team that explored the idea. The company might invest in the spinout or buy it back at a later, less-risky stage.

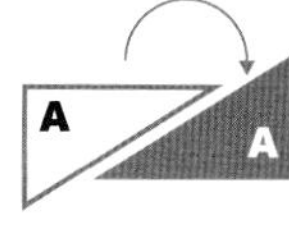

Transfer

A belongs to the Explore portfolio
↓
A is transferred to the Exploit portfolio

The decision to move a business model idea from exploration to exploitation based on strong evidence. This typically happens once you've produced strong evidence of desirability, feasibility, viability, and adaptability. Transferring requires finding a good home in the exploit portfolio. This may be as part of an existing business or as a new stand-alone business.

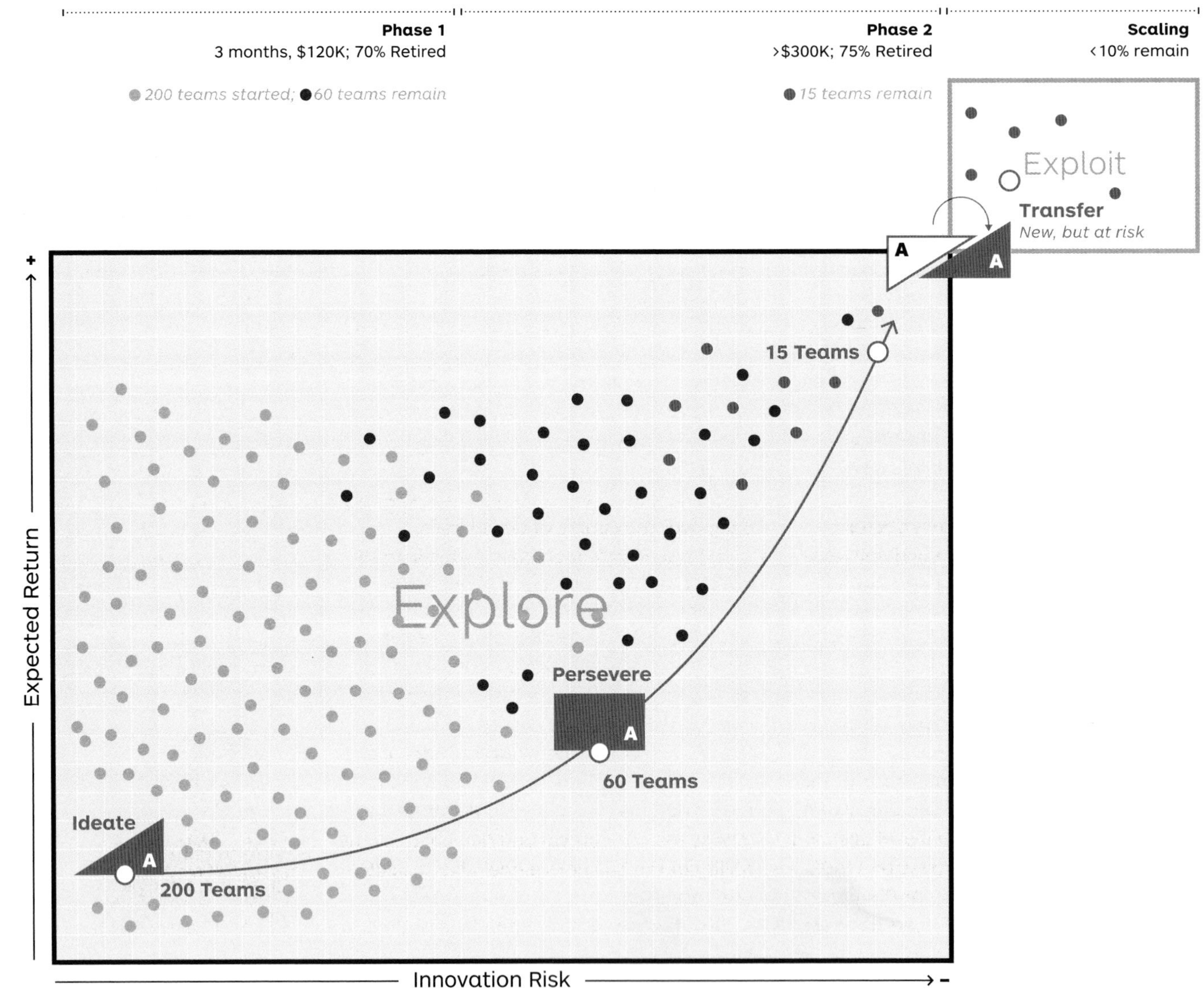
Phase 1
3 months, $120K; 70% Retired
200 teams started; 60 teams remain
Phase 2
>$300K; 75% Retired
15 teams remain
Scaling
<10% remain
Exploit
Transfer
New, but at risk
A
A
15 Teams
Explore
Persevere
A
60 Teams
Ideate
A
200 Teams
Expected Return
+
Innovation Risk
–

Portfolio Example
2017 ~~~ 2019

Bosch

To illustrate the Explore portfolio we use Bosch, the German multinational engineering and technology company founded in 1886. This illustration is based on anonymized data from the Bosch Accelerator Program between 2017 and 2019.

The Bosch Group employs 410,000 associates worldwide with annual sales of €78.5 billion (2018).[1]

Bosch has four core business sectors: Mobility Solutions (hardware and software), Consumer Goods (household appliances and power tools), Industrial Technology (including drive and control), and Energy and Building Technology.

From Products and Technology to Business Models

Since its beginnings, Bosch has been a driving force in technological innovation. Its R&D led to successes such as the diesel injection pump and the antilock brake system (ABS).

In 2014, Bosch's CEO, Volkmar Denner, sent out a communication to spur business model innovation. Bosch needed to maintain its technology and product focus but simultaneously turn more of its attention to new types of business models.

In 2015, Bosch created the Business Model Innovation Department to complement its innovation process with business model development capabilities. Bosch saw a need to create an ecosystem dedicated to exploring, nurturing, and facilitating growth innovation, moving beyond product innovation.

Bosch Accelerator Program

As part of their service portfolio Bosch's Business Model Innovation Department has created the Accelerator Program.

Teams going through the program explore either a new idea or explore a concept originating in an existing business. The program teams perform a business model deep dive and refine, test, and adapt ideas systematically over the course of two phases.

The program management selects an initial cohort of 20 to 25 teams from all over the world that work together for 2 to 10 months. Teams receive an initial funding of €120,000 and get two months to test whether their business-model ideas can scale. Depending on the results, teams can obtain an additional €300,000 or more during Phase 2 of the program. With this additional funding, teams can test minimum viable products (MVPs) with customers and demonstrate the ability of the business model idea to scale profitably.

After the successful completion of the Bosch Accelerator Program, only the teams with the best evidence move on to the incubation phase.

Since 2017, Bosch has invested in more than 200 teams. From these teams, 70% retired their projects after the first investment round and 75% of the remaining teams stopped after the second. With this process, 15 teams have successfully transferred their projects to scale with follow-on funding.

The Bosch Accelerator Program has become Bosch's global standard for validating new business ideas with batches in Europe, Asia, North America, and South America.

"The Bosch Accelerator Program has allowed Bosch to implement a fast, structured, and capital-efficient process for validating business models at scale and has led to the establishment of a Bosch-wide innovation portfolio."

DR. UWE KIRSCHNER

VP Business Model Innovation, Bosch Management Consulting

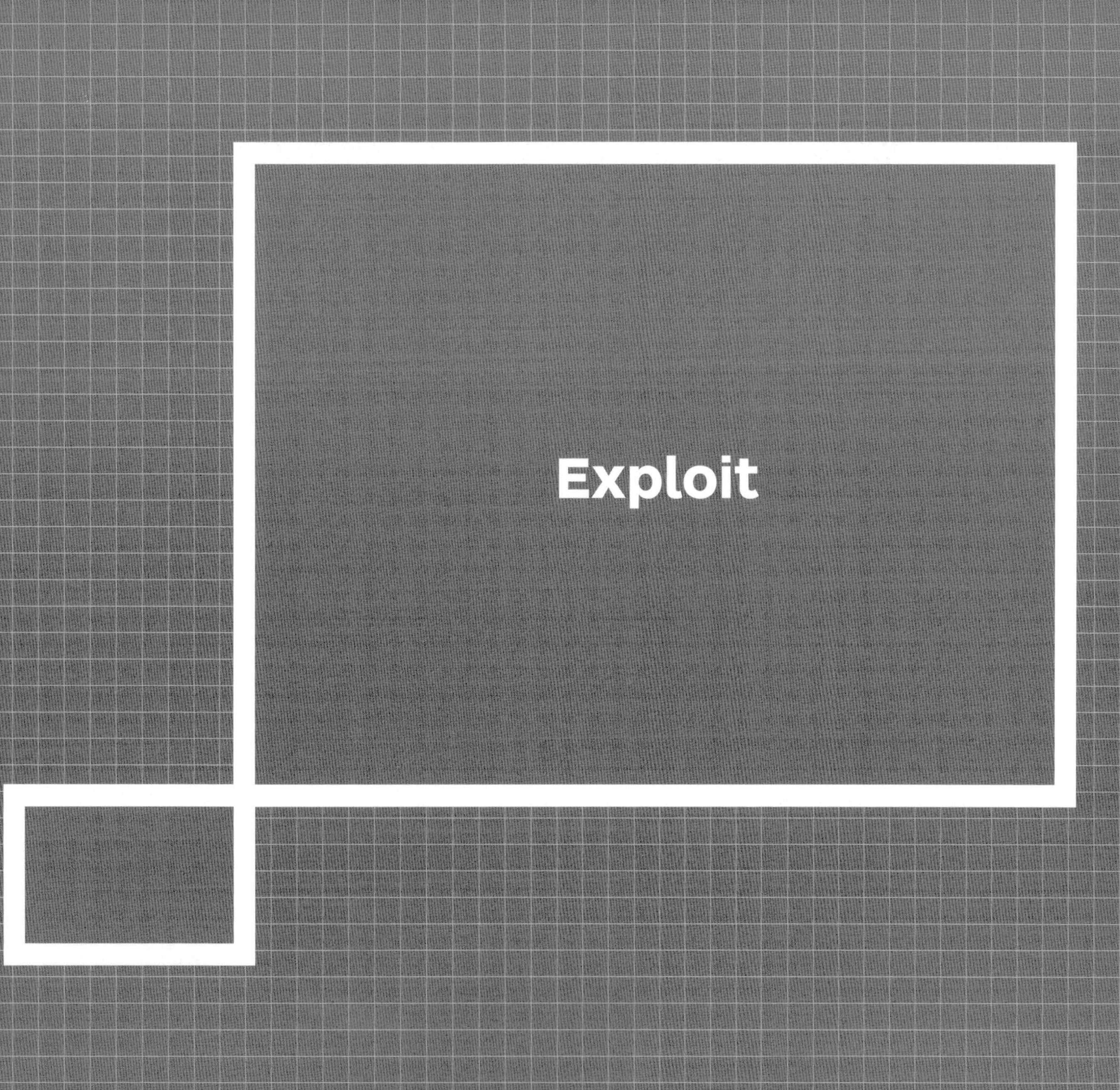
Exploit

Return and Death and Disruption Risk

Return
The financial return (or impact) of an existing business. You can pick how you define the financial return according to your preferences. This may be based on profitability, revenue, revenue growth, margins, or any other financial metric that allows you to evaluate the financial return of a business. Alternatively, you may focus on the social or environmental return rather than the financial return.

Death & Disruption Risk
There are two types of death and disruption risks that might kill a business:

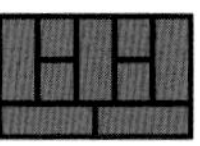

Internal Business Model Design Risk
Weaknesses

A business model can be more or less vulnerable to disruption based on its design. For example, a company that competes mainly on products, services, or price is easier to disrupt than a company that is protected by strong business model moats. The Invent and Improve sections of this book outline how you can compete with better business models.

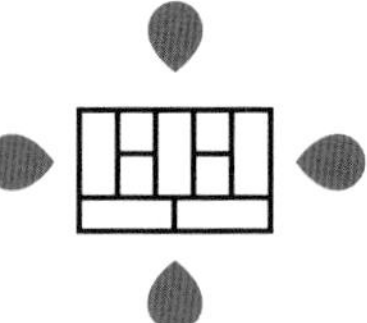

External Business Model Disruption Risk
Threats

Even the most powerful business models may be disrupted by external forces. Disruption can come from four different areas: shifting markets, disruptive trends (technological, social, environmental, regulatory), changing supply chains and competition, and changing macroeconomic circumstances.

Possible Risk Areas in Exploit Portfolio

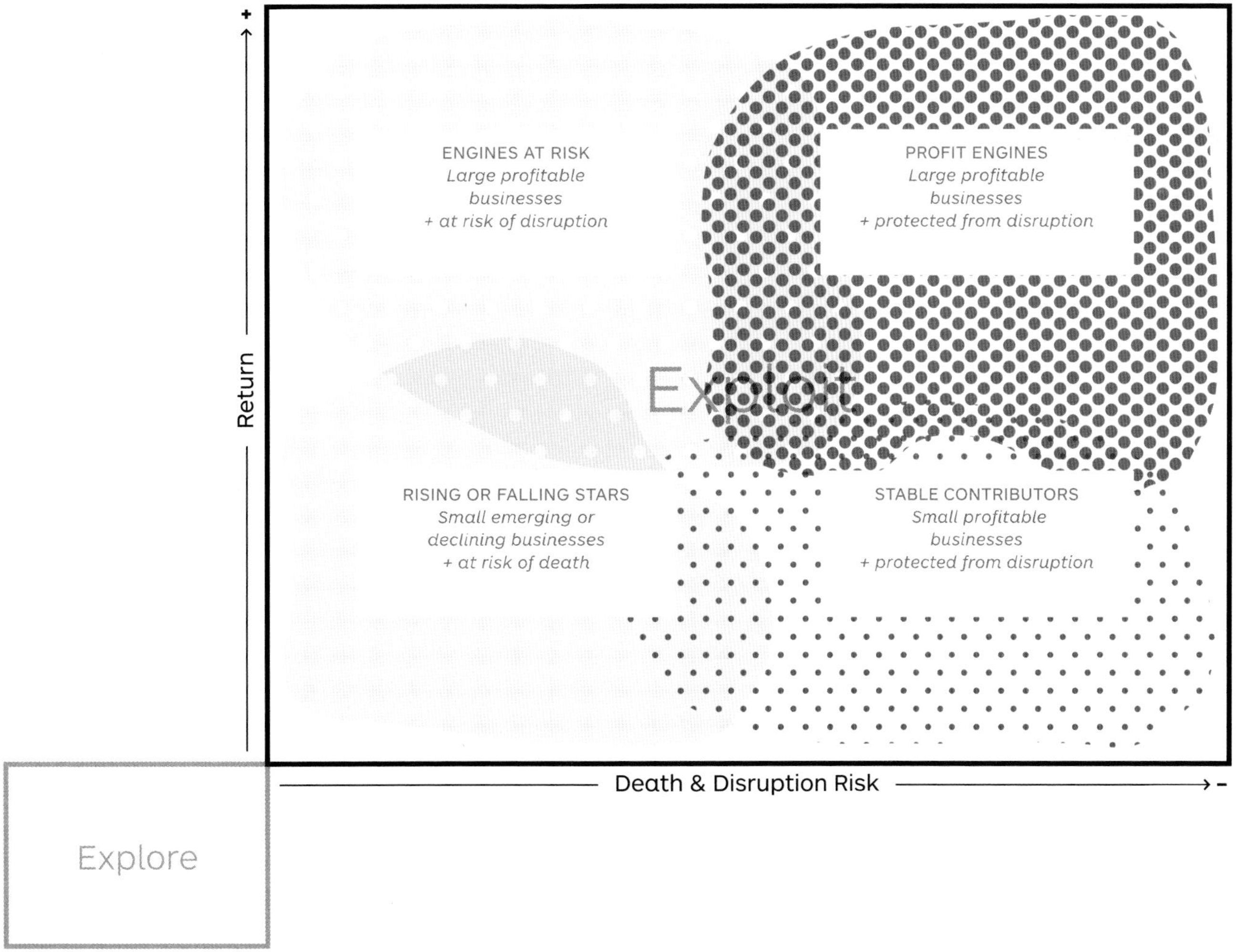

ENGINES AT RISK
Large profitable businesses + at risk of disruption

PROFIT ENGINES
Large profitable businesses + protected from disruption

Exploit

RISING OR FALLING STARS
Small emerging or declining businesses + at risk of death

STABLE CONTRIBUTORS
Small profitable businesses + protected from disruption

Return +

Death & Disruption Risk –

Explore

Growth and Decline Trajectories

The journey in the Exploit portfolio is one of growth and decline of a business. The aim is to continuously prevent existing business models from declining by protecting, improving, and reinventing them.

See p. 124 in Manage for more on testing business model shifts. See p. 228–229 in Improve for more on shifting old business models to new ones.

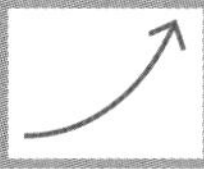

Growth Trajectory

Scale
Get the business off the ground

This is the first growth phase, when you turn a proven and promising opportunity into a real business. Main activities consist of scaling customer acquisition, retention, and product/service delivery. The entire team is focused on expansion on all fronts, including infrastructure and human resources.

Boost
Bolster the performance of an established business

In this phase you boost and maintain the growth of your proven business model with sustaining innovation. You bolster your business model with new product innovations, new channels, and the exploration of adjacent markets.

Protect
Make a business more efficient and protect it from disruption

In this phase you focus on maintaining the strong position of your business by protecting it from competition and by increasing its efficiency. Efficiency innovation usually dominates this phase. At this stage your business is large and profitable, but growth tends to stagnate.

Decline Trajectory

Disruption
Emergence of external forces that threaten your business

In this phase changes in the external environment make your business vulnerable and threaten it. Disruption may come from shifting markets; technological, social, environmental, or regulatory trends; shifting supply chains; competition; new entrants; or a changing macroeconomic environment. At this stage your business is still large and profitable, but at risk.

Crisis
External forces disrupt your business and trigger decline

Your business is disrupted by external forces and is in rapid decline. At this stage you are still heavily invested in the old business model, yet your outdated business model needs major changes to avoid obsolescence.

Shift & Reemergence
Substantial business model shift and renewed growth

You succeed in the shift from an outdated disrupted business model to a renewed one. The new business model initiates a new era of growth.

Exploit Portfolio Journey

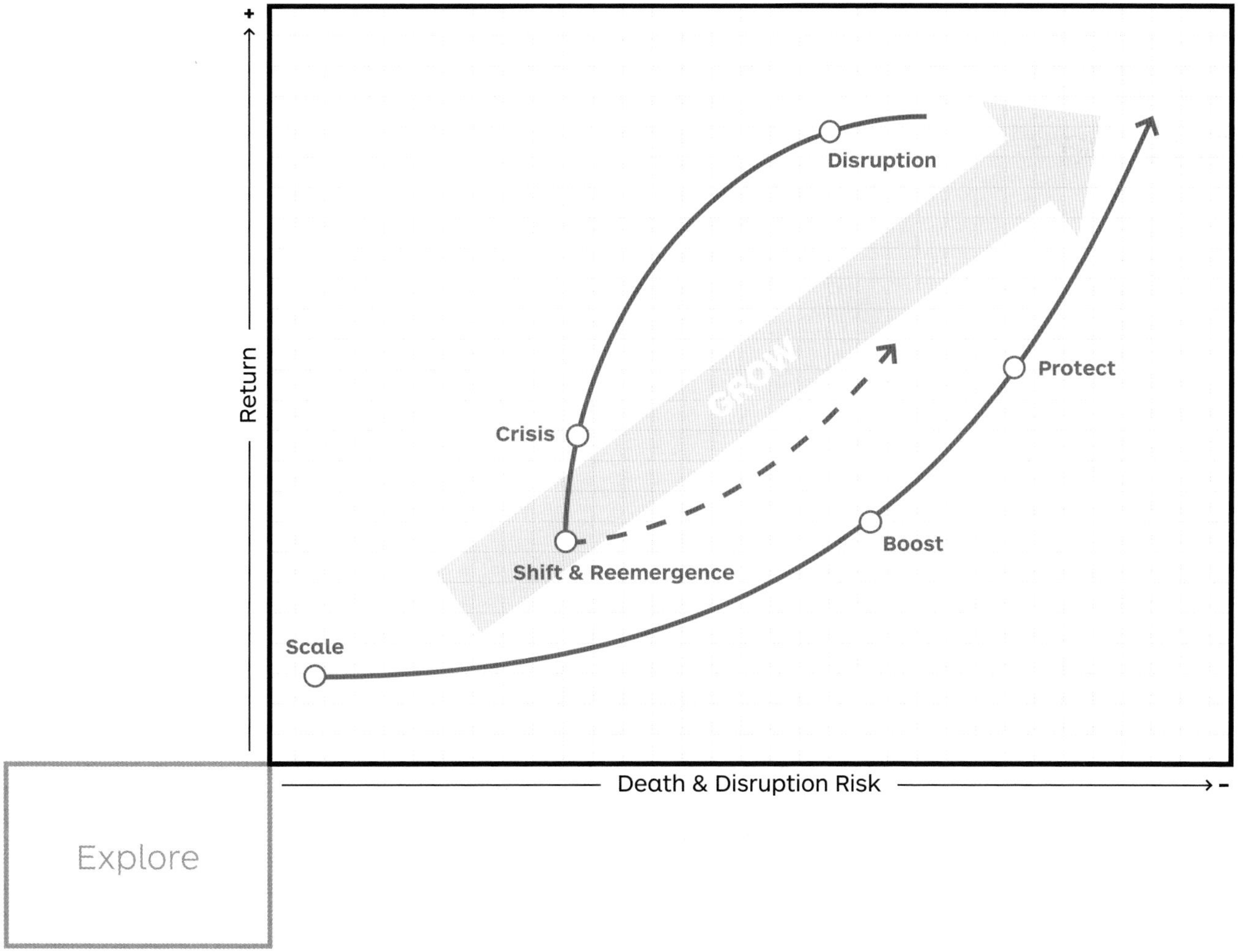

+ Return

Disruption

GROW

Protect

Crisis

Shift & Reemergence

Boost

Scale

Death & Disruption Risk -

Explore

Exploit Actions

There are seven actions you can perform in your Exploit portfolio. All of them are related to managing your existing business models and aligning it with your corporate identity. This may include everything from adding new businesses all the way to getting rid of some that don't fit anymore. It also includes improving existing business models incrementally or radically, which you will indicate in your Exploit portfolio in order to reduce disruption risk. However, you will test this improvement in your Explore portfolio, in order to reduce the innovation risk.

See p. 110 in Manage for more on Exploit portfolio actions.

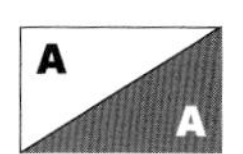

Acquire

A exists, outside the portfolio
↓
A belongs to the portfolio

The activity of buying an outside business to either create a new stand-alone business or to merge it with one of your existing businesses.

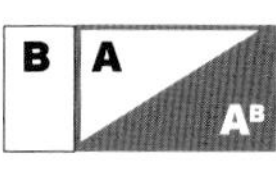

Partner

A belongs to the portfolio,
B exists outside the portfolio
↓
A still belongs to the portfolio, reinforced by **B**,
B exists outside the portfolio

The activity of partnering with an outside business to strengthen one or more of your business models.

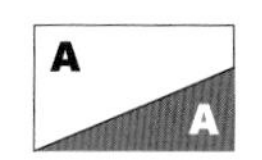

Invest

A exists, outside the portfolio
↓
A partly belongs to the portfolio

The decision to invest fully or partially in an outside business to bolster your portfolio.

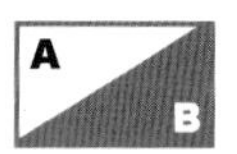

Improve

A belongs to the portfolio
↓
A is transformed into **B**, inside the portfolio

The activity of renovating an outdated business model to shift it toward a new, more competitive business model.

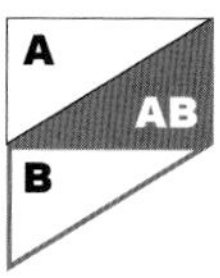

Merge

A exists, outside the portfolio,
B exists inside the portfolio
↓
A is acquired and merged with **B**, inside the portfolio

The activity of merging an acquired outside or owned inside business with one or several owned businesses.

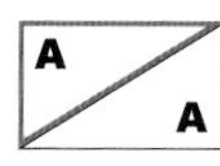

Divest

A belongs to the portfolio
↓
A still exists but outside the portfolio

The activity of disengaging from one of your business models. This can either be in the form of selling it to another company, to investors, or to the current management (management buyout).

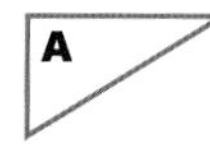

Dismantle

A belongs to the portfolio
↓
A is killed

The activity of ending and disintegrating a business.

Potential Actions in the Exploit Portfolio

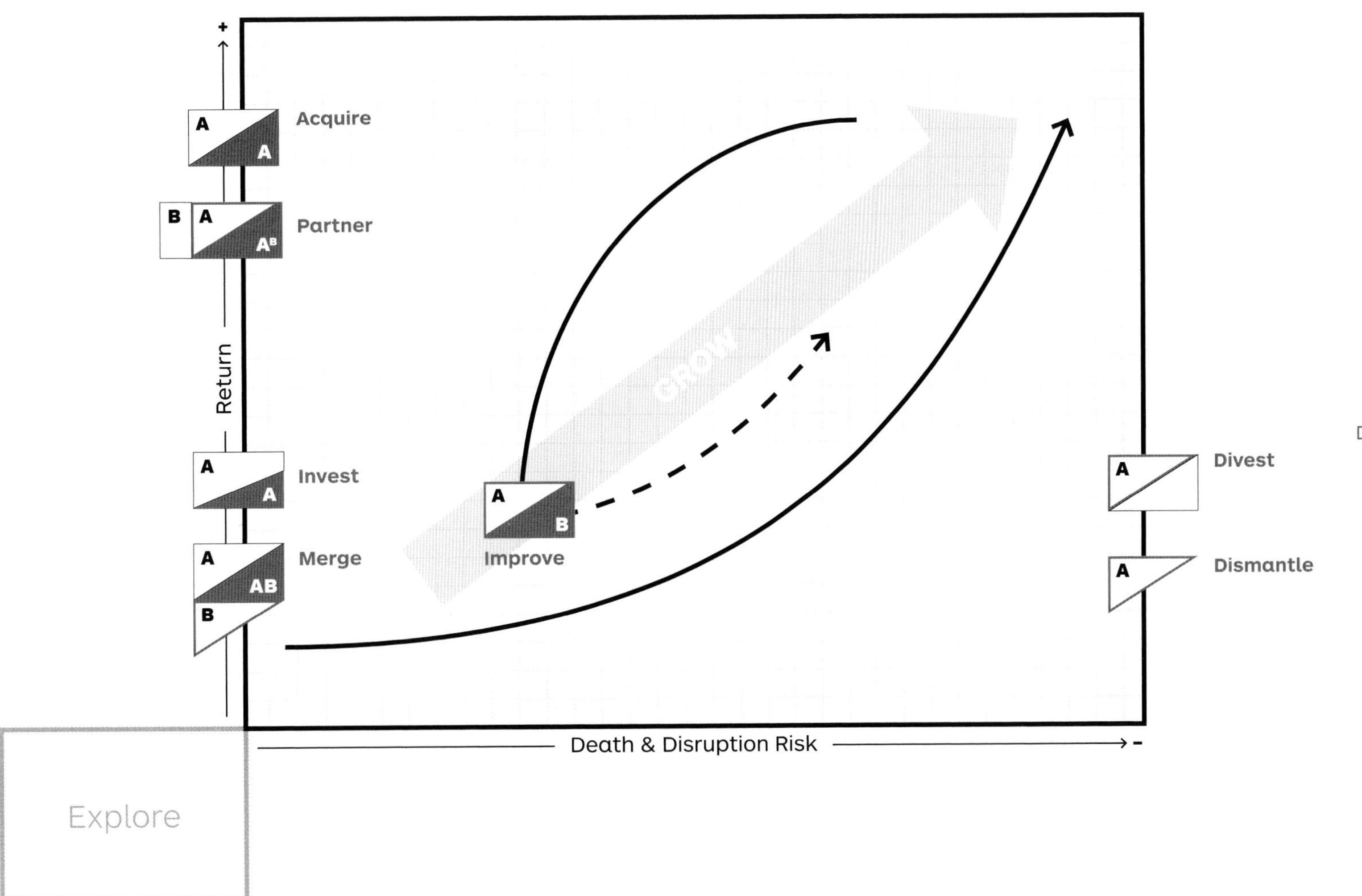

TOOL 33

Nestlé

To illustrate the use of the Exploit portfolio, we outline how Swiss food company Nestlé managed its portfolio of existing businesses over the course of 2017 and 2018. This illustration is based on CEO Ulf Mark Schneider's annual investor day presentation on February 14, 2019. Schneider had joined Nestlé in January 2017 as the first outside CEO at Nestlé since 1922.

We positioned Nestlé's main business categories vertically, based on size of total revenues of each category. Alternatively you could choose to organize the information by profitability, margins, or any other financial indicator your company uses to assess financial returns.

In the absence of clear information on death and disruption risk, we did not position Nestlé's main business categories based on risk. In his investor day presentation CEO Ulf Mark Schneider did mention, however, individual businesses and brands that were being fixed or which were under strategic review. We positioned those brands in the improve area of the portfolio map.

Acquire, Invest, Partner

Nestlé expanded its portfolio across categories by acquiring, investing in, or partnering with outside companies.

In beverages, Nestlé acquired a perpetual global license from Starbucks to market Starbucks products to consumers through retail. Previously, Nestlé acquired a majority stake in the San Fransisco–based coffee-chain start-up Blue Bottle Coffee.

In health science, Nestlé expanded with the acquisition of Atrium Innovations.

In petcare, Nestlé Purina acquired a majority stake in tails.com.

In prepared dishes, Nestlé acquired Sweet Earth, a plant-based foods manufacturer in California.[2]

Improve

Over the course of 2017 and 2018 Nestlé improved its Gerber baby food brand, Chinese food brand Yinlu, and Nestlé Skin Health. It placed Nestlé Skin Health and the food brand Herta under strategic review to potentially sell them.

Divest

Nestlé adapted its portfolio with several divestitures. It sold its U.S. confectionery business to Ferrero for $2.8 billion in cash in 2018.

It sold its Gerber Life Insurance Company ("Gerber Life"), to Western & Southern Financial Group for $1.55 billion in cash.[2]

Main Business Categories

Nestlé breaks out its results in seven main business categories. Each of those business categories holds several brands and may cover several different business models. Nestlé does not break out its results in terms of individual business models, which may differ substantially (e.g., Nespresso and Dolce Gusto both sell portioned coffee, but with radically different business models and under different brands).

Nestlé Exploit portfolio in February 2019

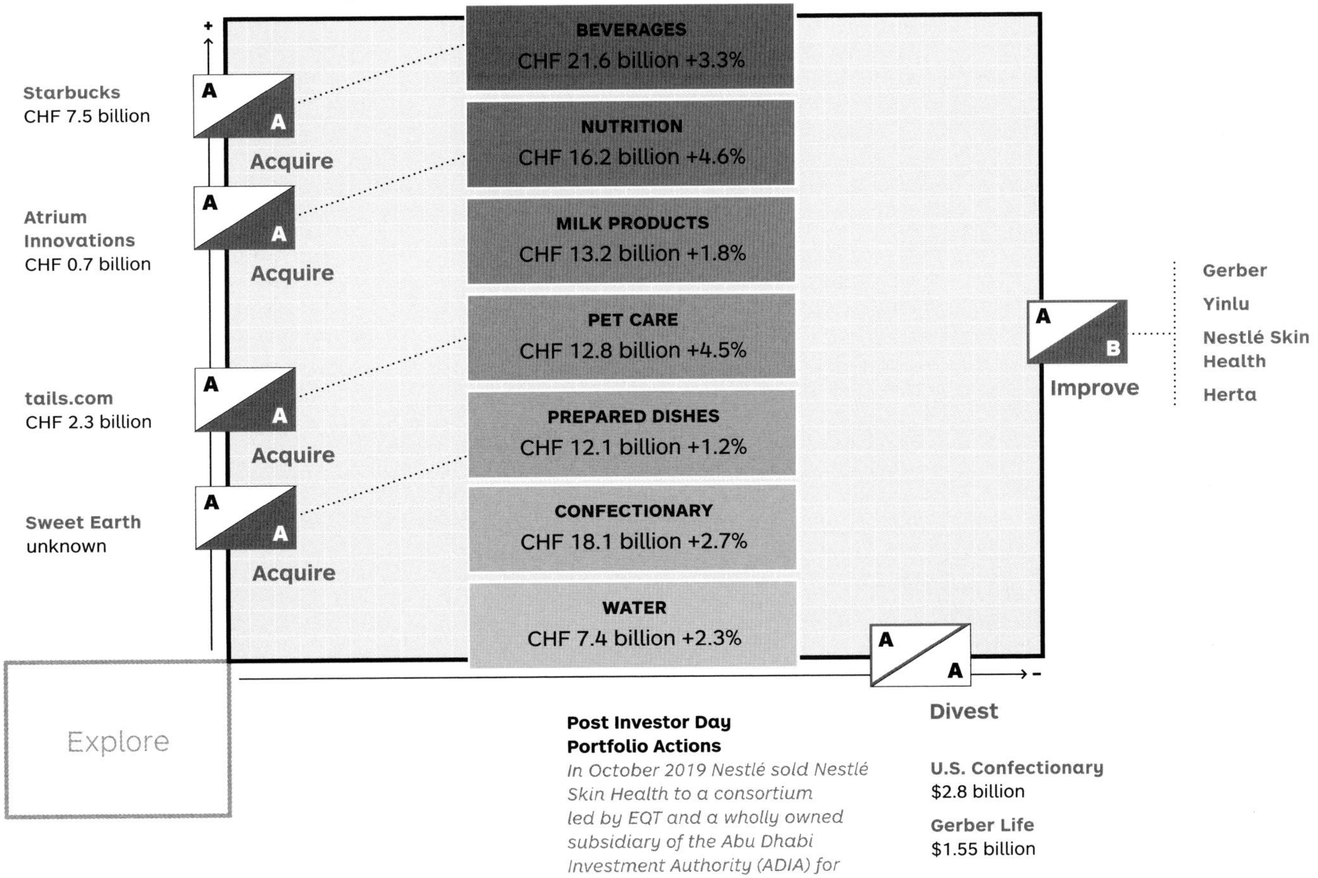

Starbucks
CHF 7.5 billion
Acquire

Atrium Innovations
CHF 0.7 billion
Acquire

tails.com
CHF 2.3 billion
Acquire

Sweet Earth
unknown
Acquire

Category	Sales
BEVERAGES	CHF 21.6 billion +3.3%
NUTRITION	CHF 16.2 billion +4.6%
MILK PRODUCTS	CHF 13.2 billion +1.8%
PET CARE	CHF 12.8 billion +4.5%
PREPARED DISHES	CHF 12.1 billion +1.2%
CONFECTIONARY	CHF 18.1 billion +2.7%
WATER	CHF 7.4 billion +2.3%

Improve

Gerber
Yinlu
Nestlé Skin Health
Herta

Explore

Divest

U.S. Confectionary
$2.8 billion

Gerber Life
$1.55 billion

Post Investor Day Portfolio Actions

In October 2019 Nestlé sold Nestlé Skin Health to a consortium led by EQT and a wholly owned subsidiary of the Abu Dhabi Investment Authority (ADIA) for a value of CHF 10.2 billion.[3]

Exploit Portfolio

Explore Portfolio

DEFINITION

Types of Innovation

Not all innovations are equal. Different types of innovations require different skills, resources, experience levels, and support from the organization. Ideally, they also live in different parts of the organization and have different degrees of autonomy in order to succeed. We distinguish between three different types of innovation heavily borrowed from Harvard professor Clayton Christensen: efficiency, sustaining, and transformative innovation.

Explore ⟷ **Exploit**

Transformative

Transformative innovation is the most difficult innovation. It's about exploring opportunities outside of the traditional field of a company. This type of innovation usually requires a radical change or expansion of a company's business model(s). It includes opportunities that help a company expand and create new growth, but also covers opportunities that disrupt the existing business(es). Transformative innovation helps position a company for the long term.

Advantage
Positions the company for the long-term; offers protection from disruption.

Disadvantage
High risk and uncertainty; rarely quick returns.

Home
Dedicated and autonomous innovation teams outside of business units, with access to skills and resources from operating businesses.

Sustaining

Sustaining innovation is about exploring opportunities that build on top of a company's existing business model(s) to strengthen it/them and keep it/them alive. Typical examples of sustaining innovation are new products and services, new distribution channels, new support and production technologies, or geographical expansions.

Advantage
Low risk and uncertainty, immediate impact, predictability; covers the entire range from small to large financial impact, depending on innovation.

Disadvantage
No protection from disruption; doesn't help position the company for the future.

Home
Across the organization and at every level, ideally with the support of professional innovators.

Efficiency

Efficiency innovation is about exploring opportunities that improve operational aspects of a company's existing business model(s). They don't change the business model in a substantial way. Typical examples include technologies that improve operations, distribution, or support, and process innovations that make an organization more effective.

Advantage
Low risk and uncertainty, immediate impact, predictability; covers the entire range from small to large financial impact, depending on innovation.

Disadvantage
No protection from disruption; doesn't help position the company for the future.

Home
Across the organization and at every level, ideally with the support of professional innovators.

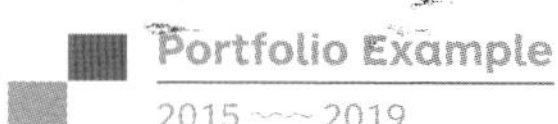

Gore

We use W. L. Gore & Associates to illustrate a balanced Explore and Exploit portfolio. Gore is an American multinational engineering and technology company founded in 1958 by husband and wife team Bill and Vieve Gore.

Gore specializes in material science and is known for creating innovative, technology-driven solutions that range from medical devices that treat aneurysms to high-performance GORE-TEX® Fabrics found in casual and professional clothing.

Gore's three main areas of focus are industrial and electronics, performance fabrics, and implantable medical devices. It has an annual revenue of $3.7 billion and is one of the 200 largest privately held companies in the United States. The company employs 10,500-plus associates in 50 facilities around the world.[4]

Trigger

Traditionally, Gore's revenue growth relied heavily on adding new divisions. It started out with insulated wire and cables, then added electronics in 1970, medical devices in 1975, and wearable fabrics in 1976. In the last decade, however, the markets for Gore's most successful products have matured. This, along with competitive, cheap alternatives, triggered Gore to be more ambitious with their innovation strategy. The organization decided to launch innovation initiatives for their core businesses, but also to explore potential future businesses.

Innovation Funnel

In 2015, Gore launched an initiative to grow its innovation funnel to explore, test, and adapt new ideas. The goal was to build a process-driven ecosystem that allowed for continuous generation and testing of potential new growth engines, while also looking for ways to constantly improve the existing businesses.

In fall of that year, the first cohort of six teams of internal entrepreneurs started their innovation journey. By the end of 2019, 12 cohorts of 103 teams in total will have been through the innovation funnel.

The process is made up of two major phases. During the first phase, called Concept Development, the teams are expected to provide evidenced based recommendations for each component of the Business Model Canvas. In the second phase, called Product Development, teams tackle the main technical and market uncertainties to reduce risk and uncertainty.

Teams are made up of engineers and other associates who dedicate 100% of their time to their internal start-up for each phase. Gore wants to build a pool of internal entrepreneurs that the organization can draw on for future exploration.

For Gore, innovation is an ongoing activity with an end-to-end process and a continuous pipeline of exploration.

"We innovate by fostering genuine curiosity, deep imagination, and courage to take risks. Our innovative culture and advanced materials expertise enables us to find the possibilities where none presently exist."

GREG HANNON

Chief Technology Officer

GORE-TEX® INFINIUM THERMIUM footwear
One of the first tested and validated products to come out of the innovation funnel was GORE-TEX® INFINIUM THERMIUM footwear. The team took an existing technology and turned it into a footwear technology that customers want. It provides the warmth of an insulated winter boot without the bulk. The launch of GORE-TEX® INFINIUM THERMIUM footwear in 2018 included multiple styles of women's footwear available through ECCO® and FRAU® with additional brands utilizing the technology in their 2019 collections.

GORE® Thermal Insulation
One innovation team spoke to over 80 industry contacts in the mobile electronics supply chain to conduct a value proposition deep dive. This resulted in an extensive collaboration with DELL to use GORE® Thermal Insulation in their latest XPS Laptops to prevent devices from overheating.

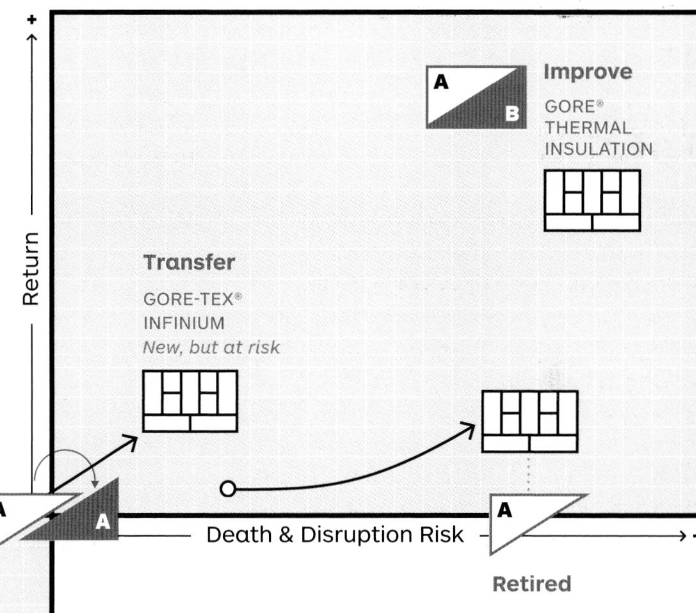

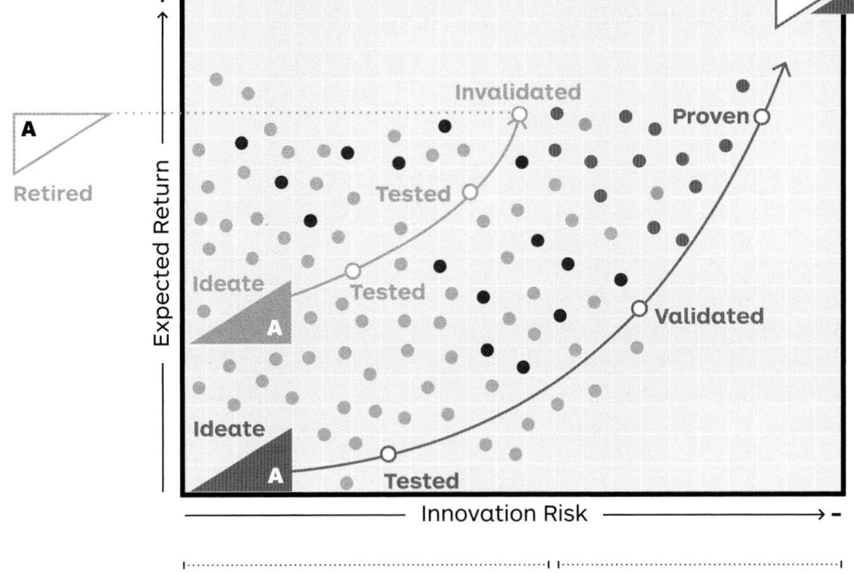

Concept Development
66% Retired

Product Development
57% Retired

103 teams started *35 teams remain* *15 teams remain*

From niche to mass market
One team explored how to potentially expand sales of an existing product from a premium market into a mid-tier segment. The hypothesis was that this new segment would value the differentiation this product provided. However, evidence from customer interviews proved them wrong and showed low demand and perceived value from end users. The idea was shelved without wasting a lot of time and energy on something that wouldn't work in the market.

Using the Portfolio Map

Use the Portfolio Map to visualize, analyze, and manage your existing businesses and the new ideas you are exploring.

	Entrepreneurs	Corporate Innovation Teams	Senior Leaders
VISUALIZE	Map all the ideas you are exploring according to expected return and innovation risk profile.	Gather all innovation leads in your organization and map the innovation projects according to expected return and innovation risk (based on evidence).	Gather your senior leadership team and map all your existing businesses (categories, units, business models, products, brands) according to return and death and disruption risk.
ANALYZE	Evaluate all ideas and identify the most promising one based on your ambitions and risk appetite.	Evaluate whether your exploration portfolio is likely to generate the returns you expect. Ask if you're exploring enough ideas and if you are de-risking them sufficiently.	Evaluate both your explore and exploit portfolios. Determine if you are exploring a sufficiently large number of new innovation projects to compensate for established businesses at risk of disruption.
MANAGE	Continue to test and de-risk your most promising idea and improve the business model to optimize the expected return.	Expand your exploration portfolio if you need to increase the expected return. Intensify testing if the majority of your projects haven't been able to reduce risk and uncertainty.	Invest more in exploration if you are at high risk of disruption. Expand or prune your exploit portfolio based on your vision and improve your businesses that are at risk.

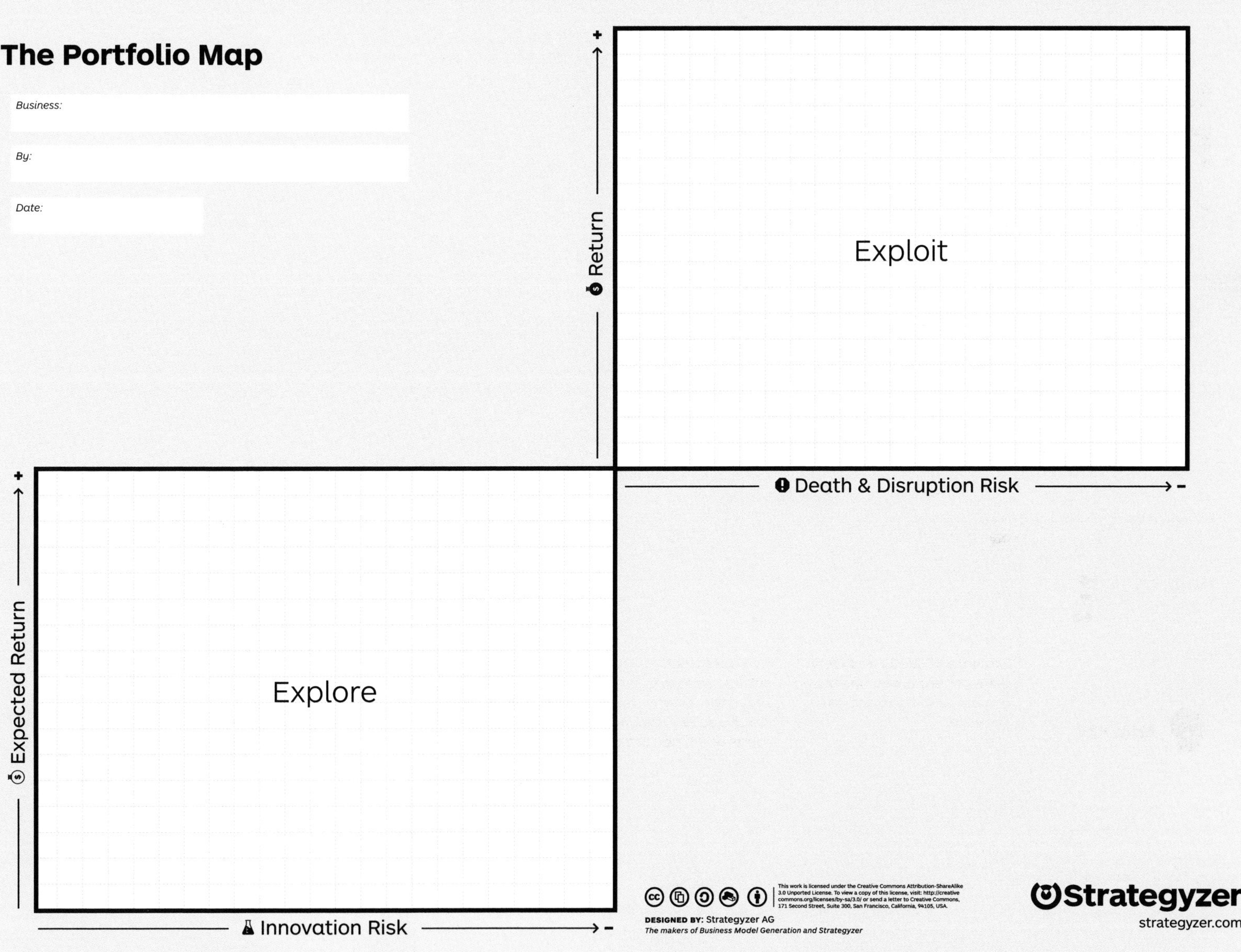
The Portfolio Map
Business:
By:
Date:
Exploit
Return
Death & Disruption Risk
Explore
Expected Return
Innovation Risk
This work is licensed under the Creative Commons Attribution-ShareAlike 3.0 Unported License. To view a copy of this license, visit: http://creativecommons.org/licenses/by-sa/3.0/ or send a letter to Creative Commons, 171 Second Street, Suite 300, San Francisco, California, 94105, USA.
DESIGNED BY: Strategyzer AG
The makers of Business Model Generation and Strategyzer
Strategyzer
strategyzer.com

CREATE TRANSPARENCY TO SEE EYE TO EYE WITH YOUR FUTURE

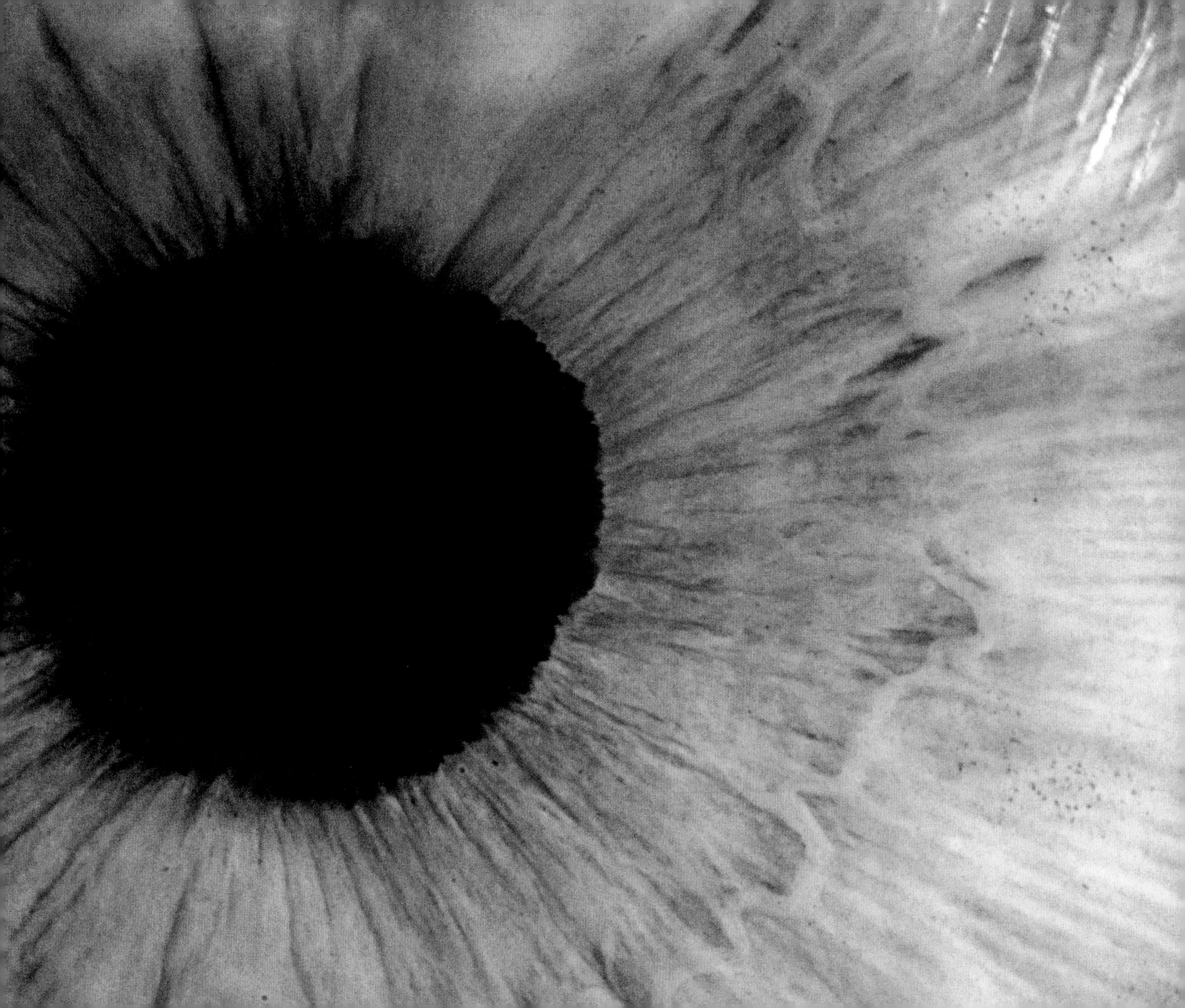

2

Manage

Manage Your Portfolio

Invincible Companies strategically guide, diversify, measure, and act upon their portfolio of existing and potential new businesses simultaneously.

GUIDE

Provide strategic portfolio guidance to make clear what type of projects, innovations, improvements, and portfolio actions are in or out.

DIVERSIFY

Create an innovation funnel, spread bets to minimize innovation risk. Let the best projects and teams emerge. Incrementally invest in teams with evidence.

MEASURE

Systematically measure and visualize innovation and disruption risk of all businesses and opportunities. Understand how fit your portfolio is for the future.

ACT

Use the full range of portfolio actions to optimize your portfolio. Grow businesses in-house, make acquisitions and divestitures, or do both depending on context.

Guidance

You need to provide a clear direction in order to design and maintain a strong portfolio. We call this strategic guidance and it consists of outlining your strategic direction, the required organizational culture, and the corporate image you would like to project to the outside world. Once you have defined this strategic portfolio guidance, you will have all you need to determine your portfolio actions.

Defines your aspirations for your organization. Here you make explicit where you want to play and what kind of financial performance you hope to achieve. Strategic direction is about defining what type of company you want to build or become.

Corporate Indentity
Who we are

Brand Image
What you say about what you do

Defines the key behaviors people in your company need to exhibit in order to implement the strategic direction you outlined for your organization. Here you describe which enablers you will put in place to facilitate the culture you want.

Defines how you want the outside world to perceive you. This includes customers, stakeholders, shareholders, and media. Your desired external image should be aligned with your strategic direction and organizational culture.

Portfolio Guidance

Your strategic guidance provides a clear context for portfolio management. It helps you define the portfolio guidance for resource allocation and portfolio actions. Portfolio guidance provides explicit boundaries to understand what to focus on and what not to, where to invest and where to divest, or what to explore and what not to explore.

OVERALL GUIDANCE

Define...

- ☐ financial performance philosophy (e.g., safe dividends, growth performance, etc.)
- ☐ arenas to play in the long term (e.g., markets, geographies, technologies, etc.)
- ☐ strategic key resources and capabilities to develop (e.g., tech resources, business model foundations, etc.)

EXPLOIT GUIDANCE

- ☐ short term financial performance targets
- ☐ business model improvement targets (e.g., technology investments, business model shifts)
- ☐ how to develop or improve value propositions for the existing portfolio

EXPLORE GUIDANCE

- ☐ performance guidelines to prioritize explore projects (e.g., size of opportunity, size of markets, size cost savings, etc.)
- ☐ exploration boundaries and strategic fit (e.g., new arenas or not, new business models or not, new technologies or not, etc.)
- ☐ key resources and capabilities to prioritize (e.g., tech resources, business model foundations, etc.)

TRANSFER GUIDANCE

Define...

- ☐ governance of how explore projects will be integrated into existing profit and loss divisions or how new ones will be set up
- ☐ governance of how explore projects will be protected from being swallowed up by dominant established business models

Portfolio Funnel Quiz

In how many project teams would a company have to invest $100,000 in order to produce at least one outsized success (e.g., a new $500+ million business)?

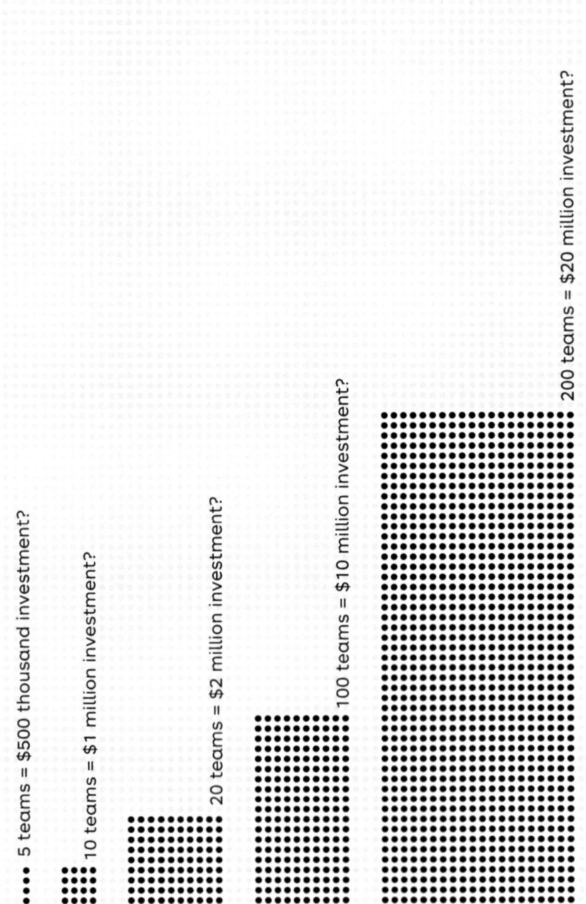

If we invest into ______ projects of $100K each, A ______ will fail, B ______ will find some success, and C ______ will become a new growth engine.

Answer on the following page →

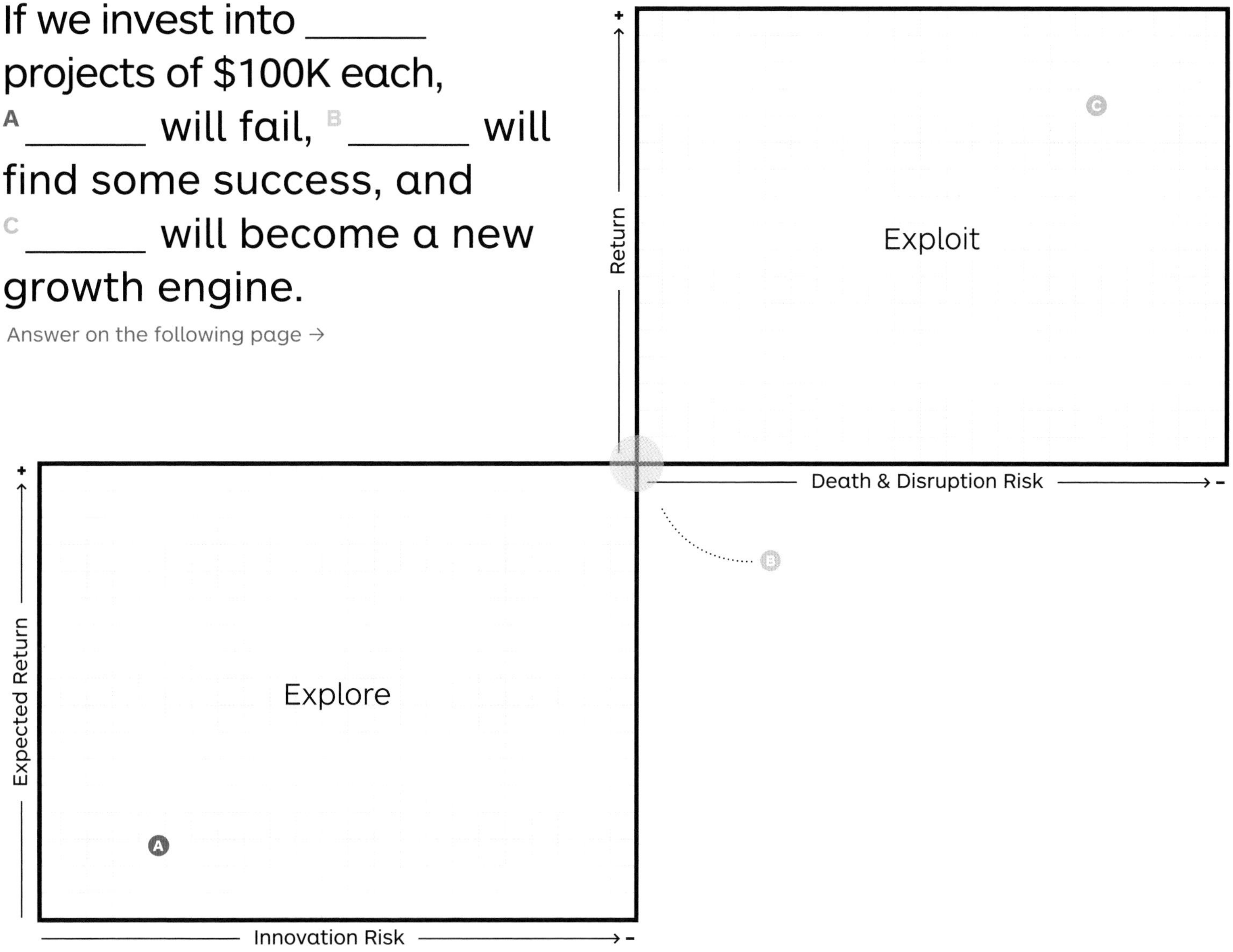

Return

Exploit

Death & Disruption Risk

Expected Return

Explore

Innovation Risk

You Can't Pick the Winner

The statistics on this page stem from early-stage venture capital investments into start-ups. This data provides a very good proxy to estimate the order of magnitude regarding the success/failure ratio in established organizations. The ratio might be even more extreme if we assume that established companies are often less innovative and more risk averse than start-ups.

Return Distribution in U.S. Venture Captial

2004–2013

Statistics from early-stage venture capital investment show that the majority of early-stage investments won't return capital or will only provide small returns.

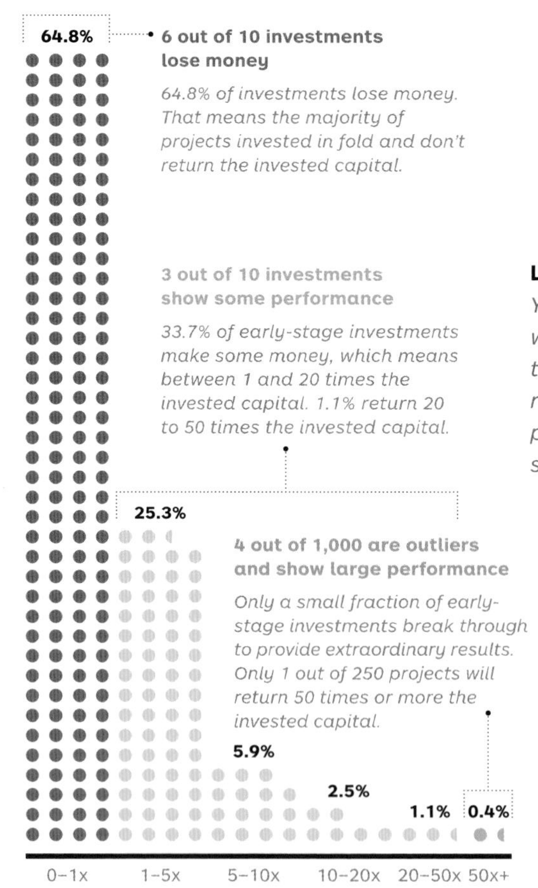
64.8%
6 out of 10 investments lose money
64.8% of investments lose money. That means the majority of projects invested in fold and don't return the invested capital.
3 out of 10 investments show some performance
33.7% of early-stage investments make some money, which means between 1 and 20 times the invested capital. 1.1% return 20 to 50 times the invested capital.
25.3%
4 out of 1,000 are outliers and show large performance
Only a small fraction of early-stage investments break through to provide extraordinary results. Only 1 out of 250 projects will return 50 times or more the invested capital.
5.9%
2.5%
1.1%
0.4%
% OF FINANCINGS
0–1x
1–5x
5–10x
10–20x
20–50x
50x+
RETURN GROUPINGS

Lessons Learned

You can't pick the winner without investing in projects that will fail. The larger the return you expect, the more projects you need to invest small sums in.

If we invest into 250 projects of $100K each, A 162 will fail, B 87 will find some success, and C 1 will become a new growth engine.

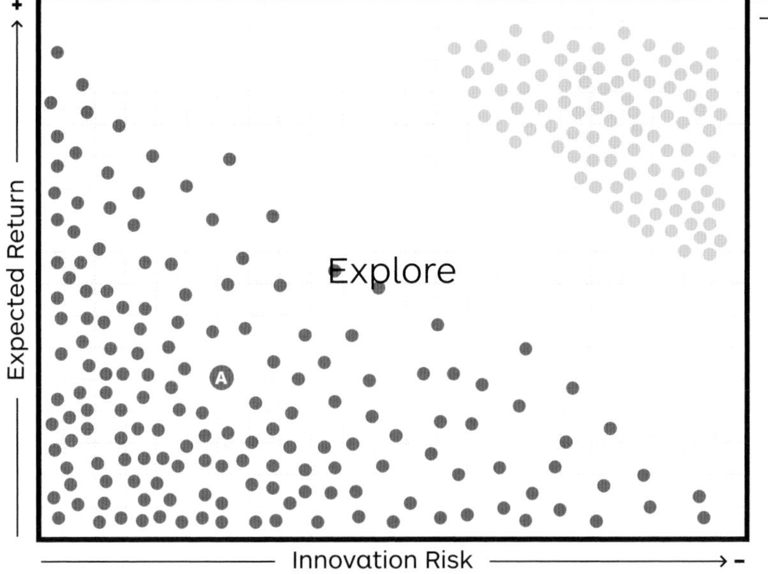

Metered Funding

The traditional investment process of established corporations equips teams with a large budget upfront to implement a full project. This leads to large risky bets with unproven ideas. In innovation you can't know what will work.

In the start-up and venture world risk and uncertainty are acknowledged and investments are spread over a portfolio of projects. This is combined with metered funding that equips teams with capital over a series of rounds. Only ideas with traction are retained and get follow-up funding to continue. In other words, a large number of ideas obtain small amounts of money to get started. Of all those ideas only those with sufficient traction and evidence receive follow-up funding. Ideas that don't work or project teams that don't have it in them are weeded out.

Smaller Outcome, Fewer Bets

Not every investment needs to produce outliers. A small- or medium-size company (SME), for example, will be happy with a new business that is in line with its current revenues and profits. Or, a division or business unit of an established company will not need to produce the growth expectations the overall company might have. What remains constant, however, is that you can't pick the winner. You have to invest in at least four projects, if you want to see any kind of return beyond the invested capital. The statistics would predict a return between 1x to 5x. Only 6 out of 100 will produce a 5x to 10x return.

If we invest into 10 projects of $100K each, A 6 will fail, B 3 will find some success, and C 1 will become a new growth engine.

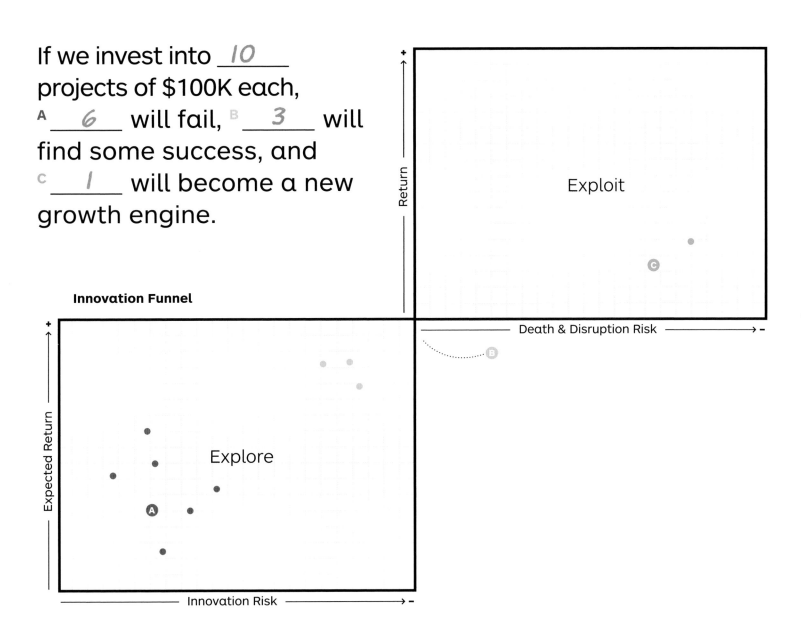

Innovation Funnel

Return +

Exploit

C

Death & Disruption Risk –

B

Expected Return +

Explore

A

Innovation Risk –

ALL YOU TOUCH WILL NOT TURN TO GOLD

MAKE MANY SMALL BETS TO CATCH ONE SUCCESS

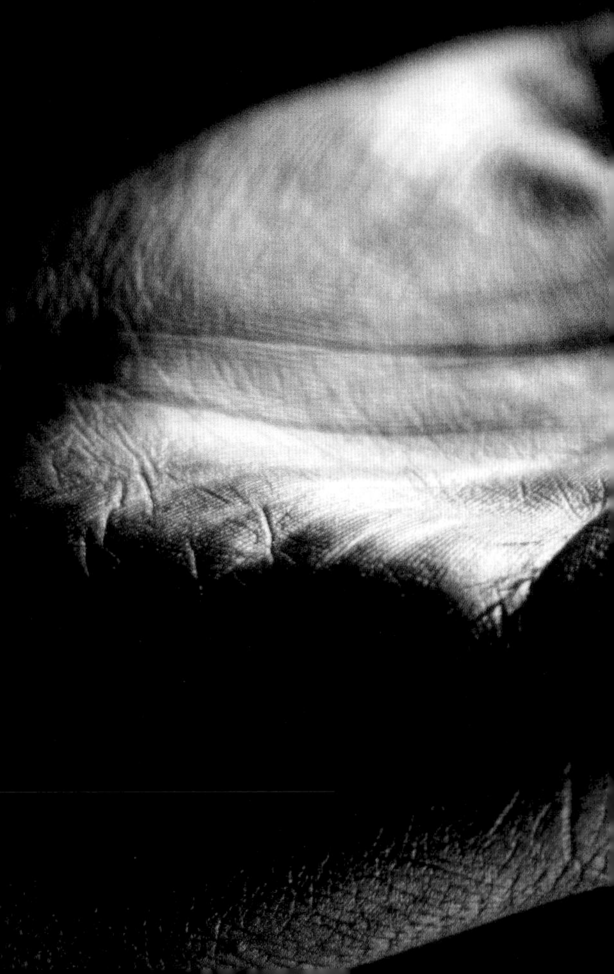

Portfolio Example
2008 ~~~ 2018

Amazon

"Failure and invention are inseparable twins," says Amazon CEO Jeff Bezos. Mistakes are where learning comes from and understanding this has been at the heart of Amazon's rampant success. Amazon has been able to build their entire organization's culture through embracing failure from leadership and incentivizing experimentation from every single employee.

Bezos understands the road to success is scattered with failures. What's clever about Amazon's strategy is its ability to create value out of a culture of failure. Externally, it has accustomed investors to its many costly failures so that the company's value is not tied to its losses but to its potential successes. Internally, it has rewarded employees who take initiative to pursue something that is far from a sure thing by making it completely "acceptable to take a risk, try hard, and fail."

Bezos has also indicated that the larger Amazon becomes, the larger its failures will be. In order for an organization to truly push its innovative boundaries, smaller "safe" failures won't really move the needle. Making a lot of mistakes, even disastrous failures (writing off $170 million for the Fire Phone), is what will keep Amazon relevant in the future.[1]

Read more about Amazon's culture of innovation on p. 302.

Amazon Marketplace		Amazon Web Service
✔ Amazon Marketplace	2007	✔ Amazon Web Service
Launches Fulfilmentby Amazon (FBA)		Launches Amazon AWS
	2005	
		Satellite hub sets up in South Africa
Launches free shipping on orders over $99	2003	Dedicates team of 57 to build "infrastructure of the world"
Auctions shuts down		
Multiple vendors exit Auctions; confusion over retail vs auctions		Bezos issues mandate for tech to be "good enough for outside use"
Launches Marketplace		
zShops shuts down	2001	Issues with timely tech/infrastructure deployment
Launches zShops mini-shops for other retailers within the Amazon site		
Creates a joint auction site for high end products with Sotheby's		Builds merchant.com for 3rd party seller to build online site
Purchases LiveBid to allow the broadcast of auctions live		
Amazon Auctions launches	1999	
Secret project to build an auction site from scratch to take on eBay		

Embrace Failure to Let Winners Emerge

This is a selection of businesses that Amazon has explored and retired since 2001.

JEFF BEZOS

Amazon founder & CEO

"The big winners pay for thousands of failed experiments."

- × Amazon Wallet
- × Endless.com
- × Amazon Music Importer
- × Amazon Destination
- × zShops
- × Amazon Local Register
- × Kozmo.com
- × Amazon Spark
- × Askville
- × Instant Pickup
- × Amazon Local
- × Dash Buttoms
- × Testdrive
- × Auctions
- × Quidsi
- × Storybuilder
- × Webpay
- × Fire Phone
- × Amazon Webstore
- × Amazon Restaurants

Portfolio Example

2008 ~~~ 2018

Ping An

In 2008, Peter Ma, founder of Ping An Insurance (Group) Company of China, Ltd., starts shifting the company from a financial conglomerate to become a technology company. Ping An builds an innovation funnel to transcend industry boundaries and compete in five distinct arenas beyond banking and insurance.

Ping An Insurance Company of China, Ltd., founded in 1988 by Peter Ma, is a Chinese financial conglomerate whose subsidiaries mainly deal with insurance, banking, and financial services. By 2007 it was China's second largest insurance provider.

In 2008, Peter Ma started Ping An's transformation from a financial institution to a technology company. Ping An built an innovation funnel to transcend industry boundaries and compete in five distinct arenas beyond banking and insurance.

In 2008, Ping An was ranked 462 on the *Fortune* Global 500 list. In 2019, it was ranked 29th and was the third most valuable global financial services company in the world.[2]

Pre-Empt Disruption

The global financial crisis of 2008 made Ping An realize how vulnerable it was to disruptions. The company decided to shift its strategic direction and business models to build resilience into the system.

PETER MA

Founder and CEO of Ping An Insurance

Strategic Direction

In 2008 Ping An shifts its strategic direction from a financial conglomerate to a tech company where their capabilities can be used a cross industries, moving from a single- to multiple-ecosystem strategy: finance, healthcare, auto services, real estate, and smart-city ecosystems.

Organizational Culture

To be a tech giant, Ping An understands they need to think and act like a start-up, prioritizing the tech start-ups in their ecosystem—now worth one-third of the company value. They even hired a Co-CEO, Jessica Tan, tasked with driving Ping An's technology transformation and dedicated to ideating and managing the start-ups in Ping An's portfolio.

Just like a start-up, Ping An acknowledges there are many areas where they have no experience, but they are not afraid of giving it a go. Ping An has founded start-ups in new sectors that have failed very quickly, learned from their mistakes, and evolved these failed start-ups into more successful versions.

Brand Image

Ping An no longer sees the company as a financial services provider; rather, it is evolving to an organization with adaptable skill sets and capabilities that can problem solve across any sector. Ping An wants to redefine industry lines and be seen as a tech company leader across an array of industries such as real estate, auto services, and even entertainment. Just like other tech start-ups, Ping An measures success in terms of online active users.

Exploit Guidance

In the last decade, Ping An has invested $7 billion into Ping An Technology, developing the four core technologies believed to be critical to the future of financial services:[3] cognitive recognition, AI, blockchain, and cloud. These technologies are breathing new life into Ping An's core financial services, increasing profits while lowering disruption risk.

Existing Businesses Change in Revenue From 2008–2018

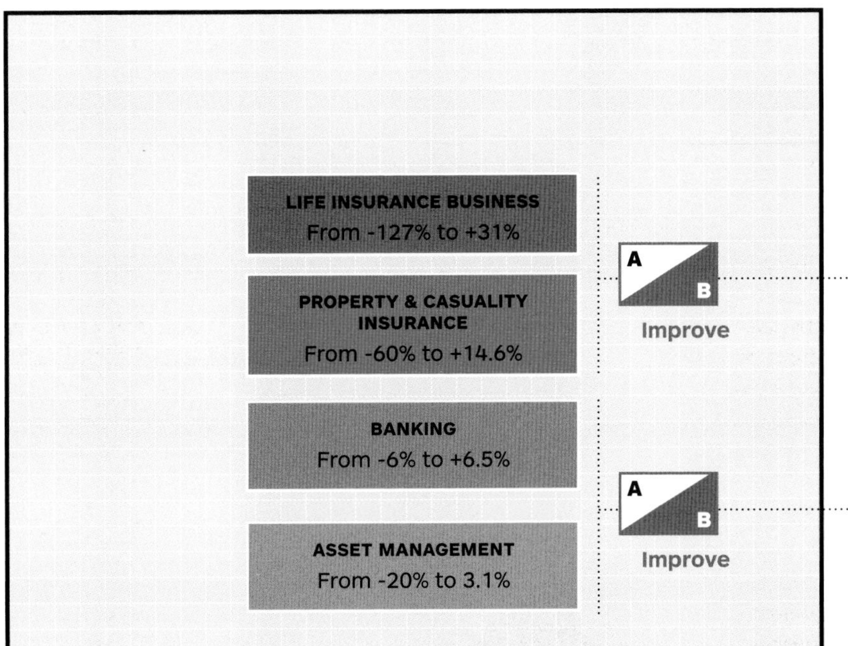

In 2014 **Ping An Property & Casualty Insurance** develops the Ping An Auto Owner app, using AI and telematics to track driver behavior in order to tailor policy pricing and risk selection. This redefines their relationship with customers by turning a passive product into a responsive personalized good that rewards good behavior. Through the app, Ping An can shorten the average turnaround time of a single claim to 168 seconds, with no back-end manual operation involved. As of 2019, the app has 16 million monthly active users, topping the list of auto service apps in China.[4]

Ping An spent four years developing proprietary technology using AI for loan application and fraud detection. By 2017 the program can read micro-expressions of applicants with 90% accuracy in detecting lies. This is used in loan approval instead of credit scores, giving Ping An access to a new customer segment: 40% of Chinese consumers who currently do not have a credit score. This technology can help reduce credit losses by 60%, with accuracy being much higher than other approaches.[5,6]

Exploring in the Future

Since Ping An's strategic shift in 2008 they have committed to spending 1% of revenue on R&D (~10% of profit) every year.[7] This was to establish Ping An Technology as the technology incubator arm of Ping An Group. Ping An Technology has been responsible for seeding the group's most successful start-ups while revolutionizing Ping An's existing financial services. By 2028, Ping An expects to have spent $21 billion in R&D to support their strategic direction of evolving into a tech giant.[8]

This steadfast commitment to R&D investment, along with an agile "can do" culture, has enabled Ping An to have a strong innovation pipeline resulting in a diverse explore portfolio that is now worth one-third of the company's brand value. These include 11 start-ups in tech. Two are listed (Lufax, Autohome) and four are valued at more than $1 billion (Lufax, Good Doctor, Autohome and OneConnect).[9]

JESSICA TAN

Ping An Group Co-CEO

Measuring Success

Ping An's most successful platforms are the ones that have fully embraced their ecosystem strategy of being a "one-stop shop" for their customers, continuously improving online user experience, and aligning use cases with user needs. Ping An tracks user engagement to measure the success of their business. In 2019, yearly active users reached 269 million, translating to 2.49 online services per user.[9]

Good Doctor (2014)

Ping An realized the medical needs in China were woefully underserved and saw an opportunity to use its capabilities to bolster the ecosystem. Good Doctor was developed by Wang Tao, previously VP of Alibaba group. He joined in 2013 as the new CEO of Ping An Health, with the objective of building China's largest medical app. Good Doctor is now the largest online healthcare platform in China, with over 265 million users. It provides users with comprehensive 24/7 online consultation through their AI doctor services. Good Doctor went public in 2018 with a $1.12 billion IPO.[11]

Ping An Net Profit Growth (2010–2018)

In billions (Yuan)

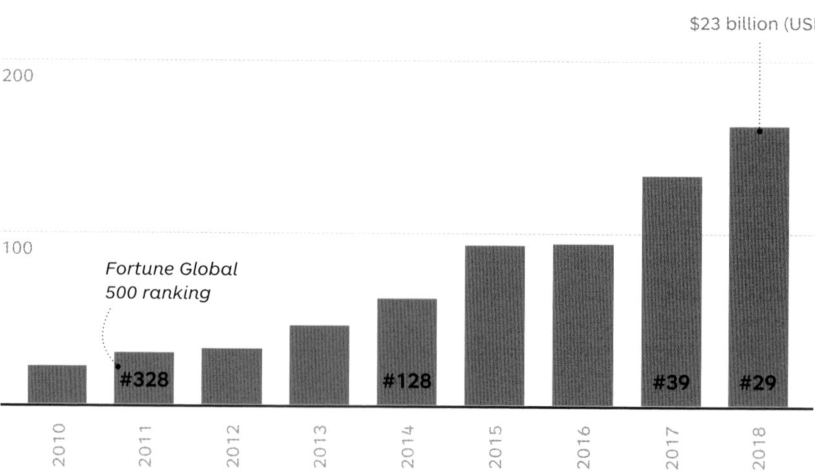

Oneconnect (2015)

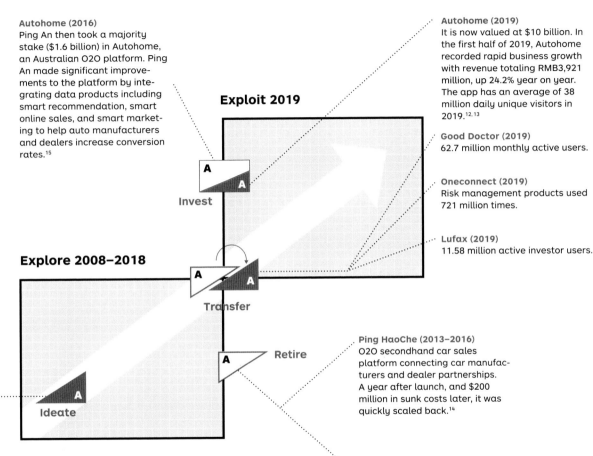

Ping An's proprietary technology has become so advanced that they have now bundled it up into a cloud platform known as OneConnect, providing fintech solutions to other financial institutions. As of 2018 OneConnect had provided services for 3,289 financial institutions, including 590 banks, 72 insurers and 2,627 non-bank financial institutions across China. It is now rolling out into the rest of Asia and Europe as well.

Autohome (2016)
Ping An then took a majority stake ($1.6 billion) in Autohome, an Australian O2O platform. Ping An made significant improvements to the platform by integrating data products including smart recommendation, smart online sales, and smart marketing to help auto manufacturers and dealers increase conversion rates.[15]

Autohome (2019)
It is now valued at $10 billion. In the first half of 2019, Autohome recorded rapid business growth with revenue totaling RMB3,921 million, up 24.2% year on year. The app has an average of 38 million daily unique visitors in 2019.[12,13]

Exploit 2019

Good Doctor (2019)
62.7 million monthly active users.

Oneconnect (2019)
Risk management products used 721 million times.

Lufax (2019)
11.58 million active investor users.

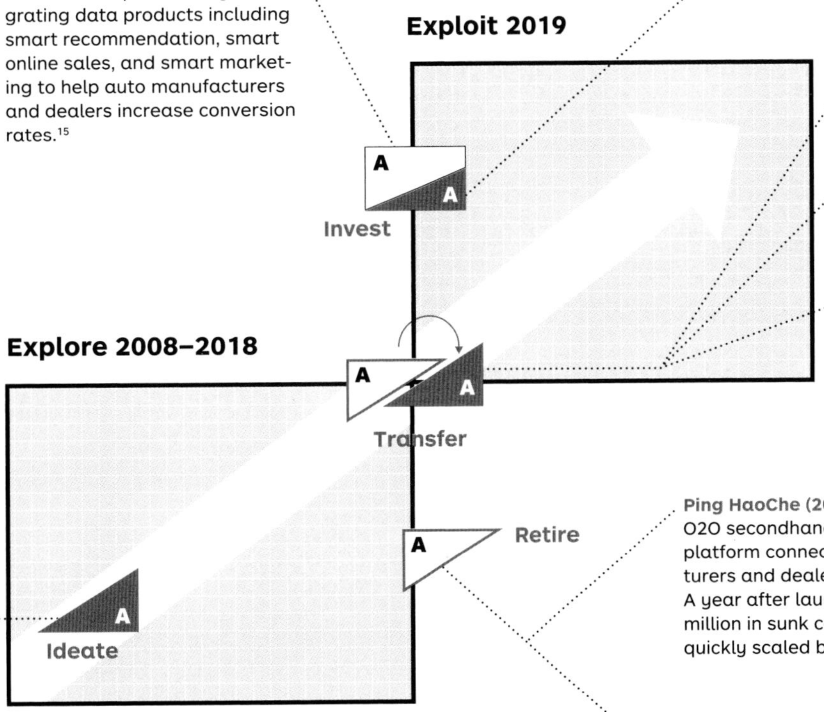

Invest

Explore 2008–2018

Transfer

Retire

Ideate

Ping HaoChe (2013–2016)
O2O secondhand car sales platform connecting car manufacturers and dealer partnerships. A year after launch, and $200 million in sunk costs later, it was quickly scaled back.[14]

Lufax
Lufax is an example of how Ping An has been able to provide financial services to a segment of the market it was unable to access until it made the transition to a tech company. It matches borrowers and lenders by providing the middle class with over 5,000 financial products for investments of as little as $1,000. Lufax uses AI (robo-advisor) to cut operating costs and optimize interactions, opening up a whole new market of investors to Ping An. Lufax is currently valued at $5 billion, with Ping An owning 41%.[10]

Ping Haufang (2014–2018)
A one-stop shop for home sales, rental, real estate investing and property developments. It failed because it was unable to capture the complexity of the real estate industry, an ecosystem Ping An does not have any experience in. Yet they were very much willing to give it a go.

Business R&D

Innovation is a young, emerging profession that substantially differs from managing a business and is not the same as traditional R&D. Because it's such a young discipline, some misconceptions persist that, unfortunately, prevent organizations from investing in innovation the right way. We outline five misconceptions that we've seen senior leaders falling for.

Misconception #1
Innovation = new technologies and R&D.
Reality
Technology may or may not play a role in a particular innovation.

Innovation is first and foremost about exploring novel ways to create value for customers and your organization. That is broader than just technology-based innovation. The Nintendo Wii, for example, was an inferior technological platform when it launched, yet it disrupted the gaming industry. (cf p. 240).

Misconception #2
Innovation = find the perfect idea.
Reality
Good ideas are easy.

The hard part of innovation is the search and iteration process of shaping and adapting ideas until you find a concrete value proposition that customers care about, embedded in a business model that can scale profitably. Finally, to reduce risk you should not bet on a few bold ideas that look good, but create a portfolio in which you explore many ideas, so the best ones emerge.

Successful Innovation = (R&D)* + Business R&D + Execution[16]

invention*
*optional

Customer Value | Business Model

Misconception #3

Innovation = build products (and services) customers love.

Reality

Products, services, and value propositions customers care about are a pillar of innovation, yet insufficient on their own.

Without a business model that can scale profitably, even the best products will die. All types of innovations, from efficiency to transformative innovation, require a sustainable business model.

Misconception #4

Innovation = creative genius that can't be learned.

Reality

Innovation is not black magic that depends on creative genius.

Turning innovative ideas into a business result is an art and a science that can be learned. Some aspects, like the tools, business model patterns, or testing can be learned "in the classroom." Other aspects, like turning evidence from testing into better value propositions and business models, are more an "art" (i.e., pattern recognition) and come from experience.

Misconception #5

Innovation = business and strategy as usual.

Reality

Most organizations have done traditional R&D for decades.

However, what worked in the past isn't fit for the future. Business models and value propositions are expiring faster than ever before, industry boundaries are disappearing, and competitors increasingly come from unexpected places. It's time for a new type of business R&D on the strategic agenda.

Guidance

The activities a company undertakes to spot, create, test, de-risk, and invest in a portfolio of novel business opportunities. Opportunities range from improving the existing business(es) to exploring radically new ones. The heart of business R&D is the art and science of shaping value propositions and business models and the identification and testing of desirability, feasibility, viability, and adaptability risks for each opportunity. It complements traditional technology and product R&D, which mainly focus on feasibility.

Innovation Performance and R&D spending

According to a 2018 study by Strategy& of PwC there is no strong direct link between innovation success and R&D spending. For example, the car manufacturer Volkswagen spent $15.8 billion on R&D and was the third largest spender in the study, yet didn't make the top 10 innovators. Tesla spent $1.5 billion on R&D or 7% of revenues and ranked fifth among the study's most innovative companies.[17]

The top two in that list also look pretty different. Top ranked Apple is only the seventh largest R&D spender with $11.6 billion or 5.1% of revenues. Second ranked Amazon is the number one R&D spender with $22.6 billion or 12.7% of revenues. Pharmaceutical companies like Roche, Johnson & Johnson, Merck, Novartis, Pfizer, and Sanofi are all top 20 spenders (14% to 25% of revenues), yet none of them made the top 10 innovators.

The Strategy& study shows that the 10 most innovative companies outperformed the 10 biggest R&D spenders on revenue growth, gross margin, and market cap growth.

Innovating vs. Spending[17]

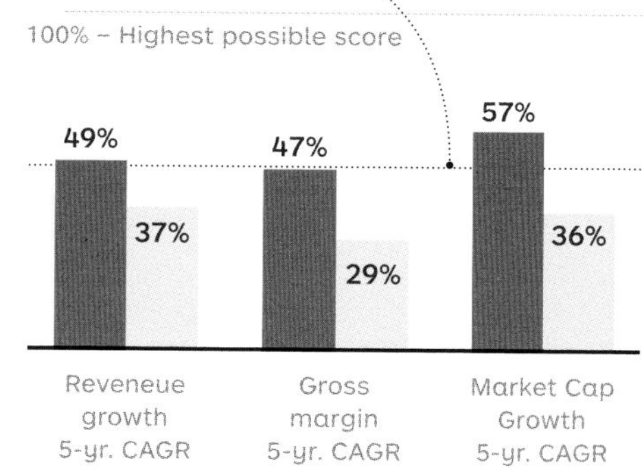

Business R&D in Action

Business R&D doesn't replace traditional technology and product R&D. It's complementary. Its purpose is to create, explore, and research new value propositions and business models and reduce the risk for the business hypotheses underlying them. Business R&D may draw on traditional R&D, which focuses more on the technological aspects of feasibility.

Main Business R&D tasks include:

1) Identification of Opportunities
This is the activity of scanning the environment for promising opportunities to improve the existing business or explore completely new ones. Opportunities may come from shifting customer needs, technology innovations, regulatory changes, societal trends, and more. It may also include the acquisition of competitors, start-ups, or complementary organizations.

2) Shaping, Testing, and Adapting Value Propositions and Business Models
The majority of Business R&D is dedicated to testing opportunities and turning them into real businesses. This consists of shaping, testing, and adapting value propositions and business models, until customers care and evidence shows you can build and scale the business model profitably.

3) Portfolio Management
This last activity of Business R&D consists of protecting your company from disruption by maintaining a business (model) portfolio. This includes spreading your innovation bets across all types of innovation projects and incrementally investing in those that produce evidence, while shelving those that don't. This diversifies risk and lets the best ideas and teams emerge.

Explore

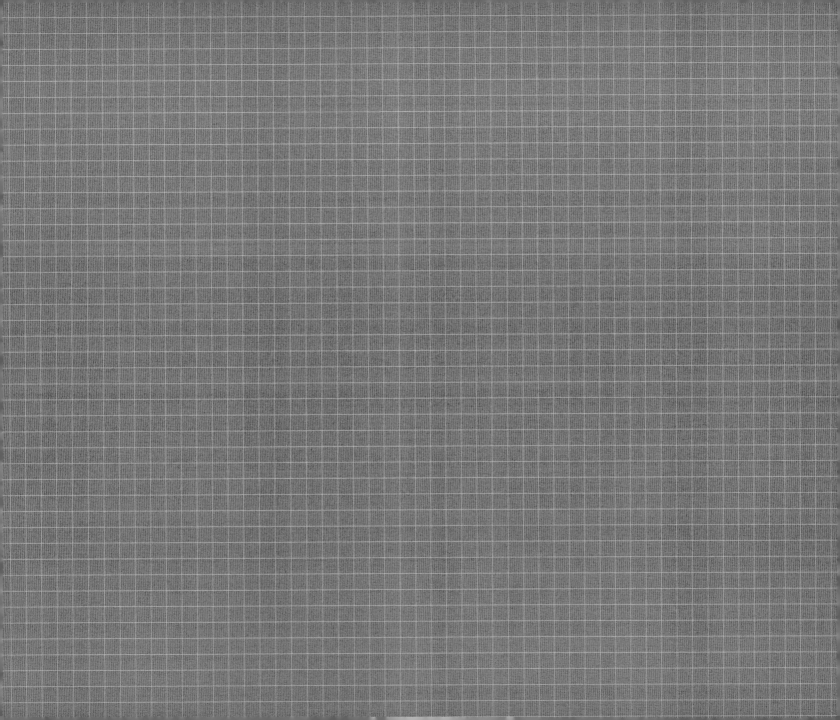

Exploration Portfolio

Your exploration portfolio serves to develop new growth engines for the future and protects you from outside disruption. It helps you either derisk new business areas you hope to develop and implement yourself or it equips you with sufficient insights to make better acquisitions.

For all your exploration projects work through two main iteration loops: the improvement of your business design to maximize expected returns and the reduction of risk and uncertainty to avoid investing in projects that won't hold up to the real world.

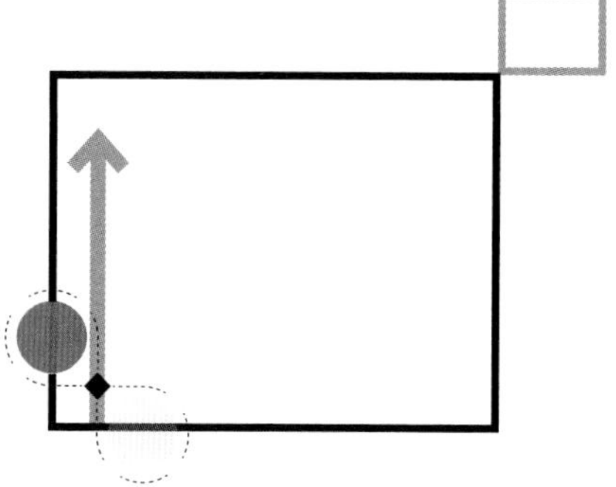

Business Design
Increase Expected Return

In the business design loop teams shape and reshape their business ideas to turn them into business models with the best possible expected return. First iterations are based on intuition and starting points (product ideas, technologies, market opportunities, etc.). Subsequent iterations are based on evidence and insights from the testing loop.

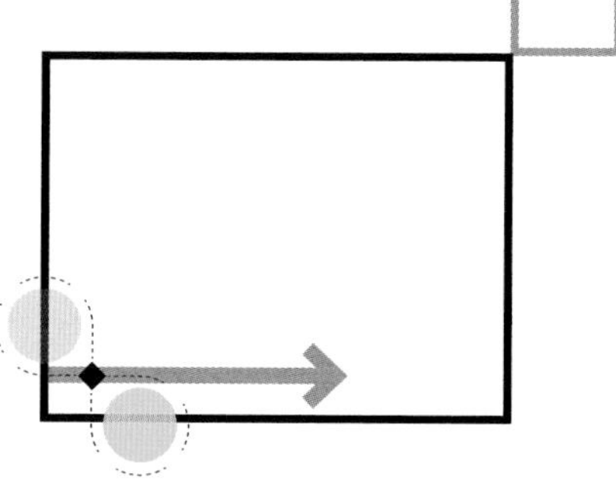

Test
Reduce Innovation Risk

In the test loop teams test and retest the hypotheses underlying their business ideas until they have sufficiently reduced the risk and uncertainty of an idea to justify larger investments. First iterations are often based on quick and cheap experiments (e.g., interviews and surveys to gauge customer interest). Subsequent, more sophisticated experiments help confirm initial insights.

A strong business model design "on paper" does not mean an idea is necessarily going to work. To figure out if your idea is going to work, you need to test your business model design "in the real world." Business design and testing are two loops that continuously feed each other.

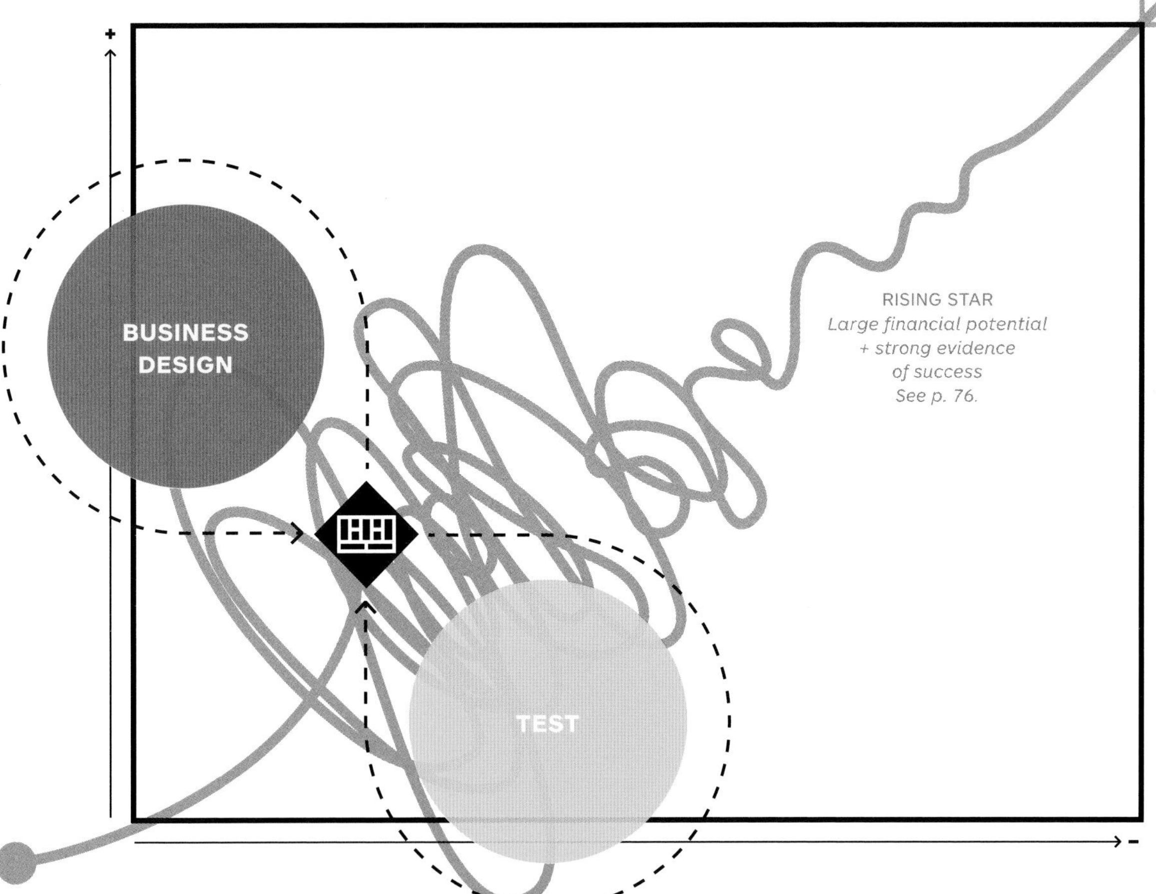

Business Model Design Performance

Good business model design is about competing beyond superior or innovative products, services, and lower prices. It is about creating business models that beat or even disrupt competition, based on superior profitability and protectability. At every stage of your innovation journey you should ask yourself how you can create a better business model, based on what you learn from the market.

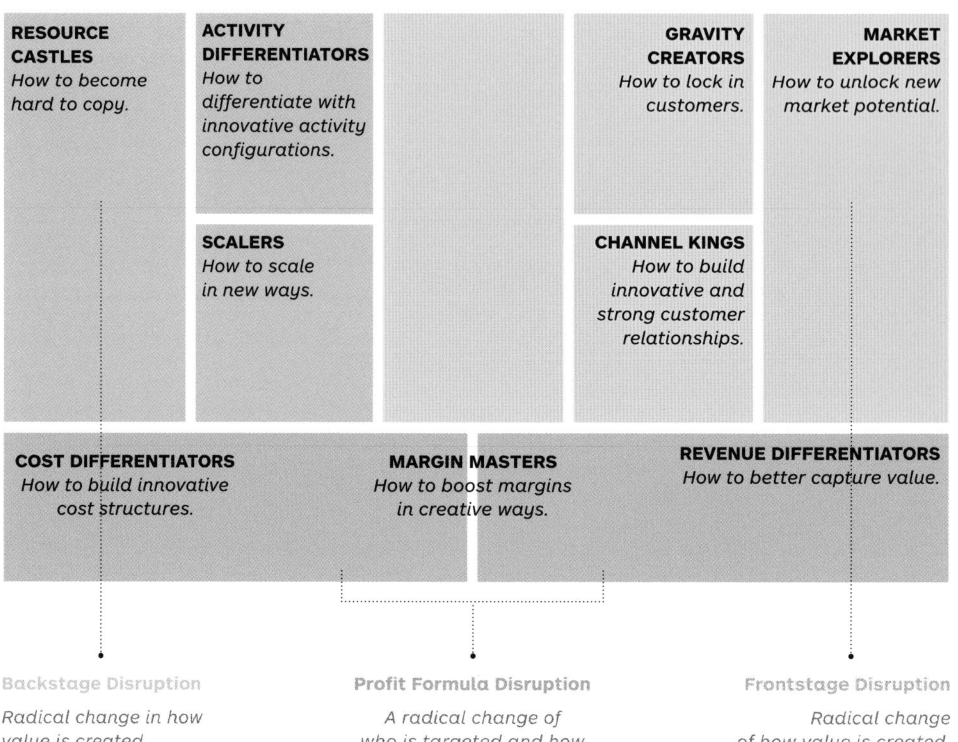
RESOURCE CASTLES
How to become hard to copy.
ACTIVITY DIFFERENTIATORS
How to differentiate with innovative activity configurations.
SCALERS
How to scale in new ways.
GRAVITY CREATORS
How to lock in customers.
CHANNEL KINGS
How to build innovative and strong customer relationships.
MARKET EXPLORERS
How to unlock new market potential.
COST DIFFERENTIATORS
How to build innovative cost structures.
MARGIN MASTERS
How to boost margins in creative ways.
REVENUE DIFFERENTIATORS
How to better capture value.
Backstage Disruption
Radical change in how value is created.
Profit Formula Disruption
A radical change of who is targeted and how value is delivered.
Frontstage Disruption
Radical change of how value is created.

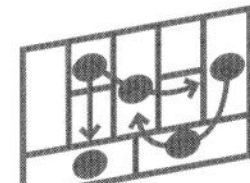

Business Model Pattern Library
To help you boost your business model performance, see the library of nine business model patterns in chapter 3. These patterns serve as a reference library or inspiration to help you compete beyond products, services, and price.

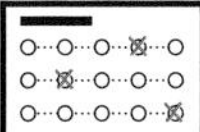

Assess Your Design
We also introduce an assessment sheet on p. 213-214 to evaluate the current design of your business model idea, existing business, or business unit. A high score indicates a strong business model. A low score indicates strong potential for improvement. You can also use this score to evaluate existing and new competitors in the market. Caveat: Good design DOES NOT EQUAL "it's going to work."

Design–Test

To explore ideas systematically, work through two iterative loops: shape ideas with business design and reduce risk with testing.

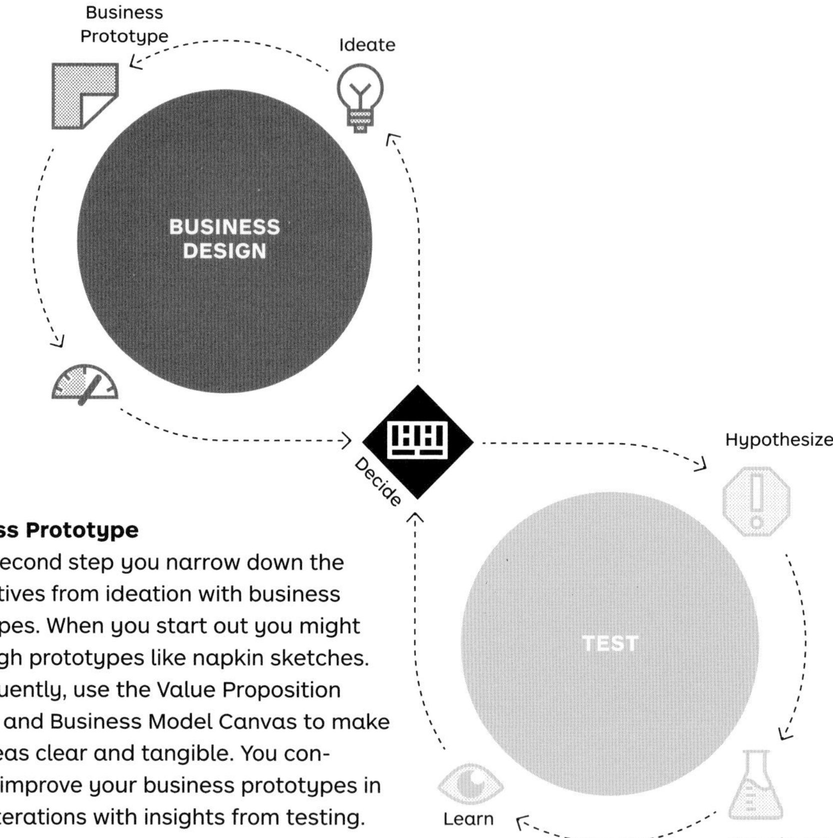

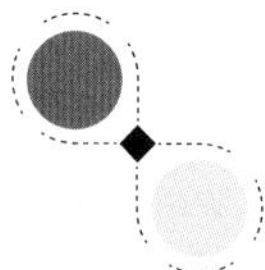

Business Design Loop

In the design loop you shape and reshape your business idea to turn it into the best possible business model. Your first iterations are based on your intuition and starting point (product idea, technology, market opportunity, etc.). Subsequent iterations are based on evidence and insights from the testing loop.

Ideate
In this first step you try to come up with as many alternative ways as possible to use your initial intuition or insights from testing to turn your idea into a stronger business. At this stage it's important to not fall in love with your first ideas.

Business Prototype
In this second step you narrow down the alternatives from ideation with business prototypes. When you start out you might use rough prototypes like napkin sketches. Subsequently, use the Value Proposition Canvas and Business Model Canvas to make your ideas clear and tangible. You constantly improve your business prototypes in future iterations with insights from testing.

Assess
In this last step of the design loop you assess the design of your business prototypes with the assessment sheet on p. 110. Once you are satisfied with the design of your business prototypes you start testing in the field or go back to testing if you are working on subsequent iterations.

STEVE BLANK

Inventor of Customer Development and Godfather of the Lean Startup Movement

"No business plan survives first contact with customers."

Testing Loop

Every (radically) new business idea, product, service, value proposition, business model, or strategy requires a leap of faith. If proven false, these important and yet unproven aspects of your idea can make or break your business.

That's why it's important to break down your idea into smaller chunks that you can test. You achieve this by making the uncertainty and assumptions underlying your idea explicit in the form of hypotheses. Then you prioritize these hypotheses to test the most important ones.

Hypothesize
The first step of testing a business idea is to understand the risks and uncertainty of an idea. Ask: "What are all the things that need to be true for this idea to work?" This question allows you to make the assumptions underlying an idea explicit in the form of testable hypotheses. In other words, you break down a big idea into smaller testable pieces.

Experiment
To reduce the risk and uncertainty of your ideas it's not sufficient to make your hypotheses explicit. Don't make the mistake of executing business ideas without evidence. Test your ideas thoroughly with experiments, regardless of how great they may seem in theory. This second step will prevent you from pursuing ideas that look good in theory, but won't work in reality.

Learn
In this last step of the testing process you analyze the evidence from experiments in order to support or refute your hypotheses. Your insights will inform your decision to persevere with, pivot, or kill your idea.

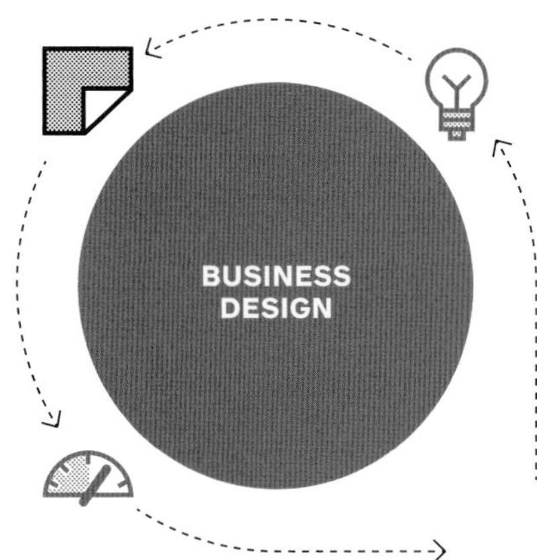

BUSINESS DESIGN

The Business Model Canvas

You don't have to be a master of the Business Model Canvas to use this book, but you can use it to shape ideas into a business model so you can define, test, and manage risk. In this book, we use the Business Model Canvas to define the desirability, feasibility, and viability of an idea. If you'd like to go deeper than the synopsis of the Business Model Canvas, we recommend reading *Business Model Generation* or going online to learn more.

Customer Segments

Describe the different groups of people or organizations you aim to reach and serve.

Value Propositions

Describe the bundle of products and services that create value for a specific customer segment.

Channels

Describe how a company communicates with and reaches its customer segments to deliver a value proposition.

Customer Relationships

Describe the types of relationships a company establishes with specific customer segments.

Revenue Streams

Describe the cash a company generates from each customer segment.

Key Resources

Describe the most important assets required to make a business model work.

Key Activities

Describe the most important things a company must do to make its business model work.

Key Partners

Describe the network of suppliers and partners that make the business model work.

Cost Structure

Describe all costs incurred to operate a business model.

The Value Proposition Canvas

Much like the Business Model Canvas, the same goes for the Value Proposition Canvas. You'll get value from this book without having a proficiency in using it, but we do reference it for framing your experimentation, especially with regard to understanding the customer and how your products and services create value. If you'd like to go deeper than the synopsis of the Value Proposition Canvas, we recommend reading *Value Proposition Design* or going online to learn more.

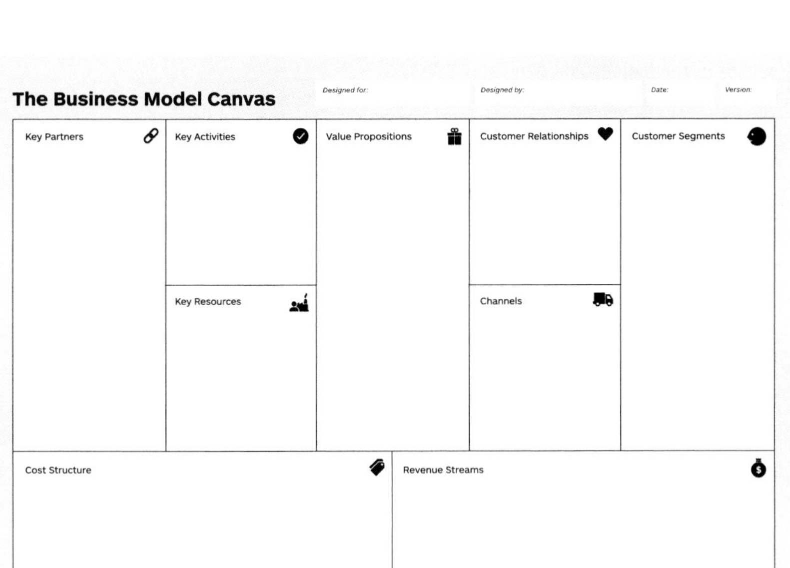

To learn more about the Business Model Canvas visit strategyzer.com/books/business-model-generation.

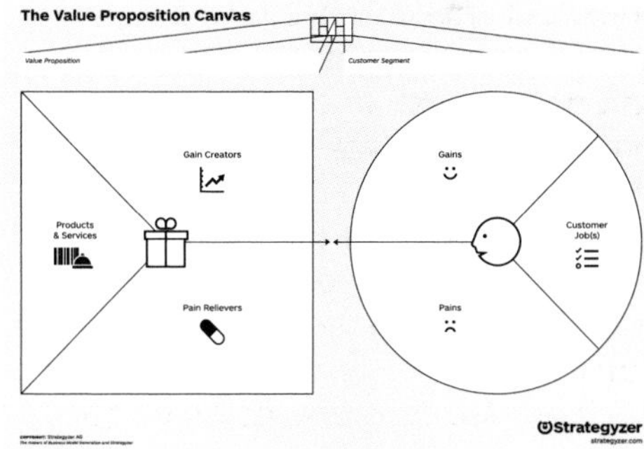

To learn more about the Value Proposition Canvas visit strategyzer.com/books/value-proposition-design.

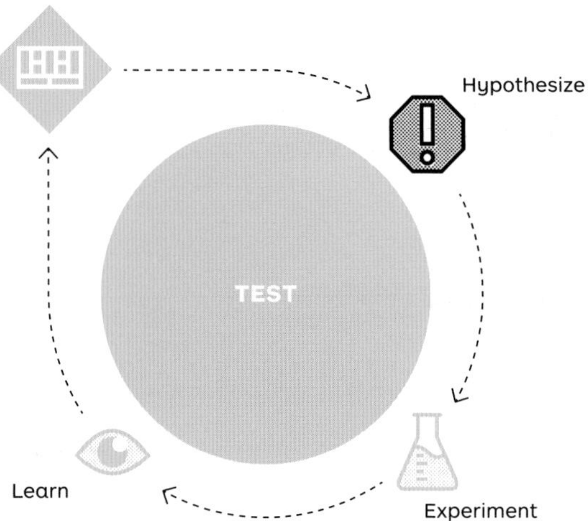

Hypothesize

The first step of the testing loop is to identify and prioritize the critical hypotheses underlying your business idea. This allows you to make the most important risks of your idea explicit so that you can test them.

Definition

- *an assumption that your value proposition, business model, or strategy builds on.*
- *what you need to learn about to understand if your business idea might work.*
- *linked to the desirability, feasibility, viability, or adaptability of a business idea.*
- *formulated so that it can be tested and supported (validated) or refuted (invalidated) based on evidence and guided by experience.*

Identify the Four Types of Hypotheses

To understand the risk and uncertainty of your idea you need to ask: "What are all the things that need to be true for this idea to work?" This will allow you to identify all four types of hypotheses underlying a business idea: desirability, feasibility, viability, and adaptability.

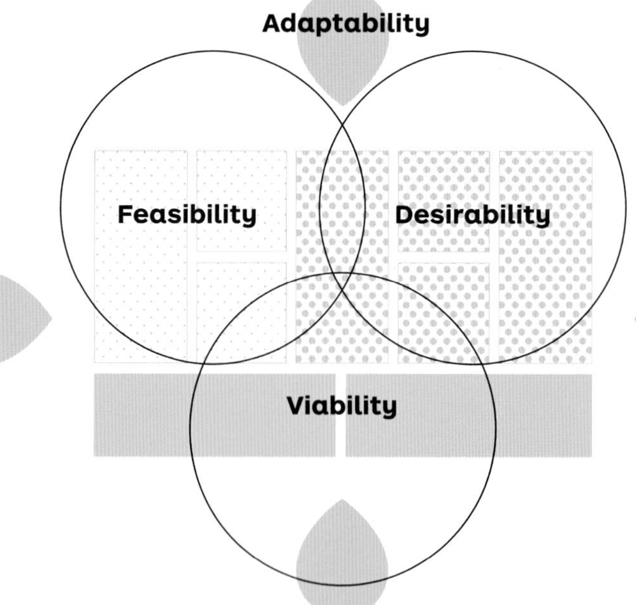

Prioritize Your Hypotheses

Not all hypotheses are equal. It is important to identify the most important hypotheses for which you have no evidence, in order to test them first. You achieve this by using a tool called the Assumptions Map that uses the following two dimensions:

Desirability
Does the market want this idea?
Use the Value Proposition Canvas and the frontstage of the Business Model Canvas to identify desirability hypotheses.

Feasibility
Can we deliver at scale?
Use the backstage of the Business Model Canvas to identify feasibility hypotheses.

Viability
Is the idea profitable enough?
Use the revenue streams and cost structure in the Business Model Canvas to identify viability hypotheses.

Adaptability

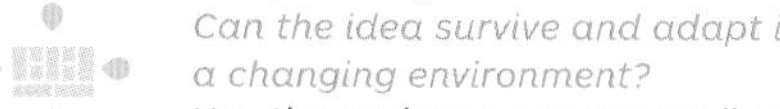

Can the idea survive and adapt in a changing environment?
Use the environment surrounding your business model to identify adaptability hypotheses.

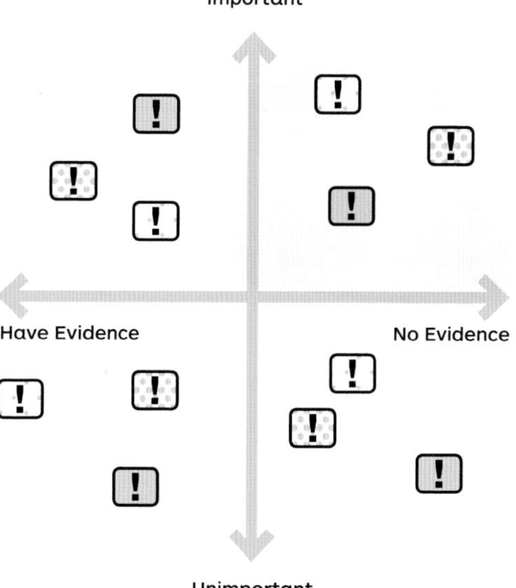

Importance
Ask how critical a hypothesis is for your business idea to succeed. In other terms, if that hypothesis is proven wrong, your business idea will fail, and all other hypotheses become irrelevant.

Existence of Evidence
Ask how much observable and recent firsthand evidence you have—or don't have—to support or refute a specific hypothesis.

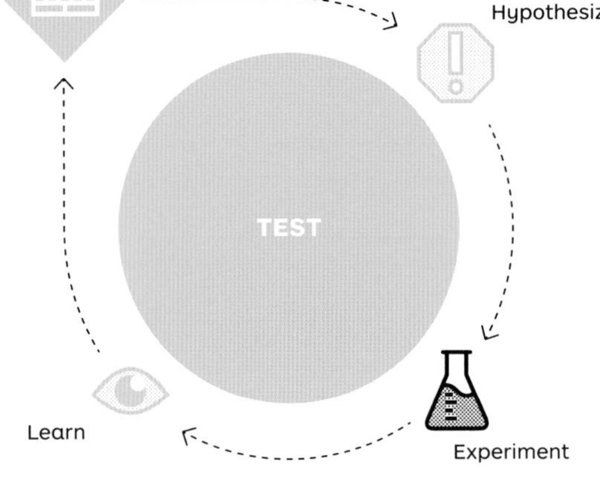

TESTING

Experiment

Reducing the Risk of Your Ideas with Experiments

To avoid building something nobody wants you need to test your ideas thoroughly with business experiments. Test your most important hypotheses first and continue until you are sufficiently confident that your idea will work.

Definition

- *a procedure to reduce the risk and uncertainty of a business idea.*
- *produces weak or strong evidence that supports or refutes a hypothesis.*
- *can be fast/slow and cheap/expensive to conduct.*

There are a multitude of experiments to test your ideas. We describe 44 different business experiments at length in our book *Testing Business Ideas* (strategyzer.com/test). Experiments can range from simple interviews over discussion prototypes, all the way to simulated sales, working prototypes (so-called minimum viable products, [MVP]), and co-creation with customers. In general, we have observed that most teams don't sufficiently test their ideas and barely go beyond interviews. We'd like to invite you to more thoroughly test your ideas over three phases before you transfer them to your execution portfolio and scale them.

To learn more about Testing Business Ideas visit strategyzer.com/test.

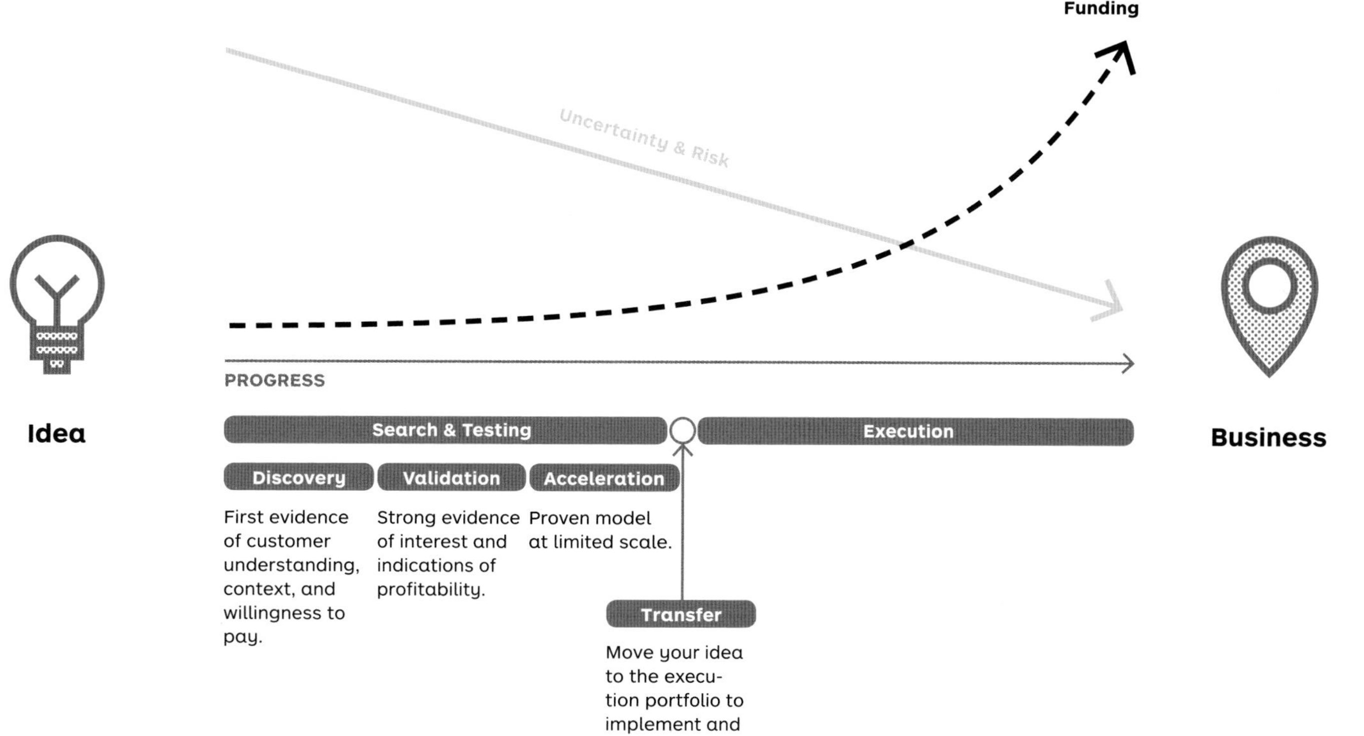
Funding
Uncertainty & Risk
Idea
PROGRESS
Business
Search & Testing
Execution
Discovery
Validation
Acceleration
First evidence of customer understanding, context, and willingness to pay.
Strong evidence of interest and indications of profitability.
Proven model at limited scale.
Transfer
Move your idea to the execution portfolio to implement and scale.

Here are four rules of thumb that we describe in Testing Business Ideas *to pick the right experiments to test your business ideas.*

1. **Go cheap and fast at the beginning.**

   Early on, you generally know little. Stick to cheap and quick experiments to detect the right direction. You can afford starting out with weaker evidence, because you will test more later. Ideally, you select an experiment that is cheap and fast, yet still produces strong evidence.

2. **Increase the strength of evidence with multiple experiments for the same hypothesis.**

   Run several experiments to support or refute a hypothesis. Try to learn about a hypothesis as fast as possible, then run more experiments to produce stronger evidence for confirmation. Don't make important decisions based on one experiment or weak evidence.

3. **Always pick the experiment that produces the strongest evidence, given your constraints.**

   Always select and design the strongest experiment you can, while respecting the context. When uncertainty is high you should go fast and cheap, but that doesn't necessarily mean you can't produce strong evidence.

4. **Reduce uncertainty as much as you can before you build anything.**

   People often think they need to build something to start testing an idea. Quite the contrary. The higher the cost to build something, the more you need to run multiple experiments to show that customers actually have the jobs, pains, and gains you think they have.

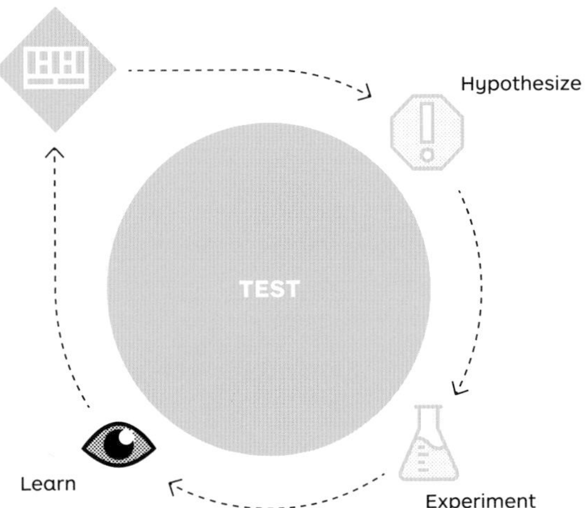

Learn

The last step of the Testing Loop is about learning if your evidence from testing supports or refutes your business hypotheses. It's the analysis of evidence to detect patterns and gain insights. The more experiments you run, the more evidence you have, the stronger it is, the more confident you can be about your insights.

Evidence

Evidence is what you use to support or refute the hypotheses underlying your business idea. It is data that you get from research or generate from business experiments. Evidence can come in many different forms, ranging from weak to strong.

Definition

- *data generated from an experiment or collected in the field.*
- *fact(s) that support or refute a hypothesis.*
- *can be of different nature (e.g., quotes, behaviors, conversion rates, orders, purchases, etc.) and can be weak/strong.*

Evidence Strength

The strength of a piece of evidence determines how reliably the evidence helps support or refute a hypothesis. You can evaluate the strength of evidence by checking four areas.

Weak	**Strong(er)**
Opinions (beliefs)	Facts (events)
What people say	What people do
Lab settings	Real-world settings
Small investments	Large investments

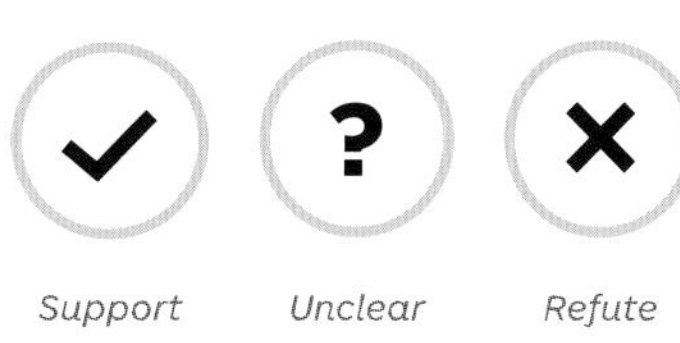

Insights

Insights are what you learn from studying the evidence. You need to search for patterns that either support or refute the hypotheses you have been testing.

Definition

- *what you learn from studying the evidence.*
- *learning related to the validity of hypotheses and potential discovery of new directions.*
- *foundation to make informed business decisions and take action.*

Confidence Level
Your confidence level indicates how much you believe that your evidence is strong enough to support or refute a specific hypothesis.

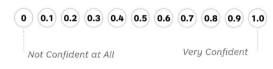

Very Confident
You can be very confident if you've run several experiments of which at least one is a call-to-action test that produced very strong evidence.

Somewhat Confident
You can be somewhat confident if you've run several experiments that produce strong evidence or a particularly strong call-to-action experiment.

Not Really Confident
You need to run more and stronger experiments if you've only done interviews or surveys in which people say what they will do. They might behave differently in reality.

Not Confident at All
You need to experiment more if you've only run one experiment that produces weak evidence, such as an interview or survey.

AVOID BIG FAILURES, OR YOU'RE DEAD

EMBRACE SMALL FAILURES, OR YOU'RE DEAD

DEFINITION

Innovation Metrics

In innovation, the main task is not to measure if you are on time and on budget, which are key metrics in an execution project. In innovation and exploration it is crucial to measure whether you are reducing the risk and uncertainty of new business ideas before you invest big and scale.

Exploration	⟷	Exploitation
Search and find	**Objective**	Execute and scale
Low	**Predictability**	High
Reduction of risk and uncertainty of new ideas	**Key Performance Indicators**	On time and on budget
Learn and adapt	**Key Activity**	Plan and implement
Okay (cheap and fast)	**Failure**	Not an option
Investment to learn	**Cost of Failure**	Loss = Punishment
Expected ROI	**Financials**	Real ROI

For every exploration project you need to track four main key performance indicators (KPIs):

- *Risk and Uncertainty*
  How much have you de-risked an idea so far? How much risk remains?
- *Expected Profitability*
  How big might the idea be in financial terms?
- *Learning Velocity and Time Spent*
  How much time have you spent so far? How much have you learned during this time?
- *Cost*
  How much have you spent to test this idea?

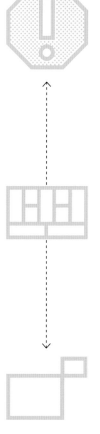

Risk and uncertainty are measured at three different levels:

1. Hypothesis Level

By breaking down an idea into smaller chunks you can understand and test risk at a more granular level. We call this the hypotheses underlying your idea. In other words, the most important things that need to be true for your idea to work. If you don't have recent evidence to support or refute a hypothesis, you need to test to reduce risk and uncertainty.

2. Business Model Level

At the business model level you look at all the important hypotheses underlying your idea. The more unproven hypotheses you have, the riskier your idea. To de-risk an idea you need to test the most important hypotheses until you are confident that the idea could work.

3. Portfolio Level

At the portfolio level you look at all the ideas you currently have and how much you've de-risked them so far. You also look at the financial potential of each one.

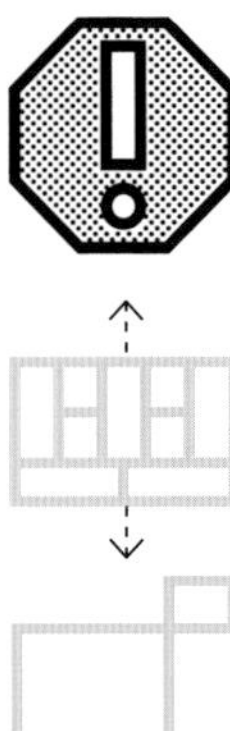

Hypothesis Level

At the hypothesis level you capture everything related to a specific hypothesis in terms of experiments conducted and insights gained.

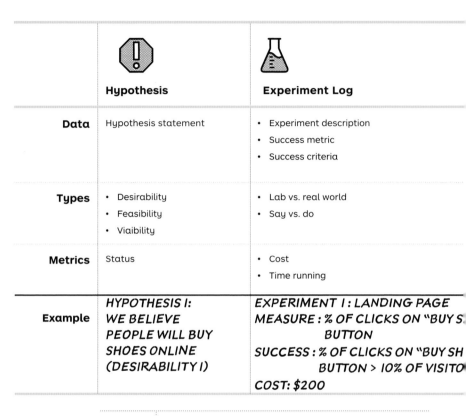

	Hypothesis	Experiment Log
Data	Hypothesis statement	• Experiment description • Success metric • Success criteria
Types	• Desirability • Feasibility • Viability	• Lab vs. real world • Say vs. do
Metrics	Status	• Cost • Time running
Example	HYPOTHESIS I: WE BELIEVE PEOPLE WILL BUY SHOES ONLINE (DESIRABILITY I)	EXPERIMENT I : LANDING PAGE MEASURE : % OF CLICKS ON "BUY S BUTTON SUCCESS : % OF CLICKS ON "BUY SH BUTTON > 10% OF VISITO COST: $200

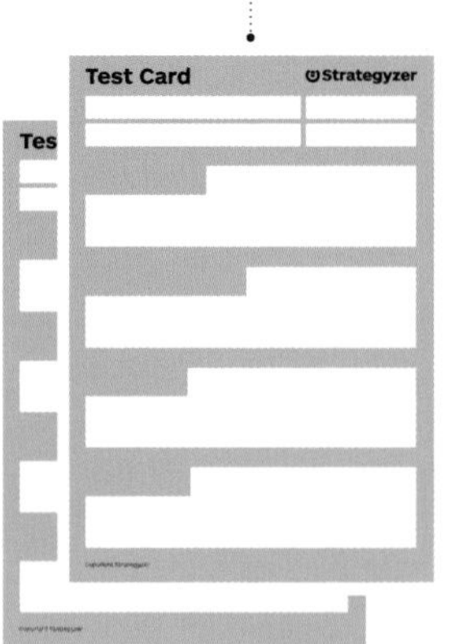

Experiment Log

Here you log all the experiments you have conducted to either support or refute a specific hypothesis. For each experiment you capture the experiment type, what you measured, the success criteria, how much time each experiment took, and what it cost.

Learning Log			Action
• Evidence • Low/medium/high strength • Number of data points	Insight ✓ Support / ? Unclear / ✕ Refute	Confidence Level 0 0.1 0.2 0.3 0.4 0.5 0.6 0.7 0.8 0.9 1.0 *Not Confident at All* … *Very Confident*	• Pivot • Shelve • Persevere • Test Again
EVIDENCE STRENGTH: HIGH *NUMBER OF DATA POINTS: 10,000+* *RESULTING EV. QUALITY: STRONG*	*✓ SUPPORT HYPOTHESIS 1*	*.75 CONFIDENT*	*PERSEVERE*

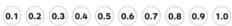

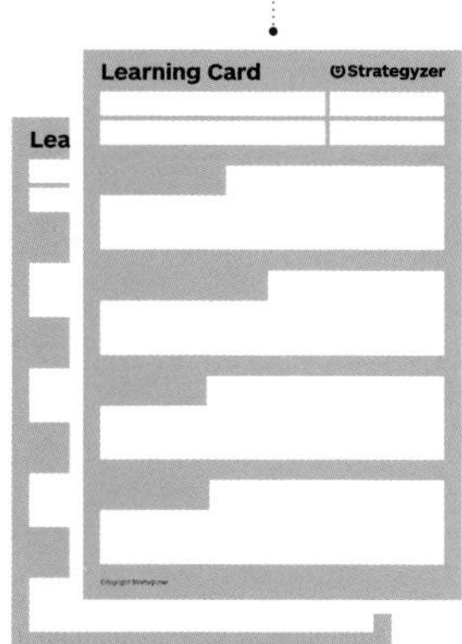

Learning Log
Here you log what you have learned from the evidence to support or refute a specific hypothesis. You specifically capture all the evidence gathered, the number of data points, the strength of the evidence, and how confident you are that your insights are true.

Insight
Indicates if we support (✓) or refute (×) a hypothesis, or if it's still unclear (?).

Confidence Level
Indicates how confident you are that the evidence is strong enough to support the insight (0 = no confidence to 1 = absolute confidence).

Action
Indicates if you kill the project, persevere and test the next hypothesis, or pivot the idea.

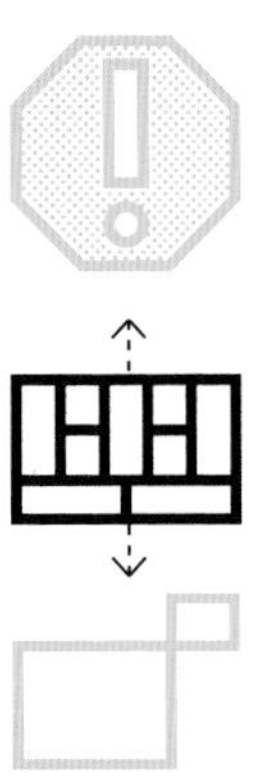

INNOVATION METRICS

Business Model Level

At the business model level, aggregate all hypotheses related to a particular project. Estimate how much risk each individual hypothesis represents of the overall risk and uncertainty of an idea. This allows you to track how much you have de-risked an idea over the course of a project.

At the aggregate project level you can now see:

- **Innovation risk level**: indicates how much you reduced the risk of the idea and how risky it still is.
- **Expected profitability**: highlights the financial opportunity of the idea.
- **Project duration**: shows how much time you've spent on testing this idea.
- **Overall cost**: outlines how much you spent to test this idea. This may or may not include the salaries of the team members.

Risk Reduction
Multiplies the percentage of risk that the hypothesis represents with the confidence level to ascertain how much you actually reduced risk for this specific hypothesis.

Once you've captured all the data, you can easily plot the change of the risk level over time and how much you have been spending to test the idea.

Pivots
Each pivot means you decided to change your previous idea. This usually leads to an increase in risk for your idea, because some of the hypotheses you already tested and de-risked are no longer relevant for your new direction. A new direction also leads to new hypotheses that you need to test again to reduce risk and uncertainty.

Cost Increase
In general, the duration and cost of your experiments will rise with the reduction of risk, because it becomes less risky to conduct expensive experiments. Later on in the life of a project, you need to produce stronger evidence and even build parts of your idea to continue to reduce risk and uncertainty. This usually increases the cost of experimentation.

Project Metrics

Name	Start Date	Project Duration
PROJECT A	9/12/2020	8 weeks

Hypotheses Log		 Experiment Log		 Learning Log			 Actions
Name	Risk %	Name	Cost $	Insight ✓ ? ✕	Confidence #0–1	Risk Reduction = Risk x Confidence	Re-test, Shelve, Perservere, Pivot
Desirability							
HYPOTHESIS 1	10%	EXP. 1	$0.2K	✓	0.75	10% x 0.75 = 7.5%	Persevere
HYPOTHESIS 2	7.5%	EXP. 2	$0.5K	✕	1	0%	Pivot
HYPOTHESIS 3	7.5%	EXP. 3, EXP. 4	$1.2K	✓	1	7.5% x 1 = 7.5%	Persevere
Feasibility							
HYPOTHESIS 7	15%	EXP. 9, EXP. 10	$0.2K	✓	0.5	15% x 0.5 = 7.5%	Persevere
HYPOTHESIS 8	10%	EXP. 11	$1K	?		0%	Re-test
Viability							
HYPOTHESIS 4	15%	EXP. 5	$1.3K	✕	1	0%	Pivot
HYPOTHESIS 5	10%	EXP. 6, EXP. 7	$0.5K	✓	0.5	10% x 0.5 = 5%	Persevere
Adaptability							
HYPOTHESIS 6	15%	EXP. 8	$0.2K	?		0%	Re-test
HYPOTHESIS 9	10%	EXP. 12	$0.7K	✓	0.25	10% x 0.25 = 2.5%	Persevere

Expected Return

Revenue Potential: $1 billion

Cost Structure: $250 million

Overall Cost $: $5,800

Innovation Risk Level %: 70%

Expected Return $: $750 million

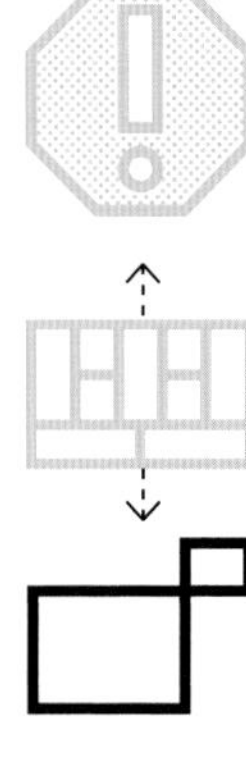

INNOVATION METRICS

Portfolio Level

You can visualize the state of your Explore portfolio once you get your teams to track the KPIs of their individual explore project. This gives you a powerful overview of the financial potential of your ideas in exploration and their current risk level. Equipped with this data and overview you can make better investment decisions and decide which projects to fund and support and which projects to retire.

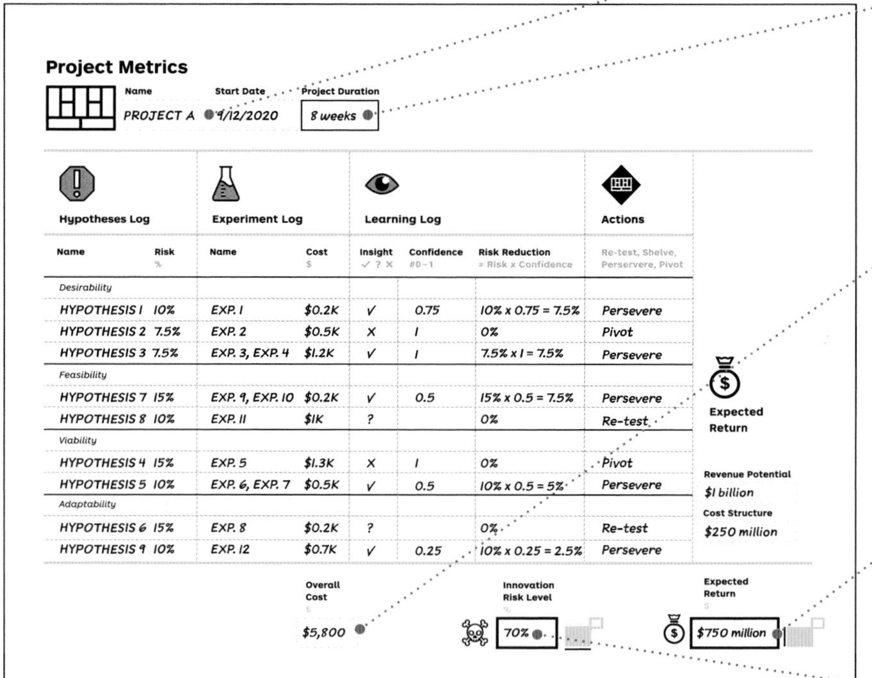

Project Metrics

Name: PROJECT A · Start Date: 9/12/2020 · Project Duration: 8 weeks

Hypotheses Log: Name	Risk %	Experiment Log: Name	Cost $	Learning Log: Insight ✓ ? ✕	Confidence #0–1	Risk Reduction = Risk x Confidence	Actions: Re-test, Shelve, Persevere, Pivot
Desirability							
HYPOTHESIS 1	10%	EXP. 1	$0.2K	✓	0.75	10% x 0.75 = 7.5%	Persevere
HYPOTHESIS 2	7.5%	EXP. 2	$0.5K	✕	1	0%	Pivot
HYPOTHESIS 3	7.5%	EXP. 3, EXP. 4	$1.2K	✓	1	7.5% x 1 = 7.5%	Persevere
Feasibility							
HYPOTHESIS 7	15%	EXP. 9, EXP. 10	$0.2K	✓	0.5	15% x 0.5 = 7.5%	Persevere
HYPOTHESIS 8	10%	EXP. 11	$1K	?		0%	Re-test
Viability							
HYPOTHESIS 4	15%	EXP. 5	$1.3K	✕	1	0%	Pivot
HYPOTHESIS 5	10%	EXP. 6, EXP. 7	$0.5K	✓	0.5	10% x 0.5 = 5%	Persevere
Adaptability							
HYPOTHESIS 6	15%	EXP. 8	$0.2K	?		0%	Re-test
HYPOTHESIS 9	10%	EXP. 12	$0.7K	✓	0.25	10% x 0.25 = 2.5%	Persevere

Expected Return: Revenue Potential $1 billion; Cost Structure $250 million

Overall Cost $: $5,800 · Innovation Risk Level %: 70% · Expected Return $: $750 million

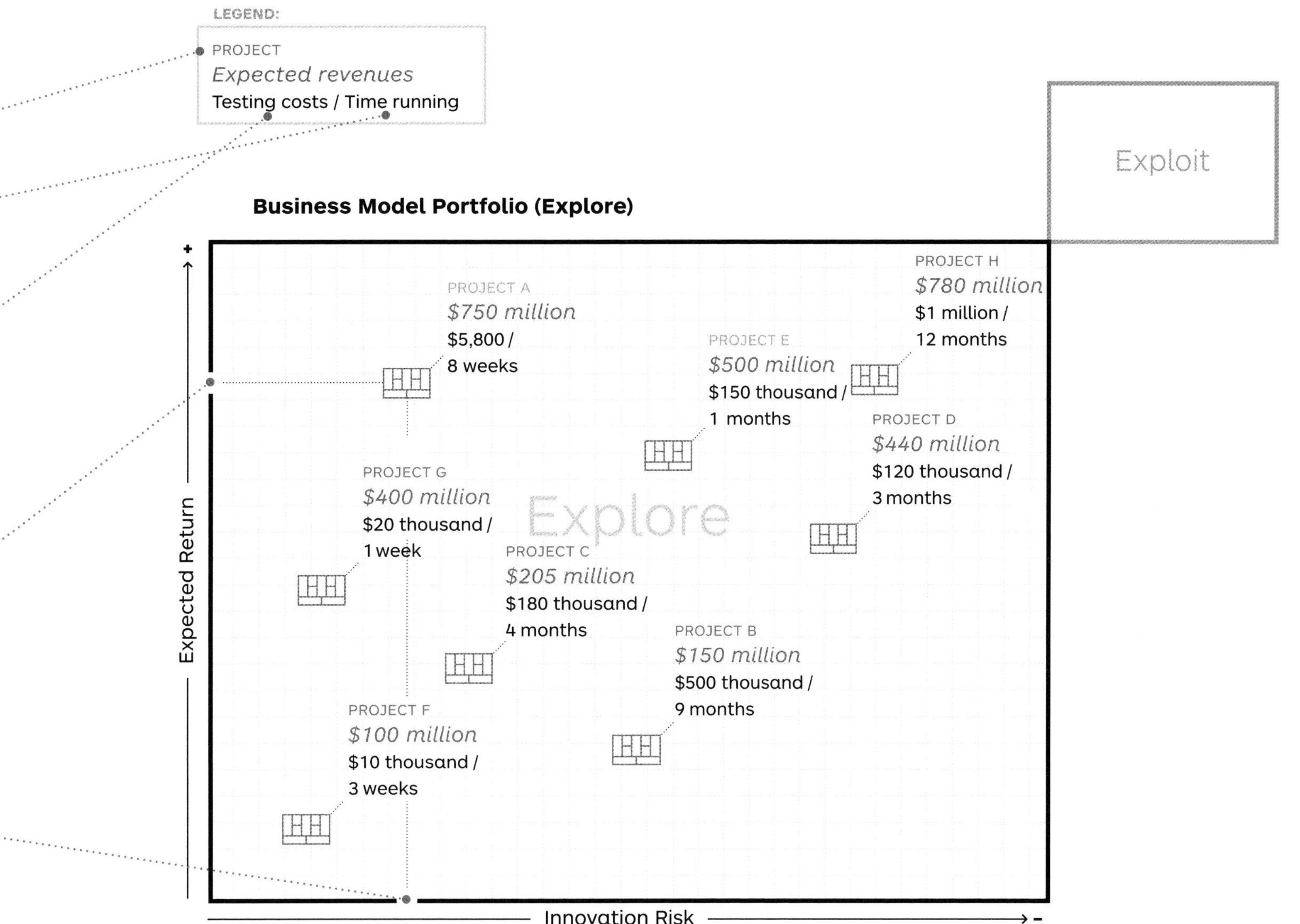

LEGEND:
PROJECT
Expected revenues
Testing costs / Time running
Exploit
Business Model Portfolio (Explore)
PROJECT H
$780 million
$1 million / 12 months
PROJECT A
$750 million
$5,800 / 8 weeks
PROJECT E
$500 million
$150 thousand / 1 months
PROJECT D
$440 million
$120 thousand / 3 months
PROJECT G
$400 million
$20 thousand / 1 week
Explore
PROJECT C
$205 million
$180 thousand / 4 months
PROJECT B
$150 million
$500 thousand / 9 months
PROJECT F
$100 million
$10 thousand / 3 weeks
Expected Return
+
Innovation Risk
-

Decisions and Actions

We developed the innovation project scorecard to systematically assess the progress that innovation and exploration teams are making in their quest to find business ideas that work. The assessment helps make better investment decisions.

The scorecard has three dimensions based on the innovation metrics and portfolio guidelines outlined previously:

Strategic Fit
The first dimension is about fit. Projects need to demonstrate they fit the vision, culture, and image of the company. They also need to fit the company's portfolio guidance and demonstrate leadership support.

Risk Reduction
The second dimension is the most important one. It is about assessing if a team is making progress in reducing the risk and uncertainty of the business idea. Teams need to produce strong evidence, beyond spreadsheets and PowerPoint slides, that their idea is likely to work in the real world.

Size of Opportunity
The third dimension is about financial fit. Teams need to show a clear understanding of the financial opportunity and provide evidence from experiments that their financial estimations are not just fantasies.

The innovation project scorecard is used by:

Leaders

- *To evaluate a pitch asking for investment.*
- *To ask better questions and guide teams.*

Teams

- *To evaluate their own progress during sprints and stand-ups.*

Leaders and teams

- *To benchmark the current status of an innovation project.*
- *To decide next steps for testing.*

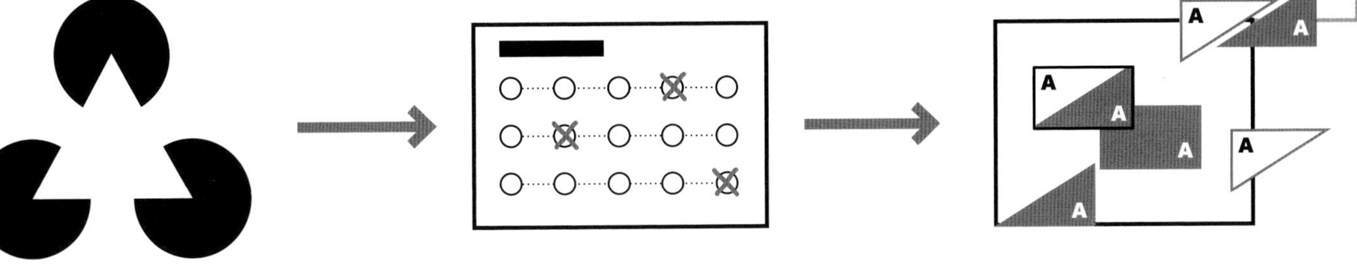

Strategic Fit
p. 50

Project Scorecard
p. 98

Explore Actions
p. 23 and 100

Project Scorecard

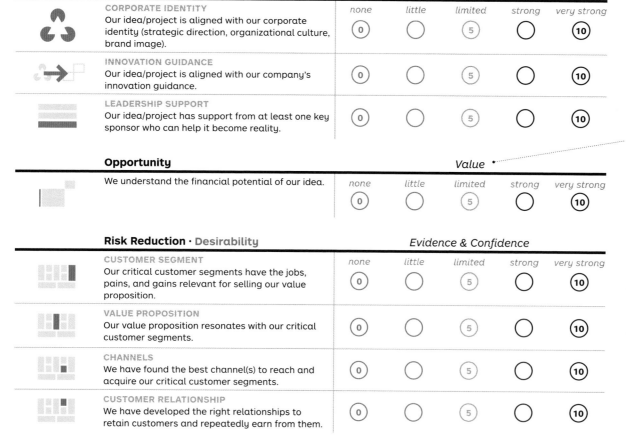

Strategic Fit	Alignment				
	none	little	limited	strong	very strong
CORPORATE IDENTITY Our idea/project is aligned with our corporate identity (strategic direction, organizational culture, brand image).	0		5		10
INNOVATION GUIDANCE Our idea/project is aligned with our company's innovation guidance.	0		5		10
LEADERSHIP SUPPORT Our idea/project has support from at least one key sponsor who can help it become reality.	0		5		10

Opportunity	Value				
	none	little	limited	strong	very strong
We understand the financial potential of our idea.	0		5		10

Risk Reduction · Desirability	Evidence & Confidence				
	none	little	limited	strong	very strong
CUSTOMER SEGMENT Our critical customer segments have the jobs, pains, and gains relevant for selling our value proposition.	0		5		10
VALUE PROPOSITION Our value proposition resonates with our critical customer segments.	0		5		10
CHANNELS We have found the best channel(s) to reach and acquire our critical customer segments.	0		5		10
CUSTOMER RELATIONSHIP We have developed the right relationships to retain customers and repeatedly earn from them.	0		5		10

Some companies sort opportunity by the geographical reach of the value created:

- *little opportunity would be an opportunity that impact a local team only*
- *very strong opportunity would be an opportunity with global impact*

Other companies sort opportunity by $ value:

- *little opportunity would be ‹ $100 thousands*
- *very strong opportunity would be › $100 millions*

Risk Reduction · Feasibility	*Evidence & Confidence*				
	none	*little*	*limited*	*strong*	*very strong*
KEY RESOURCES We have the right technologies and resources to create our value proposition.	0		5		10
KEY ACTIVITIES We have the right capabilities to handle the most critical activities for creating our value proposition.	0		5		10
KEY PARTNERS We have found the right key partners who are willing to work with us to create and deliver our value proposition.	0		5		10

Risk Reduction · Viability	*Evidence & Confidence*				
	none	*little*	*limited*	*strong*	*very strong*
REVENUES We know how much our customers are willing to pay us and how they will pay.	0		5		10
COSTS We know our costs for creating and delivering the value proposition.	0		5		10

Risk Reduction · Adaptability	*Evidence & Confidence*				
	none	*little*	*limited*	*strong*	*very strong*
INDUSTRY FORCES Our idea/project is well positioned to succeed against established competitors and new emerging players.	0		5		10
MARKET FORCES Our idea/project takes known and emerging market shifts into account.	0		5		10
KEY TRENDS Our idea/project is well positioned to benefit from key technology, regulatory, cultural, and societal trends.	0		5		10
MACROECONOMIC FORCES Our idea/project is adapted to known and emerging macroeconomic and infrastructure trends.	0		5		10

e.g. ***limited*** *would be evidence from only one experiment,* ***strong*** *would be evidence from one experiment with very strong confidence,* ***very strong*** *would be evidence from several experiments.*

From Risk Assessment to Action

We introduced Explore portfolio actions on p. 96. Here we further develop the topic to highlight decision-making in the context of exploration. In fact, there are two entities that make decisions in the context of exploration:

Teams: Teams need to constantly evaluate and reevaluate their business model and value propositions based on evidence from the testing process. Every week the team should decide about staying the course (persevere), substantially changing aspects of the idea (pivot), or killing the idea altogether.

Committee: A decision or investment committee should meet every couple of months to decide which teams and ideas to invest in and which ideas to kill. The Innovation Project Scorecard and evidence from testing should be the main drivers for decision-making. The committee should trust the process and not interfere with teams between committee meetings.

<table>
<tr><th>Action</th><th>Innovation Team/Entrepreneur</th><th>Committee</th></tr>
<tr><td>Ideate</td><td>Teams don't just ideate at the beginning of a project. During the whole journey there should be mini-ideations to create a more powerful business model and better value proposition. Ideally, ideation is based on evidence from testing.</td><td>The committee's role during the initial ideation phase is to set the exploration guidelines. It should help teams understand how to evaluate strategic fit in terms of size and direction. The committee should support the exploration of several ideas in parallel.</td></tr>
<tr><td>Invest</td><td>Based on evidence from testing, a team might suggest investing in a startup* or acquiring a technology rather than building in-house.</td><td>The committee should always ask if it's more appropriate to invest externally or explore internally. Also, internal testing leads to better investments.</td></tr>
<tr><td>Persevere</td><td>At every stage of the journey the team should evaluate evidence to justify staying the course. The stronger the evidence, the more confidently a team can persevere.</td><td rowspan="4">The committee should only make persevere, pivot, kill, or spinout recommendations on predefined dates. The committee's role is to support teams to make evidence-based decisions on their own, between committee meeting dates.

All recommendations by the committee should be evidence-based, rather than opinion-based, and grounded in strategic fit. Recommendations should be made in the context of all teams exploring. Teams exploring strategic ideas, but incapable of producing sufficient evidence, should only rarely be encouraged to persevere.</td></tr>
<tr><td>Pivot</td><td>The team should consider slightly or radically changing course when the evidence doesn't support your initial direction. Make sure your evidence is strong enough before you pivot.</td></tr>
<tr><td>Retire</td><td>Sometimes pivoting doesn't make sense and the best option is to kill an idea. Remember you are saving money, time, and energy by killing an idea that won't work.</td></tr>
<tr><td>Spinout</td><td>Teams may suggest a spinout if it believes a project could be successful, but not fit the company's portfolio guidance.</td></tr>
<tr><td>Transfer</td><td>A team should recommend to scale and execute an idea when it is sufficiently confident that the idea will work based on strong evidence from many experiments.</td><td>The committee should move an idea from exploration to execution, if one of the teams shows strong evidence that the idea will succeed.</td></tr>
</table>

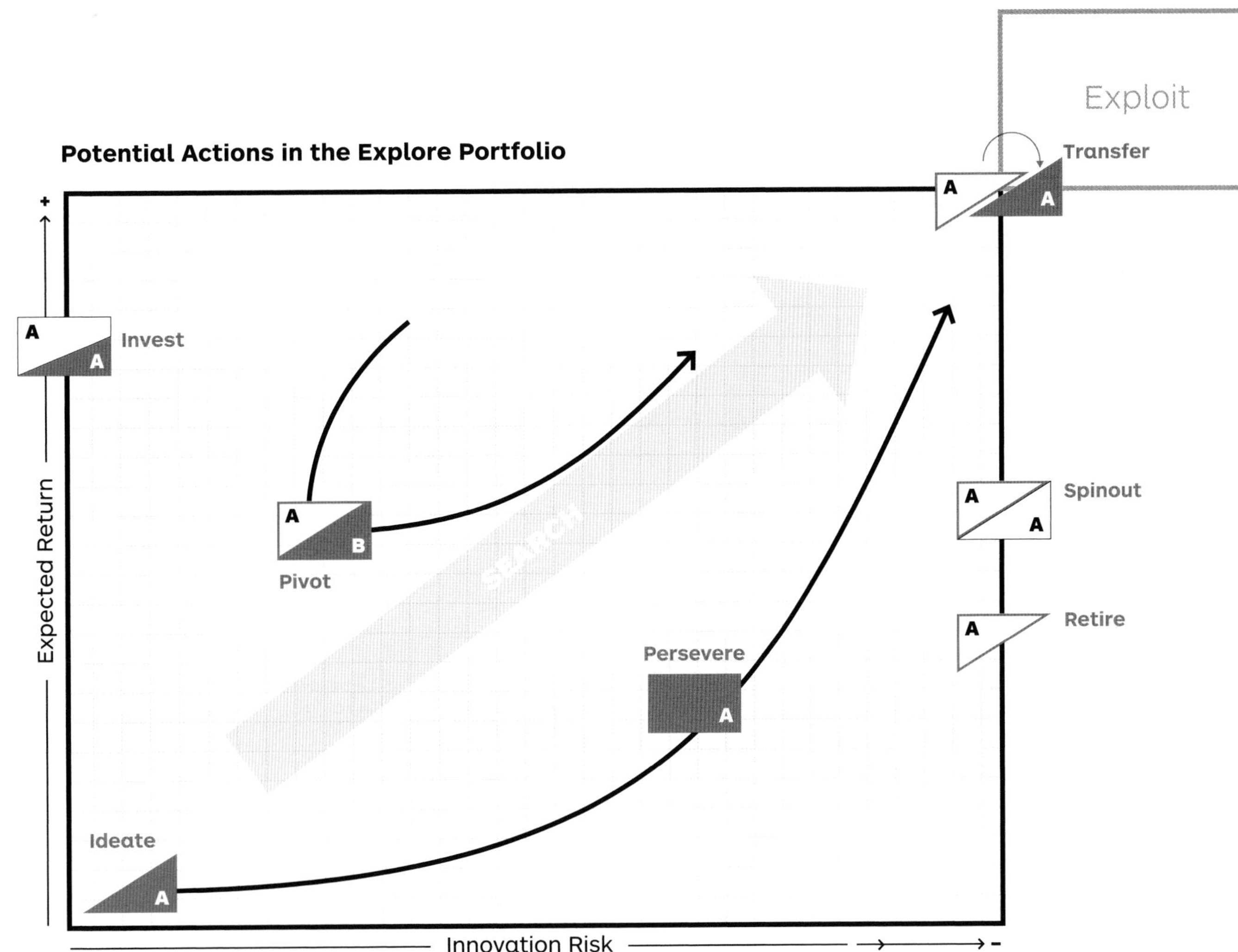

Exploit
Potential Actions in the Explore Portfolio
Transfer
A
A
+
Invest
A
A
Pivot
A
B
SEARCH
Spinout
A
A
Retire
A
Persevere
A
Ideate
A
Expected Return
Innovation Risk
-

Invest Like a Venture Capitalist

For exploration, adopt a more venture capital-style investment approach, as opposed to the relatively rigid annual budgeting cycles practiced in Exploit projects.

The Enemy of Innovation: The Business Plan

Companies that still require business plans from project teams maximize the risk of failure. The business plan is a document that describes an idea and its execution in detail. This maximizes the risk of executing an unproven idea that looks good on paper and in spreadsheets. Innovation is about admitting risk and uncertainty. It is about iterating and adapting ideas based on evidence from experiments until they are likely to work. This minimizes the risk of executing a flawed idea.

This requires the following four principles:

1. Invest in a portfolio of projects rather than individual projects to spread your bets and manage risk (see "You Can't Pick the Winner," p. 54).
2. Start with small bets (i.e., investments/funding), while risk and uncertainty of project success are high.

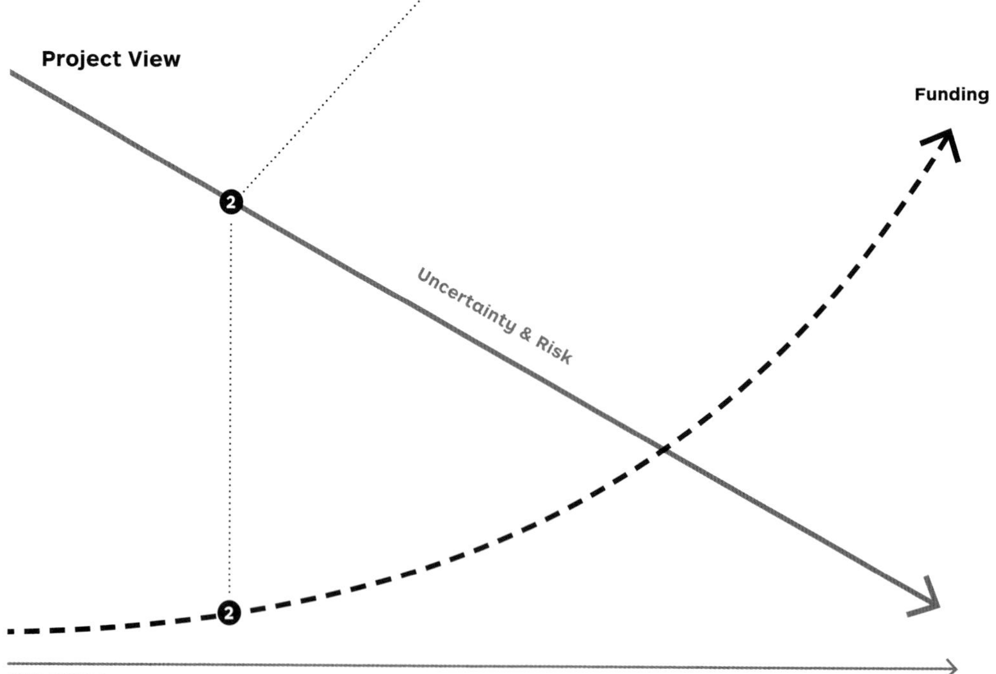

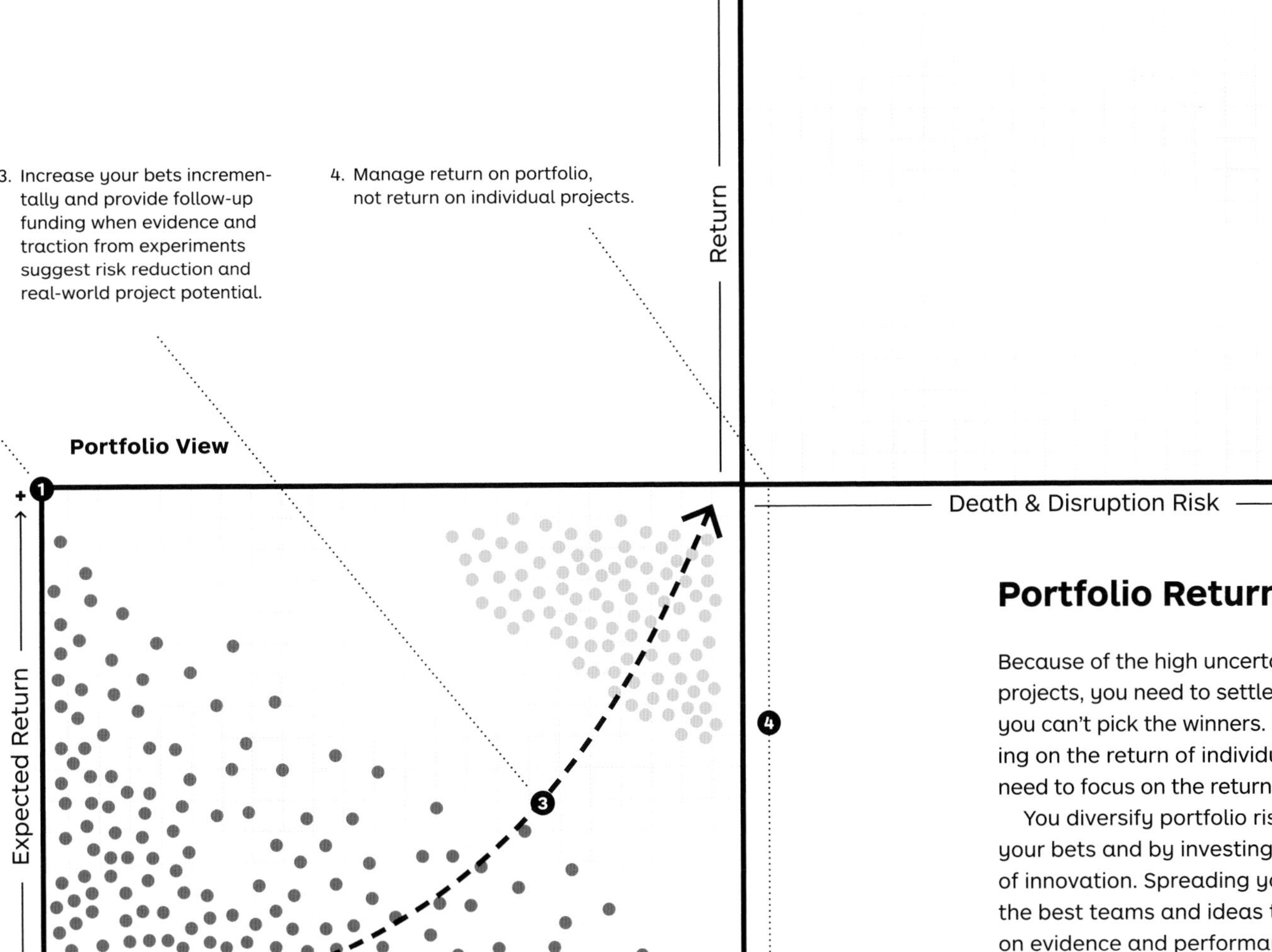
3. Increase your bets incrementally and provide follow-up funding when evidence and traction from experiments suggest risk reduction and real-world project potential.
4. Manage return on portfolio, not return on individual projects.
Portfolio View
Expected Return
Innovation Risk
Return
Death & Disruption Risk

Portfolio Return

Because of the high uncertainty of innovation projects, you need to settle with the fact that you can't pick the winners. Instead of focusing on the return of individual projects, you need to focus on the return of your portfolio.

You diversify portfolio risks by spreading your bets and by investing in different types of innovation. Spreading your bets allows the best teams and ideas to emerge, based on evidence and performance. Investing across all three types of innovation, namely, efficiency, sustaining, and transformative innovation, spreads bets across different levels of risk and return.

Growth and Innovation Investment Committee

An important aspect of funding like a venture capitalist is the constitution of an investment committee dedicated to growth and innovation. It's crucial to create a dedicated committee, because the investment logic and investment style substantially differ from investments in execution projects.

The committee is composed of a small number of leaders who have decision-making authority when it comes to budget. Ideally, it includes members who are fully dedicated to exploration, as well as members who are more preoccupied with exploitation. Investment decisions usually take place every 3 to 6 months, depending on the type of organization. Investments are mainly in internal teams, but may also include start-ups.

Project guidance and investment guidelines
Communicate portfolio guidance. Clarify which types of projects are in and which ones are out. Highlight financial expectations. Outline how teams can get initial discovery funding and what type of evidence is required to qualify for follow-up validation and acceleration investments.

Portfolio management
Maintain a balanced portfolio with the right number of projects in discovery, validation, and acceleration. Make sure your pipeline is full of projects to improve existing businesses before they are at severe risk of disruption or decline. Make sure you invest in a sufficiently large number of exploration projects of which some will be the foundation of the future of your organization.

Evidence-based Investments
Invest in projects that deliver evidence from testing, rather than ideas that look irresistible in PowerPoint presentations and spreadsheets. Make sure you give teams a chance to explore ideas, because you can't know which ones will excel. Let the best teams and ideas emerge through the process, rather than trying to pick them upfront.

Project team support and protection
Help project teams get to the next level by asking them how they might improve their business models. Help them qualify for follow-up funding by suggesting how they might further test their ideas to generate the required evidence. Protect projects from company forces that make exploration and testing difficult.

Encourage innovation behavior, not just outcomes
Make sure all teams that test their ideas feel valued, not just those that get follow-up investment. Encourage innovators and teams that show strong testing skills to come back with new ideas and projects after every failure.

Metered Funding

To fund Explore projects you should apply the metered funding practiced by venture capitalists, as opposed to the annual entitlement budgeting practiced in Exploit projects. Incrementally increase your investments in projects that produce evidence from testing and shelve those that don't. In the discovery phase you invest small amounts of money in a large number of tiny teams to explore ideas. In validation you increase your investment in those 30% to 50% of the teams that produced evidence during discovery. In acceleration you continue to trim your portfolio and again invest in only 30% to 50% of the teams.

Combining portfolio management and metered funding increases your chances to find outliers that will create exceptionally large returns and substantially reduces the risk you'd incur by making 1 to 2 large bets in bold ideas.

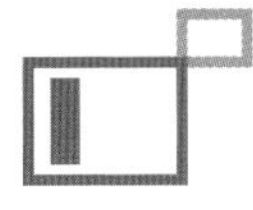
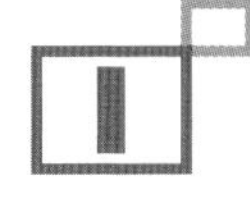

	Discover	Validate	Accelerate
Funding	Less than $50,000	$50,000 – $500,000	$500,000+
Team Size	1–3	2 – 5	5+
Time per Team Member	20 – 40%	40 – 80%	100%
Number of Projects	High	Medium	Low
Objectives	Customer understanding, context, and willingness to pay	Proven interest and indications of profitability	Proven model at limited scale
KPIs	• Market size • Customer evidence • Problem/solution fit • Opportunity size	• Value proposition evidence • Financial evidence • Feasibility evidence	• Product/market fit • Acquisition and retention evidence • Business model fit
Experiment Themes	50 – 80% / 0–10% / 10 – 30% / 0–10%	30 – 50% / 10 – 40% / 20 – 50% / 0–10%	10 – 30% / 40 – 50% / 20 – 50%

10x Rule of Thumb

Success is unpredictable and depends on organization and context. However, from experience, we recommend the 10x rule of thumb: invest 1 million into your portfolio to create 10 million in new revenue or costs savings. For example, invest $20,000 in 10 small teams. Make a $50,000 follow-up investment in the 5 teams that produce the best evidence. Finally, invest around $500 thousand, in the team with the best evidence. For a billion dollar success, invest $100 million into a much larger portfolio of projects.

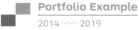

Sony Startup Acceleration Program

In 2014, Sony establishes the Sony Startup Accelerator Program (SSAP) to ideate, commercialize, and scale business ideas that live outside of Sony's traditional business units. It reports directly to the CEO.

KAZUO HIRAI

President and CEO of Sony Corporation 2012–2018

Sony, founded in 1943 by Masaru Ibuka and Akio Morita, is a Japanese multinational conglomerate with business divisions in electronics, gaming, motion pictures, music, and financial services.

In 2012 Kazuo Hirai took over as CEO and under his guidance, Sony experienced a resurgence in the 2010s. Under Hirai's One Sony policy, poorer performing divisions like mobile were downsized while the company advocated a deeper focus on products. This allowed Sony to streamline and focus on its core competencies.

As a part of this strategy, Sony created the Startup Accelerator Program (SSAP), which reports directly to the CEO. Hirai took ownership of SSAP as he envisioned a sustained innovation engine as paramount to the future of Sony. Having the CEO (and not a business division) take responsibility of SSAP ensured a long-term objective for Sony's innovation funnel and made it less prone to short-term business volatilities. In 2019, Sony brought in ¥8.66 trillion in revenue, reporting its best year ever in terms of profit in its 73-year history.[18]

Sony Startup Accelerator Program

Established in 2014 and led by Shinji Odashima, SSAP is an internal program for Sony employees to ideate, commercialize, and scale business ideas that live outside of Sony's traditional business units. Since then, SSAP has ideated over 750 business ideas and incubated 34. Out of those, 14 businesses have been successfully created.

Of the 14 businesses launched: six have continued their scaling phase under SSAP, five have moved into existing business units, two are now subsidiaries under Sony Group, and one has become wholly independent and its own company. Allowing for a variety of exit strategies means SSAP is not limited to the scope of ideas possible and is willing to accept most that can prove profitability.

Open Innovation

After five years, in 2019, the program transformed from an internal incubator to being open externally, helping anyone incubate their idea. This is because SSAP sees innovation as a numbers game. Based on their previous experience they knew the chance of success for any idea was very small (1.85%). Consequently, the more ideas running through the accelerator program, the higher the number of successes.

SSAP is also a vehicle for Sony to collaborate and partner with outside entities without disrupting its core businesses. In 2014, Sony partnered with VC firm WiL to create Qrio, a smart lock that can be easily installed in any existing door.

Crowdfunding campaigns have become a core part of SSAP testing strategy. The best way to ensure product market fit is by getting your customers to preemptively pay for it.

14 Businesses Transferred

6 continued to scale
5 merged into existing business units
2 new subsidiaries under Sony Group
1 spinout independent company

Merge

A

AB

B

Transfer

A

A

Perservere

34 business incubated

A

Spinout

A

A

Ideate

750 ideas created

A

A10 Lab

Independent and its own company

A10 Lab helps companies improve their customer lifetime value by building consumer loyalty through gamification. A10 Lab became an independent entity as A10 Lab Co., Ltd. in February 2017.

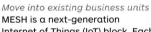

FES Watch

Move into existing business units

FES Watch U is an e-paper fashion watch that allows its wearer to change its design at any given moment. The project was initially going to be retired, since the material did not match Sony's high quality product, but the CEO protected the project, seeing it as a way for Sony to tap into a new consumer segment: young fashionistas.

MESH

Move into existing business units

MESH is a next-generation Internet of Things (IoT) block. Each block is a sensor with built-in functions to make it easy to prototype and build projects for the IoT. It is now a part of Sony Business Solutions Corporation.

SRE Holdings

Become a subsidiary of an existing business units

SRE Holdings offers comprehensive real estate services such as real estate brokerage, loan management, and renovations. SRE Holdings became a separate entity and listed on the Tokyo Stock Exchange in December 2019.

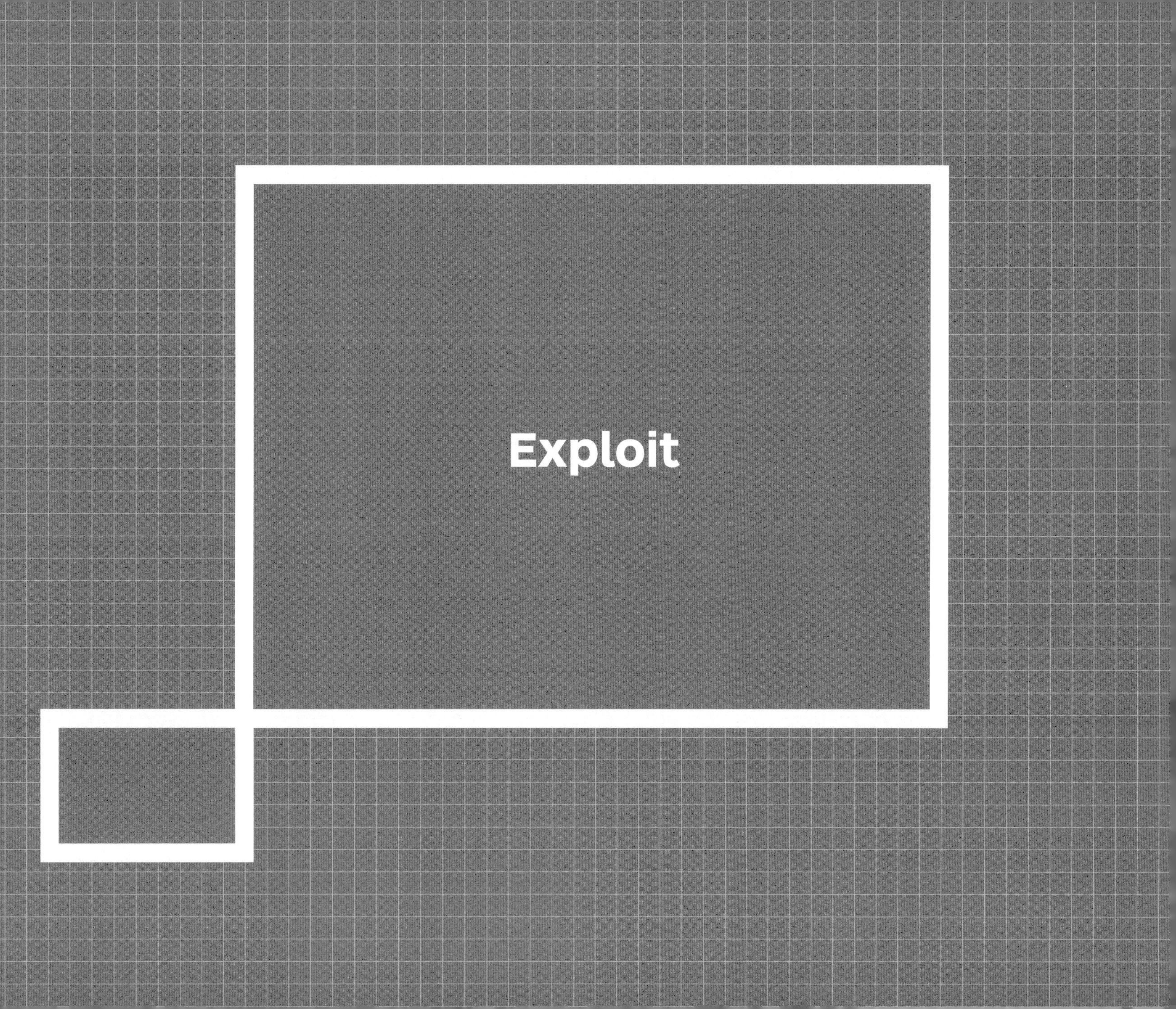
Exploit

Performance Assessment

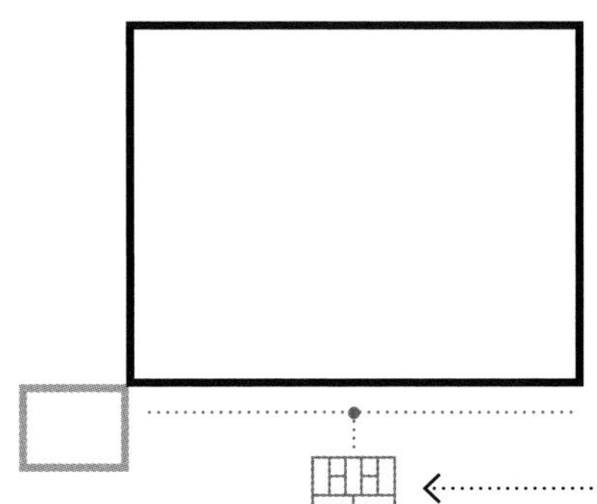

The disruption risk assessment helps identify how healthy or at risk a business model in your portfolio actually is and how much attention it needs to be improved and de-risked. The assessment includes two dimensions:

1. **Business model performance**
   strengths and weaknesses
   reveals positioning on Exploit portfolio *x*-axis

2. **Business model trend**
   opportunities and threats
   indicates likely future positioning on *x*-axis

Business Model Performance

Strength and Weakness Assessment

This assessment reveals how healthy or at risk a business model is based on recent performance. It assesses the strengths and weaknesses of the frontstage, backstage, and profit formula of a model. The resulting score ranges from -5 (highly at risk) to +5 (low risk), and allows you to place each business model on the *x*-axis of the Exploit portfolio.

Score and Positioning

The score from the business model performance assessment indicates the health of a business model based on its performance. The assessment looks at the frontstage, backstage, and profit formula of a business model. The score allows you to position each business model on the *x*-axis of the Exploit portfolio in terms of their death and disruption risk. Poorly performing business models at risk go on the left half of the Exploit portfolio. Healthy business models go on the right half of the Exploit portfolio.

Frontstage

VP	Our products and services perform worse than those of our competition.	-3	-2	-1	0	+1	+2	+3	Our products and services are highly differentiated and loved by our customers.
CS	We lost over 20% of our customer base in the last six months.	-3	-2	-1	0	+1	+2	+3	We increased our customer base by at least 50% over the last six months.
CH	We are 100% dependent on intermediaries to get products and services to customers and they are making market access difficult.	-3	-2	-1	0	+1	+2	+3	We have direct market access and fully own the relationship with the customers of our products and services.
CR	All our customers could theoretically leave us immediately, without incurring direct or indirect switching costs if they left.	-3	-2	-1	0	+1	+2	+3	All our customers are locked in for several years and they would incur significant direct and indirect switching costs if they left.

Backstage

KR	Our key resources are significantly inferior to those of our competitors and they have deteriorated over the last six months. New entrants compete with new, better, or cheaper resources.	-3	-2	-1	0	+1	+2	+3	Our key resources can't easily be copied or emulated for the next couple of years and they give us a competitive advantage (e.g., intellectual property, brand, etc.).
KA	The performance of our key activities is significantly inferior to that of our competitors and has deteriorated over the last six months. New entrants compete with new, better, or cheaper activities.	-3	-2	-1	0	+1	+2	+3	Our key activities can't easily be copied or emulated for the next couple of years and they give us a competitive advantage (e.g., cost effectiveness, scale etc.).
KP	Over the last six months we lost access to key partners.	-3	-2	-1	0	+1	+2	+3	Our key partners are locked in for years to come.

Profit Formula

RS	We lost over 20% of our revenues in the last six months.	-3	-2	-1	0	+1	+2	+3	We doubled our revenues over the last six months and are growing significantly faster than our competitors.
CS	Our cost structure grew faster than revenues and is significantly less effective than that of our competitors.	-3	-2	-1	0	+1	+2	+3	Our cost structure shrunk compared to revenue growth and is significantly more effective than that of our competitors.
Mar	Our margins shrunk by over 50% in the last six months and/or are significantly lower than those of our competition (e.g., over 50% lower).	-3	-2	-1	0	+1	+2	+3	Our margins increased by at least 50% in the last six months and/or are significantly higher than those of our competition (e.g., over 50% higher).

Trend Assessment

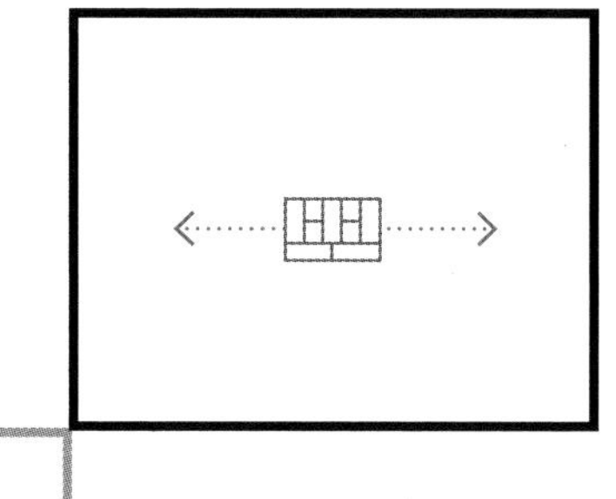

Business Model Trend

Opportunities and Threats Assessment

This assessment uncovers how a business model is trending in terms of risks coming from your external environment. It assesses how external forces represent opportunities or threats for the frontstage, backstage, and profit formula of a business model. The resulting score ranges from -5 (trending left on the risk axis) to +5 (trending right on the risk axis) and indicates how a business model is likely to perform in the future.

Score and Direction

The score from the business model trend assessment indicates in which direction a business model is likely to move based on external factors and what future performance might look like. The assessment looks at how external forces may impact and disrupt the frontstage, backstage, and profit formula of a business model. The score shows if a business model is likely to move to the left (higher death and disruption risk) or to the right (lower death and disruption risk) in the Exploit portfolio in the future.

Adding Impact Weighting

Increase the accuracy of how external forces may impact your business model by weighting each force in terms of likelihood to occur and severity of impact. For example, ask how likely new regulations are and how severely they would impact a business model. Or ask how likely new entrants are to gain traction and how severely that would impact a business model.

Trends Impact on Frontstage

	VP	New entrants are gaining traction with cheaper, better, or substitute products and services that may make our business model obsolete.	-3	-2	-1	0	+1	+2	+3	Competition for our products and services is shrinking and our products and services are likely to gain traction and benefit from that.
	CS	The markets in which we are active are projected to shrink significantly over the coming years.	-3	-2	-1	0	+1	+2	+3	The markets in which we are active are projected to grow significantly over the coming years.
	CR	Various trends (tech, cultural, demographics) are reducing the friction for our customers to leave us and never come back.	-3	-2	-1	0	+1	+2	+3	Various trends are making it harder for our customers to desert us and the friction for them to leave is increasing.
	VP/ CS	Social and cultural trends that are projected to grow are driving customers away from us (e.g., sustainability, fashion, etc.).	-3	-2	-1	0	+1	+2	+3	Various trends are making it harder for our customers to desert us and the friction for them to leave is increasing.

Trends Impact on Backstage

	KR	Technology trends that substantially undermine our business model or make it obsolete are gaining traction.	-3	-2	-1	0	+1	+2	+3	Technology trends that substantially strengthen our business model are gaining traction.
	KR/ KA	New regulations make our business model significantly more expensive or impossible to operate and give our competitors an advantage.	-3	-2	-1	0	+1	+2	+3	New regulations make our business model significantly cheaper or easier to operate and give us a competitive advantage over our competitors.
	KR/ KA	Suppliers and value chain actors are changing in a way that puts our business model at risk.	-3	-2	-1	0	+1	+2	+3	Suppliers and value chain actors are changing in a way that radically strengthens our business model.

Trends Impact on Profit Formula

ECONOMIC	An economic downturn in the next six months would be lethal to our business model (e.g., due to high cost structure, debt obligations, etc.).	-3	-2	-1	0	+1	+2	+3	Our business model is resilient and would even benefit if an economic downturn happened in the next six months (e.g., due to weak competitors).
GEOPOLITICAL	Our business model depends on key resources or other factors that may be affected by geopolitical or other external forces (e.g., commodity prices, trade wars, etc.).	-3	-2	-1	0	+1	+2	+3	Our business model does not depend on key resources or other factors that are affected by geopolitical or other external forces (e.g., commodity prices, trade wars, etc.).
VC FUNDING	There are a significant amount of venture capital funding start-ups in our arena and this has grown over the last six months.	-3	-2	-1	0	+1	+2	+3	There are little to no venture capital funding start-ups in our arena.

EXPLOIT ACTIONS

From Risk Assessment to Action

We introduced Exploit Portfolio Actions on p. 109. Much has been written about the topic in other books already. The main contribution here consists of unifying the vocabulary and creating a shared language for all actions in the context of managing a portfolio of existing businesses.

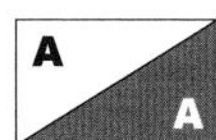
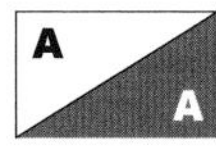

Acquire
Acquiring outside companies or business units helps boost an existing portfolio by either plugging a hole or by strengthening an existing internal business. You may either organizationally integrate an acquired business with an existing business (merge) or offer it organizational independence.

Improve
When one of your businesses is suffering decline you may decide to renovate it by substantially changing its business model. This requires testing the new business model, while operating the existing one (see p. 124). There are two types of renovation. The first consists of renovating the business to maintain it as a pillar of your portfolio. The second consists of renovating the business to divest at an attractive price.

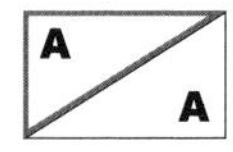

Divest
You divest when a business does not fit your portfolio guidelines anymore in terms of fit or performance. Divestiture can be immediate by closing a business down (dismantle), or by selling it to another company, investors, or the current management (management buyout). You may also divest over time after revamping the business first to make it more attractive to potential buyers.

Invest
Sometimes you are not prepared to or simply can't fully acquire an outside business. In that case, you may build up an investment stake to take advantage of its success. A joint venture is a particular type of investment where two or more companies set up a separate business and own it together.

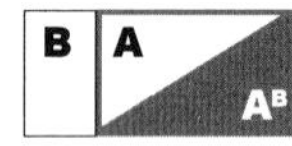

Partner
Some types of partnerships are so important that they merit mentioning at the portfolio level rather than just within a particular business model. These are partnerships that are strategic and impact several of the businesses in your portfolio in significant ways.

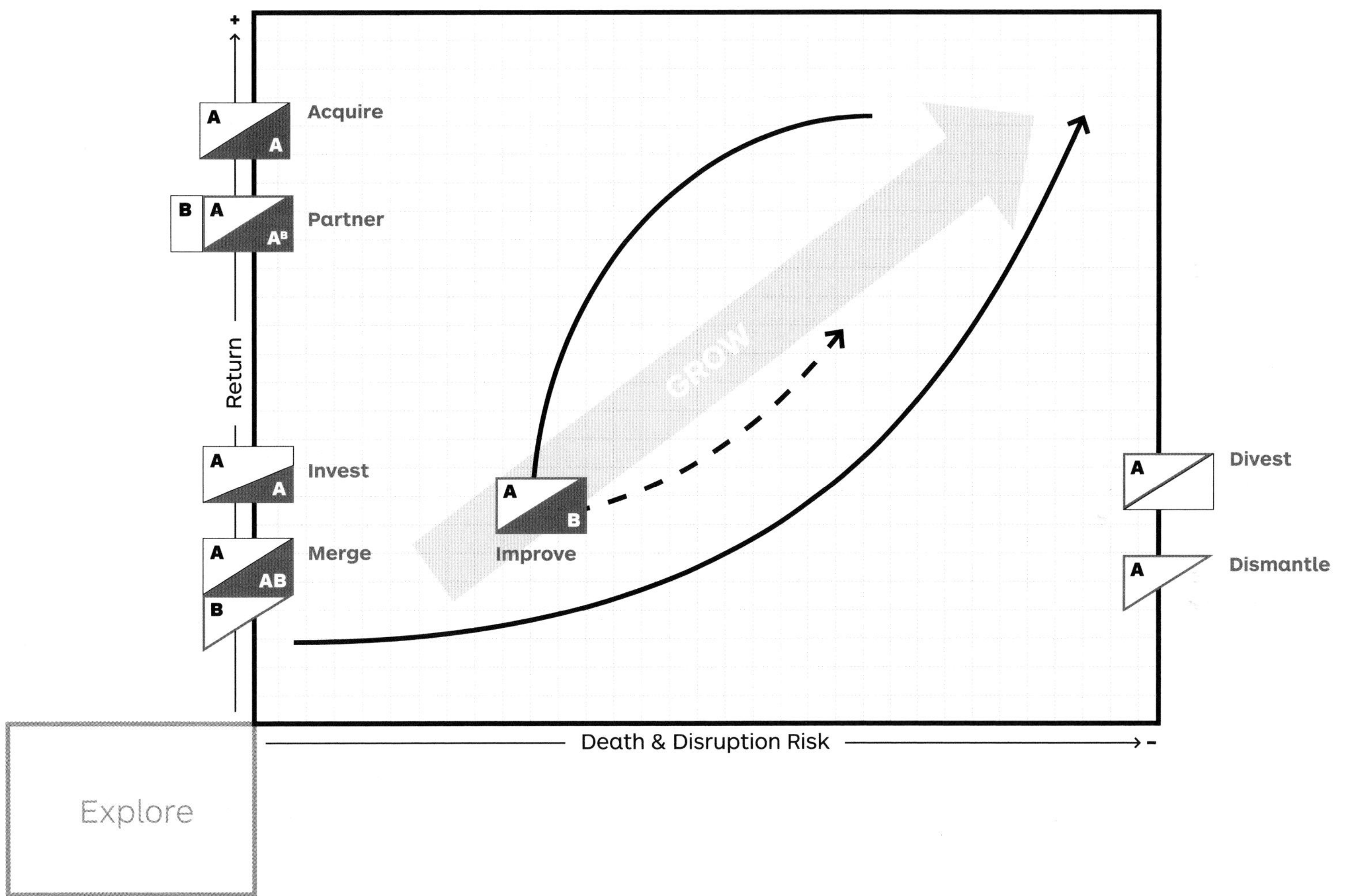
+
Return
A
A
Acquire
B
A
AB
Partner
A
A
Invest
A
AB
B
Merge
GROW
A
B
Improve
A
Divest
A
Dismantle
Death & Disruption Risk
–
Explore

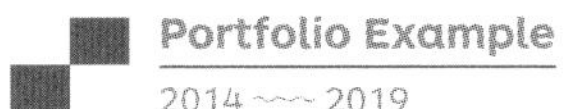

Microsoft

Satya Nadella becomes CEO of Microsoft in 2014 and radically repositions the company away from the Windows operating system to focus on enterprise users and the cloud. Nadella understands the next phase of Microsoft's growth will require an open mindset and collaboration with partners.

Microsoft was founded in 1975 by Bill Gates and Paul Allen. The company's meteoric growth came from its operating system, Windows, which came preinstalled on the majority of PCs sold. Microsoft also expanded into software and hardware that was centered around its proprietary operating system.

In 2014, Satya Nadella became Microsoft's CEO and took over from Steve Ballmer, who had led and grown the company for over a decade. Nadella profoundly changed the company's strategy to reposition it for the future. He de-emphasized the role of proprietary Windows, which was traditionally the heart and foundation of Microsoft.

Nadella focused Microsoft on enterprise users and the cloud. To accomplish that shift he established an open and collaborative mindset, a radical change from the company's traditionally closed and proprietary attitude. Nadella wanted Microsoft's technology to be running on all platforms, rather than waiting for it to "catch up" to its competitors. Technology should work with Windows, not have to be on Windows.

Demote Company's Historic Growth Engine

By 2010, the invention of the smartphone and tablet were contributing to the irreversible decline of the PC market. At that point, Windows made up 54% of Microsoft's operating income. The company needed to transform, and to do it quickly.

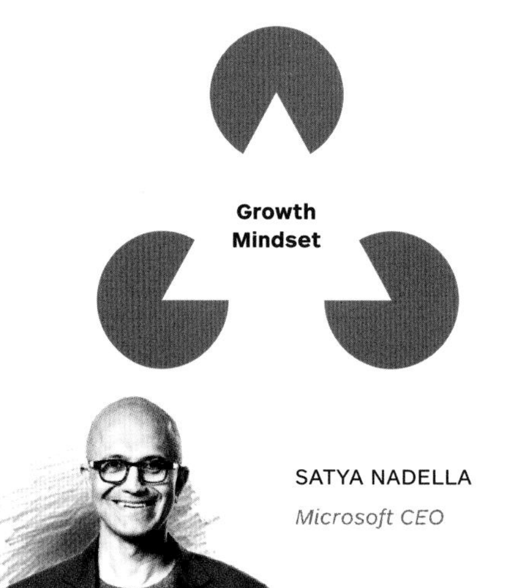

SATYA NADELLA

Microsoft CEO

Strategic Direction

The Productivity and Platform Company

A Accelerate its efforts to unchain products and services to be platform agnostic for wider adoption.

B Be an industry leader in cloud platform technology to facilitate open source collaboration across platforms.

C Help enterprise users do more and achieve more.

Organizational Culture

Collaborative and Customer Focused

Nadella shifts Microsoft's culture from a fixed to growth mindset, where leadership must be "boundary-less and globally minded in seeking solutions." This comes with the understanding that if you really want to give your customers the best products you can, then you can't do it alone.

Brand Image

Open Innovation

D Microsoft is building partnerships with "competitors" like Amazon and Sony to provide consumers with greater products and connectivity, making their software available on more platforms.

Microsoft also joins networks like Linux Foundation (2016) and Open Innovation Network (2018) to cement their commitment to open source collaboration. Developers in these networks are now able to use Microsoft's 60,000 issued patents royalty free and on any platform.[19]

Photography: *Used with permission from Microsoft*

D GitHub (2018, $7.5 billion)
GitHub is the cross-platform framework that developers can use to build for any platform and deploy to devices, the cloud, or IoT scenarios. Microsoft soon becomes one of the largest contributors to the platform.[23]

LinkedIn (2016, $26.2 billion)
Talent Solutions, Marketing, and Premium Subscriptions.[24]

B Cloud companies (2013–2018)
Microsoft acquires 23 cloud-related companies to build out their intelligent cloud division.[25]

A Windows / Office
By 2013, Windows revenue falls into third place behind office and service.[27] Consumers are choosing simpler devices like smartphones and tablets over traditional PCs. Recognizing this, one of Nadella's first tasks as CEO is to bring Office to Android and iOS, even offering free apps, including Word and Excel.[28]

2019 End of Year Results

B Azure
Many analysts compare Microsoft's Azure unfavorably to AWS. Microsoft manages to renovate it and turn it into their fastest growing business with 53% revenue growth year on year. Azure is now the world's second most used cloud infrastructure service.[29]

Project Oxford (2015)
Helps developers create smarter facial apps by integrating microsoft's advanced machine learning technology. Beta available for free to developers with an Azure account, Microsoft's cloud computing platform.[22]

B Azure Cognitive Services (2019)
Project Oxford officially releases as Azure Cognitive Services in 2019. An integral part of Azure AI services to help enterprise users solve business problems.

D Cortana
Microsoft's Cortana digital assistant (2014) lags behind Alexa and Google Assistant, largely due to the lack of hardware integration (limited to Windows 10 PCs). To leapfrog this, Microsoft partners with Amazon to integrate their digital assistants (2018).[30]

C Hololens Edition 2 (2019)
Microsoft refines Hololens' customer segment and tailors the second edition to help enterprise users of all types better do their jobs. Microsoft establishes partnerships with large companies (Saab, Airbus, Honeywell, Toyota) to optimize their production processes.[21]

Nokia (2015, $8 billion write off)
Moving out of mobile devices.[26]

Hololens (2016)
Microsoft's "mixed reality" headset is still in development phase. Sales reach 50,000 units sold by May 2018.[20]

Unilever

Paul Polman joins Unilever as CEO in 2010 and repositions Unilever to become a purpose-driven company. He believes most consumers are willing to switch their purchase to a brand that supports sustainable living—and he thinks that, as a company, you can do well by doing good.

Unilever, founded in 1929, is a British-Dutch transnational company producing products in food and beverage, home care, and personal care. Unilever now owns over 400 brands, with a turnover in 2018 of €51 billion. It has grown to be one of the most recognizable brands in the world.

By the 2000s, Unilever was struggling to overcome rising commodity prices and the financial crisis (of 2008). In 2010, Unilever picked an outsider as CEO in an effort to increase communication and transparency with the marketplace.

Paul Polman believed in focusing on the long term and set ambitious sustainability goals for Unilever, all the while doubling its business. He believed that a company's growth can decouple from its environmental impact; products with a purpose can create higher consumer demand and better constructed supply chains will be more sustainable, long term.

Incorporate Sustainability

Unilever is struggling in the 2000s to overcome rising commodity prices and then the financial crisis of 2008. When Paul Polman takes over as CEO, he creates the Sustainable Living Plan, "defining a new era of responsible capitalism."

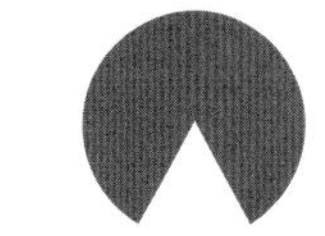

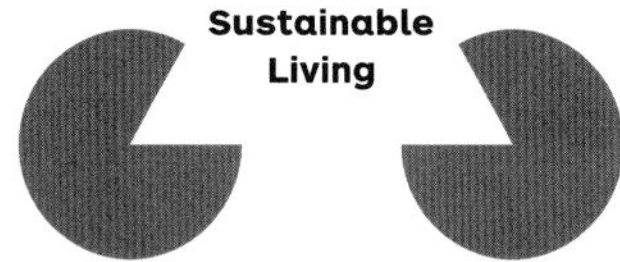

PAUL POLMAN
Unilver CEO

In 2019, Paul Polman stepped down as CEO and was replaced by Alan Jope. Jope pledged to push Unilever's sustainability objectives even further by making every one of their brands purpose led.

Strategic Direction

Make Sustainable Living Commonplace
Unilever will make all 400+ of its brands purpose led by reducing their environmental footprint, while increasing positive social impact.

Sustainability and Profits
Unilever wants to double its revenue by moving from low- to high-margin goods while halving the environmental impact of its products. These ambitious targets prove you can both do good and do well.

Long-Term Planning
Banning quarter reporting and scaling back hedge fund shareholdings reduces share price fluctuations. This, in turn, creates a more stable environment to plan for long-term growth over short-term returns.

Organizational Culture

Purposeful and Principled
At Unilever, success is defined as having "the highest standards of corporate behavior towards everyone we work with, the communities we touch, and the environment on which we have an impact." Everyone is expected to conduct operations with integrity and with respect for the many people, organizations, and environments the business touches.

Brand Image

Purpose Driven not Profit Driven
"Over 90% of millennials say they would switch brands for one which champions a cause." Unilever wants to be perceived as a company driven by the desire to act responsibly—and, to prove that sustainability is good for business.

In 2018, Unilever's purpose-led, sustainable living brands grew 69% faster than the rest of the business and delivered 75% of the company's growth.[31]

2019 End of Year Results

Schmidt's Natural (2017, Sustainability)
Natural, chemical-free deodorants

Living Proof (2016, Premium)
Premium hair care products

Mae Terra (2016, Sustainbility)
Natural and organic food business

GRAZE (2019, Sustainbility)
Healthy subscription-based snacking

Seventh Generation (2016, Sustainability)
Eco-friendly cleaning products

The Laundress (2019, Premium)
High-end, eco-friendly laundry and household cleaning products

Comfort One Rinse
A newly released version of the fabric conditioner uses 20% less water then previous editions, saving 10 million Olympic-sized pools' worth of water a year.

Lifebuoy
Creates the Handwashing Programme to prevent 600,000 child deaths every year from respiratory infections and diarrheal disease.

Dove
Dove creates the Self-Esteem Project, to ensure the next generation grow up feeling confident about the way they look—to help them reach their full potential. Since 2005, The educational tool has been improving self-esteem in more than 35 million young people.

TG Tips
In 2018 introduces fully biodegradable tea bags made with plant-based material, significantly improving their environmental impact.

Domestos
In 2017 launches Flush Less spray to market in South Africa, in response to the water shortages affecting the area.

Unilever has indicated it will drop brands that do not "contribute meaningfully to the world," even if it affects their bottom line. These include much loved brands like Marmite, Magnum, and Pot Noodle.[34]

Purpose-led

In 2014, sells SlimFast to Kaios Group. SlimFast makes shakes, snacks, and other dietary supplement foods that promote diets and weight-loss plans.[32]

Profit-led

Unilever sells off many of their food brands to make the shift to a higher-margin portfolio mix.

In 2013 sells Wish-Bone salad dressing to for $580 million and Skippy peanut butter for $700 million. In 2014, sells pasta sauce brand, Ragu for £1.26 billion.

Portfolio Example

2013 ~~~ 2019

Logitech

In 2013 Bracken Darrell takes the helm of Logitech. He unlocks growth by moving the company away from the declining PC market. Logitech builds a portfolio of design-focused consumer and enterprise accessories that benefit from the growth of the cloud.

Logitech was founded in 1981 in Switzerland. It rapidly grew, based on its innovative computer peripherals, like advanced versions of the PC mouse. Logitech came under pressure with the decline of the PC market and a $100 million failure with Google TV in 2012.[35]

Bracken Darrell re-focused the company's portfolio on consumer and enterprise accessories that would benefit from the growth of the cloud and connected devices. Logitech acquired several brands to expand its portfolio, particularly in music and gaming.

Logitech, traditionally an engineering-focused company, put design at the center of the company and its portfolio. In 2013 it hired Allistair Curtis, former head of design for Nokia, to help build a design-led organization.

Revive Entrepreneurship

In 2012 the PC market started an irreversible decline and moved toward mobile, tablets, and the cloud. Logitech, which traditionally relied on the growth in the PC industry, had to dramatically change.

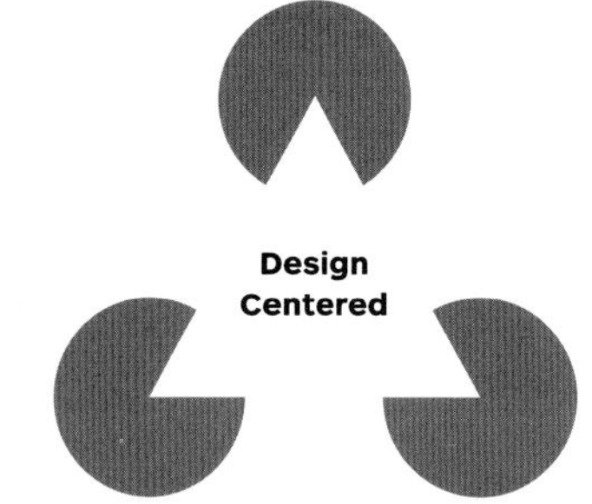

Multicategory Multibrand

Design | Engineering | Go-to-Market | Marketing

Operations

From Logitech's presentation

Strategic Direction

The Leading Cloud Peripheral Player

A Be a big fish in many small ponds and avoid giants like Apple, Google, and Amazon.

B Reinvest profits in growth, assure growth across major categories, and improve margins to high end of range.

Become a "design company."

Organizational Culture

Entrepreneural and Design Driven

Revive entrepreneurial culture where people are willing to try new things and maintain entrepreneurial independence of acquisitions.

Expand core capabilities, in particular, in-house design and customer obsession.

Design for cost early on in the process to increase operational efficiency.

Brand Image

High End Design

A Multibrand company that brings people together through music, gaming, video, and computing.

Known for innovating for the customer, to deliver exactly what they want with high-end design.

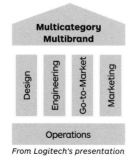

Logitech's Fiscal Year 2019 vs. 2013[36]

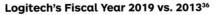

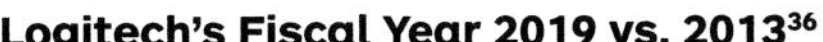

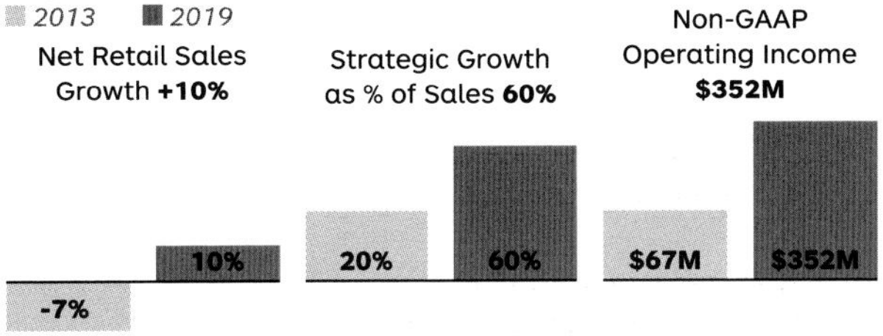

2013
2019
Net Retail Sales Growth +10%
Strategic Growth as % of Sales 60%
Non-GAAP Operating Income $352M
-7%
10%
20%
60%
$67M
$352M

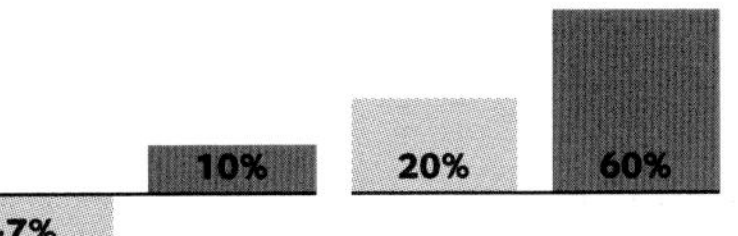

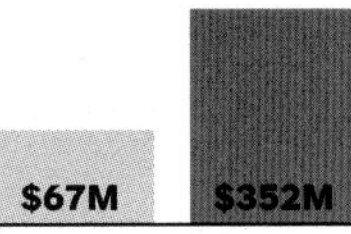

2019 End of Year Results

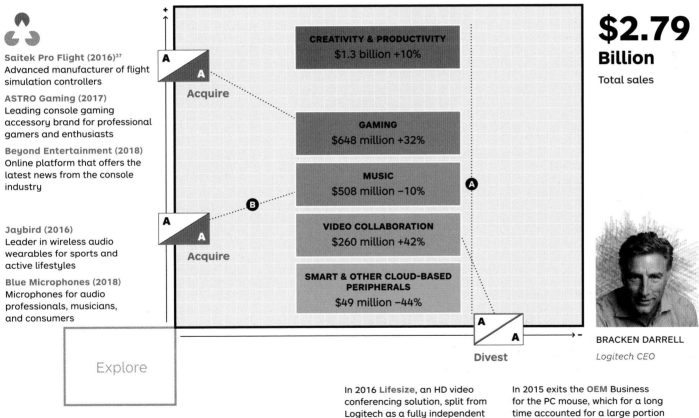

Saitek Pro Flight (2016)[37]
Advanced manufacturer of flight simulation controllers

ASTRO Gaming (2017)
Leading console gaming accessory brand for professional gamers and enthusiasts

Beyond Entertainment (2018)
Online platform that offers the latest news from the console industry

Jaybird (2016)
Leader in wireless audio wearables for sports and active lifestyles

Blue Microphones (2018)
Microphones for audio professionals, musicians, and consumers

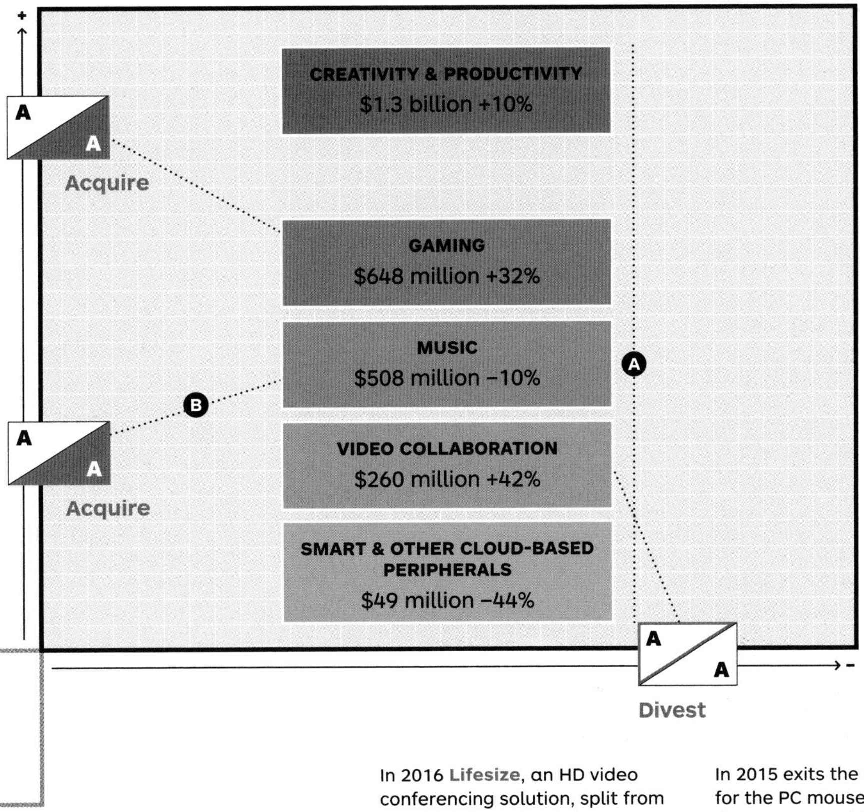

+
A
A
Acquire
CREATIVITY & PRODUCTIVITY
$1.3 billion +10%
GAMING
$648 million +32%
MUSIC
$508 million −10%
VIDEO COLLABORATION
$260 million +42%
SMART & OTHER CLOUD-BASED PERIPHERALS
$49 million −44%
B
A
A
A
Acquire
A
A
Divest
-
Explore

$2.79 Billion

Total sales

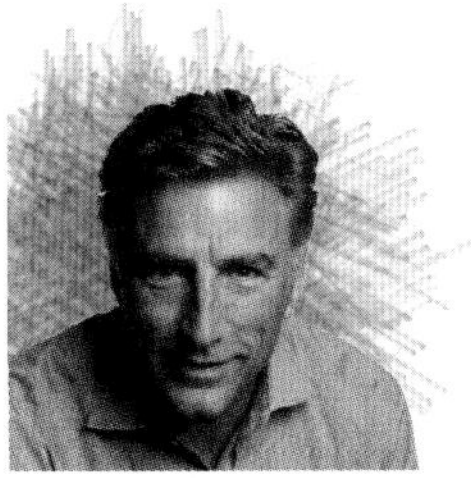

BRACKEN DARRELL

Logitech CEO

In 2016 **Lifesize**, an HD video conferencing solution, split from Logitech as a fully independent company.[39]

In 2015 exits the **OEM** Business for the PC mouse, which for a long time accounted for a large portion of Logitech's revenue.[38]

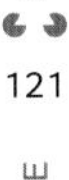

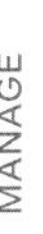

Portfolio Example

2001 ~~~ 2019

FUJIFILM Holdings

In 2003 Shigetaka Komori is appointed CEO of Fujifilm. He understands for the company to survive the digital disruption of analog film, it has to completely restructure and reinvent itself as a technology player.

Fujifilm, founded in 1934, was Japan's first producer of photofilm. By the mid-80s it dominated the industry together with Kodak. However, in the early 2000s, the digitization of film made the industry virtually irrelevant.

In 2004, CEO Shigetaka Komori came up with a 5-year medium-term management plan to "save Fujifilm from disaster and ensuring its viability as a leading company." Komori decided to downsize the photofilm business and cut almost 5,000 jobs worldwide all the while building a $400 million research facility to venture into new markets.[40] Before then, Fujifilm spent 1.5 years taking stock of their technical inventory to find a renewed appreciation of Fujifilm's capabilities nurtured in photofilm.

The new business unit Healthcare and Material Solutions now makes up 43% of total revenue and photofilms accounts for less than 1% of its revenue.[41]

Fight Disruption

By the mid 2000s, the digitization of photography had made photo film imaging virtually irrelevant. Komori understood he needed a plan to dramatically change the direction of the company, in order to ensure its survival.

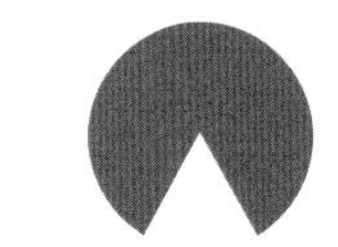

Become Tech Player

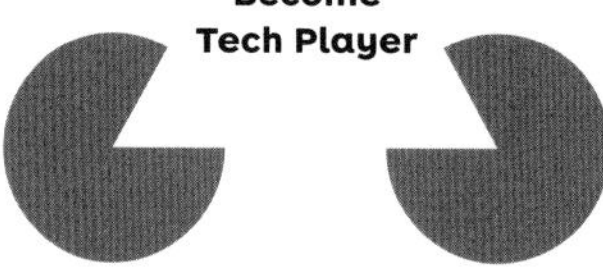

Strategic Direction

The three strategic directions outlined in Komori's 5-year plan are:

- Implementing structural reforms for cost reduction
- Building new growth strategies through a diversified portfolio
- Enhancing consolidated management for faster decision making

Organizational Culture

To ensure Fujifilm could make the rapid transformation in time, Komori understood the organization needed to create the right structure:

- Stronger individuals with greater autonomy and role flexibility that could take initiative and be more entrepreneurial
- Lean and decisive corporate leadership with rapid decision-making process[42]

Brand Image

Fujifilm is known to the world over for their state-of-the-art technology, delivering top-quality products. They want the brand image and trust they built with film to carry over to an array of care products as they make a leap to other industries.

"Fujifilm had, until then, been one of the leading companies in the photographic products industry and had continually produced big profits. I wanted to make sure it stayed that way into and through the next century. Figuring out how to do it was my job as CEO."

SHIGETAKA KOMORI

FUJIFILM Holdings Chairman and CEO

Fujifilm acquires two companies (**Diosynth RTP LLC and MSD Biologics (UK) Limited**) and renames them to Fujifilm Diosynth Biotechnologies. This is to enter into the biopharmaceutical contract development and manufacturing organization business to expand their Healthcare & Material Solutions.

The Acquisition of **Toyama Chemical** (currently Fujifilm Toyama Chemical) in 2008 signals Fujifilm's full scale entry into the pharmaceutical business.

In 2001, Fujifilm purchases an additional 25% share of **Fuji Xerox**, a joint venture with Xerox. Making it a consolidated subsidiary. The Document Solutions division now makes up 41% of annual revenue.

By 2006, the digital transformation of photography was well on its way and Fujifilm knew it had to dramatically restructure its film ecosystem, by downsizing its photographic film business. This frees up much-needed resources to fulfil their diversification plan. In 2019, **photo film** accounts for less than 1% of its annual revenue.

Building a Diversified Portfolio 2004–2019

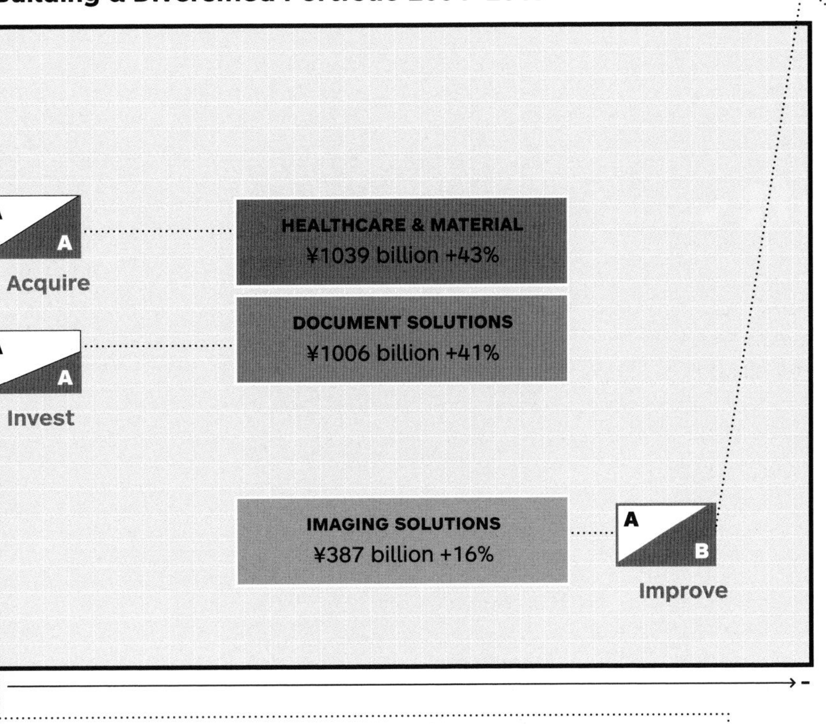

Explore

Fujifilm makes a bold decision to invest in LCD films, predicting the boom of LCD screens. Fujifilm invests over ¥150 billion in new facilities to manufacture **FUJITAC**, a high-performance film essential for making LCD panels for TV, computers, and smartphones.

Fujifilm's understanding of how photos fade and oxidizes over time helped them make the leap into the functional cosmetic realm, as the human skin ages in a similar manner. In 2007, the skincare line **Astalift** was founded.

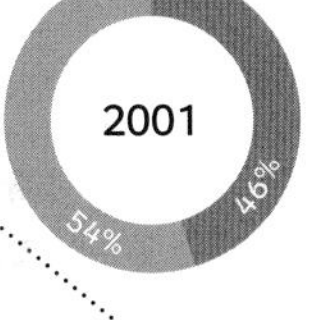

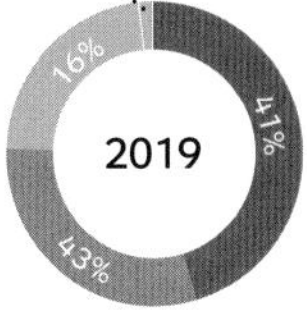

HEALTH CARE & MATERIAL SOLUTIONS
Health care & Material, Highly Functional Materials, Recording Media, Graphic Systems/Inkjet Display Materials

DOCUMENT SOLUTIONS
Office Products & Printers, Production Services, Solutions & Services

IMAGING SOLUTIONS
Photo Imaging, Electronic Imaging, Optical Devices

Business Model Shifts

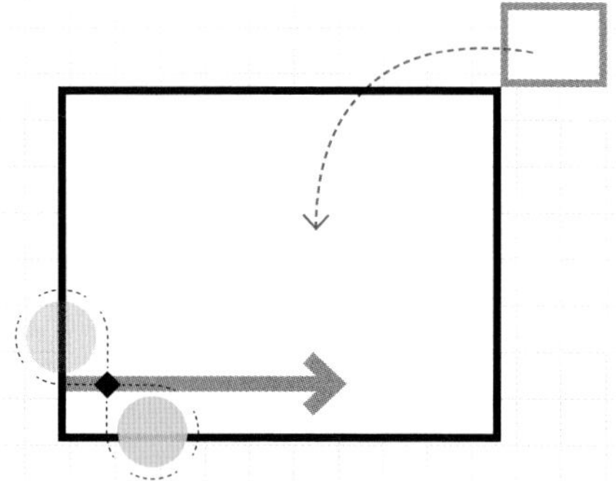

A company needs to apply the processes and metrics of the Explore portfolio when it decides to renovate one of its expiring business models in order to shift to a new one. More precisely, it needs to continue to operate the expiring business model, while simultaneously exploring and testing the shift to a new one. This is a challenging endeavor, but you will only succeed if you apply an exploration rather than an execution mindset to the testing of a potential new business model. This will reduce the risk that you shift to a new business model that won't work.

Testing Your Shift

Shifting to a new business model is very risky, because uncertainty whether it will work is high. However, if you apply the testing process and principles from the Explore portfolio you can substantially reduce the risk of shifting toward something that won't work. The main difference is that you build on top of an existing business. That has advantages and disadvantages. The main advantage is that you are likely to know customers, market, and technologies well. The disadvantage is that you might prioritize running the business as is at the expense of testing the hypotheses underlying the business model shift.

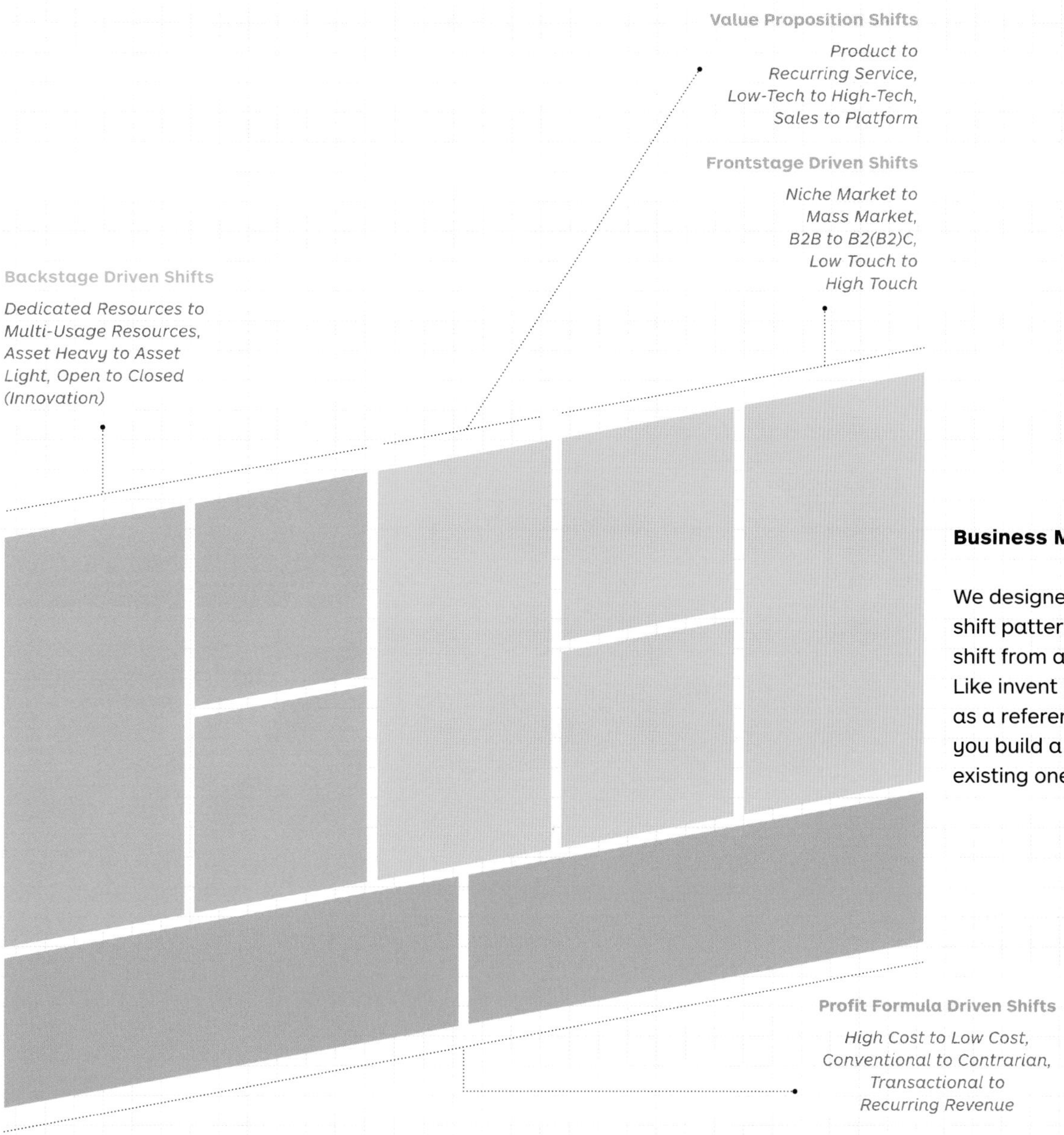

Value Proposition Shifts

Product to Recurring Service, Low-Tech to High-Tech, Sales to Platform

Frontstage Driven Shifts

Niche Market to Mass Market, B2B to B2(B2)C, Low Touch to High Touch

Backstage Driven Shifts

Dedicated Resources to Multi-Usage Resources, Asset Heavy to Asset Light, Open to Closed (Innovation)

Profit Formula Driven Shifts

High Cost to Low Cost, Conventional to Contrarian, Transactional to Recurring Revenue

Business Model Pattern Library

We designed a library of 12 business model shift patterns to help you explore how to shift from an old to a new business model. Like invent patterns, the shift patterns serve as a reference library or inspiration to help you build a new business model on top of an existing one.

Patt

erns

Business Model Patterns

A repeatable configuration of different business model building blocks to strengthen an organization's overall business model.

Help new ventures develop a competitive advantage beyond technology, product, service, or price.

Help established companies shift from an outdated to more competitive business model.

A single business model can incorporate several patterns.

Pattern Library

In the following pages we outline a pattern library that is split into two categories of patterns: invent patterns to enhance new ventures and shift patterns to substantially improve an established but deteriorating business model to make it more competitive.

Invent Patterns

Codify aspects of a superior business model. Each pattern helps you think through how to compete on a superior business model, beyond the traditional means of competition based on technology, product, service, or price. The best business models incorporate several patterns to outcompete others.

Exploit

Explore

Shift Patterns

Codify the shift from one type of business model to another. Each pattern helps you think through how you could substantially improve your current business model by shifting it from a less competitive one to a more competitive one.

Applying Patterns

Understand business model patterns to better perform the following business model activities:

Design and Assess

Use patterns to design better business models around market opportunities, technology innovations, or new products and services. Use them to assess the competitiveness of an existing business model. (p. 229)

Disrupt and Transform

Use patterns as an inspiration to transform your market. In the following pages, we provide a library of companies that disrupted entire industries. They were the first to introduce new business model patterns in their arena.

Question and Improve

Use patterns to ask better business model questions, beyond the traditional product, service, pricing, and market-related questions. Regardless of whether you are a senior leader, innovation lead, entrepreneur, investor, or faculty, you can help develop superior business models based on better questions.

THE BIGGEST THREAT TO INCUMBENTS

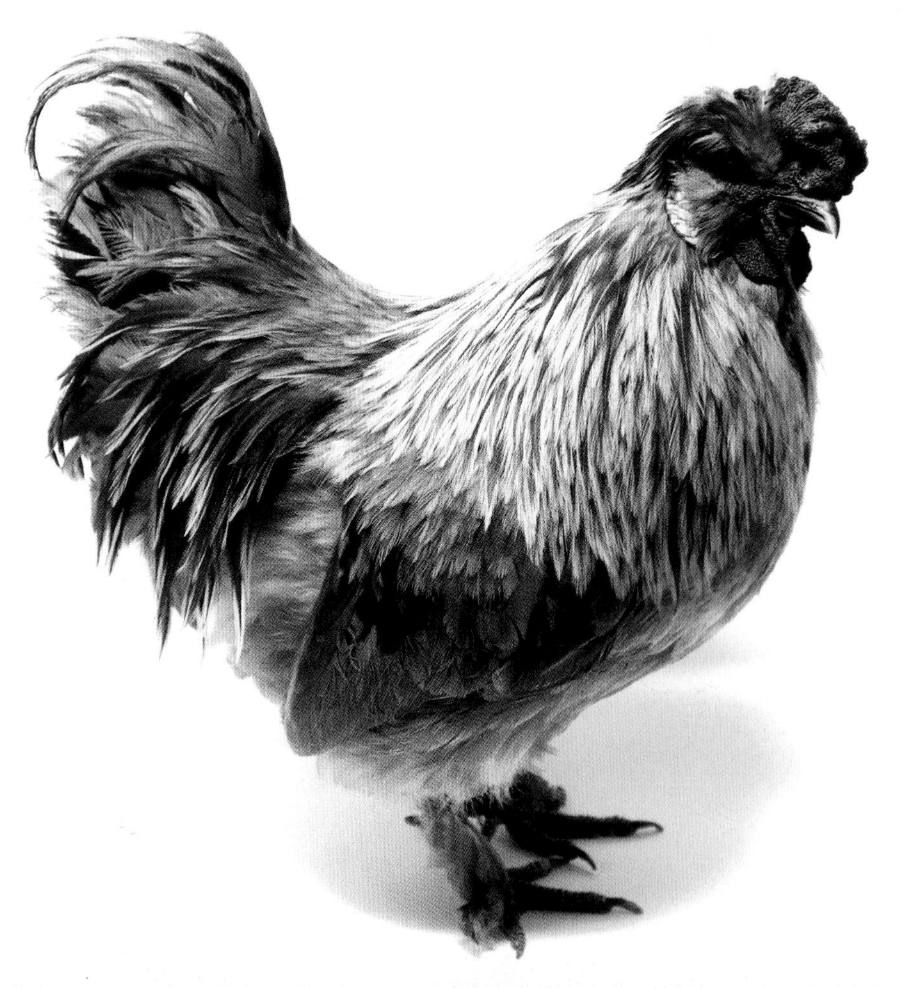

IS THE UPSTARTS

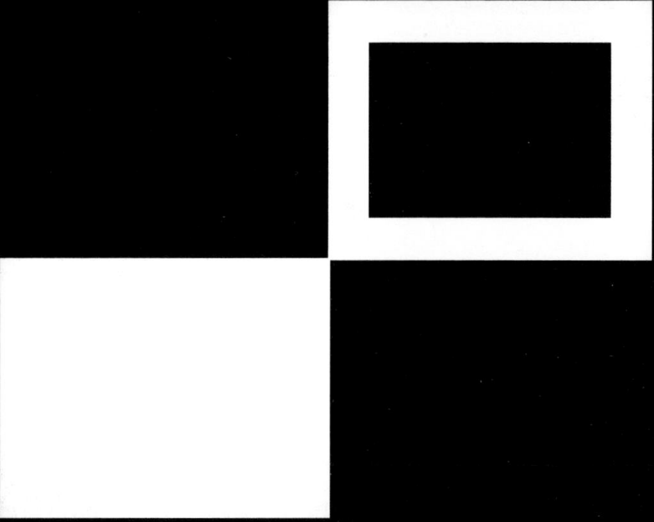

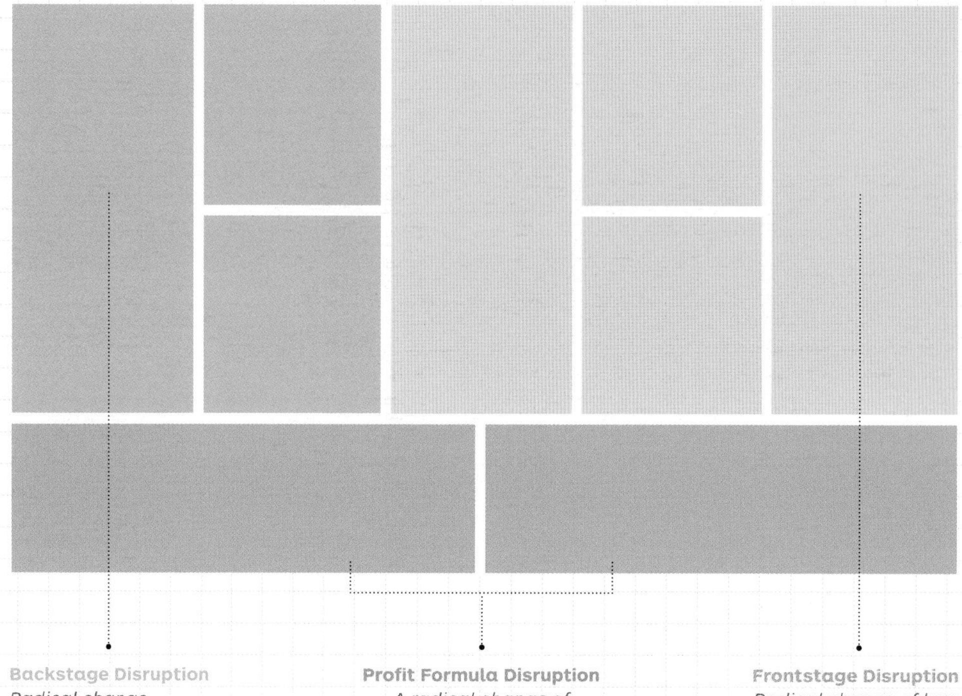
Backstage Disruption
Radical change
of how value is created.
Profit Formula Disruption
A radical change of
who is targeted and how
value is delivered.
Frontstage Disruption
Radical change of how
value is created.

Epicenters

Business model patterns can originate in the frontstage (customer-driven), backstage (resource-driven), or profit formula (finance-driven) of a business model.

Invent Pattern Library

Frontstage Disruption

Backstage Disruption

Profit Formula Disruption

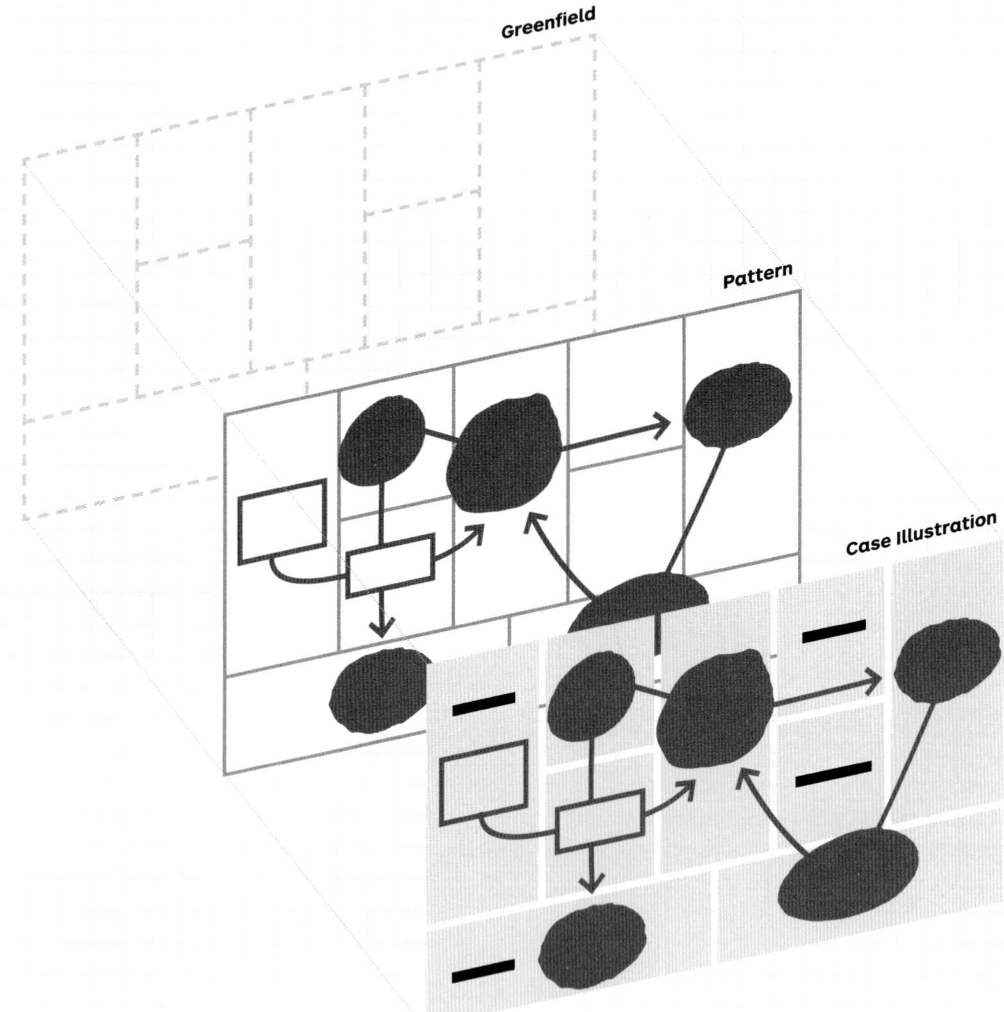

Invent Patterns

Greenfield

The companies we portray in this section all started from a blank sheet. They built business models from scratch around a technology, market opportunity, or trend. They all disrupted an industry by applying powerful business model patterns unheard of in that industry.

Pattern

We highlight nine different invent patterns with 27 flavors that new ventures and established companies can apply to build better, more competitive business models. We describe each pattern so that you can make use of it as a reference library.

Flavor
Each pattern has two or more different flavors. These are variations of a particular pattern to help you understand different ways to apply the pattern in question.

Case Illustration

Each case serves to highlight a pattern in action. We don't outline the company's entire business model—just show how it applied a particular pattern to build a more competitive business model. In reality, an entire business model might combine several patterns.

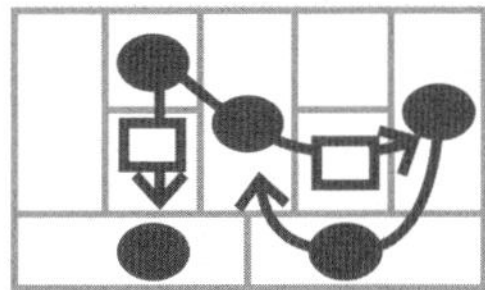

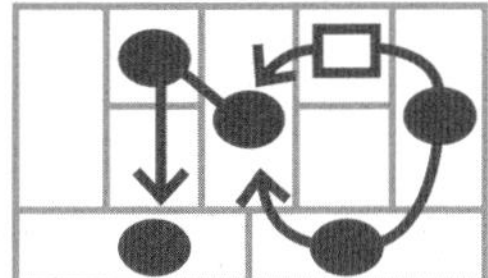

Legend

- Greenfield 
- Business Model Pattern 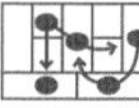
- Case Illustration 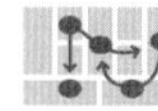
- Pattern Building Blocks 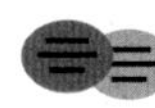
- Optional Pattern Building Blocks 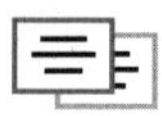
- Original Business Model Blocks 
- Other Business Model Blocks 

Frontstage Disruption

Market Explorers

Channel Kings

Gravity Creators

A radical change of who is targeted and how value is delivered.

Market Explorers

Unlock Markets

Develop innovative value propositions that create, unleash, or unlock completely new, untapped, or underserved markets with large potential. Be a pioneer and unearth new revenue potential through market exploration.

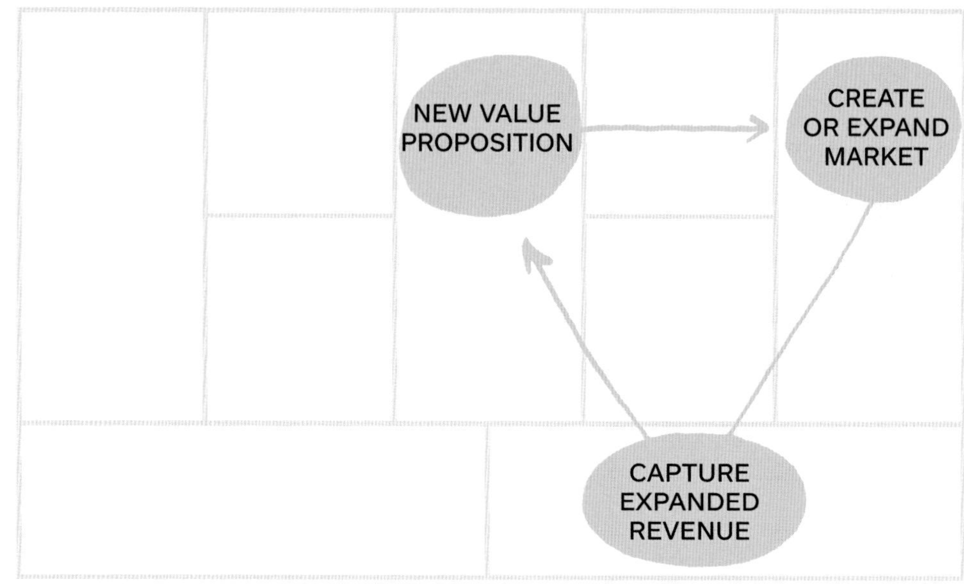
NEW VALUE PROPOSITION
CREATE OR EXPAND MARKET
CAPTURE EXPANDED REVENUE

TRIGGER QUESTION
How could we tap into new, untapped, or underserved markets with large potential?

Assessment Question
How large and attractive is the untapped market potential we are going after?

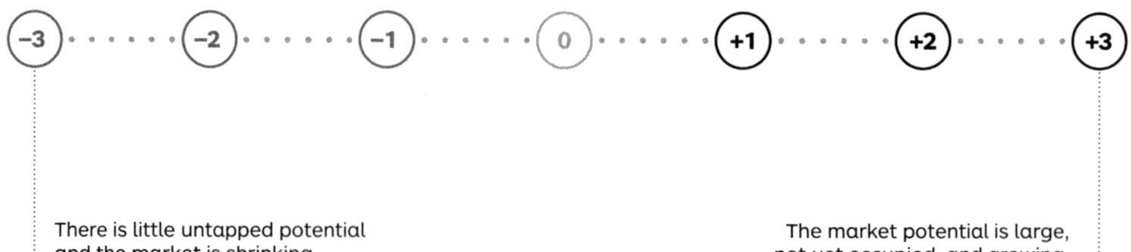
−3
−2
−1
0
+1
+2
+3
There is little untapped potential and the market is shrinking.
The market potential is large, not yet occupied, and growing.

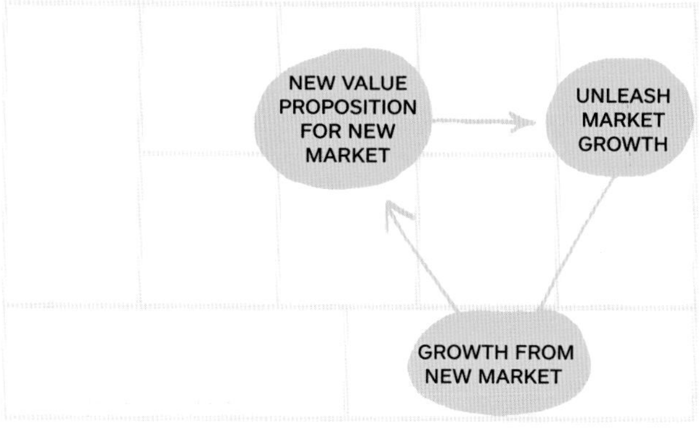

Visionaries – Use imagination to see a large market potential where others don't. Unleash growth by *exploring unproven needs* that you satisfy with a new value proposition.

EXAMPLES
Tesla, iPhone, Nintendo Wii

TRIGGER QUESTION
Which unproven needs of a large market might be worth exploring?

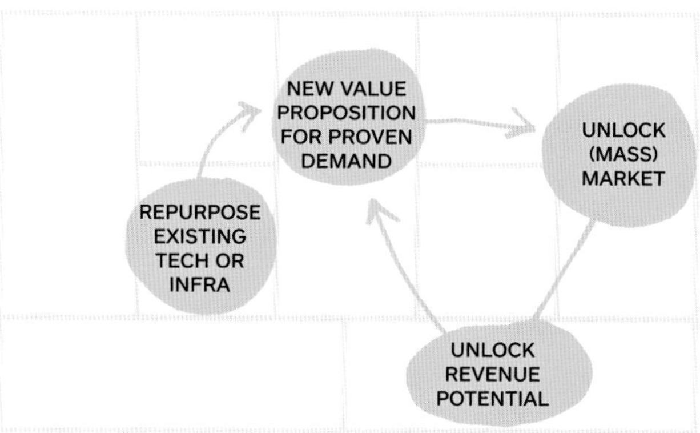

Repurposers – Find innovative ways to tap into proven market demand by *repurposing existing technology and infrastructure* that previously served other ends.

EXAMPLES
M-Pesa, AWS

TRIGGER QUESTION
How could we repurpose an existing technology or infrastructure to unlock proven, but so far inaccessible, customer needs?

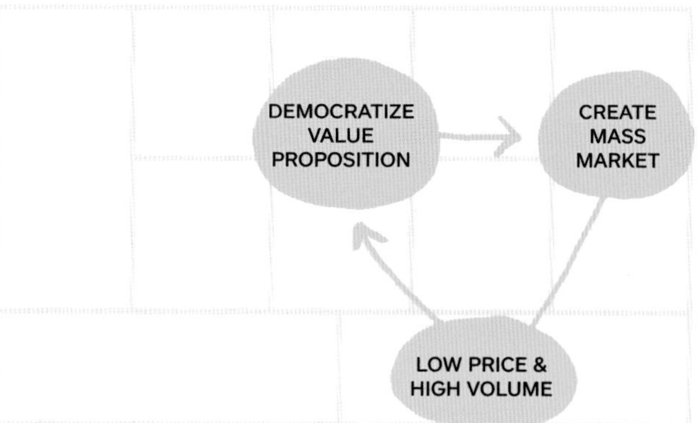

Democratizers – Find innovative ways to *democratize access to products, services, and technologies* that were previously only accessible to a small number of high-end customers.

EXAMPLES
Sears, Azuri, M-Pesa, AWS

TRIGGER QUESTION
How could we unlock products, services, and technologies that are limited to a niche market and make them more widely available for a mass market?

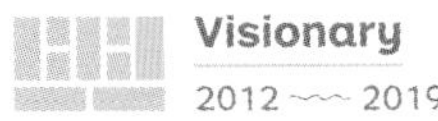

Tesla Motors

In 2012 Tesla envisions a large untapped market (high-end electric vehicles) where nobody else sees one. With the Model S they create the right value proposition to unlock the opportunity.

Tesla was founded in 2003 with the goal of commercializing electric vehicles, starting with luxury sports cars and then moving on to affordable, mass market vehicles. In 2008, Tesla began selling its Roadster. Its first breakthrough was in 2012 when it launched the Model S. Tesla's first "affordable" car, the Model 3, was announced in 2015 and produced in 2017.

Prior to Tesla, the market for electric vehicles was relatively insignificant and was served by utilitarian and unremarkable models. Tesla was the first car manufacturer to view the market for electric vehicles differently: Tesla saw a significant opportunity by focusing on performance and the high end of the market.

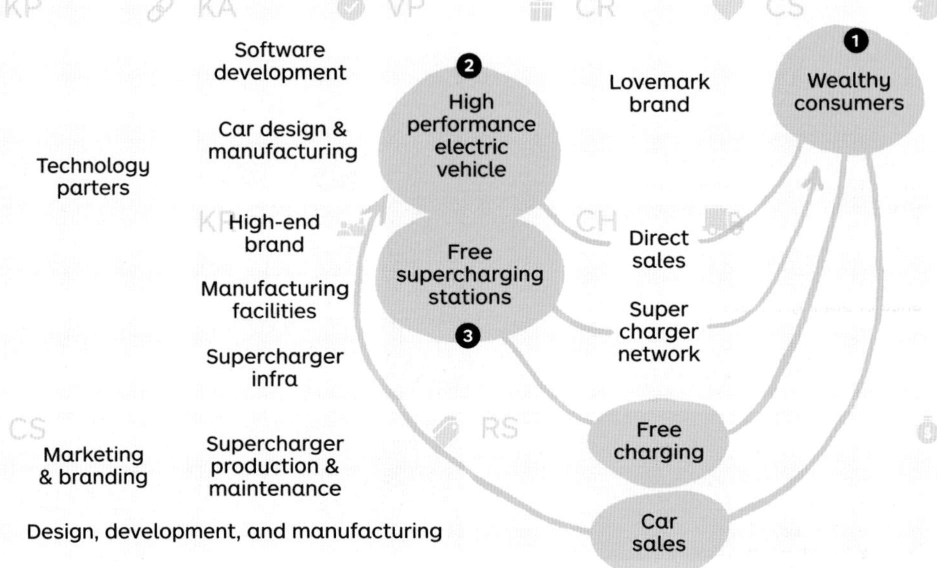

1 Envision a Large, Untapped Market, Where Nobody Sees One

Tesla identifies a potential market of environmentally conscious, wealthy consumers who are interested in electric vehicles, but not at the expense of comfort, performance, and design.

2 Create Customer Gains in New Ways

With the Model S, Tesla taps into the aspirations of its initial customer segment. In 2013, it is called the "best car ever tested," and becomes the best selling car in eight of America's 25 wealthiest zip codes.[1]

3 Relieve Customer Pains in New Ways

Tesla recognizes its customers' fears over battery range. It substantially improves the speed of charging and creates its own network of free superchargers in high traffic areas.

+ Lovemark Brand

Tesla built up a lovemark brand in record time. It inspired significant brand loyalty because of its dedication to saving the planet, high-quality vehicles, and personal customer service. In 2014, the Tesla Model S was voted the "most loved car in America."

+ Direct Distribution

From the start Tesla sold its cars directly (through the Internet, gallery-like stores in urban malls, and its owner loyalty program) to educate customers on the cars' features.

From Hardware to Software and Data

Tesla is not just a car manufacturer, it is truly a software company. Its cars run on sophisticated software that updates wirelessly. Self-driving software that constantly learns from the data of its community of drivers is introduced in 2014. Software drives the entire user experience of owning a Tesla.

Building the Backstage for Disruption

To enable its vision of unleashing the electric vehicle market, Tesla bolsters its portfolio of key resources and key activities with technology partners like Toyota, Mercedes, and Panasonic. It also manages to overcome substantial manufacturing challenges for Tesla's first affordable car, the Model 3.

14,000 Superchargers were deployed globally at 1,261 stations, as of September 2019.[3]

276 thousand Model 3 preorders in its first two days, worth more than $10 billion for Tesla as of April 2, 2016.[4]

Tesla Strategy Canvas[2]

Comparing electric cars

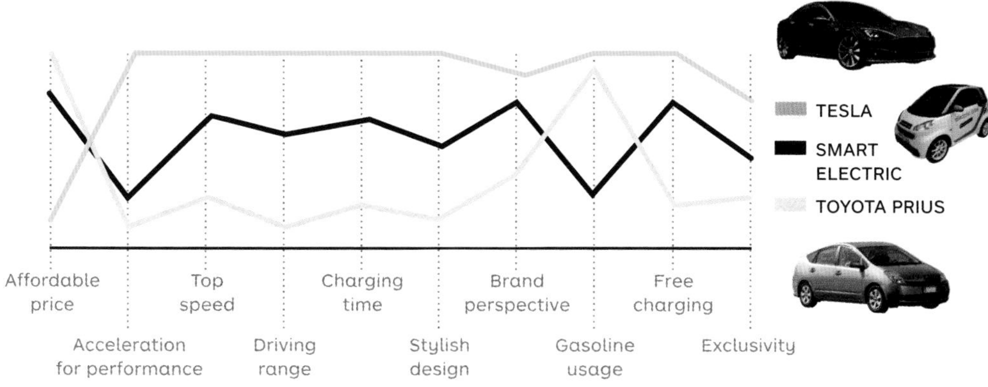

Global Electric Vehicle Sales in 2019[5]

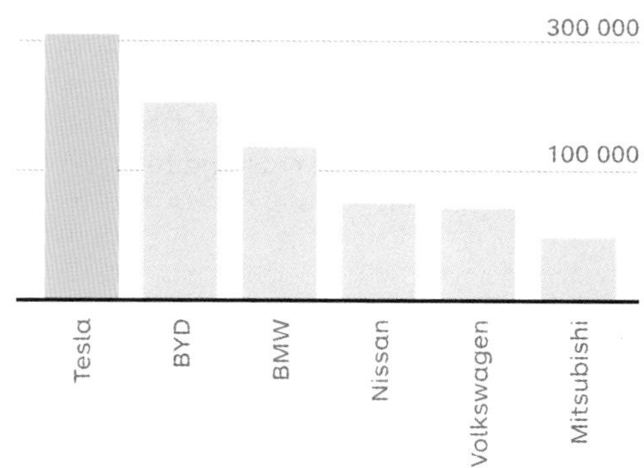

M-Pesa

In 2007, Safaricom repurposes its telecom network to create M-Pesa, a reliable money transfer solution for the masses.

Safaricom is the biggest telecom operator in Kenya. In 2007, it decided to use its telecom infrastructure to build M-Pesa, a simple mobile money transfer system. It tapped into the proven demand for mobile payments from millions of Kenyans with a mobile phone.

Existing financial services were expensive and inappropriate for small transactions. In 2009, there were only 352 ATMs and 491 bank branches in the entire country (with a population of 39 million). Most money transfers were in cash, which was expensive, unreliable, and sometimes dangerous.

M-Pesa changed that. Within two years of its introduction, M-Pesa saw 10,000 new registrant applications daily.[6] In 2010, it processed over 90% of all mobile money transactions in Kenya, and had a 70% market share of all mobile money subscribers.[7]

M-Pesa also had an impact on a national scale in Kenya with studies crediting M-Pesa for lifting an estimated 2% of Kenyan households out of extreme poverty.[8]

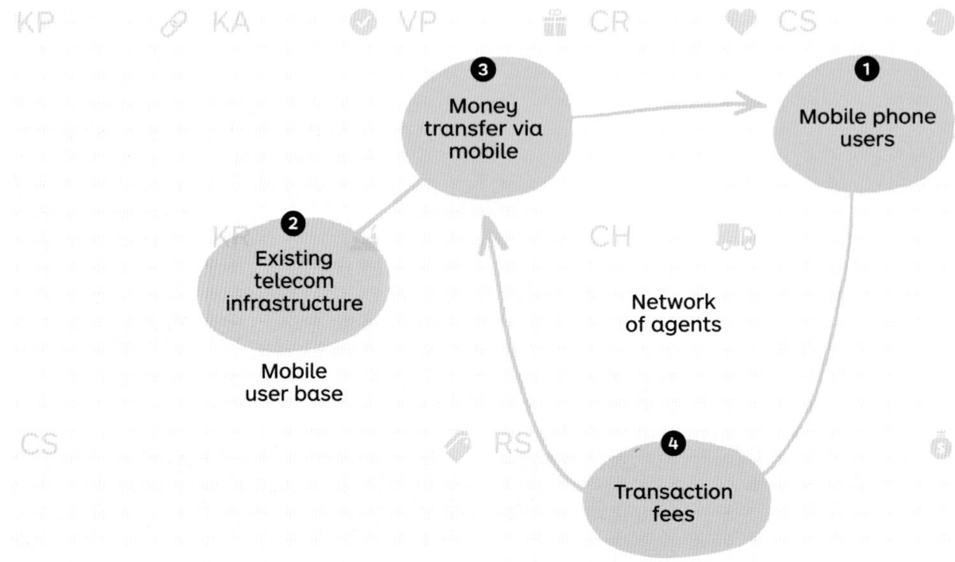

1. Identify a Proven Demand You May Unlock Based on Your Resources

Safaricom has evidence for market demand: some of their mobile customers hack their own digital payment solution by using SMS messages to share mobile airtime as a means of e-currency.

2 Repurpose Your Key Resources to Enable the New Value Proposition

In 2007, Safaricom imagines how it could repurpose its telecom network to create a reliable money transfer solution with M-Pesa. As the dominant telecom operator in Kenya, it already has a relationship with millions of Kenyans.

3 Differentiate from Competition

In the mid-2000s, financial services are expensive and do not cater to irregular and small transactions. Only a minority of Kenyans are using the banking system. With M-Pesa's affordable money transfers, Safaricom opens up the financial system to the previously unbanked.

4 Enjoy the New Revenue Stream

M-Pesa generates a new revenue stream for Safaricom reaching Sh62.9 billion ($625 million equivalent), that is, 28% of Safaricom total revenues in 2018.[9] Revenues come from small transaction fees on money transfers and other financial services.

+ Network of Agents

Through 2018, M-Pesa builds a distribution network of 110,000 agents across Kenya, allowing Kenyans to exchange cash for virtual currency and vice versa.[10] This includes small shops, gas stations, post offices, and even traditional bank branches and is 40 times the number of bank ATMs in Kenya.

23

million Kenyans

used the system by 2013 which is equivalent to

74%

of the adult population.[11]

M-Pesa Active Customers[12]

In millions as of 2019

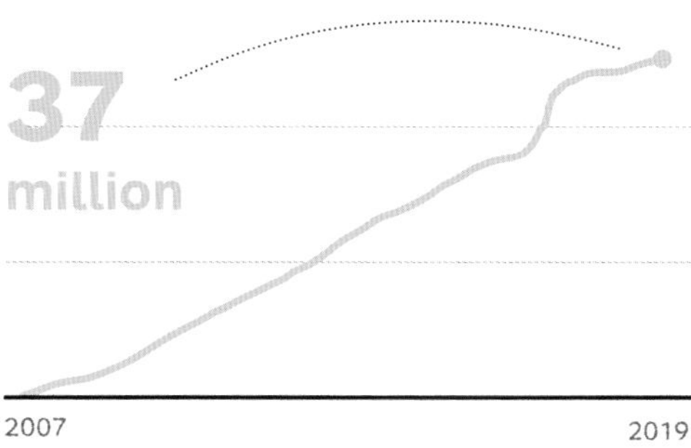

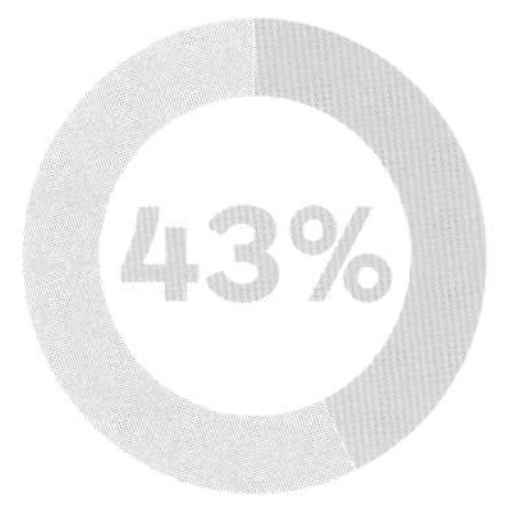

of Kenya's GDP was transferred per month over the system in 2013, up from 10% in 2009.[13]

Democratizer

1888 ~~~ 1993

Sears, Roebuck and Co.

In the late 1800s, Sears, Roebuck and Co. ("Sears") democratizes access to mass market retail with the Sears mail order catalog. By leveraging the growth in U.S. mail and delivery services, Sears was able to distribute its products to all rural areas throughout the United States.

HISTORICAL CASE

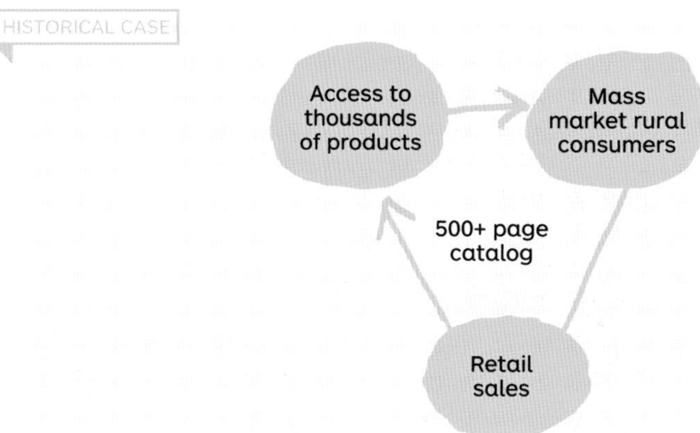

The Sears mail order catalog gave isolated settlers in the west access to a variety of low-price everyday goods that were previously inaccessible to them. By 1895 the catalog was more than 500 pages long, bringing in $750 thousand in annual sales ($23 million equivalent today).

The first Sears retail store opened in 1925 in Chicago, and Sears remained the U.S.'s top retailer until 1991. The catalog was discontinued in 1993, after over a century of use.

$23

million

Amount of sales (in today's dollars) brought in by the catalog in 1895.[14]

Channel Kings

Access Customers

Radically change how to reach and acquire a large number of customers. Pioneer innovative new channels that haven't been used in your industry before.

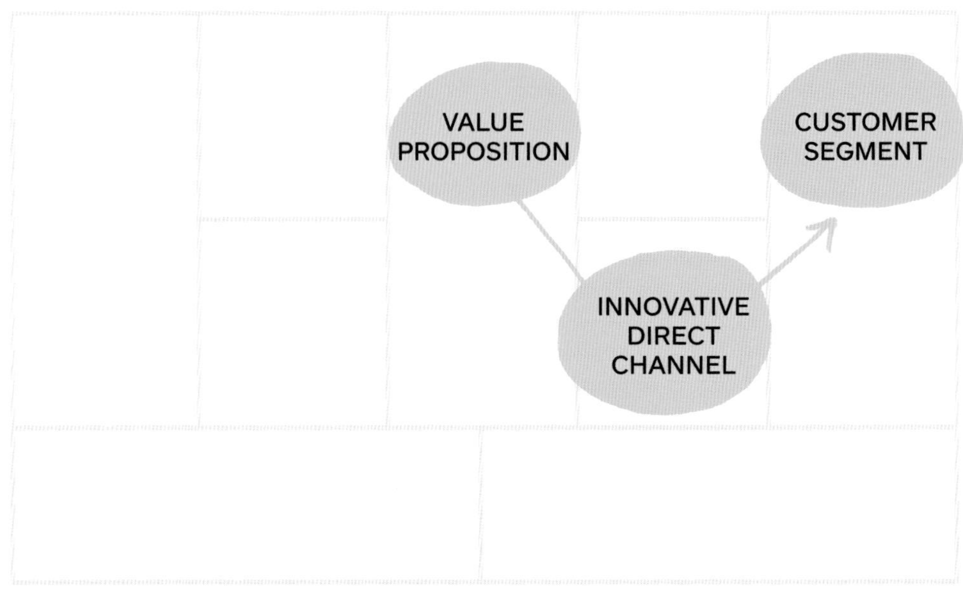

TRIGGER QUESTION

How could we increase market access and build strong and direct channels to our end customers?

Assessment Question

Do we have large-scale and, ideally, direct access to our end customer?

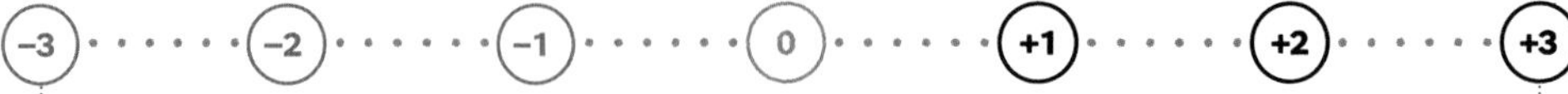

We have limited market access and depend on intermediaries to get our products and services to customers and interact with them.

We have large-scale market access and own the channel(s) and relationships with end users of our products and services.

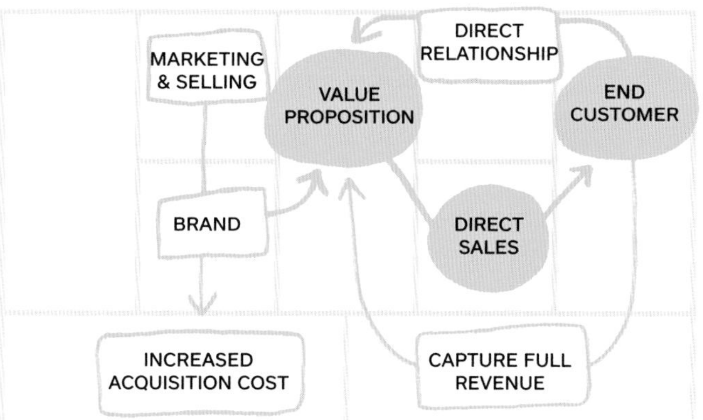

Disintermediators – Establish direct channels to customers where intermediaries previously dominated market access. Replace the reach of intermediaries with your own (often creative) marketing, customer acquisition activities, and strong brand. Develop a better market understanding, build stronger customer relationships, and capture the full revenue, which you previously shared with intermediaries.

EXAMPLES
Dollar Shave Club (DSC), Nespresso, Gore-Tex

TRIGGER QUESTION
How could we cut out the middleman and create a direct access to our end-customers?

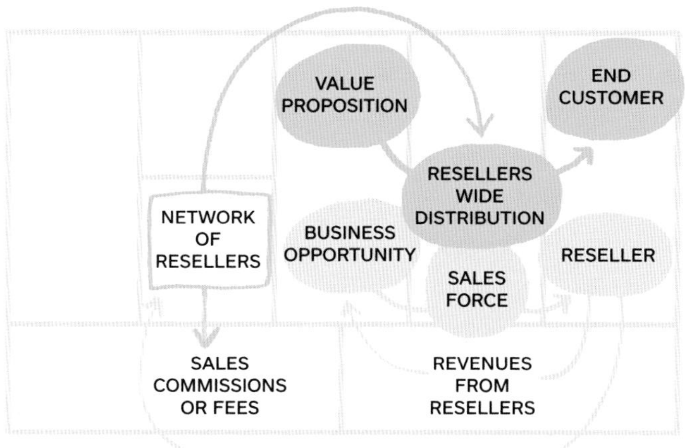

Opportunity Builders – Create business opportunities for others to sell the company's products and services. Help others make money and/or gain status, which is a powerful incentive to help you increase your market reach.

EXAMPLES
Tupperware, Grameen Phone, J. Hilburn

TRIGGER QUESTION
How could we make it attractive for a large number of people or third-party businesses to sell our products and services?

Disintermediator

2012 ~~~ 2016

Dollar Shave Club

In 2012, Dollar Shave Club (DSC) launches with a viral marketing campaign and disrupts the market for men's shaving products by selling directly to consumers.

Dollar Shave Club spotted consumer inconveniences, where most saw an over-served market. In the shaving market, men had to choose between (supposedly) high-tech razors or low-cost, low-functionality tools. DSC aimed to change this by providing an end-to-end customer experience with affordable shaving products.

In 2012, DSC launched its online store and quickly disrupted the overpriced men's razor blade market. It purchased its products from wholesalers, removed the traditional physical retail channel, and sold razors and blades online at a lower price.

DSC focused heavily on online marketing to replace the reach of the eliminated middleman. Its launch video with founder Michael Dubin showcased the brand's sense of humor and went viral. Editorial content accompanies each delivery, often with a humorous twist.

The company was acquired by Unilever in 2016 for approximately $1 billion.[15]

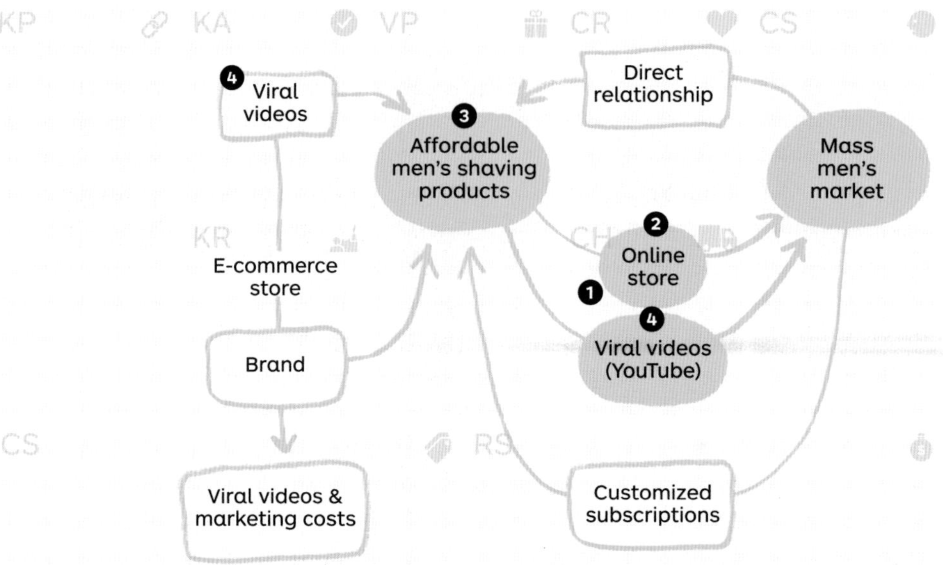

1 Eliminate (or Go Around) the Middleman

DSC cuts out retail stores to sell directly. On the upside, this means saving margins traditionally paid to retailers. On the downside, it means losing the broad market reach of retailers.

2 Build an Optimized Direct Channel

The company launches its online store in 2012, which gives it full control over the customer experience, relationships, and data. DSC uses this channel to continuously test its product line and optimize its value proposition.

3 Differentiate Your Value Proposition

DSC competes on an end-to-end customer buying experience with affordable products. Its flexible subscription plans allow members to buy their first product for just $1 and then choose the products and shipping frequency.

4 Replace the Reach of the "Historic" Middleman with Innovative Marketing

Because DSC can't rely on the reach of a retailer, it creates visibility and brand recognition with its viral videos. DSC keeps consumers coming back with educational videos and editorial content delivered with its unique brand voice.

As of November 2019
Dollar Shave Club's first video has

26,525,768
views[16]

69%
retention rate

Portion of customers that come back and transact in the first month after making an initial purchase.[17]

Disruptive Direct to Consumer Brands

Brands with a singular product focus and an elevated customer experience have led the recent growth in direct-to-consumer (DTC) brands.

DTC companies have used disintermediation to become successful by controlling: (1) their relationship with the customer, (2) the presentation of their products whether online or instore, (3) the collection of customer data, and (4) the speed to market of new products.

Increasingly, DTCs are also moving out of an online-only presence into physical stores (Warby Parker, Bonobos, and Glossier, for instance). These physical stores further cement the brand relationship (customers can actually try before they buy) and allow the brands to tailor a physical experience.

Incumbent	Product and Global Market Size (USD)	D2C Brand
Nike	SNEAKERS **$62.5 billion**	Allbirds
Colgate	ORAL CARE **$28 billion**	Quip
Luxottica	EYEWEAR **$123.58 billion**	Warby Parker

Tupperware

In 1948, Tupperware takes off when it starts selling through Tupperware Home Parties, empowering women to sell to other women, using their social networks.

Although Earl Tupper invented his now-ubiquitous Wonderlier Bowl in 1946, it wasn't until he partnered with Brownie Wise to create Tupperware Home Parties in 1948 that the innovative, bell-shaped plastic containers took off.

Brownie Wise pioneered the Hostess Group Demonstrations (aka Tupperware Parties) in order to tap into the power of women's social networks for personalized, in-home demonstrations.

Tupperware turned the initial challenge of selling plastics into an opportunity for women to make money independently from their husbands. The independent dealers were so successful that Tupperware abandoned in-store sales completely in 1951.

Tupperware was a women-focused business, empowering women to sell to other women, using their social networks as a means of expanding their reach and building trust.

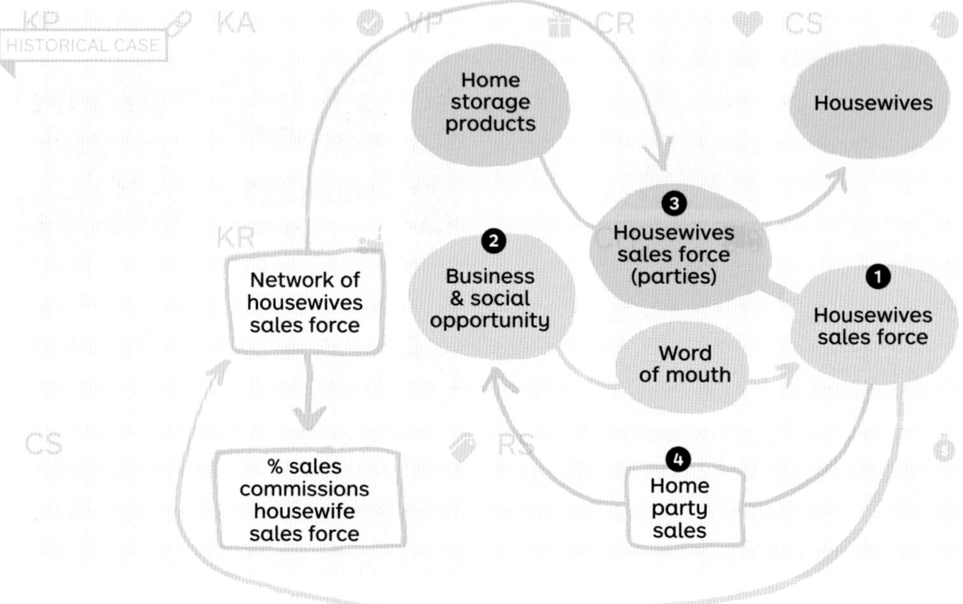

1 Identify Who You Can Create an Opportunity for to Help You Sell

After their contribution to the WW2 war effort, women are often told to go back to the kitchen. Brownie Wise sees how Tupperware can offer housewives an opportunity to become independent Tupperware dealers.

2 Design the Opportunity

Wise pioneers Tupperware Parties, where a hostess opens up her social network and the Tupperware dealer demonstrates the products. Hostesses receive products as a reward for hosting, and dealers get a cut of the sales.

3 Develop the Channel

By 1954 there are 20,000 people in the network of dealers and none of them are employees of Tupperware: they are private contractors who collectively act as the channel between the company and the consumer.[18]

4 Earn from Helping Others

Women are convinced of the utility of the product by seeing it in person and by receiving persuasive recommendations from friends. This channel is so successful that Tupperware decides to abandon in-store sales completely in 1951.

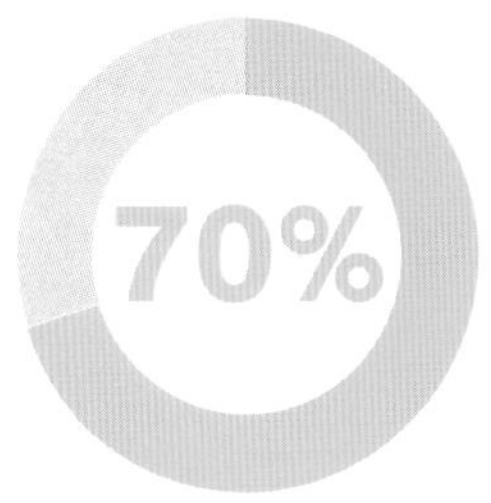

In the 1950s, 70% of U.S. homes included a working husband and a stay-at-home wife.[19]

Sales Force Growth[20]

Tupperware dealer growth during 1954

20,000

7,000

January

December

Peggy Allison shows delight as Brownie awards her a new Ford, at Tupperware's Jubilee.

Rita Richardson receives her Pontiac, presented by Tupperware Sales Counselor Homer Wilson.

A Tupperware Career

Ruth Acker and her distributor Leonard Kopowski admire her new Ford, awarded by Tupperware.

I'll never forget my First Tupperware Party! I was nervous, of course, but thrilled to find I was really a Tupperware dealer at last. It's wonderful to be a part of our national "family" and yet be in business for myself!

Fledo Segraves receives a $5,000 mink coat from Brownie.

Put yourself in the Tupperware Picture

$233 million

Tupperware sales of home storage products soar and hit $25 million in 1954 (more than $233 million in 2019's money), driven entirely by the sales efforts of Tupperware dealers.[21]

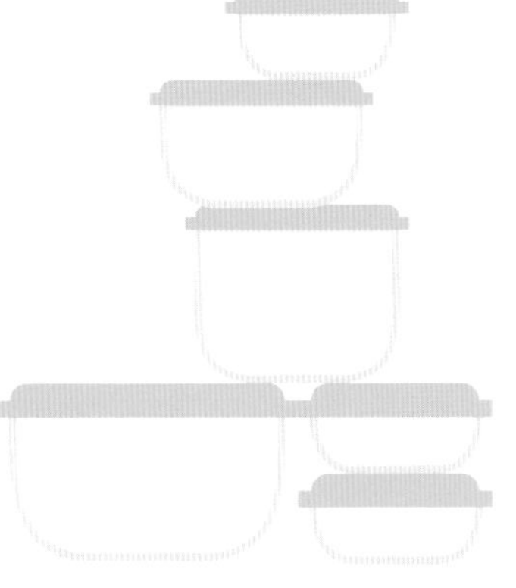

By the 1990s, the percentage of U.S. homes that owned at least one item of Tupperware was[22]

Natura

The modern-day version of Tupperware is Natura, one of the largest cosmetics companies in Latin America. It has been using a direct selling model called Selling through Relationships since 1974.

1.7 Million

number of sales consultants in the Natura network[23]

Hundreds of thousands of female entrepreneurs act as brand ambassadors and beauty advisors and sell Natura products. In 2005, Natura expanded to retail stores with its first boutique in Paris, France. In 2012, it added a digital platform to support sales consultants globally, with online courses and support features.

In May 2019, Natura agreed to purchase Avon, its largest direct selling competitor, in a share swap.

Gravity Creators

Lock In Customers

Make it difficult for customers to leave or switch to competitors. Create switching costs where previously there were none and turn transactional industries into ones with long-term relationships.

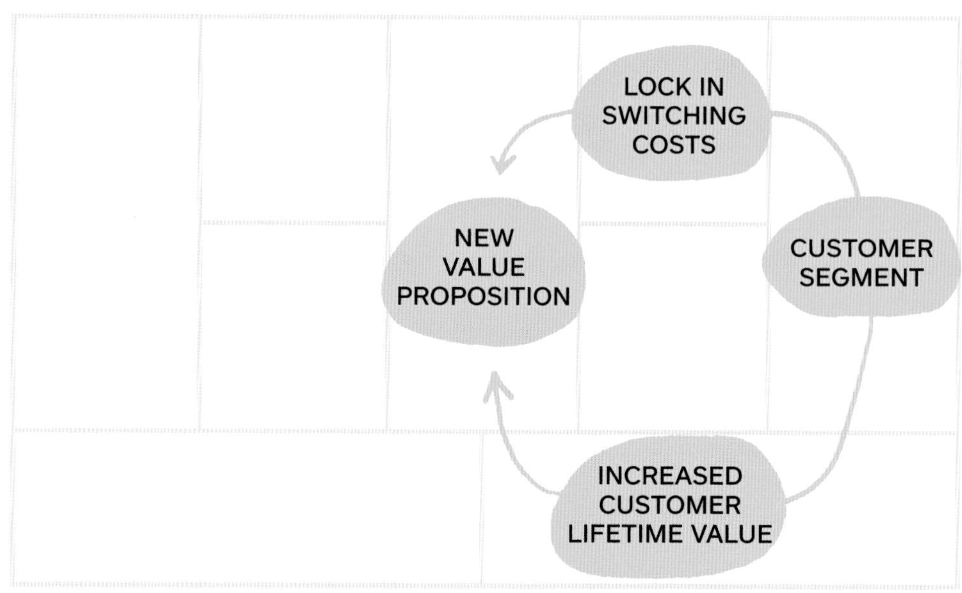

TRIGGER QUESTION

How could we make it difficult for customers to leave and increase switching costs in a positive way?

Assessment Question

How easy or difficult is it for our customers to leave or switch to another company?

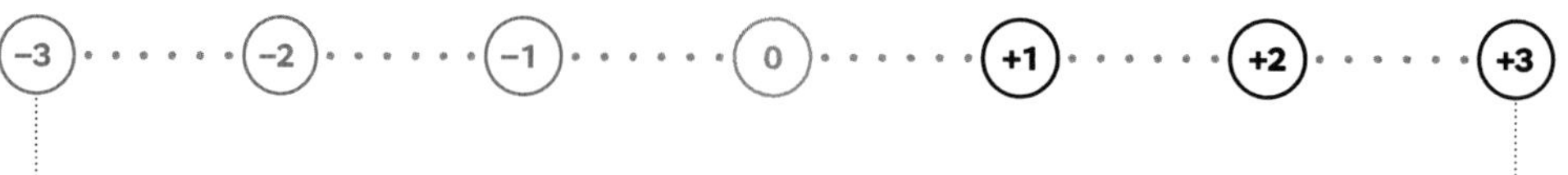

All our customers could theoretically leave us immediately without incurring direct or indirect switching costs.

Our customers are locked in for several years and they would incur significant direct and indirect switching costs if they left.

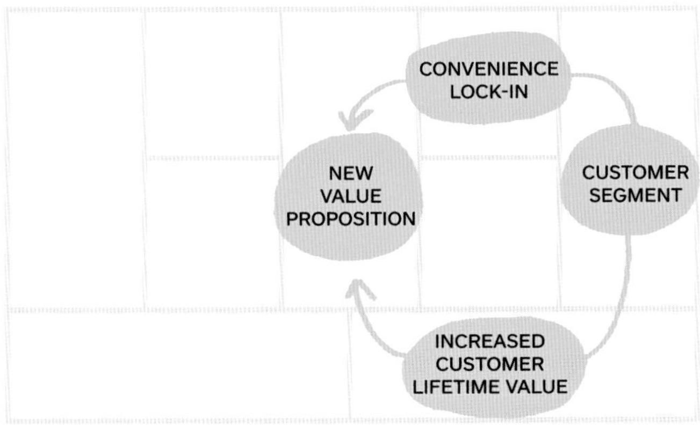

Stickiness Scalers – Increase stickiness by making it inconvenient for customers to leave. Inconvenience may be related to the difficulty of transferring data, steep learning curves, onerous departure procedures, or other customer pains if they decide to leave.

EXAMPLE
Microsoft Windows

TRIGGER QUESTION
How can we increase customer stickiness?

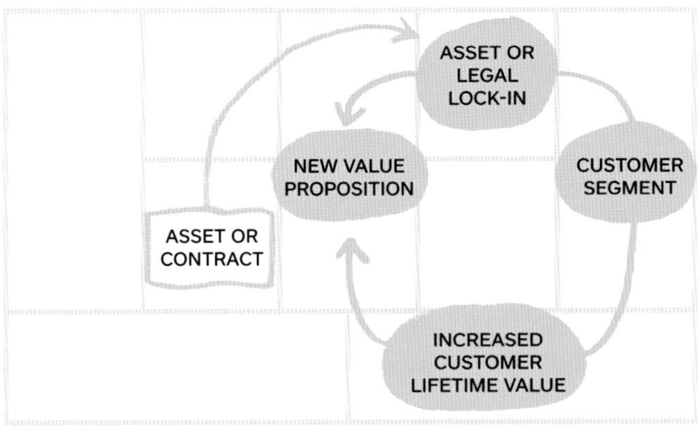

Superglue Makers – Make it difficult for customers to leave by locking them in. Lock-in may occur based on multiyear contracts, upfront sunk costs, cancellation fees, elimination of alternatives, and other techniques.

EXAMPLES
Microsoft Xbox, Nespresso

TRIGGER QUESTION
How can we lock in customers?

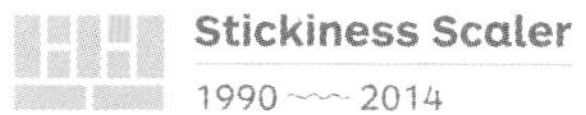

Microsoft Windows

In 1990 Microsoft got 30 PC manufacturers to preinstall Windows 3.0 on their machines. That move effectively locked in millions of users into the Microsoft ecosystem and generated recurring revenues for over two decades.

Microsoft originally launched Windows in 1985 as an add-on to MS-DOS, the original operating system of the PC. However, in 1990, when Microsoft launched Windows 3.0, it leveraged its relationships with PC manufacturers to preinstall the operating system (rather than shipping it separately). More than 30 manufacturers agreed to include the program for free and preinstalled it with every machine. As a result Windows rapidly gained in popularity—shipping over one million copies just two months after launch.[24]

Once consumers had learned how to use Windows and compatible programs, most of them were reluctant to invest the time, cost, and effort to learn a new operating system and new programs. PC users effectively got themselves locked into the Microsoft ecosystem once they purchased their first Windows-equipped PC.

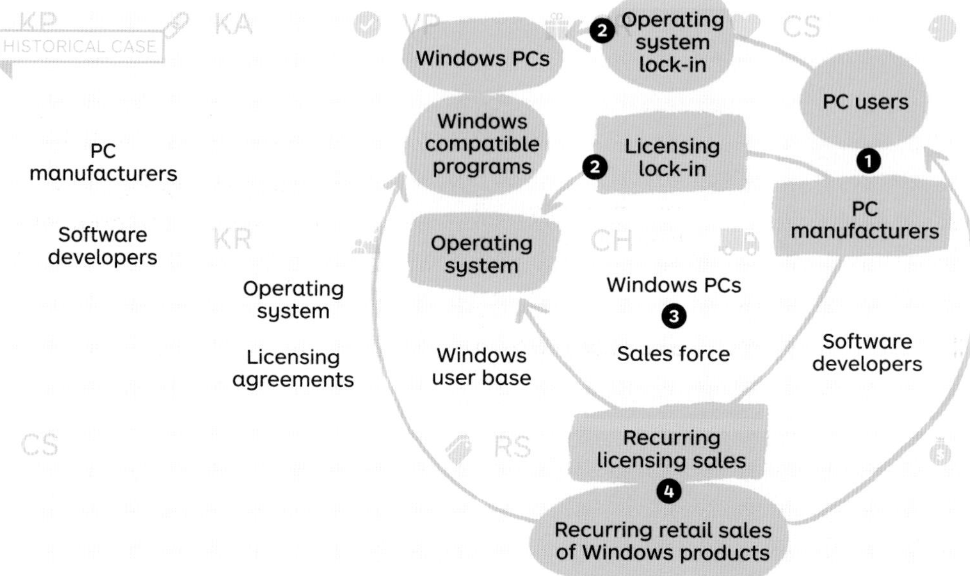

1 Spot a Market with Low Switching Costs for Customers

The early computer market is rather fragmented, and each computer manufacturer operates their own unique operating system. At this time it is relatively easy for customers to switch from one system to another.

2 Create a Value Proposition That Locks Customers In

Windows 3.0 increases switching costs in three ways: (1) PC manufacturers preinstall Windows, increasing the effort needed to switch, (2) the graphical interface and new features steepen the learning curve, (3) Microsoft builds an ecosystem of Windows-compatible software to lock customers in via interoperability.

3 Focus on Scaling First-Time Customer Acquisition

Microsoft scales first-time customer acquisition of Windows 3.0 users in 1990 by getting 30 of the main PC manufacturers to preinstall Windows 3.0 and sign long-term licensing agreements. That puts Windows in the hands of millions of users and effectively locks them in.

4 Enjoy the Benefits of Lock-in

Due to the learning curve and software compatibility advantages, customers continuously come back to buy Windows PCs. This lock-in guarantees recurring licensing royalties from PC manufacturers and Windows sales to retail customers for over two decades.

+ Boost Windows Compatible Software

A key component of Microsoft's lock-in strategy is to boost acquisition of developers to quickly increase the number of software applications available for the Windows ecosystem: Windows-compatible software rises from 700 before the launch of 3.0 to 1,200 one year later, and 5,000 by 1992.[25]

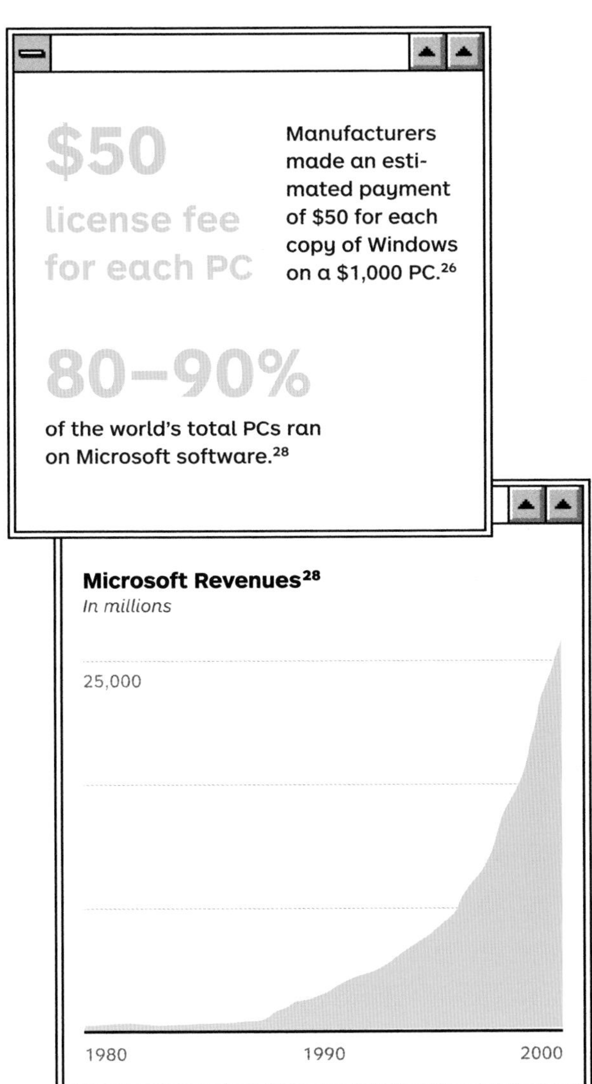

$50
license fee for each PC
Manufacturers made an estimated payment of $50 for each copy of Windows on a $1,000 PC.[26]
80–90%
of the world's total PCs ran on Microsoft software.[28]
Microsoft Revenues[28]
In millions
25,000
1980
1990
2000

Microsoft Xbox

In 2001, Microsoft makes its first foray into the living room and releases the original Xbox game console. The subsidized console locks gamers in and increases their lifetime value from game sales and royalty payments from third-party game developers.

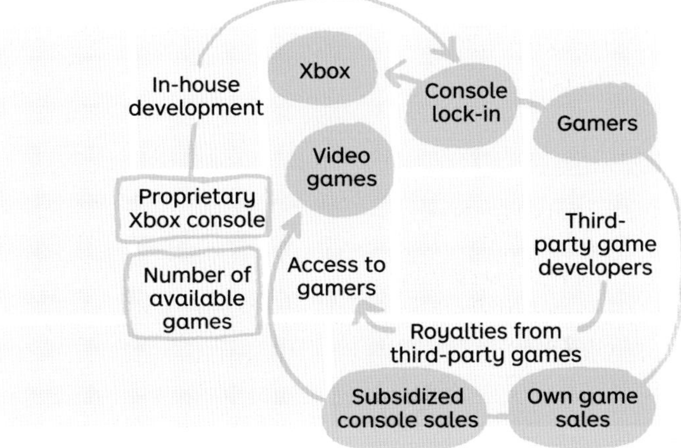

Microsoft developed the Xbox in 2001 as a closed-system gaming console. They attracted and locked in a large number of gamers by subsidizing console sales. Microsoft monetized the Xbox by selling exclusive in-house games like *Halo* and from royalties paid by third-party game developers for every game sold. Gamers have been unlikely to switch due to their upfront investment in the console and the library of games they purchased for the platform. Microsoft successfully adopted this business model from the competing Sony PlayStation 2.

$5 billion

The *Halo* franchise has made in games and hardware sales as of 2015.[29]

FRONTSTAGE DISRUPTION

Questions for Leaders

Market Explorers

TRIGGER QUESTION

How could we tap into new, untapped, or underserved markets with large potential?

Assessment Question

How large and attractive is the untapped market potential we are going after?

There is little untapped potential and the market is shrinking.

The market potential is large, not yet occupied, and growing.

Channel Kings

TRIGGER QUESTION

How could we increase market access and build strong and direct channels to our end customers?

Assessment Question

Do we have large-scale and, ideally, direct access to our end customers?

We have limited market access and depend on intermediaries to get our products and services to customers and interact with them.

We have large-scale market access and own the channel(s) and relationships with end-users of our products and services.

Gravity Creators

TRIGGER QUESTION

How could we make it difficult for customers to leave and increase switching costs in a positive way?

Assessment Question

How easy or difficult is it for our customers to leave or switch to another company?

All our customers could theoretically leave us immediately without incurring direct or indirect switching costs.

Our customers are locked in for several years and they would incur significant direct and indirect switching costs if they left.

Backstage Disruption

Resource Castles

Activity Differentiators

Scalers

A radical change in how value is created.

Resource Castles

Build Moats

Build a competitive advantage with key resources that are difficult or impossible for competitors to copy.

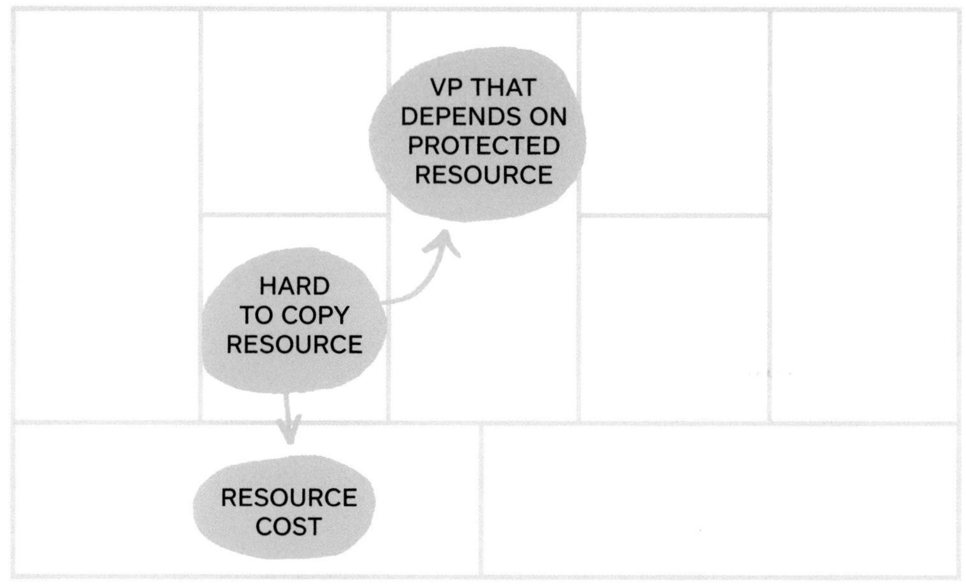

TRIGGER QUESTION

How could we make difficult-to-copy resources a key pillar of our business model?

Assessment Question

Do we own key resources that are difficult or impossible to copy and which give us a significant competitive advantage?

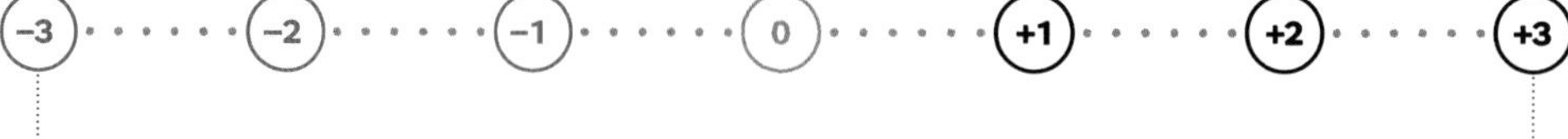

Our key resources are significantly inferior to those of our competitors.

Our key resources can't easily be copied or emulated for the next couple of years and they give us a significant competitive advantage (e.g., intellectual property, brand, etc.).

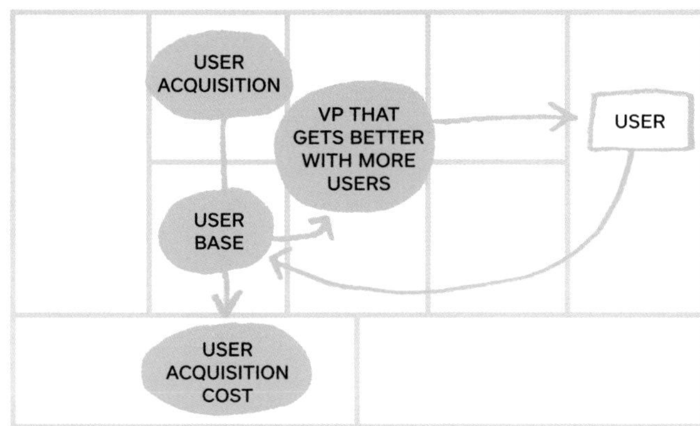

User Base Castles – Create a business model with network effects in which a large number of users equals the relative value for other users. Acquire a large user base to establish a competitive advantage that makes it hard for anybody else to catch up.

TRIGGER QUESTION
How could we establish a competitive advantage rooted in a large user base and network effects in our value proposition?

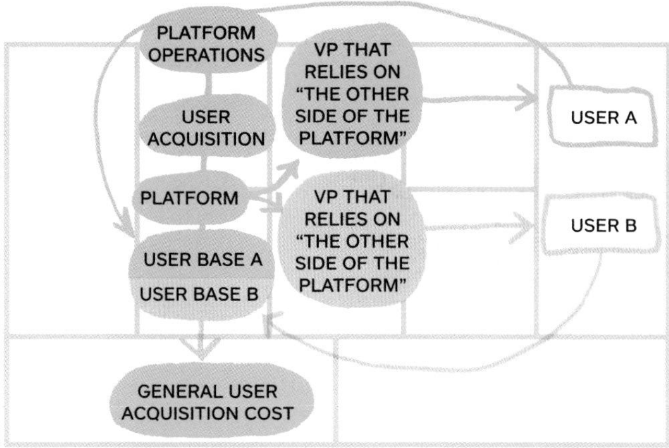

Platform Castles – Create a business model with network effects in which a large number of users represents value to one or more other distinct sets of users, and vice versa. That makes it hard for anybody else with fewer users to compete or to catch up.

TRIGGER QUESTION
How could we create a multisided platform that depends on the existence of two or more large user bases?

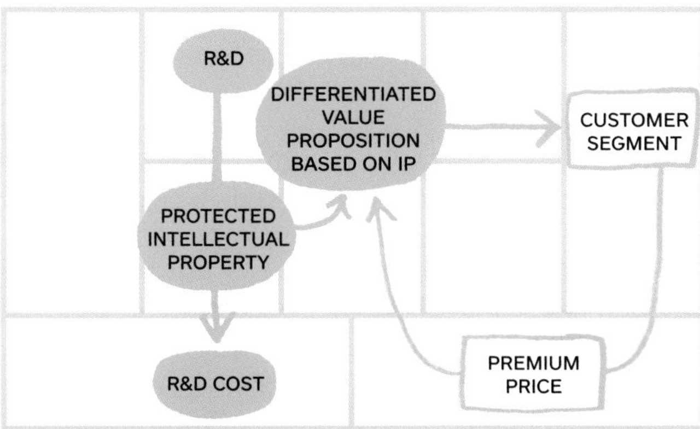

IP Castles – Use protected intellectual property (IP) to outcompete others. Offer distinct value propositions that are hard or impossible to copy if you don't own the IP.

TRIGGER QUESTION
How could we use protected intellectual property as a competitive advantage (in arenas where it hasn't mattered before)?

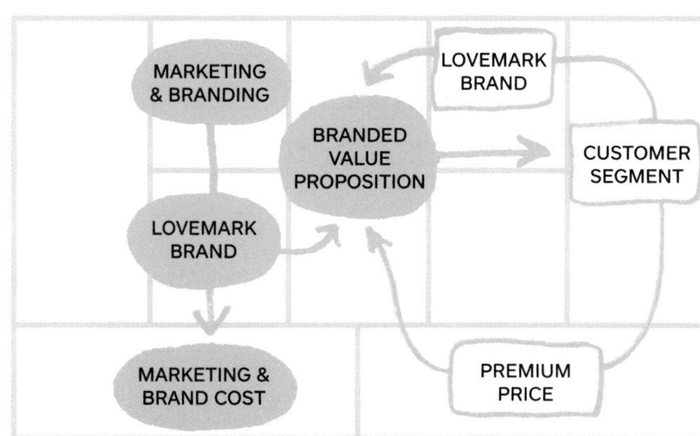

Brand Castle – Use a strong brand to outcompete others. Focus on value propositions in which a strong brand is an essential component.

TRIGGER QUESTION
How could we make brand a relevant competitive advantage (in an area where it hasn't been so far)?

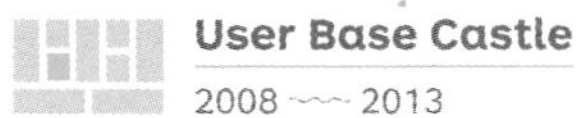

User Base Castle
2008 ~~~ 2013

Waze

In 2008, Waze develops a traffic navigation system that gets better with every additional user. Real-time information from users helps shorten commutes and reduce traffic congestion.

Ehud Shabtai, Amir Shinar, and Uri Levine founded Waze in 2008. The business idea originated from a crowdsourced project developed by Ehud Shabtai in 2006. The project aimed to create a free digital map of Israel with free updates and distribution.

Waze then evolved into a traffic navigation app that combines the reach of a social network with GPS data to shorten the commutes of its users and reduce traffic congestion globally. It's a great example of network effects, where the service becomes more valuable as more people use it.

Waze had more than 50 million users globally when Google purchased it in 2013 for $966 million, to improve its mapping service.[30]

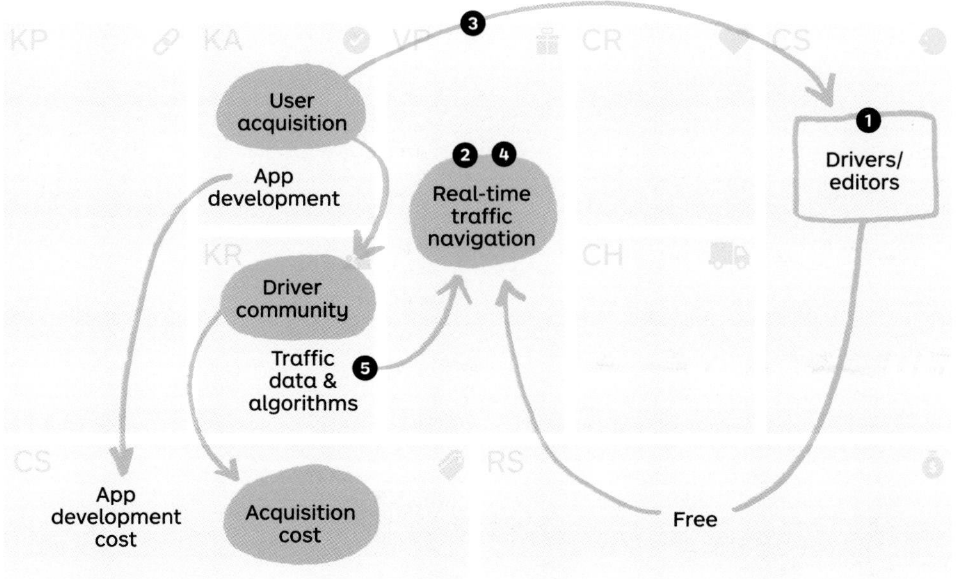

1 Identify User Base for Competitive Advantage

Waze identifies its users as a critical resource to improve its digital maps. They instrumentalize users by collecting the data they generate and by asking them to actively help improve maps.

2 Solve Pains and Create Gains for Those Users

Waze is not just a voice navigation system. Its traffic algorithm optimizes routes to help users avoid congestion and solves the pain of long delays in commutes for millions of drivers globally.

3 Acquire Users Aggressively

To build its user base quickly, Waze makes the strategic choice to offer the app for free. Users are drawn to the free tool and then stay for the steadily improving value proposition (i.e., the effectiveness of the algorithm).

4 Use Users in Your Value Proposition

Users contribute in three ways: (1) Waze collects driving times and GPS data from all users, (2) active users post traffic updates, and (3) a volunteer army of editors update maps and translate them into other languages.

5 Reap Competitive Advantage

With every new user, Waze algorithms become smarter, creating an even more attractive value proposition to existing and new users. Waze's large and active global user base is difficult to replicate by a competitor.

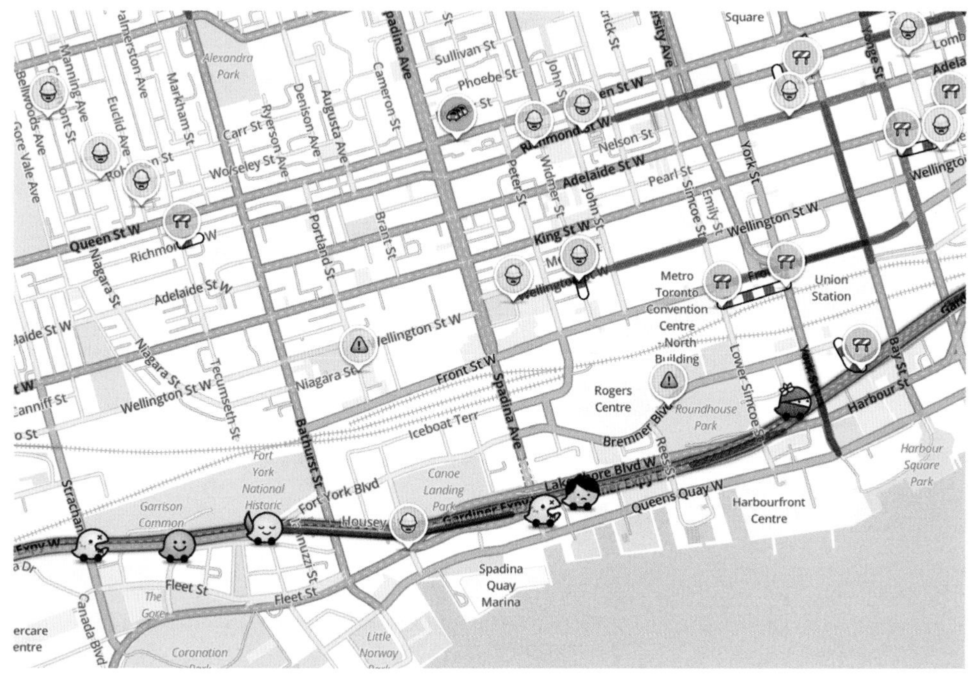

Example of a live Waze map of Toronto, generated from information reported by their user base.

Waze User Base[31]
In millions

120
80
40

2011 2012 2013 2017 2018 2019

130 million

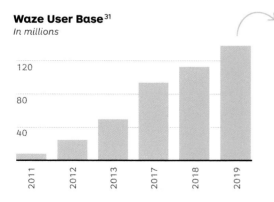

monthly active users in 2019. Waze's user base has grown from 7 million in 2011.[32]

Volunteer editors Waze counted in 2016:

420 thousand[33]

Network Effects

A network effect occurs when a product or service becomes more valuable to its users as more people use it.

A *direct network effect* occurs when the increase in the user base of a product or service creates more value based on the increased number of direct connections between these users. Examples include the telephone, WhatsApp, Skype, or Facebook.

2 Active Users
= 1 Connection

5 Active Users
= 10 Connections

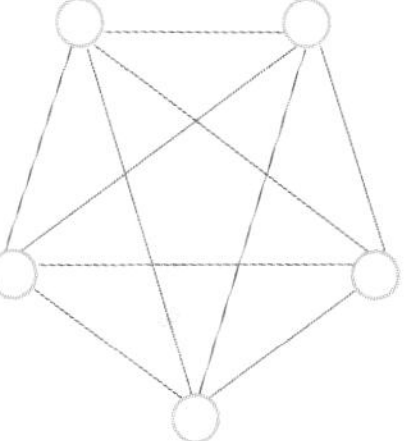

12 Active Users
= 66 Connections

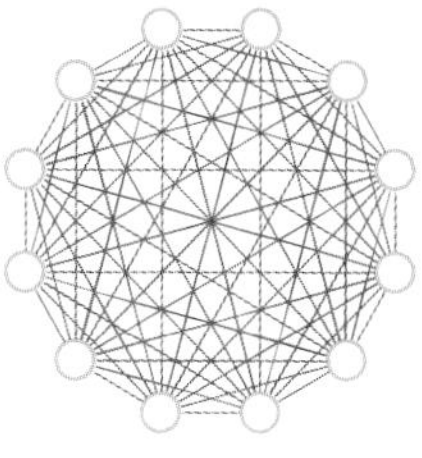

Adapted from Andreessen Horowitz

Platform Castle

2012 ~~~ 2019

DiDi

In 2012, DiDi launches a ride-hailing service and rapidly acquires the largest pool of drivers and passengers in the industry, making it hard for anyone else to compete in this space.

DiDi — the Chinese equivalent to America's Uber — was born out of the desire to fix the enormous traffic congestion and transportation problem in Beijing. Prior to the introduction of ride-hailing services in China, passenger brawls over taxis and exorbitant fares charged by illegal taxis were commonplace in crowded, urban centers. China had a unique problem: a massive population that was already connected through mobile combined with highly congested cities in need of traffic relief.

The word *DiDi* itself means "honk honk" in Chinese, a nod to the perpetual traffic congestion. While it was founded as a taxi-hailing service, it rapidly transformed to a ride-hailing platform.

DiDi's dominance is the result of an aggressive strategy of acquisitions. DiDi purchased its two main rivals (Uber China and Kuaidi Dache) and now matches the largest base of connected passengers with the biggest pool of drivers.

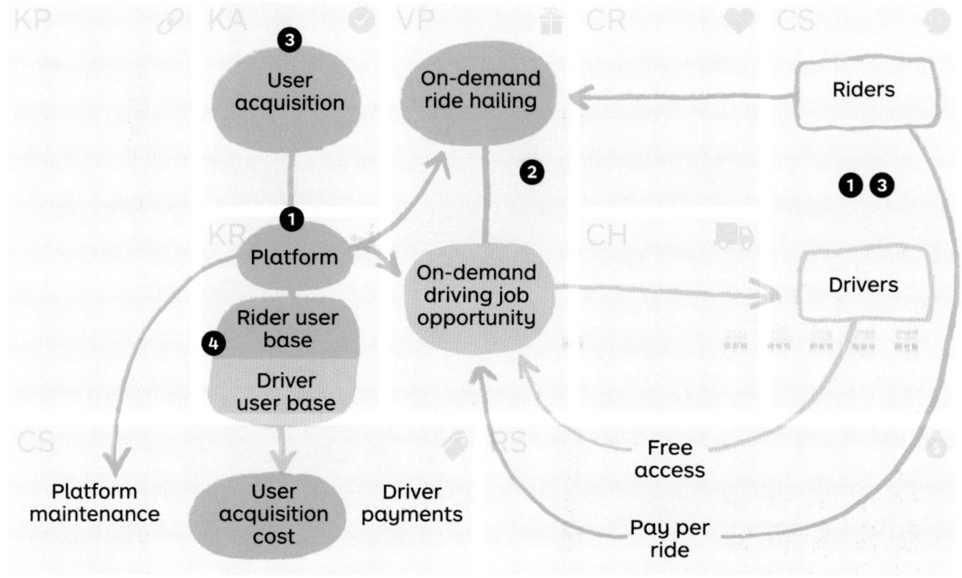

1 Identify How You Can Connect Two Groups via a Platform

DiDi identified the opportunity of improving personal mobility by matching riders and drivers. Originally, DiDi started as a taxi-hailing service, but rapidly expanded to occasional drivers to expand its available cars.

2 Create the Value Proposition for Each Group

DiDi attracts passengers with its large pool of drivers, consistent pricing, reduced wait times, and WeChat and Alipay integrations. It attracts drivers with a large pool of passengers, reduced idle time, and discounts (e.g., gas, insurance, etc.).

3 Aggressively Acquire Both Groups

DiDi pursued a very aggressive strategy to grow its passenger and driver pools, in particular, by purchasing its two main rivals (Uber China and Kuaidi Dache). As of January 2019, DiDi had more than 31 million drivers servicing 550 million registered passengers.

4 Reap Competitive Advantage

The sheer size of the two interdependent customer groups has created a competitive advantage for DiDi, which makes it hard for anyone else to compete in the transportation sector in China.

550
million registered users[35]

= 13.75 million users

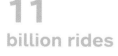

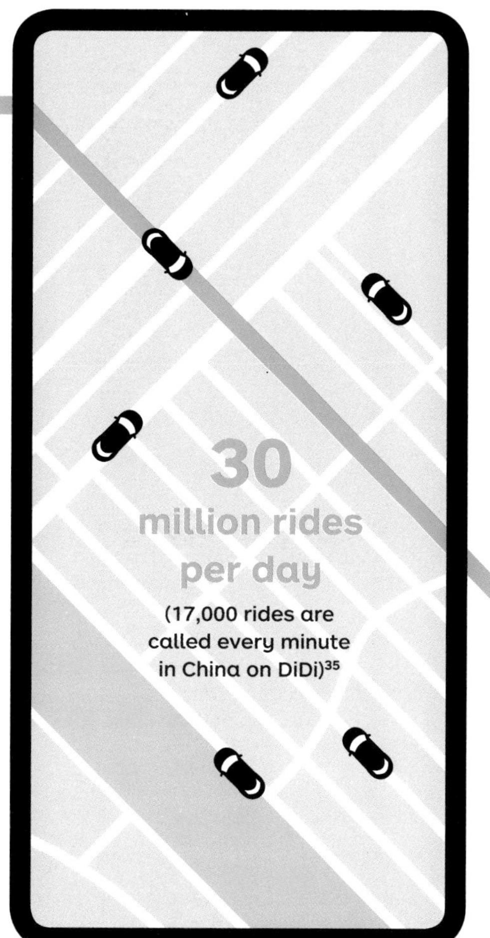

30
million rides per day
(17,000 rides are called every minute in China on DiDi)[35]

Network Effects

Two-sided network effects occur when increases in usage by one set of users increases the value of a complementary product to another distinct set of users. Examples include DiDi, Uber, Open Table, Airbnb, eBay, and Craigslist.

23 million
Private cars

3 million
Carpooling

3 million
Taxis

340 thousand
Chauffeured rides

31
million registered drivers[36]

11
billion rides

In 2018 DiDi handled an estimated 11 billion rides — up from 7.4 billion in 2017.[34]

48.8
billion km

DiDi users traveled in 2018, of which...

800
million km

...800 million kilometers on pooled trips, saving 43 million liters of fuel and 97,000 tons of CO_2 emissions.[36]

IP Castle

1993 ~~~ 2019

Dyson

Starting with a vacuum in 1993, Dyson tackles a wide range of product engineering challenges with an ingenious approach. It invests heavily in R&D to launch innovative, best-in-class products that it sells at a premium and protects with patents.

In the 1980s, James Dyson developed revolutionary, bagless, cyclonic vacuum technology. He attempted to license it to vacuum manufacturers, but the companies rejected his ideas. The technology was indeed better but this product would remove the recurring revenues from bag and filter sales.

Dyson didn't give up and manufactured his own vacuum in 1993, fighting off several patent infringement lawsuits along the way. Subsequently, Dyson's business portfolio grew by continuing to manufacture superior products from patented IP. The company expanded into hand dryers, fans, air purifiers, hair dryers, robot vacuums, and even electric cars. Each product is the result of a leap in technology (with patented IP).

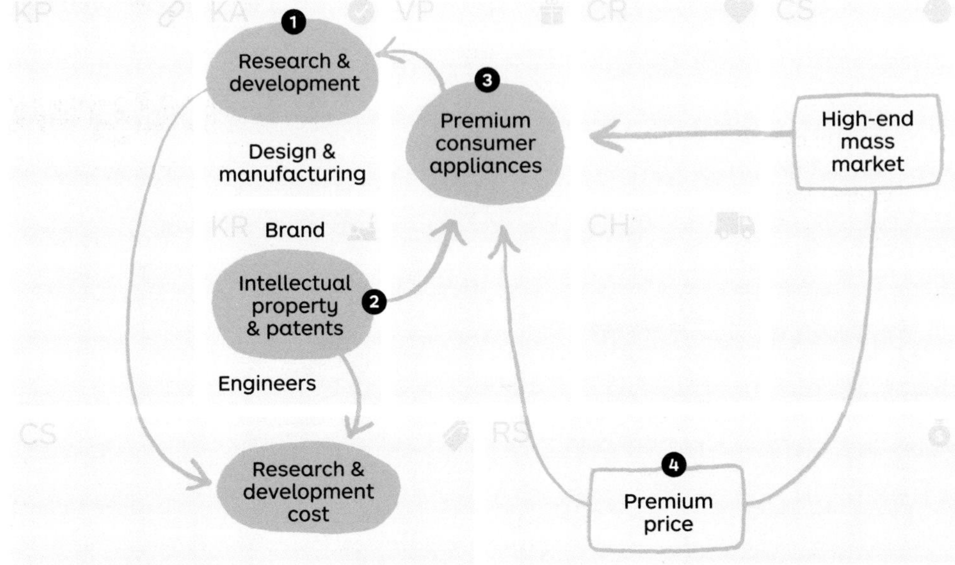

1 Invest Heavily in R&D

Dyson's ambition is to produce the best in class or nothing in each product range it enters. The company reinvests approximately 20% of its earnings into research and development.

2 Patent Aggressively

Dyson protects its product innovations with many patents. For the development of the Supersonic Hair Dryer, Dyson spent $71 million and filed 100 patent applications. The company reportedly spends over $6.5 million per year on patent litigation.[37]

3 Differentiate with the Best Products and Services

Dyson uses its IP to create the best product within each category it competes. Its vacuums, for instance, include technologies that have never been incorporated into its competitors' products.

4 Sell at a Premium

Dyson sells its home appliances at a premium price point. With a $700 price tag for its upright vacuum, Dyson is the most expensive vacuum on the market, with the cheapest alternative selling for $40.

+ Brand

Dyson developed a strong brand by transforming the sleepy home appliance market into one filled with cutting edge technology and sleek industrial design. Dyson has often been dubbed the "Apple of home appliances," as the company strives for perfection before releasing a product.

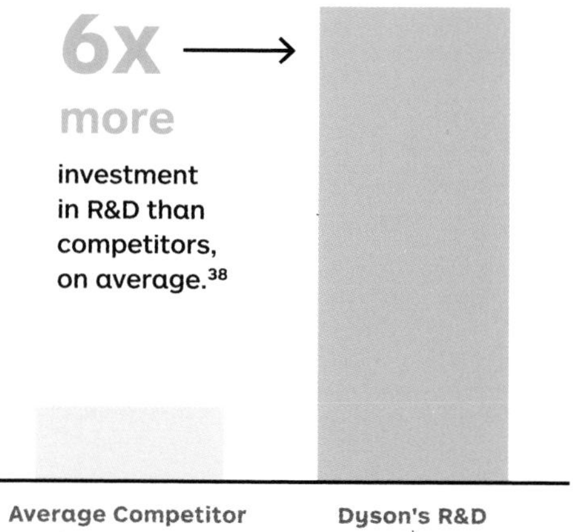

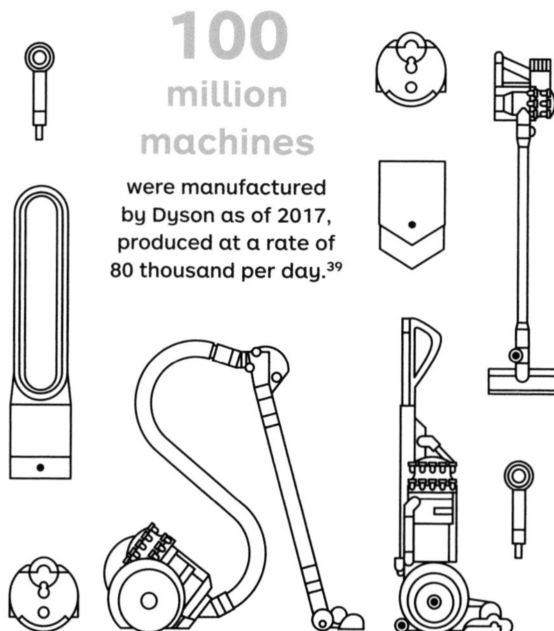

100
million
machines
were manufactured by Dyson as of 2017, produced at a rate of 80 thousand per day.[39]

Brand Castle

1765 ~~~ 2019

Wedgwood

In 1765, Josiah Wedgwood wins a royal pottery competition and is declared Her Majesty's Potter. He uses that recognition to build a strong and defensible brand, markets his pieces as Queensware, and generates a fortune of $3.4 billion in today's market value.

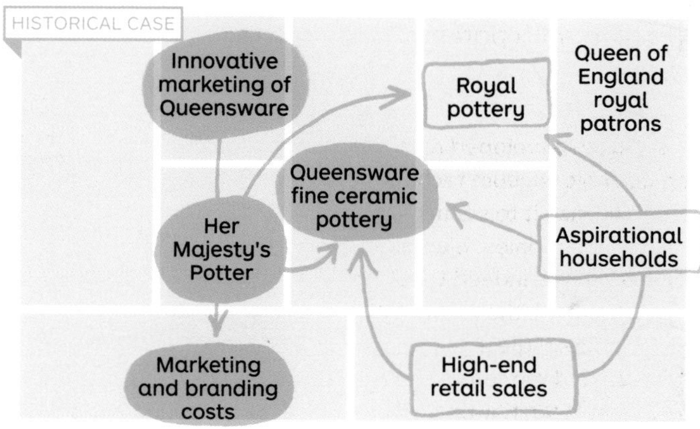

Wedgwood used his royal recognition to target aspirational consumers who wanted to drink tea like the upper class, but could not necessarily afford expensive porcelain. He created a brand in an area where there was none previously. Wedgwood also convinced consumers to buy pottery for display rather than use and used the strength of his brand to protect his business from competition for decades.

245 years

Wedgwood's Jasper vases have stayed in continuous production since 1774.[40]

Activity Differentiators

Better Configure Activities

Radically change which activities they perform and how they combine them to create and deliver value to customers. Create innovative value propositions based on activity differentiation.

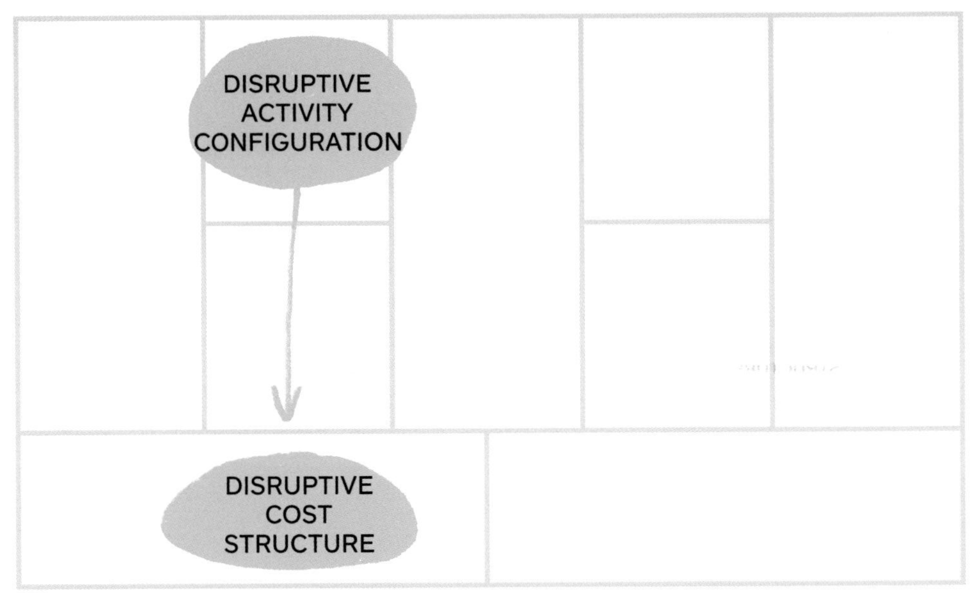

TRIGGER QUESTION

Could we create (significantly more) value for customers by performing new activities or configuring activities in innovative ways?

Assessment Question

Do we create significant value for customers because we perform and configure activities in disruptively innovative ways?

We operate conventional activities that perform similarly or worse than comparable organizations.

Our key activities can't easily be copied or emulated for the next couple of years and they give us a significant competitive advantage (e.g., cost effectiveness, scale, etc.).

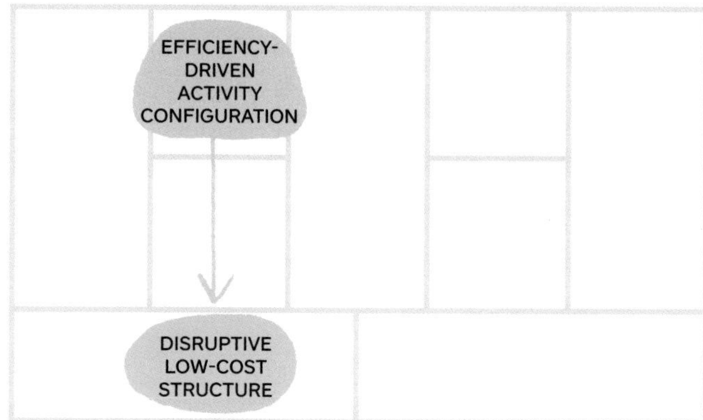

Efficiency Disruptors – Substantially change which activities you perform and how you configure them in order to become radically more efficient. Use this to create a disruptively low cost structure. You may or may not pass the cost savings onto customers.

TRIGGER QUESTION
How can we radically change the configuration of our activities to compete with a disruptive cost structure?

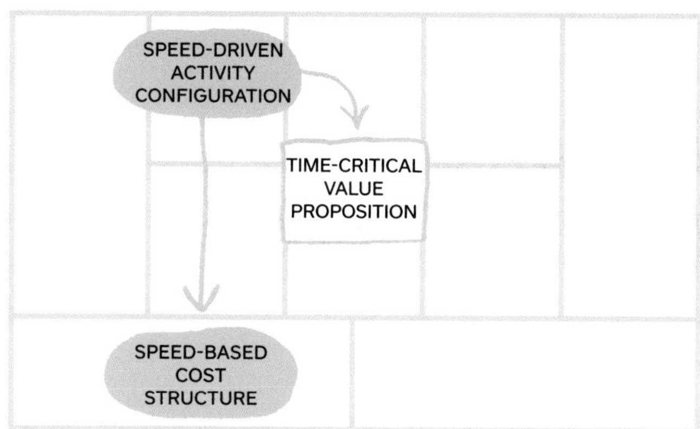

Speed Masters – Build radically new activity configurations focused on speed. Create new, time-critical value propositions and accelerate time to market.

TRIGGER QUESTION
How might we put speed at the center of our activity configuration to develop new, time-critical value propositions?

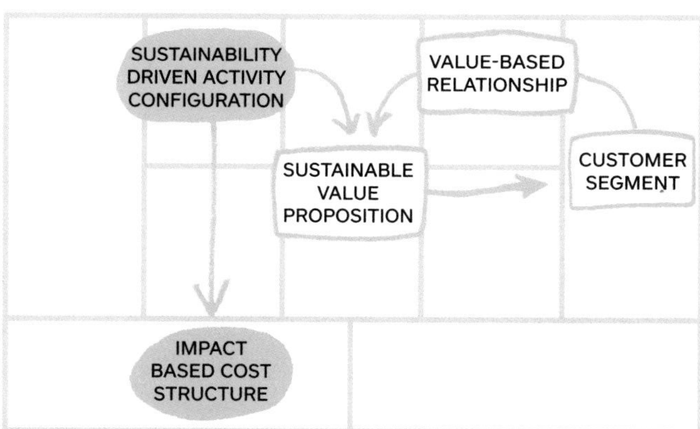

Sustainability Masters – Adjust activities such that they are environmentally friendly and positively impact society, even if it may lead to higher costs. Cut out activities that hurt the planet and society while engaging in those that add benefits.

TRIGGER QUESTION
How might we reconfigure our activities to have a positive environmental and social impact?

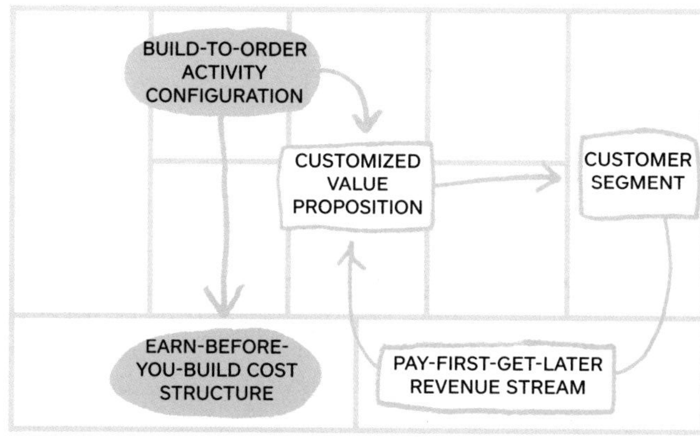

Build-to-Order – Configure products or services to match the exact specifications of customers. Adjust activities such that they only go into motion when an order is received.

TRIGGER QUESTION
How might we reconfigure our activities to build to order and only start building after order confirmation and payment?

Ford Model T

In 1913, Henry Ford introduces the assembly line to automobile production, slashes the cost of production by a factor of three, and disrupts the industry in the process.

In the early 1900s, automobiles were considered toys for the rich, and they were often overly complicated, requiring a trained chauffeur. Henry Ford was determined to build a safe, affordable automobile for the masses, and he sought any production efficiency to deliver it. Ford looked outside of his own industry, which led him to invent the assembly line.

The introduction of the assembly line reduced the time to assemble each car from over 12 hours to about 90 minutes. Training employees on just one task in the assembly line also allowed Ford to hire lower-skilled workers and further slash costs. Model T production went from 100 cars a day to up to 1,000 — which is similar to a modern factory — and enabled a price drop from $850 to $300.[41]

After just 10 years of using the assembly line, Ford's 10 millionth Model T rolled off the line.[42]

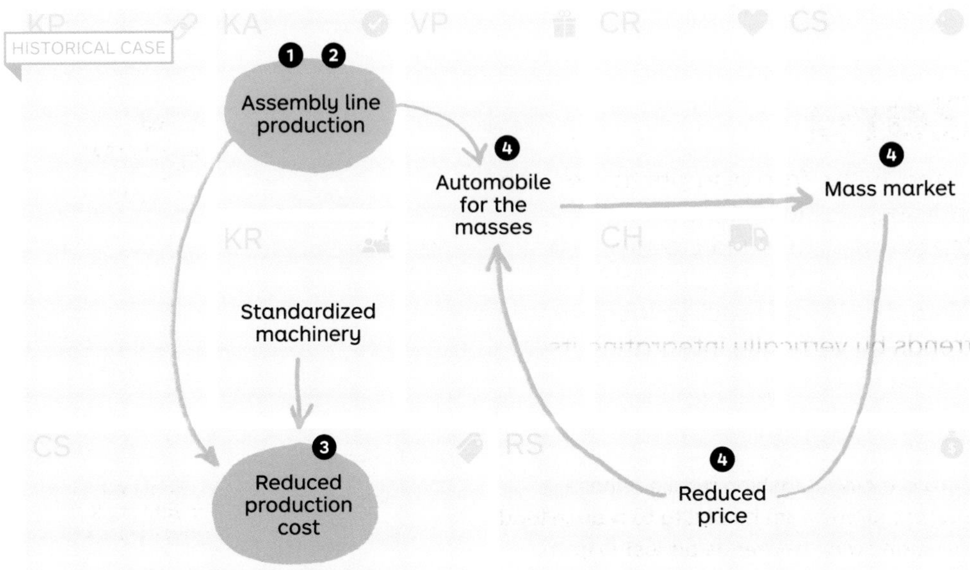

1 Scout Other Industries for Innovative Efficiency-Driven Activity Configurations

Ford is inspired by the continuous-flow production methods used by flour mills, breweries, canneries, and meat packers of the time. He believes he can adapt these activity configurations to the automobile industry.

2 Adapt Outside Ideas to Your Industry

Ford introduces the assembly line to the automobile industry. The car assembly process is standardized and broken into 84 steps.[44] Workers remain at one station and focus on one task while the car moves down a mechanized line — as opposed to working in a team to assemble each car.

3 Reap the Benefits

Rapidly, car production costs go down with this new way of working, while productivity goes up. Standardized machines lead to higher quality and more reliable production cost. Workers can now assemble a car in about 90 minutes compared to over 12 hours previously.[43]

4 Disrupt Your Industry

In 1914 Ford's 13,000 workers build around 300,000 cars — more than his nearly 300 competitors manage to build with 66,350 employees.[45] As he lowers production costs, he lowers the price of an automobile from $850 to less than $300 and disrupts the car industry.

Speed Master

1980 ~~~ 2019

Zara

In the 1980s Zara disrupts the fashion industry by radically reconfiguring the supply chain and creating the fast-fashion category. It is able to almost instantly react to fashion trends by vertically integrating its supply chain.

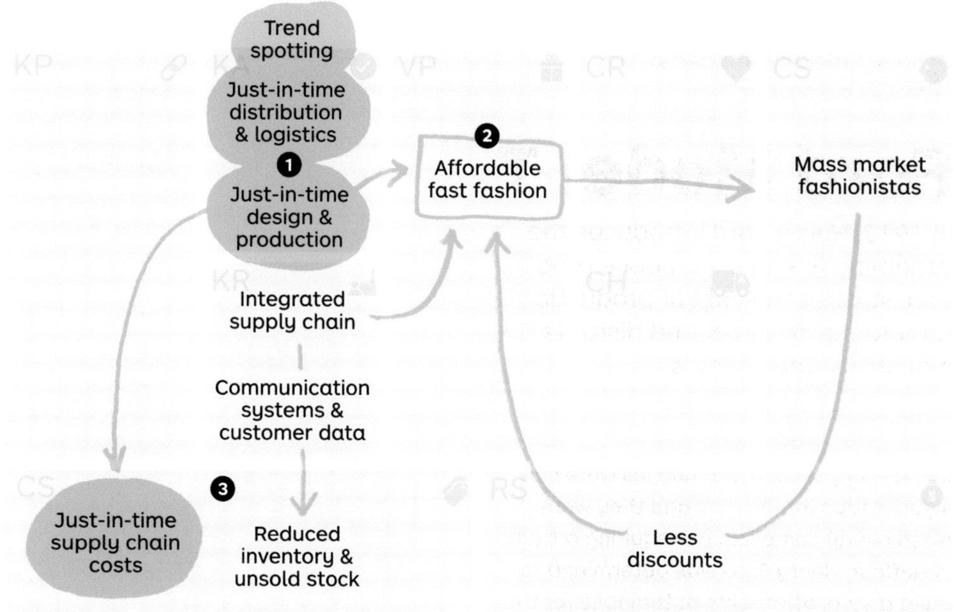

Zara is a global fashion retailer whose success stems from its ability to reduce lead times and react to trends almost instantaneously. Zara is owned by Inditex, the world's biggest fashion group.

The company was not afraid to go against conventional wisdom, vertically integrate its supply chain, and move its production to Europe (near-shoring), while many players in the fashion industry chose to outsource production to lower-cost factories in Asia.

Zara disrupted the fashion industry by shortening the time to market to less than three weeks from inspiration to retail. Zara created a new category of affordable fast fashion. This model allowed the company to become a heavyweight in the highly competitive fashion industry: as of 2018, Zara was active online and in 96 countries, managed 2,238 physical stores and €18.9 billion annual revenue.[46]

1 Radically Reconfigure Activities for Speed

Zara decides to produce more than half its fashion items locally and in its own facilities to achieve speed. At the time, most large fashion players rely on outsourcing production to Asia for cost reasons. This activity differentiation allows Zara to effectively react with lightning speed to fashion trends.

2 Develop Time-Critical Value Proposition

Zara's value proposition focuses on keeping up with fast-changing fashion trends. Its activity configuration allows it to spot trends and launch new pieces in less than three weeks. Competitors show two collections per year and take over nine months to get items to stores. Zara ships only a few items in each style to its stores, so inventory is always scarce. This leads to constantly changing collections and customers tend to "buy it when they see it," because the clothes won't be around for long.

3 Embrace a New Cost Structure

Higher labor cost was the price to pay for flexibility, full control, and the required speed in its design and production processes. Zara reserves 85% of its factory capacity for in-season adjustments and over 50% of its clothes are designed and manufactured mid-season.[47]

+ Trends, Data, and Communication

Zara trains its retail employees to relay customers' preferences and real-time sales data to designers through effective communication systems. The latest designs and production forecasts are adjusted accordingly. Because Zara manufactures only a limited supply of items, it doesn't have to deal with excess inventory or constant markdowns.

+ Pricing Power

Each store has a limited inventory of items in each style that are replenished based on demand. New styles based on latest trends arrive constantly. As a consequence Zara rarely discounts clothes, contrary to most fashion houses.

Patagonia

In 1973, Yvon Chouinard creates an outdoor apparel company whose activities are configured through the lens of environmental protection.

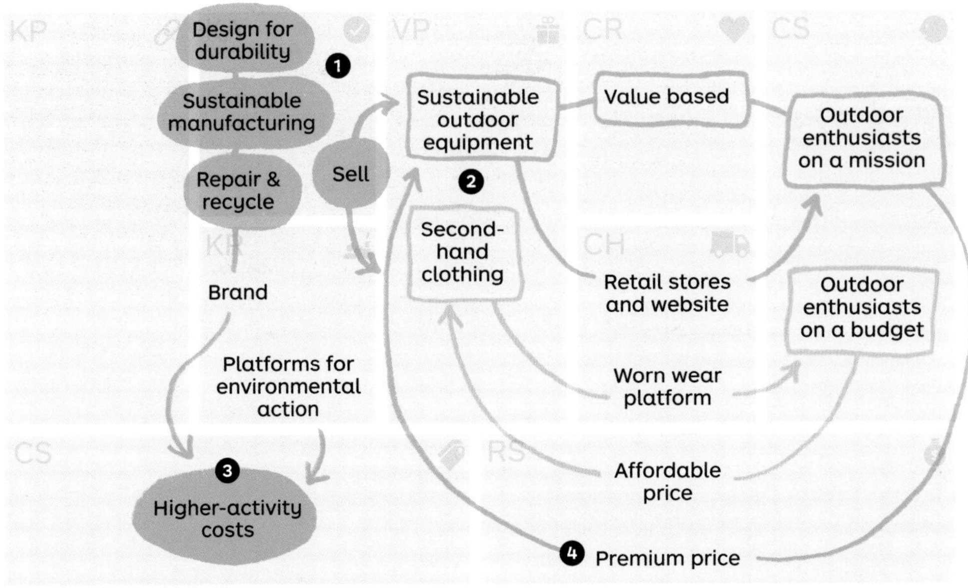

Patagonia was founded by Yvon Chouinard in 1973 to make clothing and equipment for rock climbers. Chouinard was an avid climber who believed in clean climbing with little impact on the outdoors.

From the start Patagonia had a clear focus on environmental protection that reflected the personal ethics of its founder. It was the first California company to use renewable energy sources to power its buildings and one of the first to print its catalogs on recycled paper. Patagonia switched to 100% organically grown cotton in 1994 and removed chlorine from its wool products.

Patagonia's commercial success enabled it to become a visibly activist company. In 2018 it changed its mission statement to "We're in business to save our home planet." It also provides tools and funding to grass-roots organizations.

Growth is not the ultimate goal for Patagonia, yet their differentiation and environmental focus has helped them grow sustainably.

1 Align Activities to Environmental Objectives

Patagonia makes durability a strong constraint in the design and manufacturing of its outdoor clothing equipment, in order to align with its environmental objectives. The goal is to reduce consumption and waste. In addition, the company limits its environmental impact by maximizing the use of organic and recycled materials, by repairing damaged clothes, and by complying with strong environmental protection standards for its entire supply chain.

2 Develop Sustainable Value Propositions

Patagonia makes customers feel they are contributing to protecting the environment by extending its value proposition beyond the functional value proposition of high quality outdoor clothing and equipment. By buying Patagonia products, customers feel they are contributing to the highest environmental standards. Patagonia even launches a second-hand clothing value proposition to limit its environmental footprint and make its products accessible to a larger market.

3 Accept Higher Activity Costs

Patagonia's high sustainability standards lead to higher costs. It uses more costly organic cotton, develops the infrastructure to recycle materials, and educates the public (Footprint Chronicles). It also bears the cost of making its supply chain more environmentally friendly by educating suppliers on sustainable practices.

4 Apply Premium Pricing

Patagonia can charge a premium, because customers accept that environmental friendly production comes at a cost. The company's customers are more environment-conscious than price-conscious.

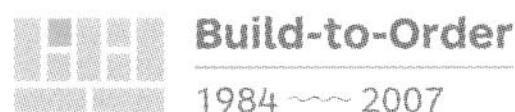

Build-to-Order

1984 ~~~ 2007

Dell Computers

In 1984, Dell disrupts the personal computer market with high quality, low-cost machines that are built-to-order and sold directly to customers.

In 1984, Michael Dell launched his company out of his college dorm room. He recognized that sophisticated computer buyers wanted customized, high quality, technical machines at an affordable cost. This is not something they could get from IBM, which dominated the market at the time.

Dell targeted users by offering customized machines that were built-to-order. Customers would simply dial a toll-free number, place a customized order, and wait for their computer to be delivered by mail.

Dell turned the traditional PC sales model on its head with build-to-order and direct sales. He disrupted the PC industry with customized, high quality, affordable PCs by avoiding retail locations, high-touch sales, and minimizing inventory and inventory depreciation costs.

Dell grew from PCs assembled in a dorm room in 1984 to a $300 million business just five years later.[48]

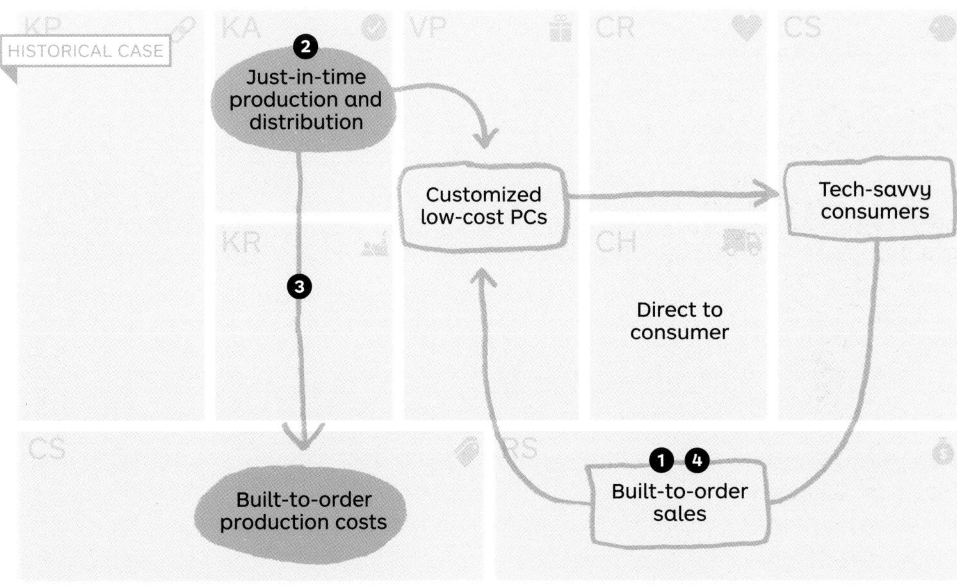

1 Take Customized Orders and Get Paid

In 1984 Dell begins to take customized PC orders over the phone. Buyers determine their exact specifications and pick from a variety of PC components. In 1996, the company brings its direct model to the Web and automates build-to-order.

2 Build the Product

Dell purchases components from PC equipment wholesalers and builds the customized machine himself (just-in-time production) based on the customer's order. He is able to keep the cost of his machines under $1,000.

3 Manage Your Just-in-Time Supply Chain

Contrary to a traditional PC manufacturer, Dell stays away from heavy costs of inventory management, retail, and logistics. Products are built-to-order. This requires Dell to develop excellence around a new set of activities: just-in-time supply chain and production.

4 Pass on Cost Savings to Customers and Disrupt the Market

Dell's build-to-order model avoids unsold PCs and value depreciation. In addition, Dell's direct model and wholesale component purchases further reduce production and distribution costs. This allows him to pass on cost savings in the form of disruptive prices for high quality PCs.

Scalers

Grow
Faster

Find radically new ways to scale where others stay stuck in conventional nonscalable business models.

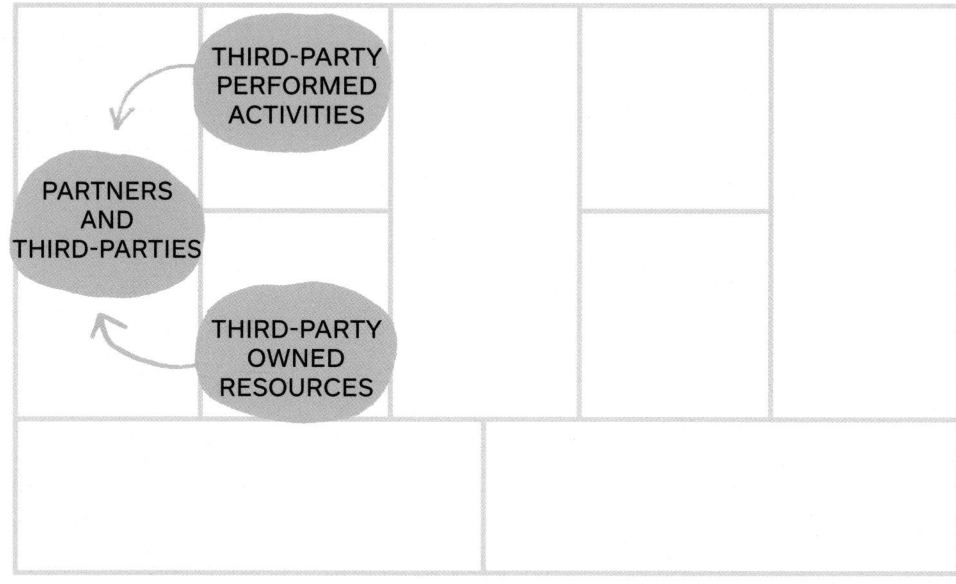

TRIGGER QUESTION

What could we do differently to make our business model more scalable (e.g., eliminate resource and activity bottlenecks)?

Assessment Question

How rapidly and how easily can we grow our business model without substantial additional resources and activities (e.g. building infrastructure, finding talent)?

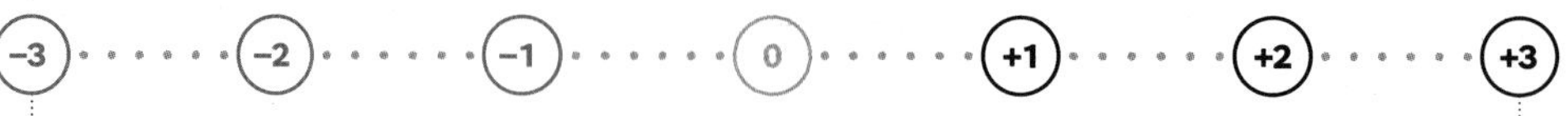

Growing our business and customers is resource intensive (e.g. more people) and requires a lot of effort (e.g., nonscalable activities).

Our revenues and customer base can easily grow and scale without a lot of additional resources and activities.

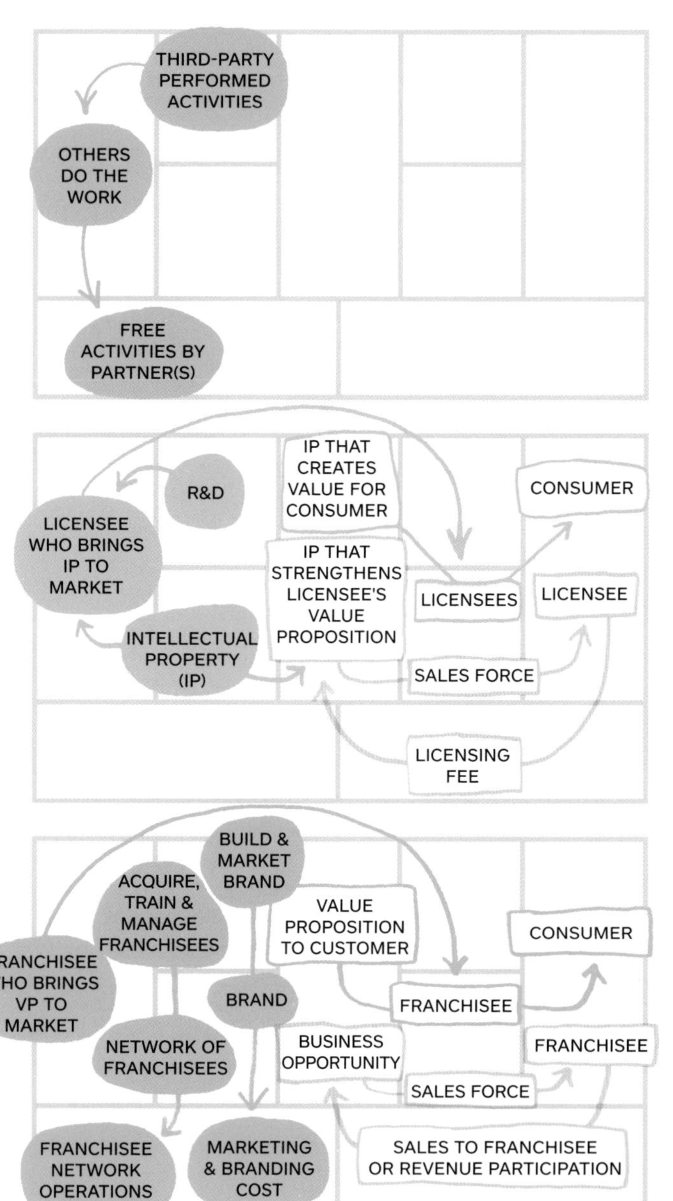

Delegators – Increase scalability by getting others to do some of the key activities (for free) that you have previously performed internally yourself.

EXAMPLES
IKEA, Facebook, Twitter, Instagram, Red Hat, Zinga

TRIGGER QUESTION
In which areas could we leverage customers or third parties to help us create value for free?

Licensors – Increase scalability by getting licensees to perform the bulk of value-creating activities like product manufacturing and commercialization.

EXAMPLES
ARM, Disney

TRIGGER QUESTION
How could we use licensing to make our business model more scalable and/or monetize intellectual property (e.g., brand, patents, etc.)?

Franchisors – Create scalability by licensing your business concept, trademarks, products, and services to franchisees who run franchise locations.

EXAMPLES
Harper, Ritz Carlton, McDonald's

TRIGGER QUESTION
How could we use franchising to make our business model more scalable and increase our market reach?

IKEA

In 1956, IKEA introduces "flatpacking" and turns customers into a free workforce that takes over part of the traditional furniture manufacturing value chain. Customers buy furniture in pieces in stores and assemble it in a DIY fashion at home.

IKEA was founded in 1943 on a vision of offering "a wide range of well-designed, functional home furnishing products at prices so low, that as many people as possible will be able to afford them."

In 1956, the stores introduced furniture through the "flatpacking" method: furniture was sold in pieces and customers assembled it at home. By reducing transportation, assembly, and inventory costs, IKEA was able to scale aggressively, locating wherever it had willing customers.

IKEA's ability to leverage the work done by its customers enabled it to grow to 433 stores in 49 global markets, serving more than 957 million customers for a retail revenue of €41.3 billion in 2019.[49, 50]

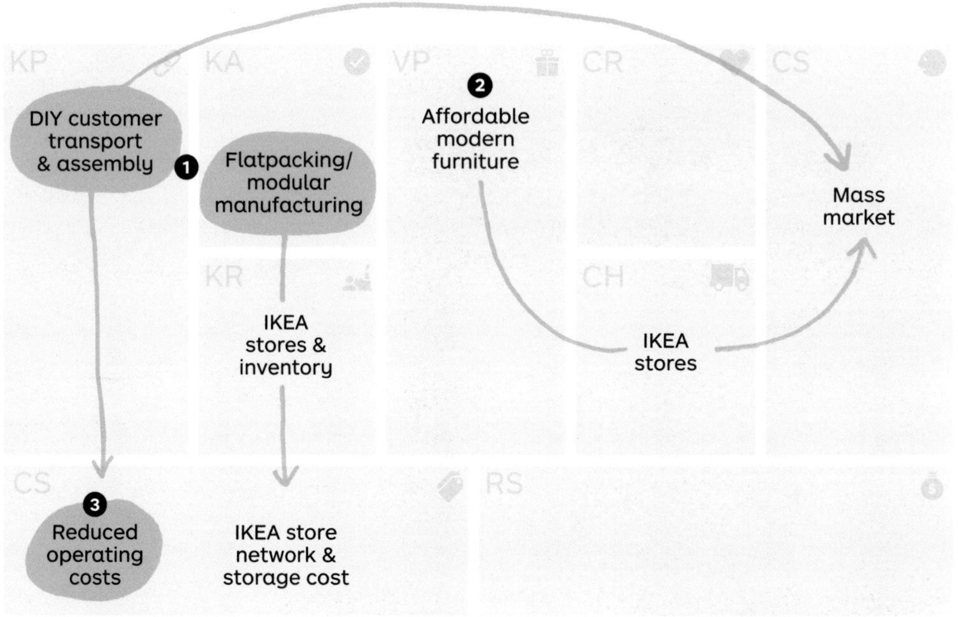

1 Identify How Others Can Create Value for You for Free

In 1956 IKEA adopts flat-pack, ready-to-assemble furniture that is easier and cheaper to transport from factory to retail centers. The company sees an opportunity in getting the customer to take over that part of the value chain.

2 Develop a Value Proposition

Because of flatpacking, IKEA can keep more furniture in stock and offer more affordable prices than competitors. Customers find the modular pieces they want to purchase in IKEA's open storerooms, then transport and assemble them at home.

3 Reap the Operational Savings from Getting Others to Do the Work

IKEA reaps substantial operational cost savings from getting customers to perform part of the work. Since storerooms also act as warehouses, customers select furniture, pick up the flatpacks, then transport and assemble them all at their own cost.

+ Modular Design and Manufacturing

Flatpacking, price differentiation, and customer assembly encourage IKEA to embrace a very modular, simple, clean, and minimalist design for which the company is known globally, which also simplifies manufacturing.

+ Overall Savings from Flatpacking

Flatpacking doesn't just enable cost savings from enlisting customers to do part of the work: it leads to overall cost savings in the manufacturing, storage, and mass transportation of furniture from factories to retail centers.

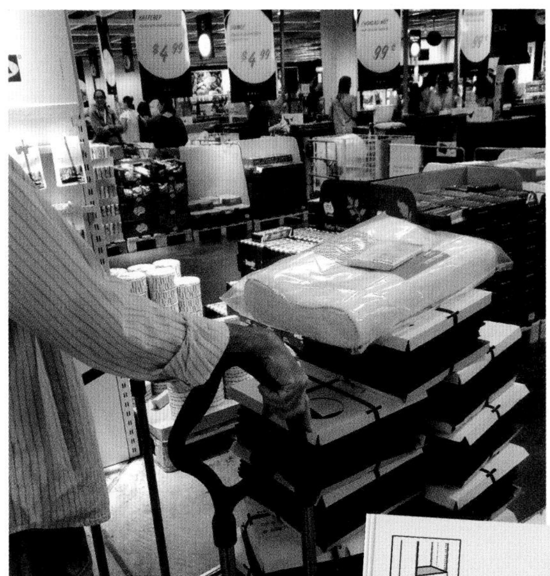

In 2010 IKEA changed the design of its Ektorp sofa, reducing the size of the flatpack by

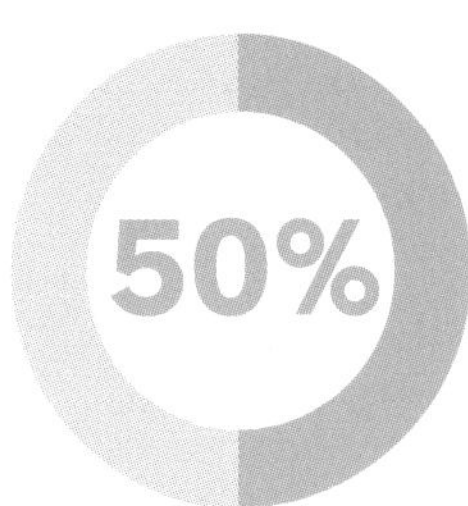
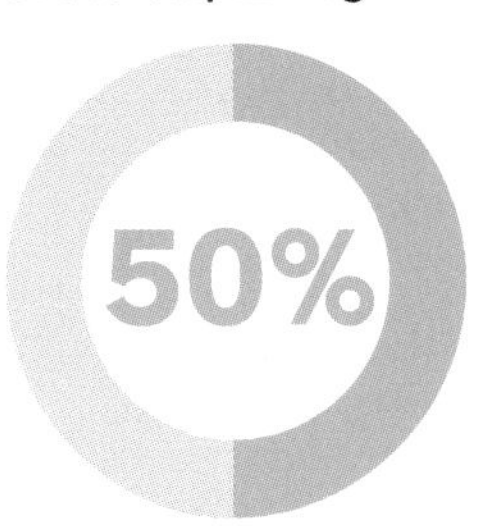

50%

and charging a 14% lower retail price.[52]

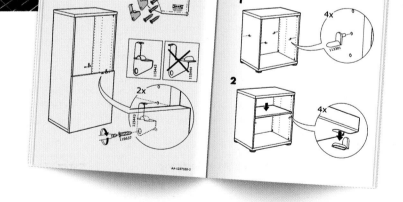

$500

The cost of shipping a sofa in the U.S. depending upon the size and distance traveled.

$20

The cost of shipping a truckload of IKEA couches can be as low as $20 for each sofa.[51]

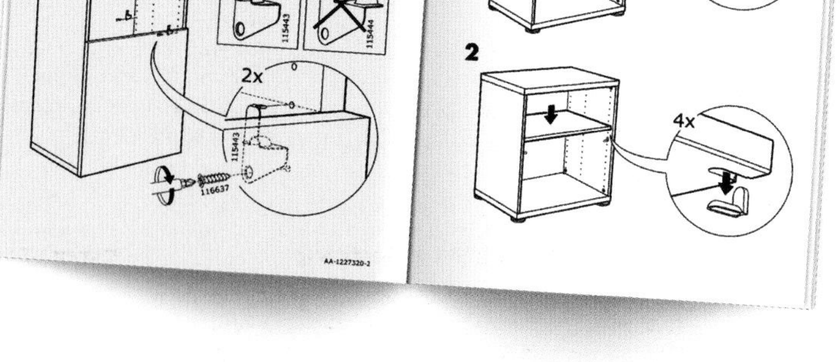

16% of surveyed U.S. homeowners have purchased more than 1/4 of their furniture from IKEA in the last 10 years.[53]

Red Hat

Red Hat launched in 1993 as a software company. Its main value proposition builds on the freely available Linux open-source operating system. The particularity of open-source software like Linux is that it is created by a community of developers and made available to anybody for free.

Red Hat found a way to create a business model on top of Linux, as the operating system became more complicated. It recognized that there were significant barriers to its adoption by enterprise customers. It made Linux more accessible to the enterprise by offering them a subscription for the testing, certification, and support of Linux.

Red Hat found a way to effectively monetize the work done by the Linux developer community in a way that was mutually beneficial to Red Hat and the developer community.

In 2019, IBM completed its acquisition of Red Hat for $34 billion.[54]

ARM

In 1990, ARM launched as a spinoff of a computer manufacturer to focus entirely on designing and licensing intellectual property for silicon chips. Today, almost all of the world's smartphones and tablets contain ARM designs.

ARM Holdings develops intellectual property (IP) used in silicon chips. It was founded in 1990 as a spinoff of British computer manufacturer Acorn Computers. The first time ARM designs were used in a cell phone was in 1994 for the Nokia 6110.

Semiconductor manufacturers combine ARM IP with their own IP to create complete chip designs. Chips containing ARM IP power most of today's mobile devices, due to their low power consumption. In 2014, 60% of the world's population used a device with an ARM chip on a daily basis.[55] In 2012, 95% of the chips found in smartphones and tablets were ARM designs.[56]

ARM licenses IP to over 1,000 global partners (including Samsung, Apple, Microsoft). The company doesn't manufacture or sell chips, unlike semiconductor manufacturers such as Intel or AMD.

SoftBank purchased ARM in 2016 for £24.3 billion.[57]

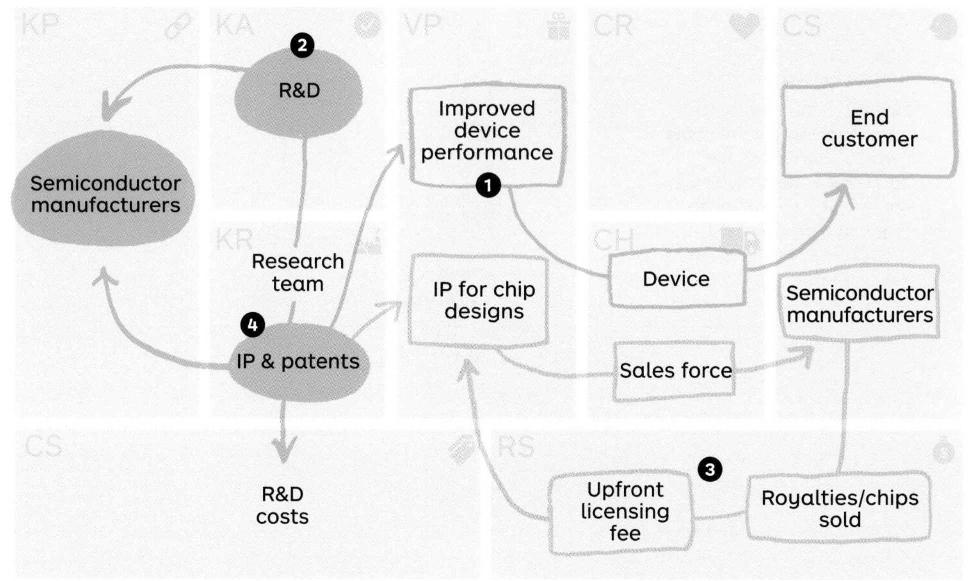

1 Detect and Solve Difficult Problems

ARM recognizes that tablets, laptops, and smartphones are the next wave of technology. To create attractive chips and intellectual property for portable devices, ARM focuses on faster processing speeds, lower power consumption, and lower costs.

2 Invest Heavily in R&D

In 2018, ARM invests $773 million in R&D (42% of 2018 revenues).[58] ARM is able to incur R&D costs many years before revenue starts (eight years on average). In 2008, ARM's R&D expenditure was £87 million or 29% of revenues. Expenditures continue to grow over time.[59]

3 License Intelligently

ARM earns fixed upfront license fees when they deliver IP to partners and variable royalties from partners for each chip they ship that contains ARM IP. The licensing fees vary between an estimated $1 million to 10 million. The royalty is usually 1 to 2% of the selling price of the chip.

4 Scale without Manufacturing

Licensing enables ARM to scale the business efficiently. Designs can be sold multiple times and reused across multiple applications (e.g., mobile, consumer devices, networking equipment, etc.). ARM has no manufacturing costs.

+ **Growing Base Yield Royalties Over a Long Period**

Licensing and royalty fees earn revenues over multiple years. In particular, the sales-dependent royalties constitute a sort of recurring revenue. License and royalty from new IP build on top of existing ones, creating a powerful long-term revenue engine.

+ **Growth of the Smartphone Industry**

ARM-based chip architectures are particularly suited for mobile devices, because of their low power consumption. That allows ARM to surf the exponential growth of the mobile industry.

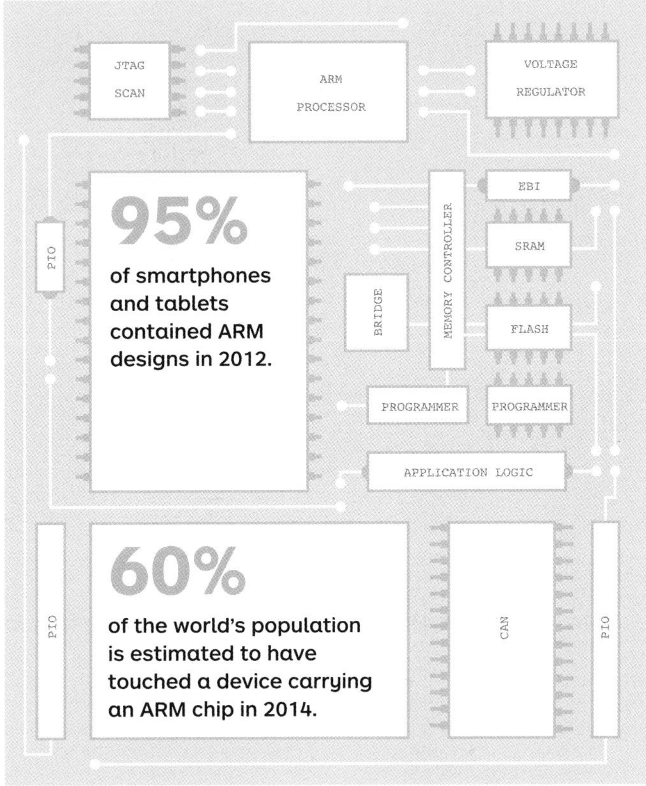

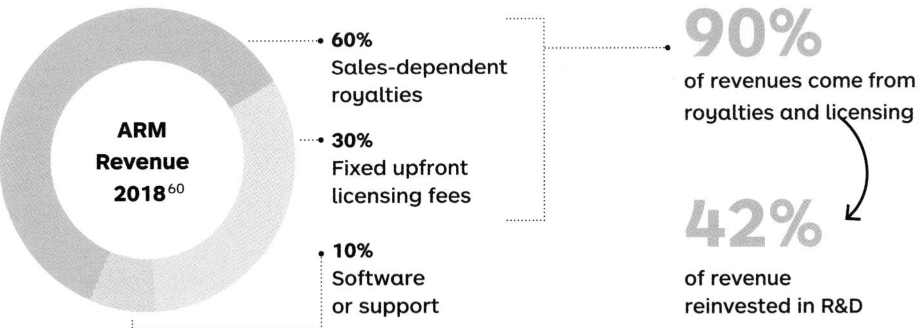

90%

of revenues come from royalties and licensing

42%

of revenue reinvested in R&D

Disney

Walt Disney created Mickey Mouse in 1928, and quickly licensed the iconic character in 1930 for the cover of a writing tablet. In 1929, Disney created Walt Disney Enterprises for the purpose of separating merchandising from studio productions.

6 out of 10

The Walt Disney Company had 6 of the top 10 entertainment merchandising franchises in the world in 2017.[61]

Disney began by licensing toys, dolls, and watches. Then in 1934, Mickey Mouse became the first licensed character on a cereal box. Walt Disney Enterprises effectively became the precursor to Disney Consumer Products.

Disney Consumer Products continues to grow, especially through its Princess franchises (established in 1999). Licensing today is not limited to traditional kids, toys and books. Disney sells food, apparel, home goods, targeting "children of all ages."

Franchisor

1888 ~~ 1956

Harper

In 1891, Martha Matilda Harper creates the modern franchising system, empowering female entrepreneurs to run their own beauty salons under the Harper brand.

Martha Matilda Harper opened her first beauty salon in 1888, and her focus on customer service and pampering led to the initial success of her business. Harper created the modern franchising system by creating a network of salons in order to scale her business while empowering female entrepreneurs.

Harper's clients were both suffragettes and socialites, and word of mouth helped to build her market reach. Soon women were asking her to open satellite salons across the country.

Harper was determined to create a network of franchises owned and operated by working-class women like herself. By 1891, the first two franchise salons had opened. In the 1930s, Harper scaled to 500 active salons across the globe, along with a chain of training schools.[62]

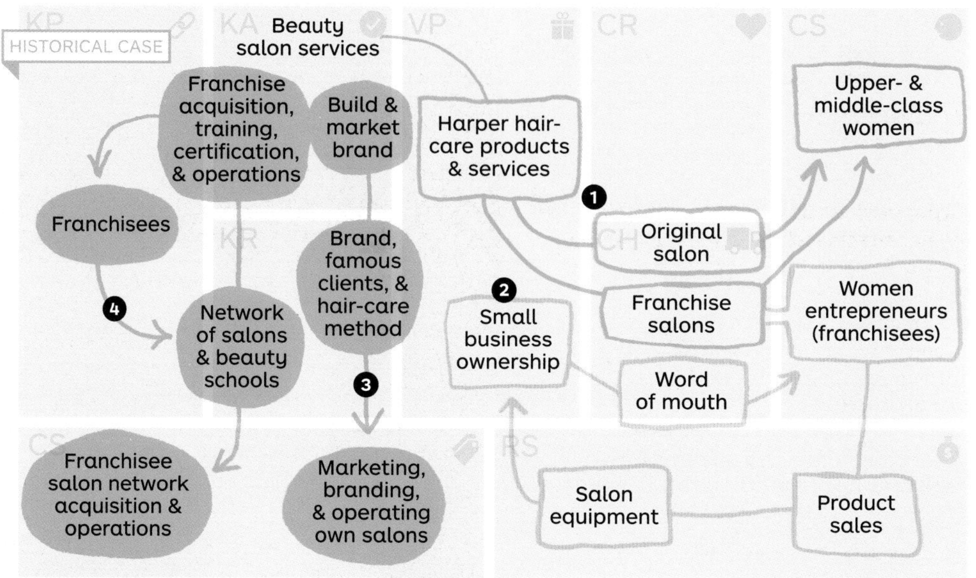

1 Create a Successful Reference Business and Value Proposition

Harper starts with a single salon where she offers hair-care services and products. The initial salon is a success and demand develops rapidly for other salons.

2 Create a Franchising Opportunity for Entrepreneurs

Harper uses this demand to grow a network of salons operated by working-class women like herself. She supports these franchise owners with start-up loans, marketing support, and training in the Harper Method of beauty.

3 Invest in Your Brand

The Harper brand becomes famous thanks to the publicity around the faithful clientele of high caliber politicians, Hollywood stars, and the British royal family. To assure brand consistency, Harper asks franchises to go through salon inspections and continual refresher courses.

4 Scale through Franchisees

With the franchising model Harper is able to scale rapidly. To generate revenues she sells her hair-care products and salon equipment to 500 salons across the globe at the height of her business in the 1930s.

+ Innovative in Hair Care

Harper disrupts existing habits and social norms around hair care. She introduces the scientific approach to hair care. Her invention of the reclining salon chair and her focus on customer service also remove some stigma around getting one's hair done outside of the home and triggers the expansion of the beauty salon market.[63]

$360

Life savings to open first store in 1888.[64]

Harper grew up as a poor servant girl and her clients include significant women in the suffragist movement. She decides that her first 100 salons should be opened and operated by women like herself to empower them. She provides them with start-up loans and training on her hair-care method and customer service.[65]

Profile of Harper's Franchisees

Jobs:

- Achieve financial independence
- Obtain a skilled job outside the home or factory

Pains:

- Lack of skills and education
- Lack of job opportunities

Gains:

- Empowerment
- Financial independence

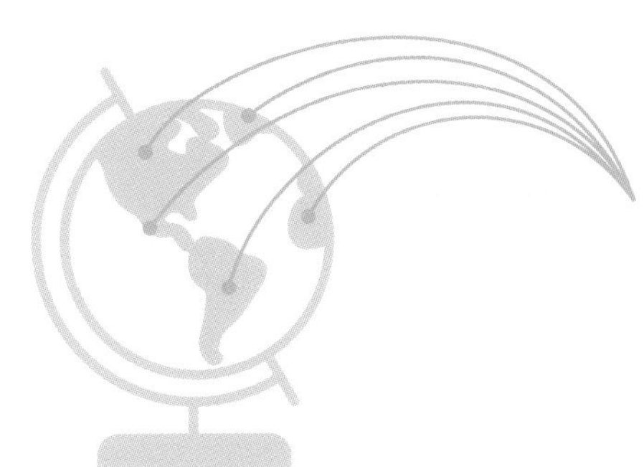

Harper used her famously long tresses as a marketing tool to demonstrate the health of her hair and the efficacy of her products.

500

Salons Worldwide

Harper grew her network of salons to 500 across the globe at the height of her success in the 1930s.

Franchising

Franchising has remained a popular tool for scaling across industry sectors and geographies. In 2018, in the U.S. alone, there are close to 740 thousand franchises employing 7.6 million people and putting over $800 billion into the economy.[66]

Franchises are a substantial source of economic growth and stability. During the first five years 50% of new businesses fail, whereas franchises are much more likely to be operating after five years.

Number of Franchises in U.S. since 1900

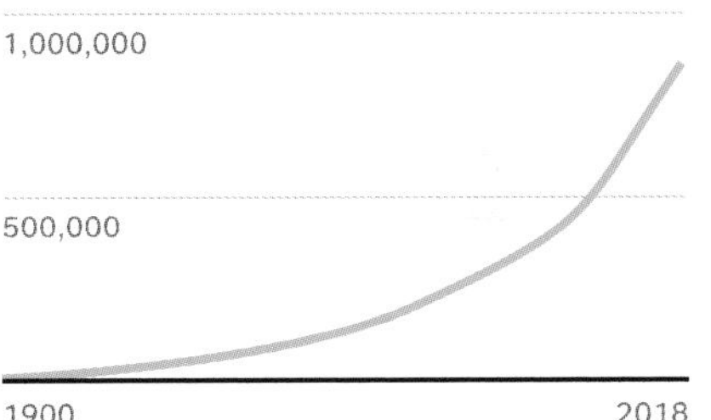

750 Thousand Establishments

7.6 Million Jobs

$800 Billion Output

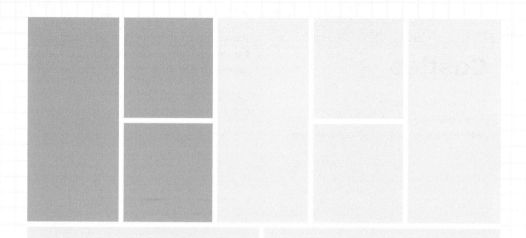

BACKSTAGE DISRUPTION

Questions for Leaders

Resource Castles

TRIGGER QUESTION

How could we make difficult-to-copy resources a key pillar of our business model?

Assessment Question

Do we own key resources that are difficult or impossible to copy and which give us a significant competitive advantage?

Our key resources are significantly inferior to those of our competitors.

Our key resources can't easily be copied or emulated for the next couple of years and they give us a significant competitive advantage (e.g., intellectual property, brand, etc.).

Activity Differentiators

TRIGGER QUESTION

Could we create (significantly more) value for customers by performing new activities or configuring activities in innovative ways?

Assessment Question

Do we create significant value for customers because we perform and configure activities in disruptively innovative ways?

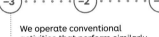

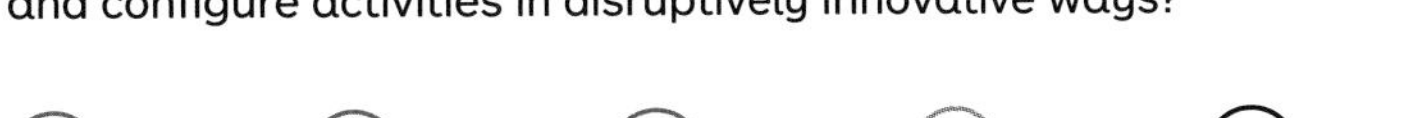

We operate conventional activities that perform similarly or worse than comparable organizations.

Our key activities can't easily be copied or emulated for the next couple of years and they give us a significant competitive advantage (e.g., cost effectiveness, scale etc.).

Scalers

TRIGGER QUESTION

What could we do differently to make our business model more scalable (e.g., eliminate resource and activity bottlenecks)?

Assessment Question

How rapidly and how easily can we grow our business model without substantial additional resources and activities (e.g., building infrastructure, finding talent)?

Growing our business and customers is resource intensive (e.g., more people) and requires a lot of effort (e.g., nonscalable activities).

Our revenues and customer base can easily grow and scale without a lot of additional resources and activities.

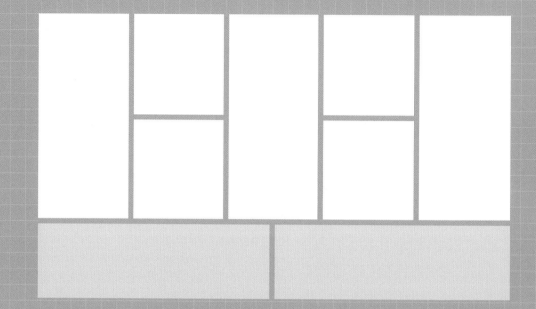

Profit Formula Disruption

Revenue Differentiators

Cost Differentiators

Margin Masters

A radical change in how profits are made in terms of revenues and costs.

Revenue Differentiators

Boost Revenues

Find innovative ways to capture value, unlock previously unprofitable markets, and/or substantially increase revenues.

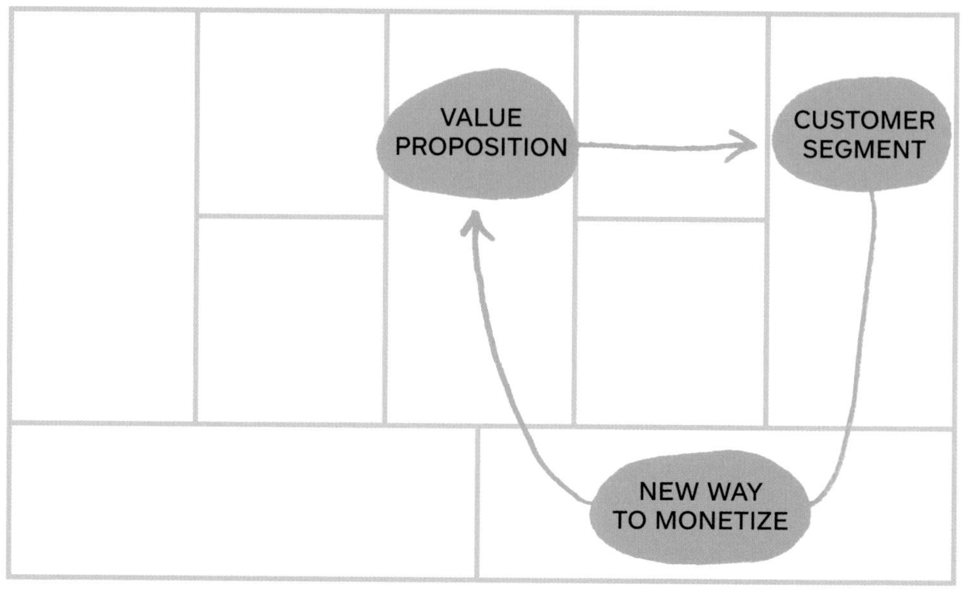

TRIGGER QUESTION

Which new revenue streams or pricing mechanisms could we introduce to capture more value from our customers or unlock unprofitable markets?

Assessment Question

Do we use strong revenue streams and pricing mechanisms to monetize value creation for customers?

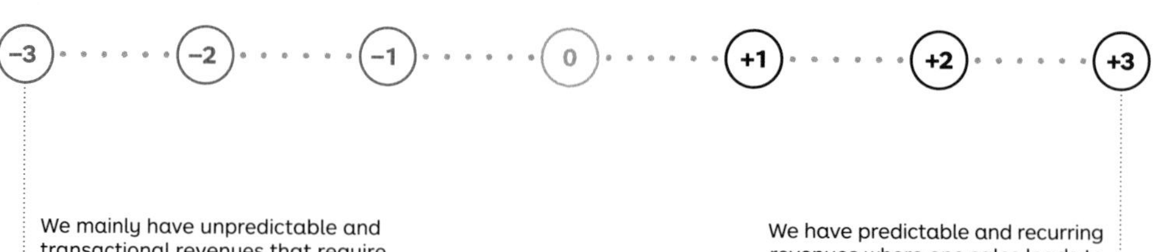

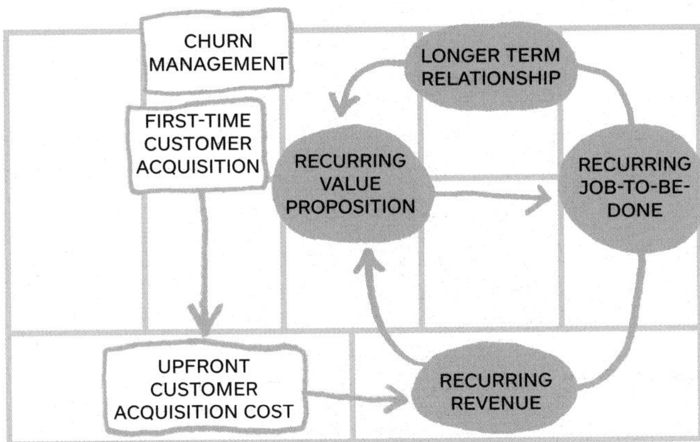

Recurring Revenue – Generate recurring revenues from one-time sales. Advantages include compound revenue growth (new revenues stack up on top of existing revenues), lower cost of sales (sell once and earn recurrently), and predictability.

TRIGGER QUESTION
How could we generate long-term recurring revenues rather than transactional ones?

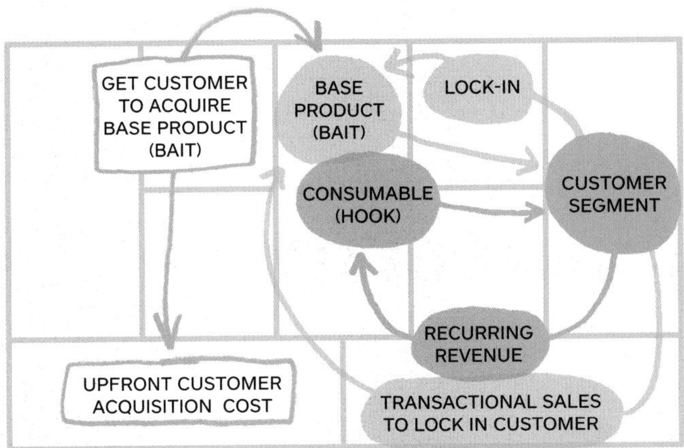

Bait & Hook – Lock customers in with a base product (the bait) in order to generate recurring revenues from a consumable (the hook) that customers need recurrently to benefit from the base product.

TRIGGER QUESTION
How could we create recurring revenues with a base product or service and a consumable?

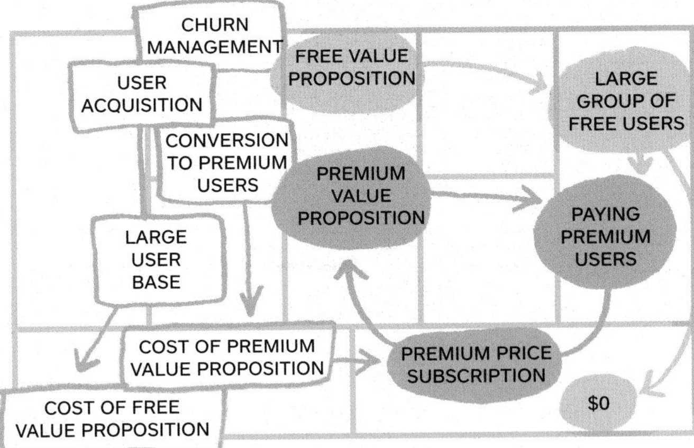

Freemium Providers – Offer basic products and services free of charge and premium services and advanced product features for a fee. The best freemium models acquire a large customer base and excel in converting a substantial percentage to paid users.

TRIGGER QUESTION
How could we split our value proposition into a free and a premium offer?

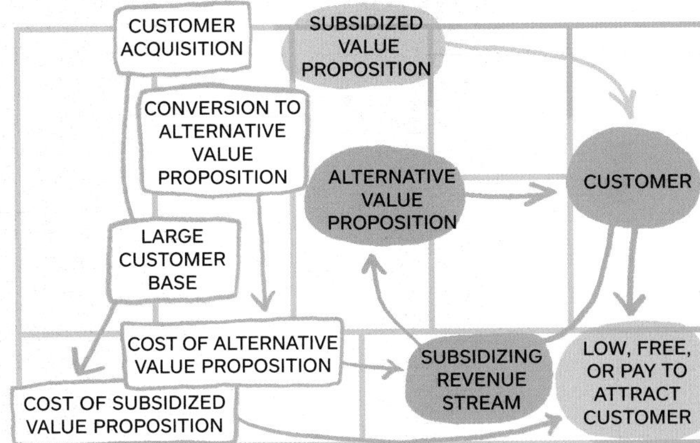

Subsidizers – Offer the full value proposition for free or cheaply by subsidizing it through a strong alternative revenue stream. This differs from freemium, which only gives free access to a basic version of products and services.

TRIGGER QUESTION
How could we give away our main value proposition for free by generating sufficient alternative revenue streams?

Xerox

In 1959, Xerox launches the first plain paper photocopier, the Xerox 914. Rather than just selling the machine, they generate long-term, recurring revenues from each photocopy made.

In 1959, Xerox revolutionized access to information by inventing and commercializing the first plain paper photocopy machine, the Xerox 914. The 914 took over a decade and a significant R&D budget to develop.

The machine was revolutionary: averaging 2,000 copies a day or 100 times more than the average business copier at the time.[67]

Because the 914 was expensive, it adopted a leasing model to make it more affordable. Customers were able to cancel the lease with only 15 days' notice, demonstrating Xerox's confidence in its value proposition.

Xerox added a pay-per-copy plan in order to monetize what they believed would become a copy addiction, but included the the first 2,000 copies for free. It's thanks to this innovative business model that earnings from the technology far exceeded earnings had they just sold the machine.

By 1962, the commercial copying business was worth $400 million, up from $40 million a decade before. By then the Xerox name had become synonymous with photocopying.[68]

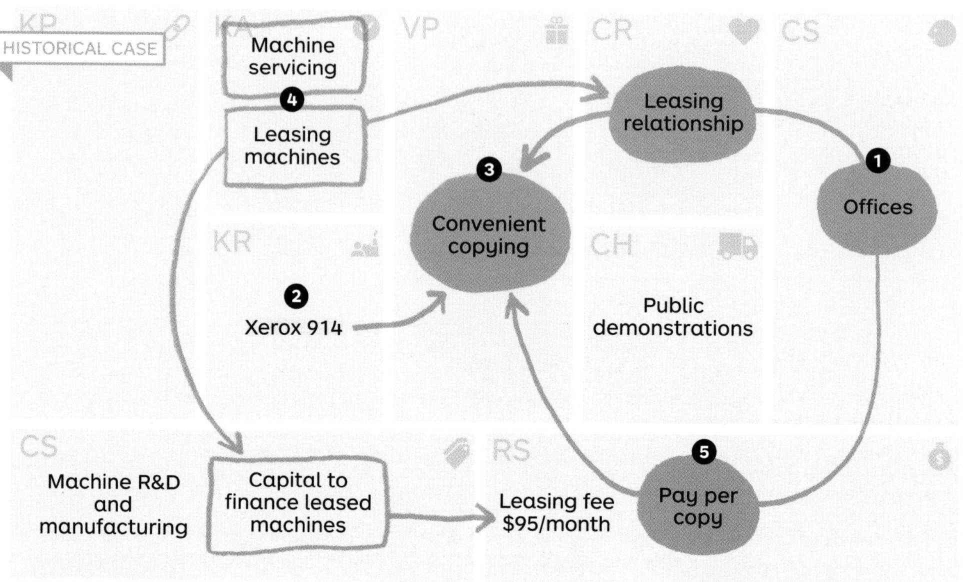

1 Identify Recurring Job-to-Be-Done

Chester Carlson, a patent office employee, struggles with the cumbersome job of copying documents. At the time, the average business copier produces 15 to 20 copies per day.

2 Create Asset to Monetize Continuously

To address the challenge, Carlson invents and patents a new technique called xerography. Together with what later becomes Xerox, he develops the first plain paper photocopying machine, the Xerox 914, which averages 2,000 copies per day.

3 Design the Value Proposition

Xerox believes that once workers become familiar with the power of photocopies, they will be addicted to the convenience and copy more than ever before. Xerox offers the first 2,000 copies for free and a pay-per-copy plan after that.

4 Acquire Customers

Xerox recognizes that its copier is too expensive and new for mass adoption. It adopts a leasing model to make the machine affordable and get it into offices. Instead of Xerox selling it for $29,500, customers lease it for $95 a month.[69]

5 Earn Recurring Revenue

Each machine is fitted with a counter to tally the monthly usage. After the first 2,000 copies, customers pay 4 cents a copy. This allows Xerox to continuously monetize its value proposition through recurring revenue.

+ Public Demonstrations to Boost Adoption

The Model 914 is large and difficult to transport, and the technology has to be seen to be believed. Rather than using a traditional sales model, Xerox chooses to hold public demonstrations (including in NYC's Grand Central Terminal). These events help exhibit the machine's productivity and spur adoption.

100 thousand

The average monthly copy volume of the 914, which was originally designed to produce an average monthly copy volume of 10 thousand copies.[70]

$12.5 million

Development cost of the 914 (the equivalent of $110 million today). That was more than the company's total earnings from 1950 to 1959.[71]

650 lbs.

The weight of the original Model 914, which had to be tilted and squeezed through most office doors.[71]

Xerox Revenue[72]

In millions of U.S. dollars

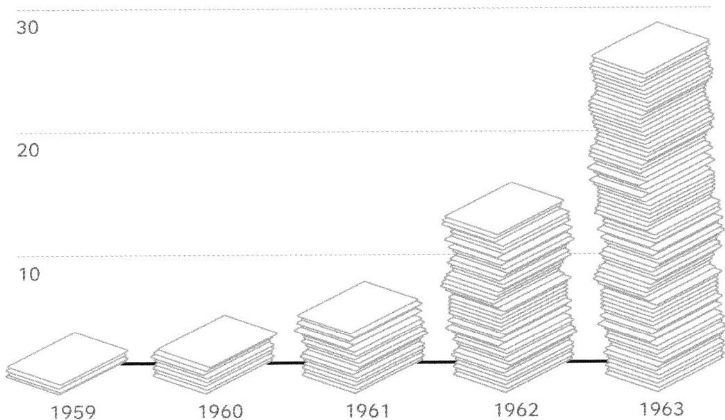

The Rise of Recurring Revenue through Subscriptions

A more conventional way to generate recurring revenues is through subscriptions. Historically popularized through newspaper subscriptions, the model has spread to countless domains.

15% product subscriptions

15% of online shoppers have signed up for one or more subscriptions to receive products on a recurring basis.[73]

In particular, with the rise of the Internet, the subscription model has boomed. In 2018 Interbrand attributed 29% of the total value of the top 100 brands to subscription-based businesses versus 18% in 2009.[74]

Customers can subscribe to countless replenishment or curation services (food, clothing, etc.), or subscribe to services where access replaces ownership (e.g., software-as-a-service [SaaS], clothing, entertainment). The subscription model has conquered not just the consumer market, but also business-to-business and industrial markets.

Bait & Hook
1900 ~~~ 2012

Kodak

In 1900, Kodak "baits" consumers with cheap cameras to generate significant follow-on revenues from selling high margin film and photo processing.

George Eastman founded Kodak in 1888 with a goal of making "the camera as convenient as the pencil." One can argue that he succeeded with the introduction of the Brownie, an inexpensive camera, in 1900. With the Brownie, Kodak made cameras accessible to the masses: affordable, portable, and easy to use.

Kodak created the amateur photography market and held a dominant position through most of the twentieth century. Only the introduction of the digital camera in 1999—which it helped invent—triggered the end of Kodak's dominance over photography.

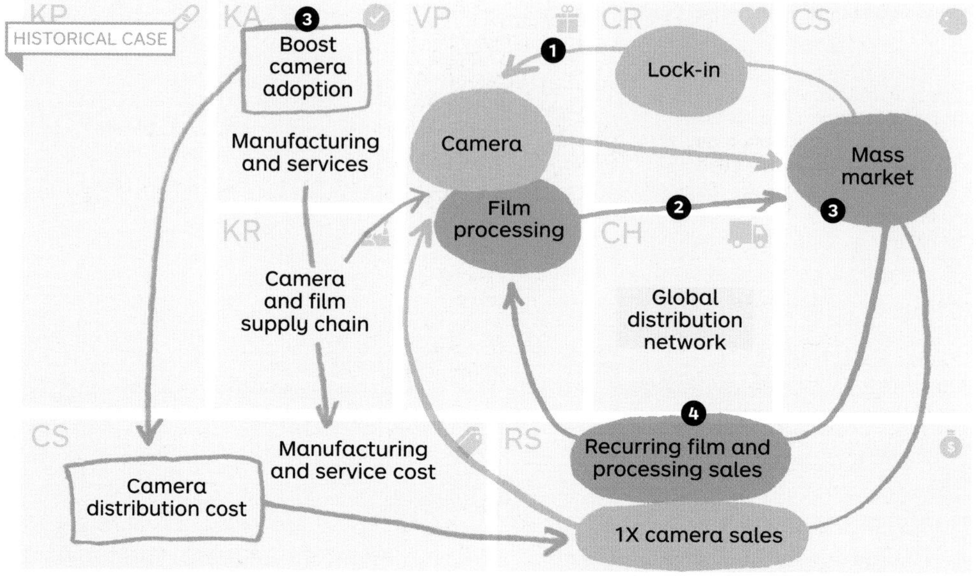

1 "Bait" and Lock In Customer with Base Product

In 1900, Kodak introduces the Brownie, the first mass market camera. It sells for only $1 (equivalent to $30 in 2019) and introduces amateur photography to the masses.[75]

2 "Hook" Customers with a Consumable Product and Service

The Brownie comes preloaded with film. Once the film is used, amateur photographers send the film back to Kodak for processing. Photographers get hooked and need to come back if they want to continue their hobby.

3 Acquire Customers

In 1900 photography is very new. Kodak uses low pricing for the Brownie and extensive marketing campaigns targeted at amateur photographers, including women and children, to spur customer acquisition. It sells 250,000 cameras the first year.[76]

4 Enjoy Recurring Revenues from Consumable

At the time, film costs 15¢ a roll. For an extra 10¢ a photo plus 40¢ for developing and postage, users can send their film to Kodak for development. Repeat purchases of film and processing generate significant recurring revenues for Kodak.

+ **Building the Backstage for Film and Processing**

Kodak builds up a backstage to support the complex process of manufacturing film. Kodak owns most of its supply chain, including raw materials such as processing chemicals, which create significant barriers to entry.

+ **Distribution and Brand**

Over the decades, Kodak establishes a global distribution network of dealers, which it supports with a strong brand and substantial marketing investments.

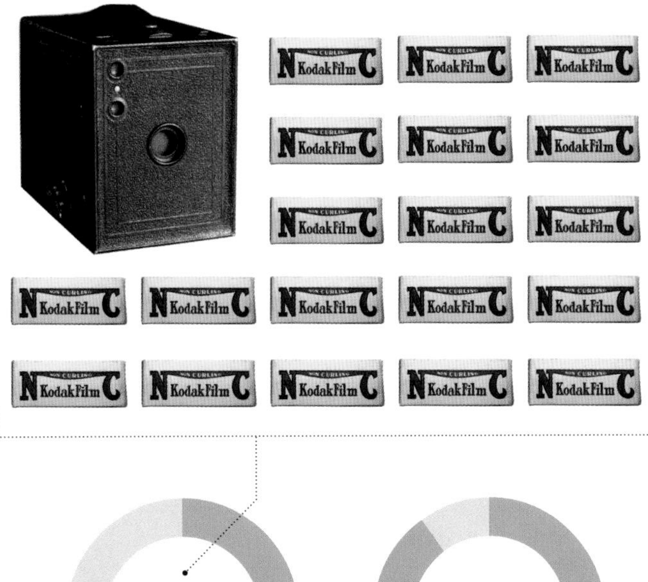

5th most valuable brand globally (in 1996).[79]

70% profit margin on film Kodak enjoyed in the 1980s.[77]

90% of film sales in the U.S. were by Kodak in 1976.[78]

Photos Taken Each Year

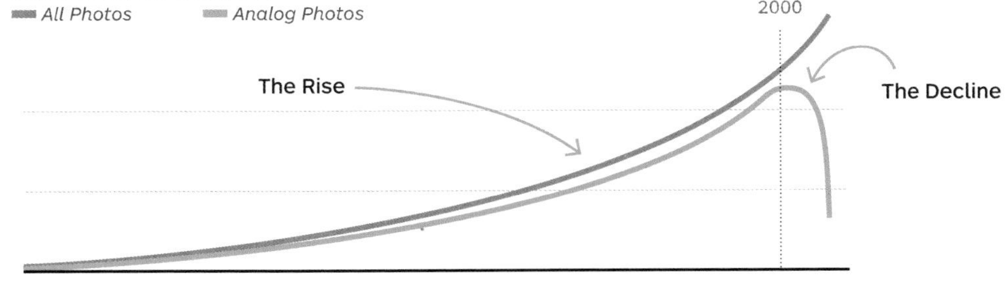

Disruption of an Innovator

Kodak filed for bankruptcy in 2012 due to the disruption of Kodak's business model by digital cameras and smartphones. They made Kodak's major revenue engine (analog film) obsolete. Ironically, Kodak engineer Steven Sasson invented the first digital camera in 1975.

Kodak failed to adapt its camera, and film-based business model to the digital world. In 2001, it acquired a photo-sharing site called Ofoto. Instead of using an advertising-based business model (like Facebook), Kodak positioned Ofoto to attract more people to print digital images, when the printing market was already highly competitive and in decline.

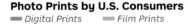

Photo Prints by U.S. Consumers

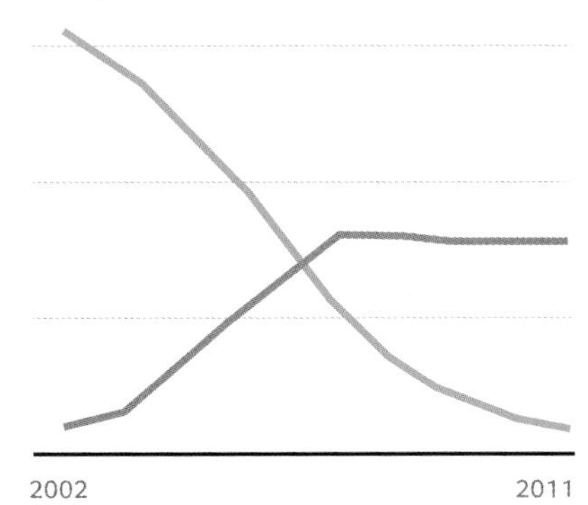

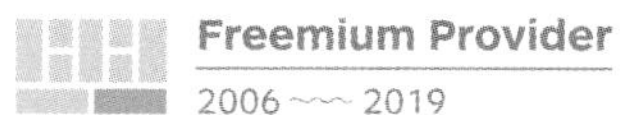

Freemium Provider

2006 ~~~ 2019

Spotify

In 2006, Spotify launches a free online music service to compete against freely available, pirated music. Its main revenue source comes from users upgrading to a premium subscription.

Spotify is a music streaming platform that gives users access to a large catalog of music. It uses a freemium revenue model that offers a basic, limited, ad-supported service for free and an unlimited premium service for a subscription fee.

Spotify relies heavily on its music algorithms and its community of users and artists to keep its premium experience delightful. Its premium subscriber base has grown from 10% of total users in 2011 to 46% in 2018.[80]

From the start Spotify saw itself as a legal alternative to pirated music and paid song purchases on iTunes. Spotify pays a significant portion of its revenue in the form of royalties to music labels. It has paid close to $10 billion in royalties since its launch in 2006.[81]

The company accelerated the shift from music downloads to streaming and disrupted Apple iTunes in the process.

For the first time in company history, Spotify made a profit in 2019.[82]

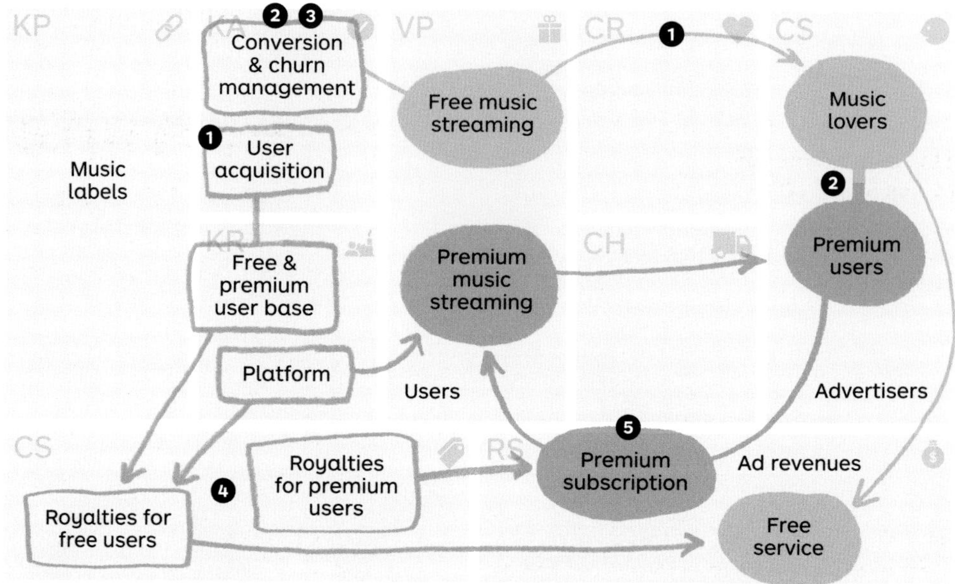

1 Attract a Large Base of Users with a Free Service

Spotify's free music streaming service gives users access to a catalog of millions of songs. The free service has basic functionality and users have to listen to messages from advertisers that partially subsidize the free service.

2 Convert Free Users to a Premium Value Proposition

Spotify has been extremely successful at converting free users to paid users. Its premium service has additional features and it removes advertising. In 2018, 46% of Spotify's users are premium users, who generate 90% of its total revenues.

3 Manage Retention and Churn

Like in any subscription model a user's lifetime value (LTV)—how much Spotify can earn from a user over time—increases the longer the company can retain users. This is called managing customer churn. In the first half year of 2019, Spotify's premium subscriber churn rate fell to a record low of 4.6%.[83]

4 Balance Cost of Free and Premium

Spotify pays record labels close to 52% of the revenue generated by each stream. Over 85% of music streamed from Spotify belongs to four record labels: Sony, Universal, Warner, and Merlin. In 2018, Spotify pays €3.5 billion in royalties for premium users and €0.5 billion for free users, which equates to 74% of overall costs.[84]

5 Finance It All with Your Revenue Stream from Premium

The particularity of the freemium model is that you need to be able to cover the costs of free and paying users. Spotify's user base grows to over 248 million users in 2019 for which it needs to pay royalties. Of those users, 54% consume (limited) music for free.[85]

#1

most downloaded music streaming app

in the United States on the App Store in 2018.[86]

U.S. On-Demand Audio Song Streams[87]

In billions

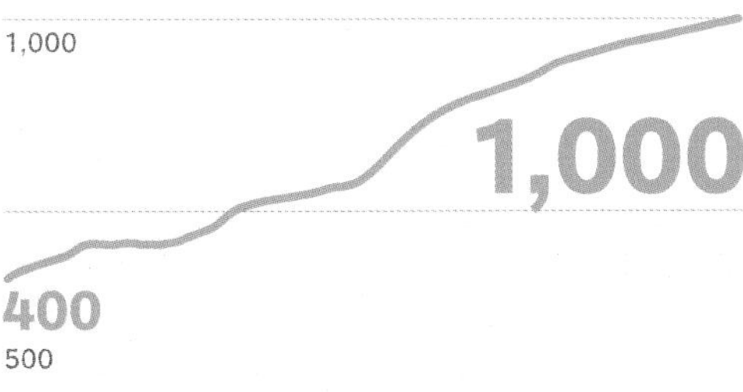

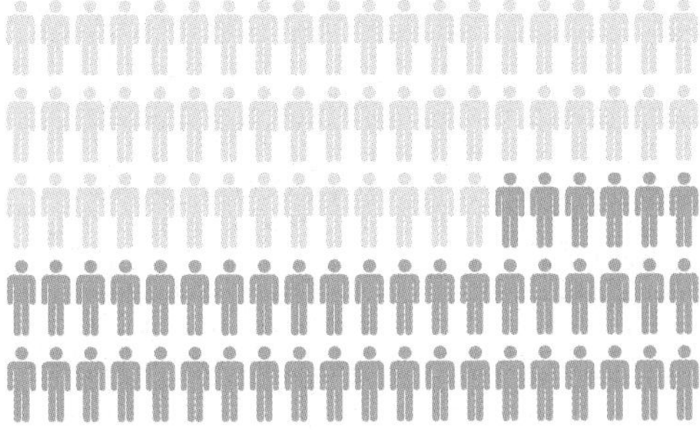

46%

conversion rate to paid services

compared to 30% for Slack, 4% for Evernote, 4% for Dropbox, and 0.5% for Google Drive.[88]

Subsidizers

2017 ~~~ 2019

Fortnite

In 2017, Epic Games releases *Fortnite: Battle Royale*, a completely free, multiplatform, online video game that is subsidized by in-app purchases for digital goods.

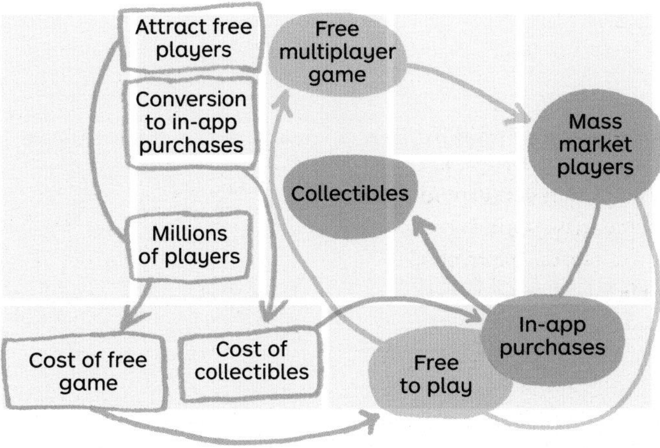

Fortnite: Battle Royale became a cultural phenomenon after its release. It is a free-to-play, multiplayer video game where hundreds of players fight to the death on an island.

Epic Games monetizes through in-app purchases, allowing players to buy collectibles like fashion statements or dance moves, but which provide no strategic edge to advance in the game. *Fortnite* was originally released as a paid version for $40 in July 2017 before switching to a free version subsidized by in-app purchases.[89]

Festivals

Festivals often use subsidizer mechanics. For some festivals, the sale of food and drinks subsidizes the festival free-entry fee. In other instances, a paid festival can subsidize an off or free festival such as the Montreux Jazz Festival in Switzerland.

Cost Differentiators

Kill Costs

Build a business model with a game-changing cost structure, not just by streamlining activities and resources, but by doing things in disruptive new ways.

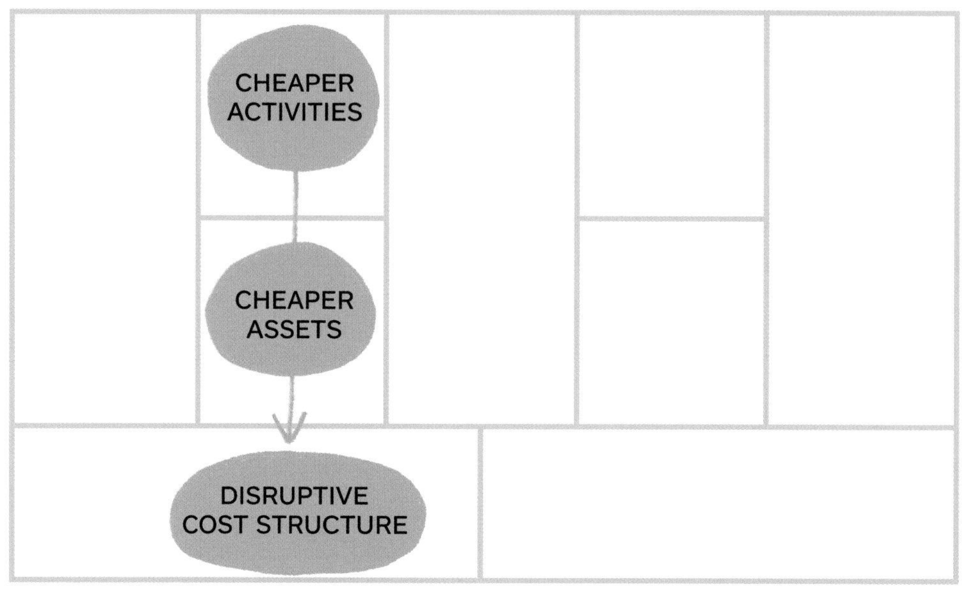

TRIGGER QUESTION

Could we change our cost structure significantly by creating and delivering value with different and differently configured resources and activities?

Assessment Question

Is our cost structure conventional or disruptive?

We have a conventional cost structure that performs similarly or worse than comparable organizations (e.g., worse by a factor of two).

We have a game-changing disruptive cost structure that performs differently and substantially better than comparable organizations (e.g., better by a factor of two).

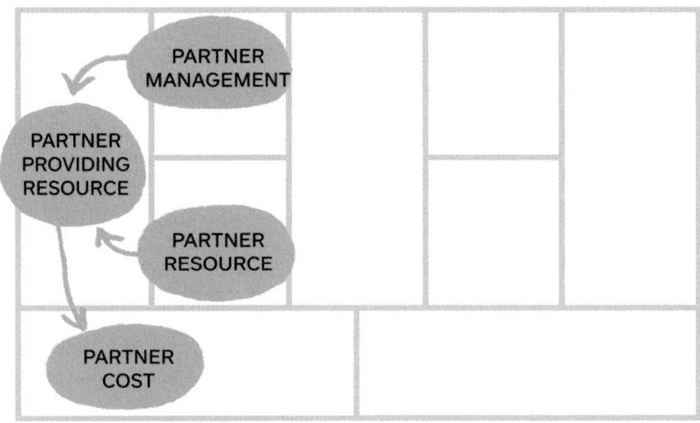

Resource Dodgers – Eliminate the most costly and capital-intensive resources from your business model to create a game-changing cost structure.

EXAMPLES
Airbnb, Uber, Bharti Airtel

TRIGGER QUESTION
How could we create a resource-light business model and get rid of the most costly and capital intensive resources?

TECHNOLOGY DEVELOPMENT & MAINTENANCE
TECH-BASED VALUE PROPOSITION
TECHNOLOGY
DISRUPTIVE COST OF TECHNOLOGY

Technologists – Use technology in radically new ways to create a game-changing cost structure.

EXAMPLES
WhatsApp, Skype

TRIGGER QUESTION
How could we use technology to replace activities and resources to create a game-changing cost structure?

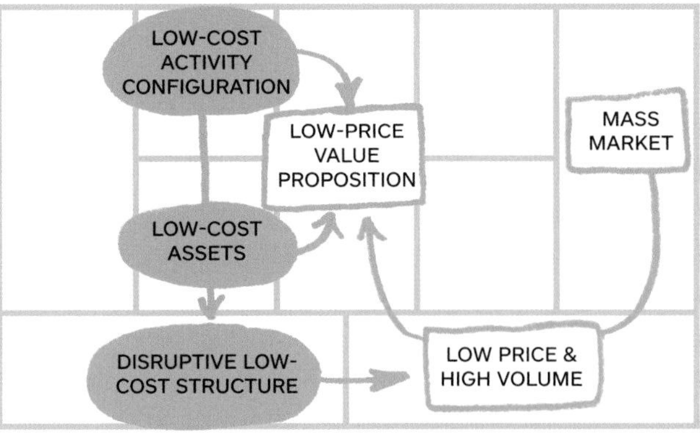

Low Cost – Combine activities, resources, and partners in radically new ways to create a game-changing cost structure with disruptively low prices.

EXAMPLES
easyJet, Ryanair, Trader Joe's

TRIGGER QUESTION
How could we radically recombine activities, resources, and partners to significantly lower costs and pricing?

Resource Dodger

2008 ~~~ 2019

Airbnb

In 2008, Airbnb launches a platform that feels like a hotel chain but owns no properties. It connects travelers with owners of idle assets.

Airbnb was founded in 2008 as an online marketplace to connect travelers looking for an authentic, unique place to stay with hosts that had extra room to rent. Airbnb operates as an intermediary, matching these two distinct customer segments.

The company has a radically lighter cost structure than the hotel chains with which it competes, because it does not own any of the rooms it lists on its website, nor does it manage a large hospitality staff. Airbnb's main costs are platform management and marketing, which explains how they have scaled so quickly.

The success of Airbnb's business model is based on a resource-light cost structure. It found an innovative way to partner with owners of idle assets (empty rooms) and help them monetize those assets via their matchmaking platform.

Airbnb differs from other matchmaking sites like booking.com or hotels.com, in that travelers associate the listed properties and rooms with the Airbnb brand as if it was a traditional hotel chain.

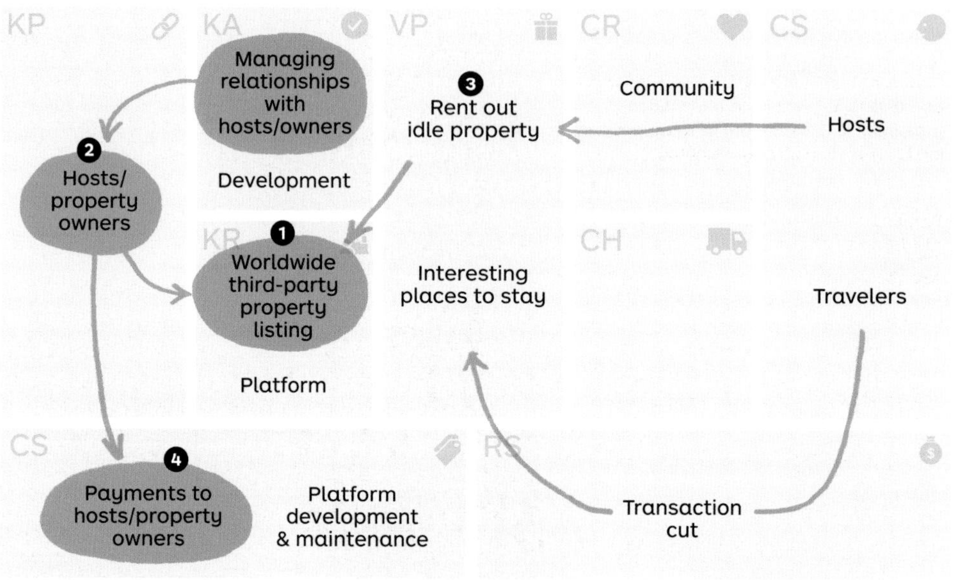

1 Identify the Most Costly Resource in your Business Model or Industry

The most costly elements in the hotel industry are the properties, their maintenance, staff, and services. Also, when hotel rooms are not rented out on a given night, they are a sunk cost. The hotel industry is very capital intensive.

2 Identify Asset Owners That Could Provide You with the Required Resource

Airbnb recognizes that many property owners have idle assets (unused bedrooms, apartments, beach houses, etc.) that are relatively difficult for an individual to rent out continuously for short periods of time.

3 Develop an Innovative Value Proposition to Acquire Resources from Partners

Airbnb offers property owners the opportunity to become hosts to generate extra income (average $924/month in 2017).[90] Airbnb gives hosts access to a pool of travelers through the platform and relieves one of the biggest pains for property owners.

4 Compete on a New Cost Structure

Airbnb competes on a much lighter cost structure than hotels, because it owns no hotels, nor employs cleaning or service staff. Airbnb's operational costs are mostly platform management, marketing and promotion, and other host and traveler support activities.

+ Double-Sided Platform

For Airbnb to be attractive to hosts, it needs a large pool of travelers. Developing this "other side of its platform" is a key success factor in the value proposition to hosts.

Lovemark Brand

Airbnb develops a very strong brand for this particular type of travel experience. It deeply changes social norms and habits. While it is commonplace now, in 2008 it is unheard of to be willing to sleep in a stranger's home.

The Importance of Community and the Sharing Economy

Airbnb fosters the connection of hosts and travelers on a more personal level than what they'd experience at a hotel, in order to build a global Airbnb community. This type of connectivity gives rise to the sharing economy, also known as collaborative consumption.

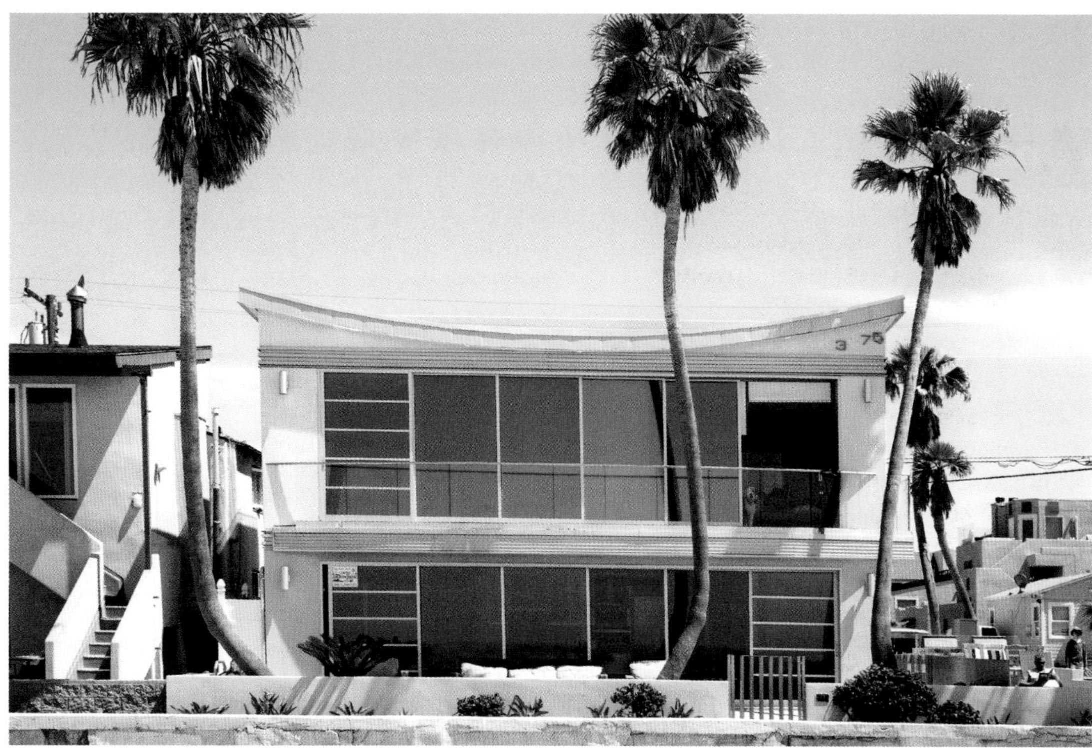

7

million global listings

Airbnb indicates 7 million global active listings on its platform in early 2019, which was more rooms than the top 5 hotel rooms combined.[91]

2

million+

Average number of people staying in an Airbnb per night in 2019.[91]

Zero

Number of properties Airbnb owns.

Share of Travelers Using Airbnb[92]

Percentage of leisure and business travelers in the U.S. and Europe

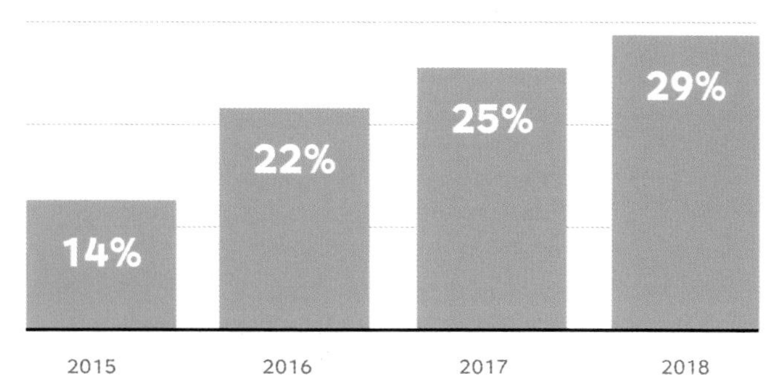

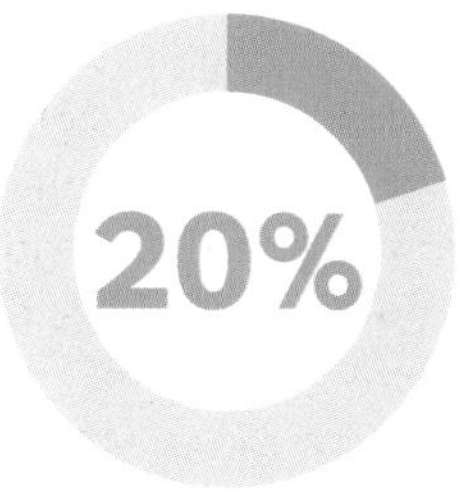

Airbnb's 2018 percentage of U.S. consumer spending for lodging.[93]

WhatsApp

In 2009, WhatsApp launches a device-agnostic free messaging service and platform that disrupts SMS and free desktop messaging.

WhatsApp was originally, in 2009, a status update app before it transformed into a free, unlimited messaging service. The company targeted anyone with a smartphone and an Internet connection, regardless of device and location.

When WhatsApp launched, it disrupted a very competitive messaging market. Text messaging was dominated by paid SMS services by telecom operators and free desktop messaging like Yahoo! Messenger, MSN Messenger, and Skype.

WhatsApp used software and the Internet to externalize the hardware and proprietary infrastructure costs that telecom operators bear in order to offer SMS services. This allowed them to benefit from the growth of smartphone users globally, operate at a radically lower cost structure, and pass on cost savings to users in the form of a free service. In February 2013, WhatsApp serviced 200 million active users with only 50 staff members. By December that year, it had 400 million users.[94, 95]

In 2014, Facebook acquired WhatsApp for more than $19 billion.[96]

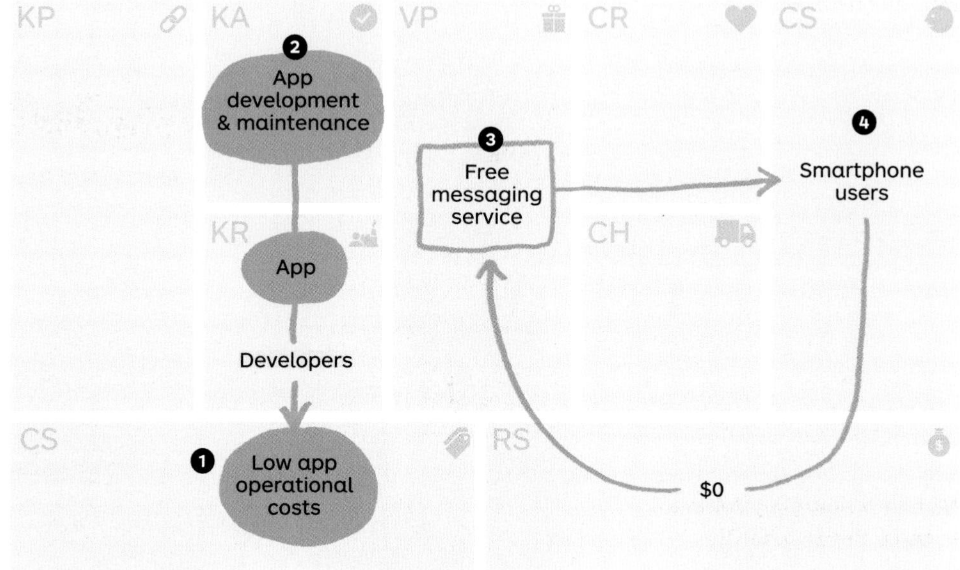

1 Identify an Industry Cost and Revenue Structure That You Can Disrupt with Tech

Telecom operators charge an estimated 6,000% markup for SMS messages. WhatsApp disrupts this revenue stream with a free service.[97]

2 Build the Technology

In early 2009 Jan Koum starts working on a new type of Internet-based iPhone messaging app. Unlike SMS messages, which use a telecom operator's network infrastructure, WhatsApp piggybacks on a user's smartphone connection to deliver messaging for free.

3 Disrupt with a Radically Different Cost Structure

WhatsApp incurs no variable or fixed costs for messages sent by users. Its main costs are in software development, not infrastructure. With only a few software developers, it serves millions of users and destroys billions of dollars of lucrative SMS revenues for telecom operators in the process.

4 Reap the Benefits

WhatsApp grows at a breathtaking speed without having to grow its cost structure substantially. In December 2013 WhatsApp claims they've reached 400 million active users with only 35 engineers.

+ Smartphone Growth

WhatsApp focuses on mobile first and benefits from the rapid growth of the smartphone market. WhatsApp expands to multiple platforms and devices, but contrary to their free, desktop messaging competitors (like Yahoo! Messenger, MSN Messenger, and Skype) WhatsApp's primary focus always remains mobile.

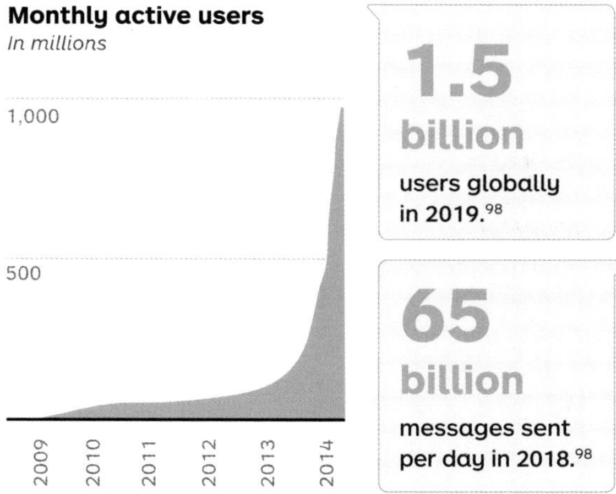

1.5 billion users globally in 2019.[98]

65 billion messages sent per day in 2018.[98]

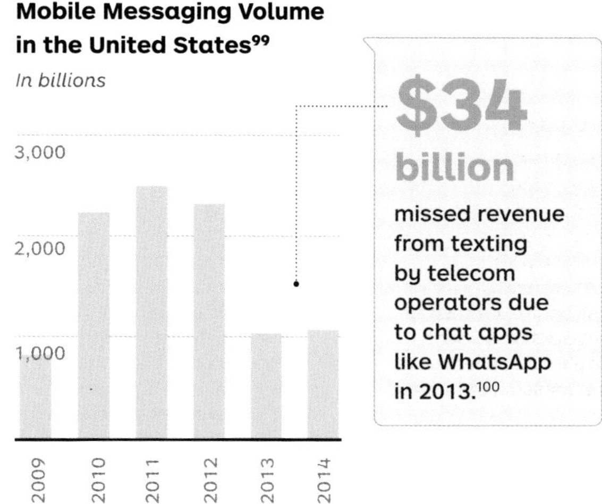

$34 billion missed revenue from texting by telecom operators due to chat apps like WhatsApp in 2013.[100]

$19 billion Amount Facebook paid to acquire WhatsApp in February 2014, five years after launch.

Low Cost
1995 ~~~ 2002

easyJet

In 1995, easyJet disrupts European travel with a low-cost, no frills air travel experience.

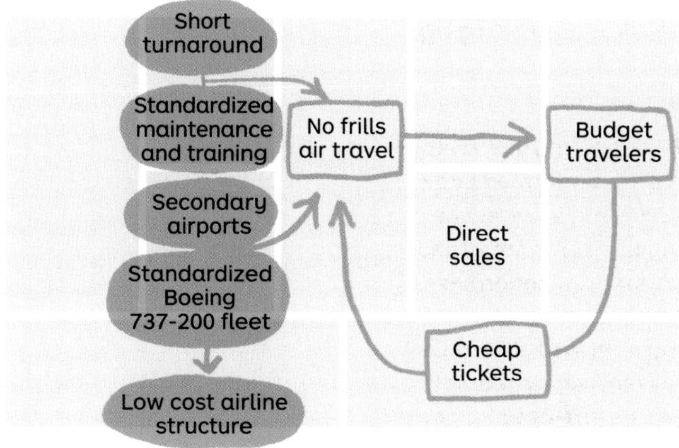

easyJet launched in 1995, popularizing the low-cost carrier model in the European market. easyJet's business model applies the following low-cost blueprint until it diversifies in 2002:

- No-frills airline experience for budget travelers.
- **Secondary airports**: often land in secondary airports that charge lower fees.
- **Fleet standardization:** one model of aircraft with simple cabin configuration to reduce maintenance and training costs.
- **Short turnaround times:** minimizing the time aircraft are on the ground not generating revenues.
- **Direct sales:** selling directly to customers to bypass travel agent fees.

Margin Masters

Boost Margins

Achieve significantly higher margins than competitors by focusing on what customers are willing to pay for most, while keeping your cost structure in check. Prioritize profitability over market share.

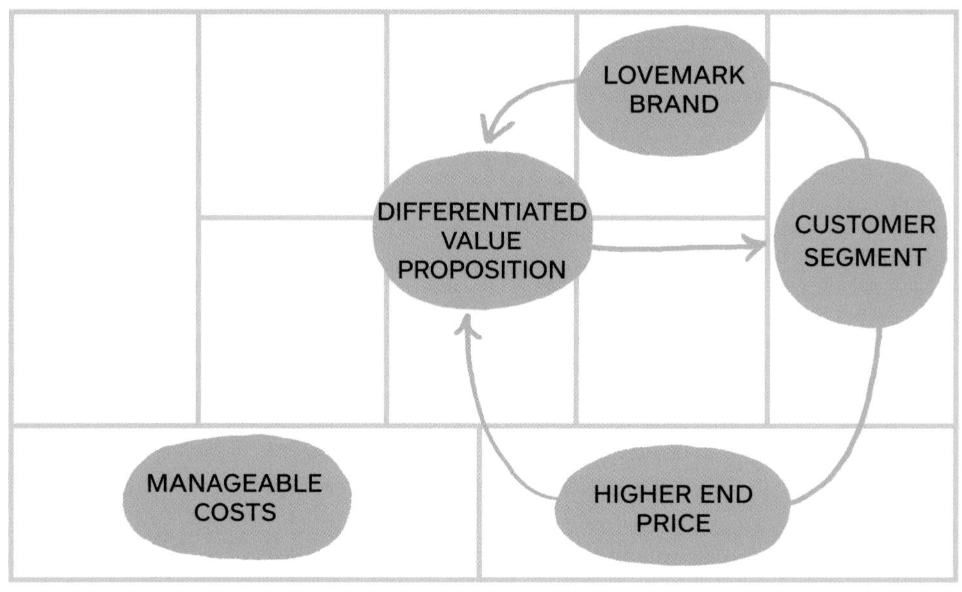

TRIGGER QUESTION

How could we find innovative ways to eliminate the most costly aspects of our business model, while focusing on value that matters to customers most and which they are willing to pay a high price for?

Assessment Question

Do we have strong margins from low costs and high prices?

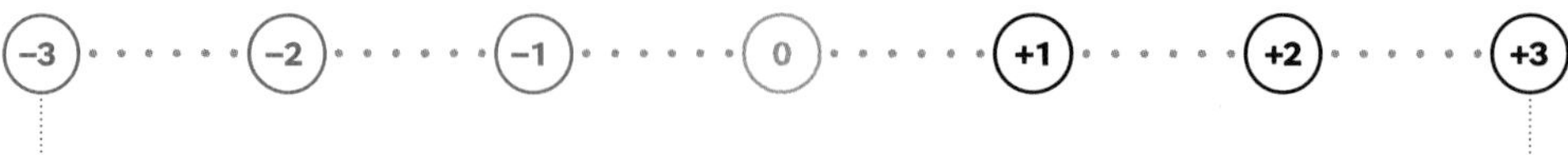

We have very thin margins due to our cost structure and weak pricing power (e.g., we perform worse than comparable organizations by at least 50%).

We have very strong margins from an optimized management of costs and strong pricing power (e.g., we perform better than comparable organizations by at least 50%).

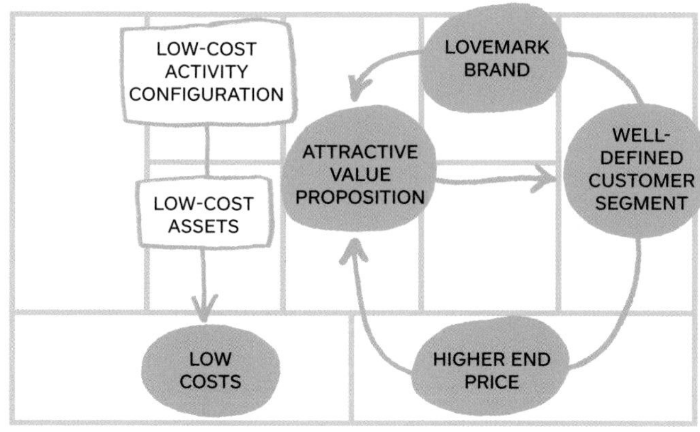

Contrarians – Significantly reduce costs and increase value at the same time. Eliminate the most costly resources, activities, and partners from your business model, even if that means limiting the value proposition. Compensate by focusing on features in the value proposition that a well-defined customer segment loves and is willing to pay for, but which are relatively cheap to provide.

EXAMPLES
CitizenM, Cirque de Soleil, Nintendo Wii

TRIGGER QUESTION
Which costly elements of our business model and value proposition could we eliminate and make up for with extremely valuable but affordable elements?

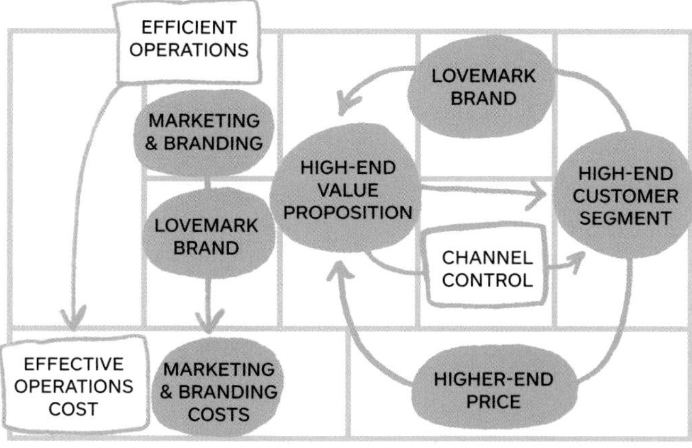

High Enders – Create products and services at the high end of the market spectrum for a broad range of high-end customers. Use these to maximize margins and avoid the small size and extreme cost structure of a luxury niche.

EXAMPLE
iPhone

TRIGGER QUESTION
What could we modify in our business model to significantly increase customer value and price without substantially increasing our cost structure?

Contrarian

2005 ~~~ 2019

citizenM

In 2005, citizenM launches a hotel concept with reduced costs but increased value for "mobile citizens."

In 2005, the founders of citizenM realized that the modern hotel industry hadn't changed in decades, despite the changing tastes and habits of the global traveler.

citizenM focused on the "mobile citizen"—the person who travels often and depends upon mobile technology. citizenM recognized that global travelers have a few essential conveniences and luxuries that they are willing to pay for, while other traditional amenities are not always necessary.

Based on these insights, the founders launched a hotel concept at Schiphol Airport in Amsterdam that minimized costs and maximized value for the mobile citizen without making it feel cheap. citizenM found a way to create more for less and was able to maintain high profit margins per room.

In 2019, the privately owned citizenM operated 20 hotels in 13 cities on three continents with an additional 10 hotels planned.

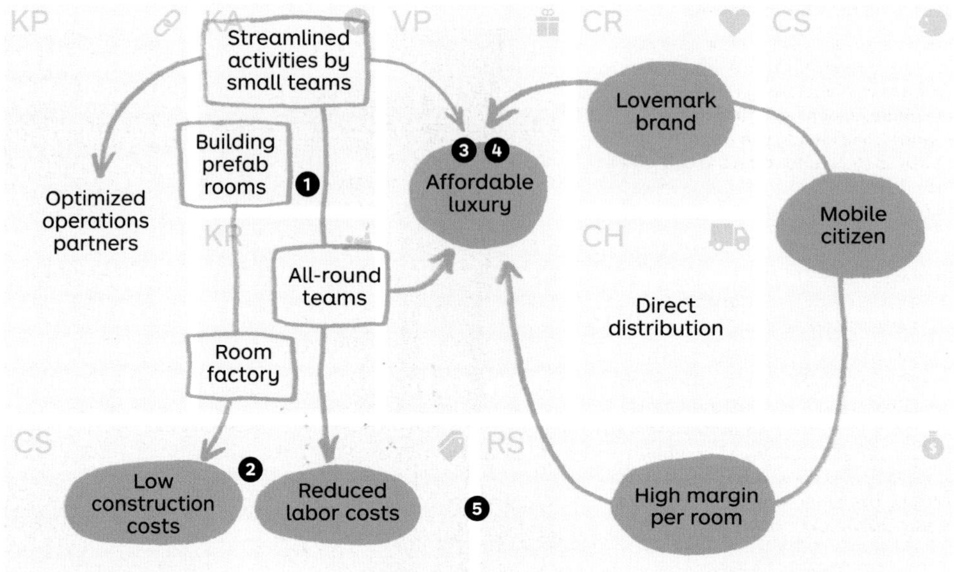

1 Eliminate Most Costly, Desirable Elements, Yet Not Essential to Customers

citizenM launches in Amsterdam in 2008. It removes the most costly elements of a high-end hotel, not essential to the mobile citizens it targets: no fine dining, no spa or sophisticated gym, no minibar, and no room service.

2 Reduce Costs without Making It Feel Cheap

citizenM drastically reduces construction and maintenance costs by building highly standardized 14-square-meter rooms in a room factory, which are then stacked like shipping containers to form the hotel.[101] It reduces HR costs by working with small, cross-functional teams.

3 Increase Value That Customers Care about at Low Cost

citizenM focuses on what really matters to mobile citizens: great mattresses, pillows, and sound-proof rooms. Its small staff has only one task: make customers happy. The lobby is vibrant, equipped with designer furniture, and 24-hour food and drinks.

4 Create New Elements That Boost Value at Less Cost

CitizenM launches its own room factory to fuel low-cost expansion from Amsterdam to New York and Taipei. It streamlines cleaning and linens with new operations partners.[102] Rooms are equipped with free broadband WiFi and movies-on-demand.

5 Reap Benefits of Creating More Value at Less Cost

citizenM's profitability per square meter is twice that of comparable upscale hotels.[103] It achieves that by eliminating the most costly elements from the hotel business without making it feel cheap for its customer, the mobile citizen.

Optimized for Mobile Citizens

From the start, citizenM optimizes its hotel experience for the mobile citizen: travelers who visit a city for 1 to 3 days for culture, shopping, entertainment, or work. They mainly use the hotel as a base to sleep and roam the city. They don't need many of the services embedded in other hotels.

Empowered Employees, Strong Customer Relationship, and Lovemark Brand

citizenM hires people who are highly customer oriented and then gives them the autonomy to deliver a great guest experience. It has one of the lowest staff turnovers in the industry. In addition, citizenM encourages teams to establish a strong customer relationship in order to establish a lovemark brand.

A. Build

99% of each room is finished at the factory.[104]

2x profitability CitizenM's profitability per square meter is twice that of comparable upscale hotels.

B. Assemble

C. Enjoy

7,000 rooms in **30** hotels on **3** continents[105]

High Ender
2007 ~~~ 2019

iPhone

In 2007, Apple launches the iPhone and combines an Internet browser, a music player, and a mobile phone in one high-end, multitouch device without a keyboard. It ushers in the era of the smartphone.

In 2007, Apple founder Steve Jobs famously introduced the iPhone at the Macworld 2007 convention as a revolutionary device that "would change everything." Its initial selling price was a hefty $499, but 270 thousand units sold its first weekend and 6 million units in its first year of production.[107,106]

Apple's iPhone ushered in the era of the smartphone, the world of mobile-first and constant connection, leading the way for mobile technology to dominate and reform day-to-day existence. Apple's iPhone has consistently been more expensive than competing devices. However, Apple continually packs new features and technology into its iPhone in order to keep its products from seeming like a commodity.

Despite high prices, Apple maintains a high degree of control over production costs in its supply chain. This combination of controlled costs, high-end positioning, and continuous technology innovation have resulted in gross margins of 60 to 70% in the last 10 years.[108]

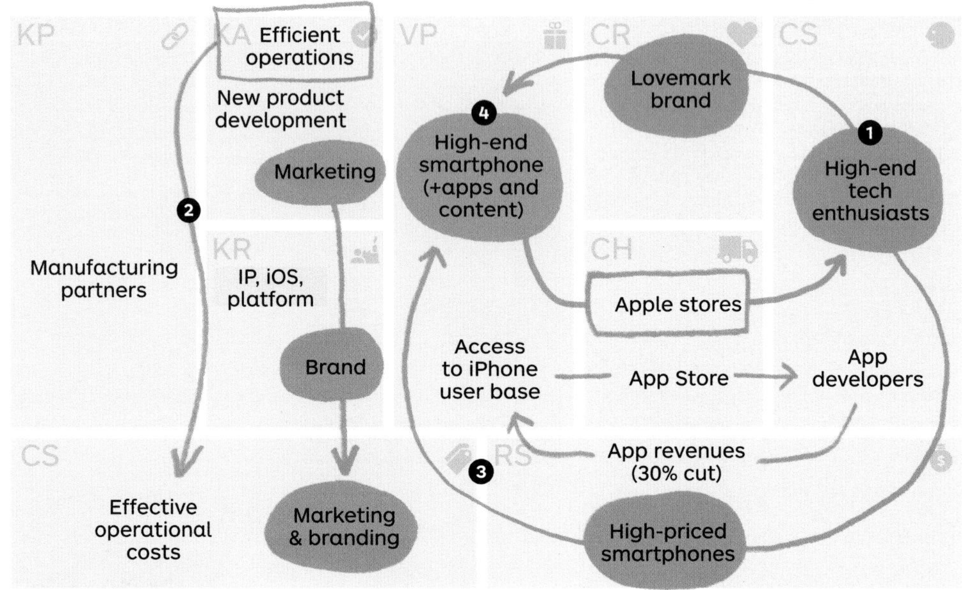

1 Delight and Surprise the High End of the Market

Apple positions the iPhone at the high end of the spectrum, knowing that the price will put it out of reach for the majority of the market. The phone combines an aspiration feel with design, technology, and simplicity, and capitalizes on its lovemark brand.

2 Control Costs

Apple does not manufacture the iPhone, but keeps its production costs low by controlling its supply chain. Due to the popularity of the device, Apple forces its suppliers to keep costs low as well as maintain privacy and secrecy over their devices.

3 Maximize Margins and Profits from High End Market Share

The iPhone's profit margins have remained between 60 to 70% over the past 10 years. At its peak, Apple captured 94% of the smartphone industry's profits, despite only accounting for 14.5% of sales.[109]

4 Continuously Reinvent and Surprise the High End of the Market

Since 2007, Apple has released 12 generations of iPhones. While Apple isn't always the first to develop many of the iPhone's technological innovations, it often delivers the best: multitouch screen, dual cameras, Apple Pay, Siri, iMessage, FaceTime, facial recognition.

+ The App Store

The iPhone initially launched without the App Store, which was opened in 2008 with 500 applications. As of 2019, the store featured over 1.8 million apps. The available applications and number of developers provide Apple with an additional competitive advantage as described in the Resource Castle Platform (p. 164).[110]

2.2 billion

iPhones sold as of November 2018.[111]

60–70% profit margins

on iPhones in the past 10 years.

...at its peak in 2015, Apple captured 94% of smartphone profits in the industry.

The Cost of iPhones (USD)[108]

Bill of materials *Retail cost*

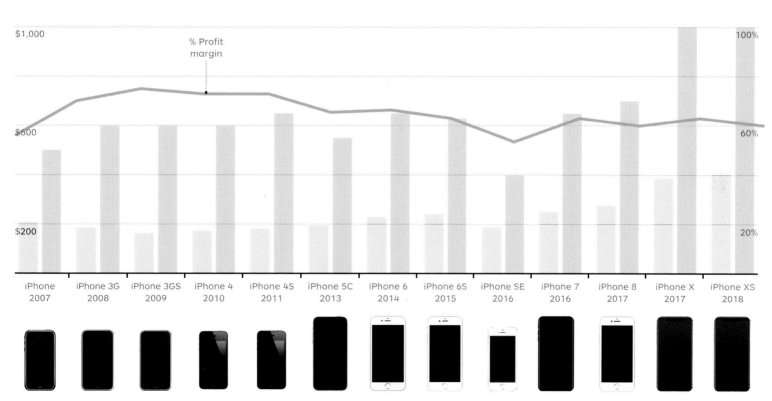

$1,000
$600
$200

% Profit margin

100%
60%
20%

iPhone 2007
iPhone 3G 2008
iPhone 3GS 2009
iPhone 4 2010
iPhone 4S 2011
iPhone 5C 2013
iPhone 6 2014
iPhone 6S 2015
iPhone SE 2016
iPhone 7 2016
iPhone 8 2017
iPhone X 2017
iPhone XS 2018

PROFIT FORMULA DISRUPTION

Questions for Leaders

Revenue Differentiators

TRIGGER QUESTION

Which new revenue streams or pricing mechanisms could we introduce to capture more value from our customers or unlock unprofitable markets?

Assessment Question: Do we use strong revenue streams and pricing mechanisms to monetize value creation for customers?

We mainly have unpredictable and transactional revenues that require constant cost of sales.

We have predictable and recurring revenues where one sale leads to several years of revenue.

Cost Differentiators

TRIGGER QUESTION

Could we change our cost structure significantly by creating and delivering value with different and differently configured resources and activities?

Assessment Question: Is our cost structure conventional or disruptive?

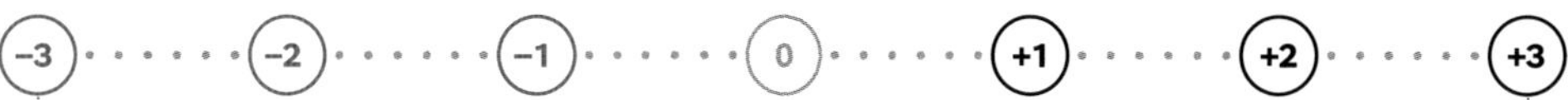

Our cost structure is significantly less effective than that of our competitors (e.g., by a factor of two).

Our cost structure is significantly more effective than that of our competitors (e.g., by a factor of two).

Margin Masters

TRIGGER QUESTION

How could we find innovative ways to eliminate the most costly aspects of our business model, while focusing on value that matters to customers most and which they are willing to pay a high price for?

Assessment Question: Do we have strong margins from low costs and high prices?

We have very thin margins due to our cost structure and weak pricing power (e.g., we perform worse than comparable organizations by at least 50%).

We have very strong margins from an optimized management of costs and strong pricing power (e.g., we perform better than comparable organizations by at least 50%).

Assessment Questions for Leaders

Assess your existing and new business models with the Assessment Questions for Leaders. Visualize your strengths and weaknesses and unearth opportunities with the resulting score. No business model achieves a perfect score. Simply be conscious about where you score well and where you don't and use the trigger questions continuously to spark ideas for improvements.

Assessment Questions for Leaders

Frontstage

Question	Score
Market Explorers: How large and attractive is the untapped market potential we are going after?	−3 −2 −1 0 +1 +2 +3
Channel Kings: Do we have large-scale and, ideally, direct access to our end-customer?	−3 −2 −1 0 +1 +2 +3
Gravity Creators: How easy or difficult is it for our customers to leave or switch to another company?	−3 −2 −1 0 +1 +2 +3

Backstage

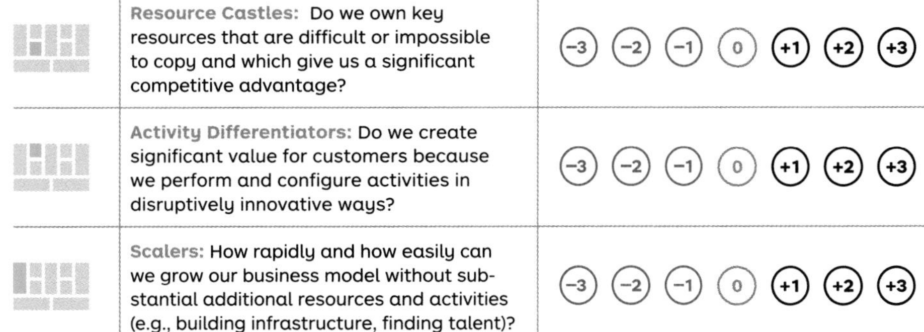

Question	Score
Resource Castles: Do we own key resources that are difficult or impossible to copy and which give us a significant competitive advantage?	−3 −2 −1 0 +1 +2 +3
Activity Differentiators: Do we create significant value for customers because we perform and configure activities in disruptively innovative ways?	−3 −2 −1 0 +1 +2 +3
Scalers: How rapidly and how easily can we grow our business model without substantial additional resources and activities (e.g., building infrastructure, finding talent)?	−3 −2 −1 0 +1 +2 +3

Profit Formula

Question	Score
Revenue Differentiators: Do we use strong revenue streams and pricing mechanisms to monetize value creation for customers?	−3 −2 −1 0 +1 +2 +3
Cost Differentiators: Is our cost structure conventional or disruptive?	−3 −2 −1 0 +1 +2 +3
Margin Monsters: Do we have strong margins from low costs and high prices?	−3 −2 −1 0 +1 +2 +3

Assessment

CitizenM

citizenM streamlined its entire hotel experience to focus on what it calls mobile citizens, the short-term business, party, culture, or shopping traveler visiting a city. It performed the remarkable feat of substantially reducing costs and simultaneously increasing customer satisfaction.

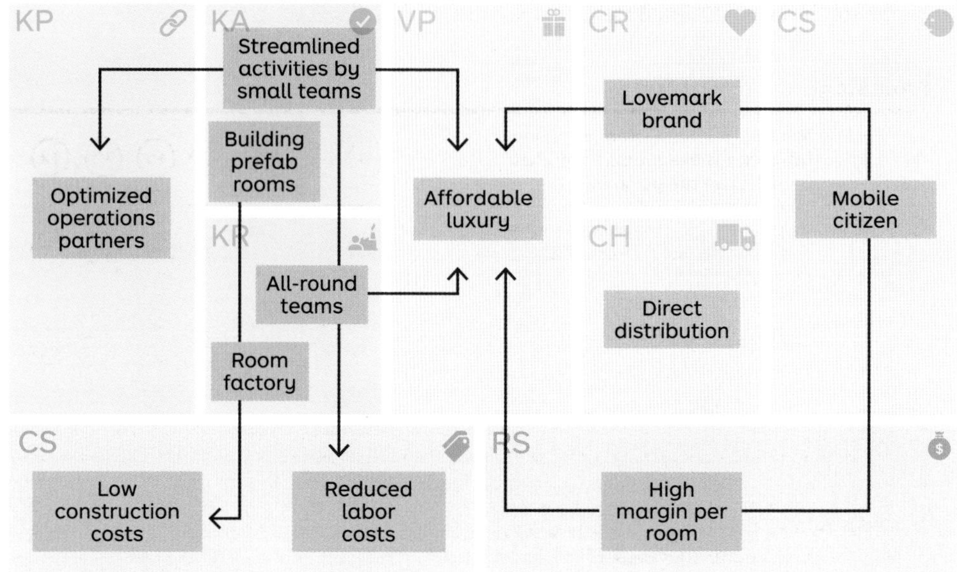

citizenM Business Model

Assessment
The citizenM business model performs extremely well on cost differentiation and does well on revenue differentiation, which leads to an overall extremely high margin business model. The weak spots are the business model's low customer switching costs and slow scalability, due to large capital and construction requirements. The low switching costs and heavy capital requirements mean that citizenM has to carefully monitor customer satisfaction to keep its business model in shape.

Four Actions Framework
Adapted from Blue Ocean Strategy

Eliminate (–)
- Minibar and room service
- Fine-dining table-seated restaurant
- Focus on traditional star rating
- Fitness, wet areas, spa

Raise (↗)
- Occupancy rate and revenue per room
- Effective use of space
- Focus on narrow customer segment
- Margins
- Customer satisfaction and service ratings
- Level of standardization
- Free broadband WiFi and video-on-demand

Reduce (↘)
- Construction costs
- Maintenance costs
- HR and operations costs

Create (+)
- Empowered all-round staff
- New segment: mobile citizens
- Room factory and prefab construction

Assessment Questions for Leaders

Frontstage

Question	−3	−2	−1	0	+1	+2	+3
Market Explorers: How large and attractive is the untapped market potential we are going after?			X				
Channel Kings: Do we have large-scale and, ideally, direct access to our end-customer?						X	
Gravity Creators: How easy or difficult is it for our customers to leave or switch to another company?		X					

Backstage

Question	−3	−2	−1	0	+1	+2	+3
Resource Castles: Do we own key resources that are difficult or impossible to copy and which give us a significant competitive advantage?					X		
Activity Differentiators: Do we create significant value for customers because we perform and configure activities in disruptively innovative ways?						X	
Scalers: How rapidly and how easily can we grow our business model without substantial additional resources and activities (e.g., building infrastructure, finding talent)?			X				

Profit Formula

Question	−3	−2	−1	0	+1	+2	+3
Revenue Differentiators: Do we use strong revenue streams and pricing mechanisms to monetize value creation for customers?						X	
Cost Differentiators: Is our cost structure conventional or disruptive?							X
Margin Monsters: Do we have strong margins from low costs and high prices?							X

citizenM performs poorly on locking in customers. Little prevents them from switching to another hotel chain. Investment in hotel city plots and construction costs make the business model relatively difficult to scale.

citizenM's high occupancy rate and effective use of space lead to higher revenues per room and square meter than those of their competitors.[112]

Due to an innovative activity configuration and extremely high level of standardization, citizenM is able to keep construction and maintenance costs extremely low.[113] A small, empowered, and all-round hotel staff magically keeps HR costs low, despite high customer service ratings.[114]

The combination of lower costs and higher revenues per room leads to a margin level unheard of in the hotel industry.

OneConnect

In 2015 the financial service conglomerate Ping An launches OneConnect to sell the technology it uses internally to other financial institutions.

OneConnect is a subsidiary of China's largest banking and insurance conglomerate. It launched OneConnect as an internal start-up to market cutting edge end-to-end financial technology solutions to small and medium-sized financial institutions. As of June 30, 2019, OneConnect has served over 600 banks and 80 insurance companies in China.[115]

The technology and platform that OneConnect sells to clients was initially developed for PingAn's internal use. OneConnect prides itself on being an industry leader in terms of technical capabilities, with a focus on preparing its clients for the ensuing digital transformation in the financial sector. Solutions range from credit checks and interbank transactions to biometric services, product sales, and mobile retail banking applications.

After a successful launch in China, in 2018, OneConnect established subsidiaries in Hong Kong, Singapore, and Indonesia to service local financial institutions. OneConnect[116] also partners with other fintech institutions to offer its software-as-a-service (SaaS) to the global market.[117]

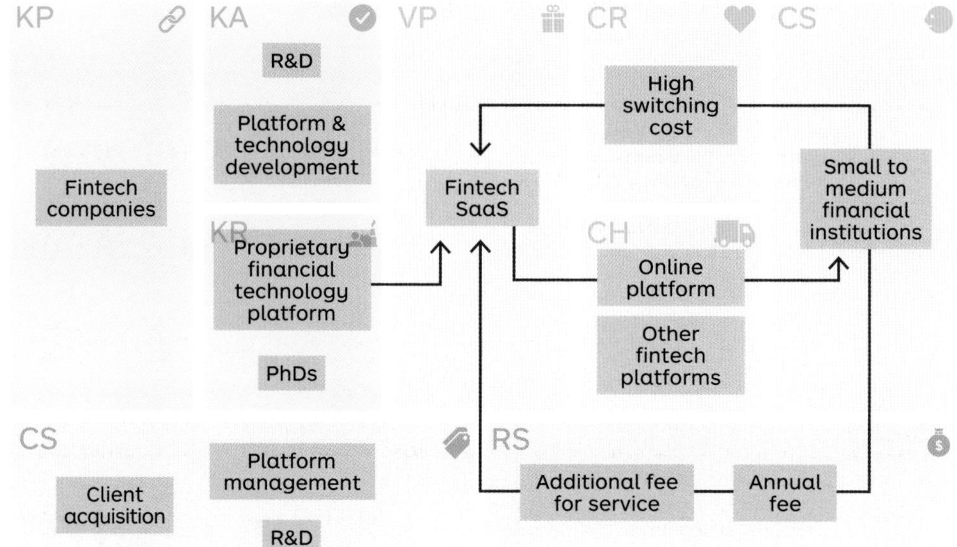

OneConnect Business Model

Assessment

OneConnect built a powerful SaaS business model that performs well on several dimensions. The substantial investments in hiring top developers, conducting fintech R&D, and building and maintaining its platform are compensated by customer lock-in, scalability of its services, recurring revenues, and strong protection of its business model.

Assessment Questions for Leaders

Frontstage

Question	−3	−2	−1	0	+1	+2	+3
Market Explorers: How large and attractive is the untapped market potential we are going after?				X			
Channel Kings: Do we have large-scale and, ideally, direct access to our end-customer?						X	
Gravity Creators: How easy or difficult is it for our customers to leave or switch to another company?							X

Backstage

Question	−3	−2	−1	0	+1	+2	+3
Resource Castles: Do we own key resources that are difficult or impossible to copy and which give us a significant competitive advantage?							X
Activity Differentiators: Do we create significant value for customers because we perform and configure activities in disruptively innovative ways?						X	
Scalers: How rapidly and how easily can we grow our business model without substantial additional resources and activities (e.g., building infrastructure, finding talent)?							X

Profit Formula

Question	−3	−2	−1	0	+1	+2	+3
Revenue Differentiators: Do we use strong revenue streams and pricing mechanisms to monetize value creation for customers?						X	
Cost Differentiators: Is our cost structure conventional or disruptive?				X			
Margin Monsters: Do we have strong margins from low costs and high prices?				X			

Financial institutions that adopt the OneConnect technology platform incur significant switching costs if they leave. Moving to another platform could create substantial downtime and re-training costs for clients.[118] Like for any SaaS, provider lock-in can be substantial. In the finance industry it is even higher, due to security reasons, data confidentiality, and regulation.

OneConnect's proprietary technology is very hard to copy and it constantly innovates. The initial platform was built for Ping An before the organization decided to leverage it for external clients through OneConnect's services. This expansion allowed OneConnect to invest substantially in advanced intellectual property and infrastructure, because its investments serve hundreds of financial institutions, including its owner Ping An.

The company employs legions of data scientists and holds thousands of patents. It constantly develops and updates its technology and platform in order to stay ahead of the curve. OneConnect has one of the most accurate biometric identification systems in the world with 99.8% accuracy.[119]

The SaaS business model requires substantial upfront investments to put the platform in place. However, after this initial investment phase, OneConnect can easily expand into new geographical territories with relatively low investments. OneConnect's hundreds of products can be deployed anywhere around the world.[120]

Assessment Questions

Salesforce

In 1999 Salesforce.com disrupts the customer relationship management (CRM) arena by offering CRM-as-a-service over the Internet. Salesforce unlocks a new market and continuously strengthens its business model with new innovations.

Salesforce.com was founded in 1999 with the goal of "making enterprise software as easy to use as a website like amazon .com." Salesforce pioneered the software-as-a-service (Saas) for customer relationship management tools. The company didn't stop there and has constantly improved its services and business model. We distinguish between two, nonexhaustive, business model phases: the early business model in 1999 and extensions starting in 2005.

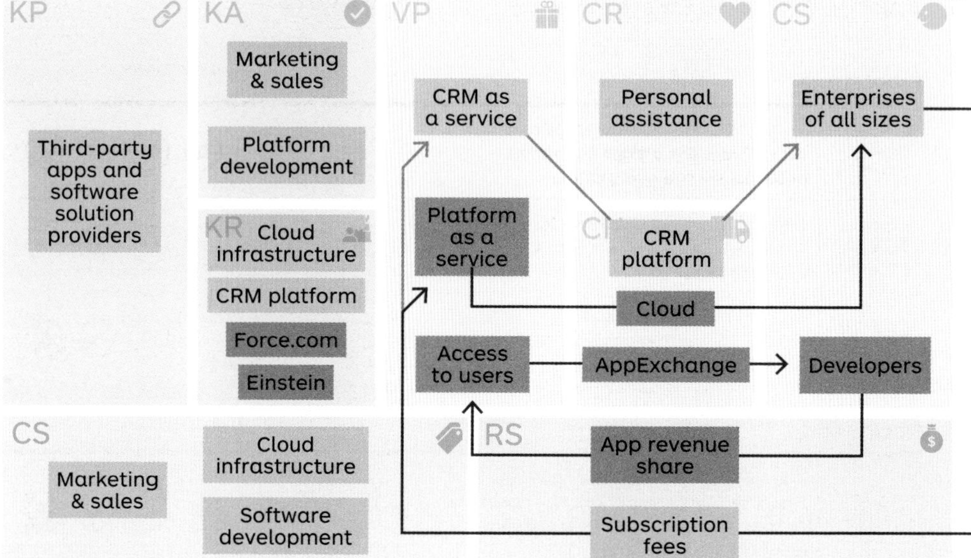

Salesforce.com Business Model

Assessment
Salesforce pioneered the SaaS model, which performs well on several business model dimensions that largely compensate for some of its shortcomings. Once its platform is in place it can scale its services easily and maintain a constant and direct relationship with its customers. The subscription model leads to predictable and recurring revenues and higher customer lifetime value. This compensates for the lower margins due to infrastructure costs.

Salesforce expands its business model in 2005, which addresses some of its initial weaknesses like relatively low switching costs and low protectability of its business model.

Early Business Model (1999) – No Software
Salesforce's platform was unique to the CRM world in that its services could be deployed rapidly without infrastructure investments. Customers didn't require hardware investments and software installations like incumbent CRM providers. Salesforce customers accessed the CRM service through the cloud and payed a recurring subscription fee.

Business Model Extensions – AppExchange, Force.com, and Einstein
Salesforce didn't stop at trailblazing the software-as-a-service model. The company continuously evolved and strengthened their business model over time.

Assessment Questions for Leaders

X = Early business model

X = Business model extensions

Frontstage

Question	Score
Market Explorers: How large and attractive is the untapped market potential we are going after?	−3 −2 −1 0 +1 +2 +3
Channel Kings: Do we have large-scale and, ideally, direct access to our end-customer?	−3 −2 −1 0 +1 +2 +3
Gravity Creators: How easy or difficult is it for our customers to leave or switch to another company?	−3 −2 −1 0 +1 +2 +3

Backstage

Question	Score
Resource Castles: Do we own key resources that are difficult or impossible to copy and which give us a significant competitive advantage?	−3 −2 −1 0 +1 +2 +3
Activity Differentiators: Do we create significant value for customers because we perform and configure activities in disruptively innovative ways?	−3 −2 −1 0 +1 +2 +3
Scalers: How rapidly and how easily can we grow our business model without substantial additional resources and activities (e.g., building infrastructure, finding talent)?	−3 −2 −1 0 +1 +2 +3

Profit Formula

Question	Score
Revenue Differentiators: Do we use strong revenue streams and pricing mechanisms to monetize value creation for customers?	−3 −2 −1 0 +1 +2 +3
Cost Differentiators: Is our cost structure conventional or disruptive?	−3 −2 −1 0 +1 +2 +3
Margin Monsters: Do we have strong margins from low costs and high prices?	−3 −2 −1 0 +1 +2 +3

Salesforce was visionary in predicting the potential of the cloud. A pioneer of SaaS, it opens up CRM services from Fortune 500 companies to the wider market of organizations of all sizes.

Since customers access Salesforce directly via the cloud, the company maintains a permanent customer relationship. Salesforce can continuously push upgrades and new functionalities to its entire customer base.

Because Salesforce provides its service in the cloud it can easily scale and with minimal cost.

Salesforce shifts the transactional license sales models of incumbents to recurring revenues from a service subscription. It increases the customer lifetime value of each customer.

Salesforce's net margins are significantly lower than those of its incumbent competitors. Offering CRM-as-a-service requires investments in hosting, monitoring, customer support, and account management. However, strengths in other areas largely compensate for this weakness.

In 2008 Salesforce releases Force.com (now called Lightning Platform) that allows customers to build their own custom applications on the platform. This substantially scales stickiness and increases switching costs. It extends stickiness by launching Einstein, a service that delivers artificial intelligence (AI) capabilities and allows developers to build apps.

In 2005, Salesforce launches AppExchange, a platform for third-party software that integrates with its CRM. It builds up a large library of hard-to-copy third-party software and shifts from a simple service provider to a platform castle.

Industry	Disruptor
Messaging	WhatsApp, WeChat
Auto	Tesla
Retail	Amazon, Alibaba
Hotel	Airbnb
Taxi	Uber, DiDi
TV & movie	Netflix
Mobile phones	Apple, Xiaomi
Music	Spotify
Telecommunications	Skype
Recruitment	LinkedIn
Travel booking	Expedia
Venture Capital	Andreessen Horowitz

...to be disrupted

Banking
Pharmaceuticals
Legal services
Education
Manufacturing
Healthcare
Insurance
Real estate
Construction
Energy production and distribution
Transport and delivery

What about your industry?

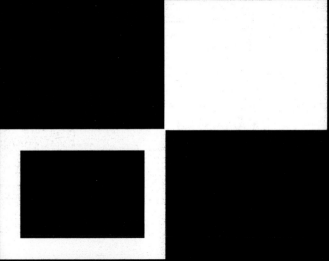

Business Model Shifts

A business model shift describes an organization's transformation from a declining business model to a more competitive one. For example, the shift from product to service. However, in some contexts, the reverse shift, from service to product, might make just as much sense.

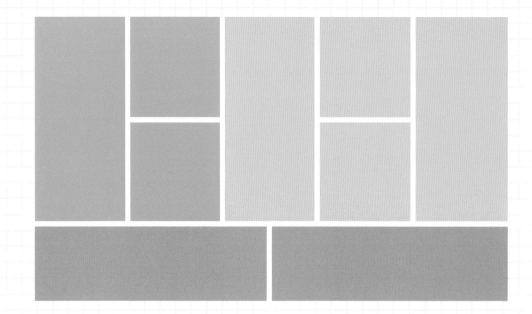

Shift Pattern Library

Value Proposition Shifts

Frontstage Driven Shifts

Backstage Driven Shifts

Profit Formula Driven Shifts

Shift Patterns

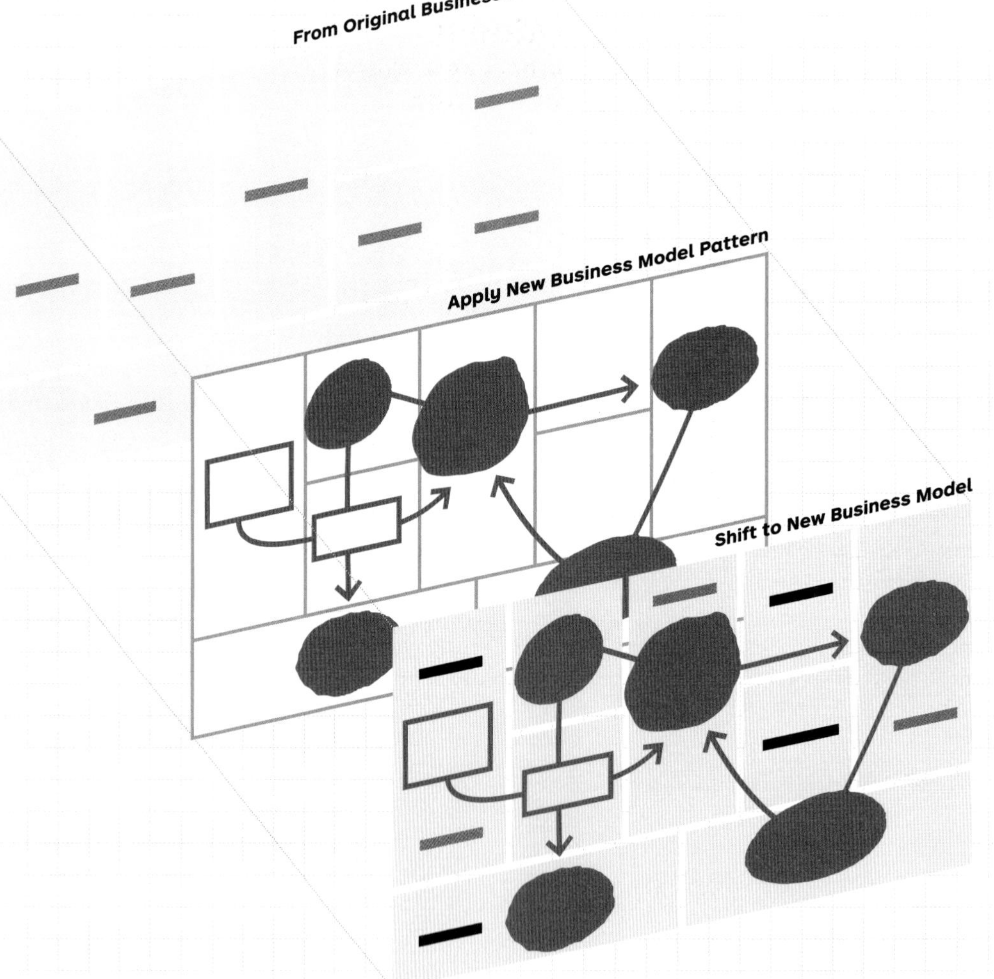

From Original Business Model...

The companies we portray in this section all started from an existing business model. This existing business model is often outdated and in decline and requires an overhaul.

Apply New Business Model Pattern

Twelve different shift patterns that established companies can apply to substantially improve and boost an existing business model are highlighted. We describe each pattern so that you can make use of it as a reference library.

...Shift to New Business Model

Each case serves to highlight a pattern in action. The company's entire business model isn't outlined, we just show how it applied a particular pattern to shift from an old business model to a new, more competitive business model. In reality, an entire business model has many more building blocks that we omit to focus on the shift.

Legend

- From Original Business Model 
- Apply New Business Model Pattern 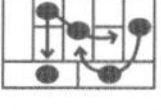
- Shift to New Business Model 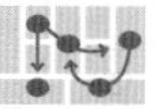
- Pattern Building Blocks 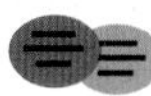
- Optional Pattern Building Blocks 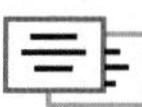
- Original Business Model Blocks 
- Other Business Model Blocks 

From Product to Recurring Service

p. 232 Hilti

From Low Tech to High Tech

p. 236 Netflix

From Sales to Platform

p. 238 The App Store

Value Proposition Shifts

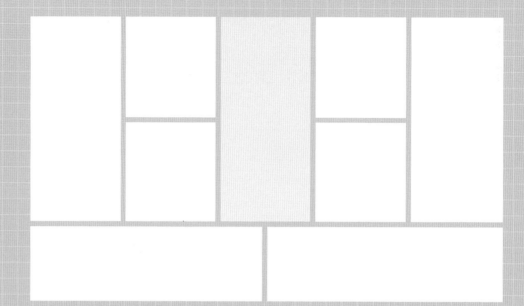

A radical shift of the value created for customers

From Product to Recurring Service

is the shift from manufacturing (and/or buying) and selling products toward providing a recurring service. Selling products on a transactional basis requires a continuous effort for every sale and it is often unpredictable. Recurring services require upfront customer acquisition costs that lead to recurring revenues. Revenues become more predictable and grow exponentially, because you build on top of a continuously growing base of customers.

STRATEGIC REFLECTION
How might we grow recurring and predictable revenues by providing a recurring service, rather than selling a product?

Upfront acquisition costs per customer might be higher, but revenues become more predictable and the lifetime value of customers often increases. Product and/or technology innovation can often provide the foundation for new services.

EXAMPLE
HILTI

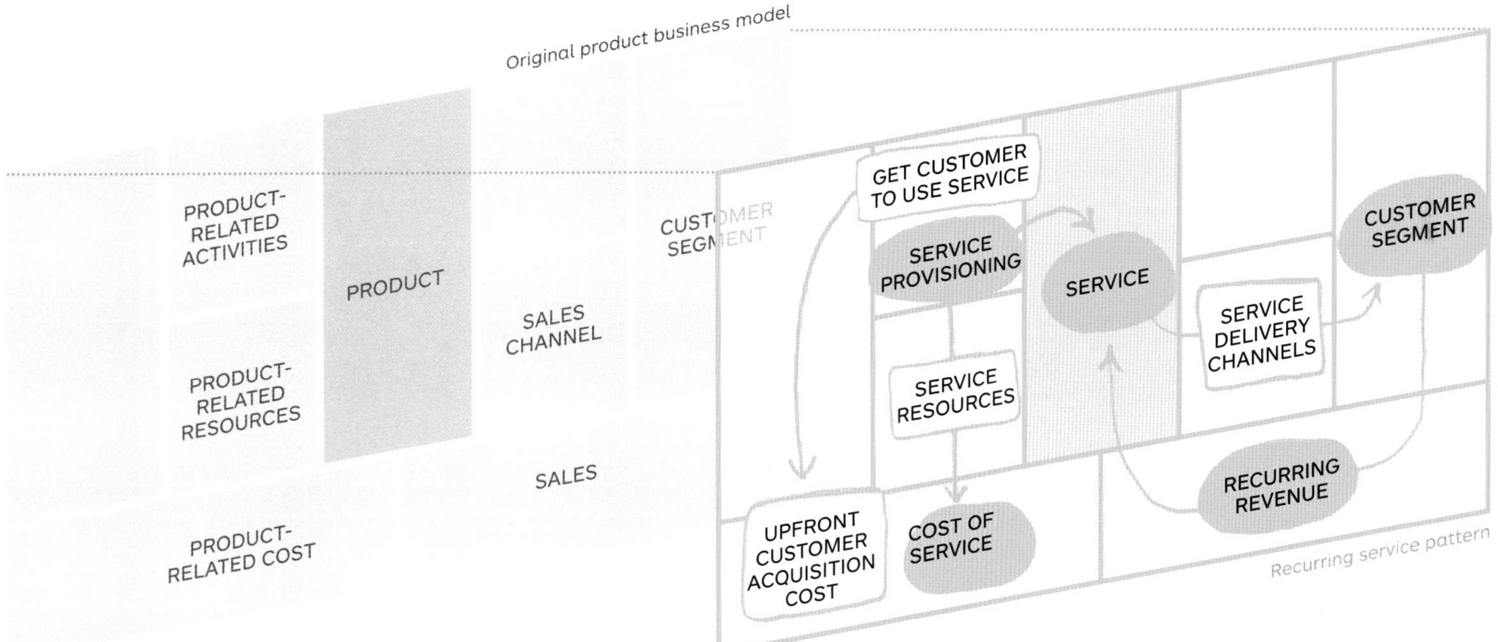

From Product to Recurring Service
2000 ~~~ 2003

Hilti

Hilti shifts from selling high quality tools to selling tool fleet management services to construction companies, after a key customer requests a holistic tool management system to increase productivity.

In 2000, one of Hilti's customers asked for a holistic tool management solution. That made Hilti realize that customers didn't want to own tools, but always wanted their workers to work productively. Hilti began an initial pilot program for tool fleet management in Switzerland and eventually rolled out the service worldwide in 2003.

With tool fleet management, Hilti became more relevant to construction companies by reducing nonproductive time for workers and adding a gain of taking on more customer jobs (e.g., tool repair).

Hilti also discovered that customers were willing to lease more tools than they had ever purchased. Some even asked Hilti to include non-Hilti tools in the service to completely prevent nonproductive time due to broken tools.

When the 2008 financial crisis hit the construction sector, many stopped purchasing new equipment. Yet Hilti's business model shift from a product to a recurring service allowed it to overcome the crisis and it has continued to grow since.

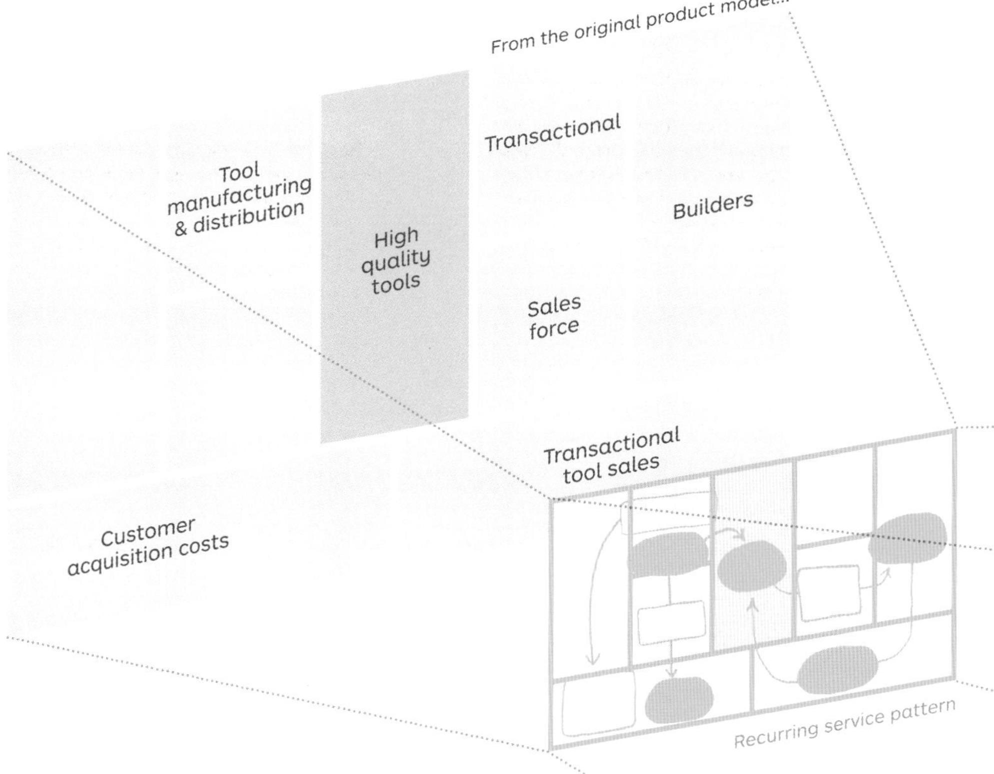

1 From Product to Recurring Service and Revenues

Managers of building companies have a lot more to worry about than just buying tools. Hilti recognizes that in 2000 and starts offering to track, repair, replace, and upgrade the whole tool fleet for their clients. This increases their productivity by ensuring they always have the right tools, properly maintained and reliable at all times. Hilti allows customers to lease the tools through a monthly subscription rather than paying for them upfront – enabling predictability of costs for building company managers and recurring revenues for Hilti.

2 From Product-Related Activities to Service Provisioning

Hilti evolves its key activities from its core of manufacturing and sales to fleet management activities that enable tool tracking, repairing, replacement, and upgrading.

3 From Sales Channel to Service Delivery Channels

Hilti retrains its sales force to speak to executives rather than project managers, and about logistics and efficiency rather than tools. It adds new online service channels to the traditional sales channel, raising awareness about the service, helping fleet customers access their inventory online, and enabling them to access Hilti easily in case of a problem with their tools.

4 From a Product to a Service Cost Structure

Hilti's cost structure adapts to this new service orientation with new fleet management costs. To date, this shift has added over CHF1 billion worth of receivable volume to Hilti's balance sheet. Even customer acquisition costs (CAC) increase, due to the longer sales and contracting process with building company managers. The CAC, however, is now a one-time cost, leading to recurring revenues and opportunities for additional revenues with the long-term relationship.

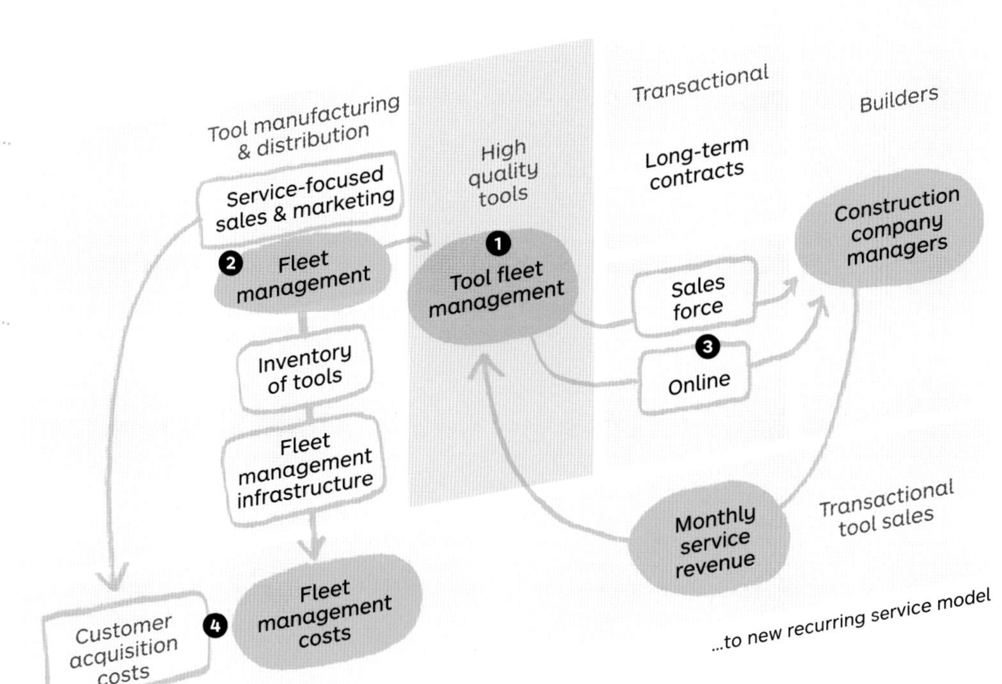

1.5

million tools

Hilti had 1.5 million tools under fleet management in 2015.[1]

2

billion CHF

Total contract value of all tools under fleet management in 2018.[2]

"The big benefit of recurring service revenues helped us to stabilize our business during the [global financial] crisis—a time when most contractors wouldn't purchase new equipment"

—DR. CHRISTOPH LOOS

CEO of Hilti

From Low Tech to High Tech

is the shift from basic, often labor-intensive, low-tech value propositions toward technology-based value propositions. This shift allows scaling reach and increasing price, which leads to a boost in revenues. The increase in price and revenues compensates for new technology-related costs and often leads to higher margins.

STRATEGIC REFLECTION
How might we scale our reach, increase price, and boost revenues by transforming a low-tech value proposition into a high-tech value proposition? Which new technology activities, skills, and resources are required to accomplish this shift? Which new tech costs does this create? How attractive are the resulting margins?

EXAMPLE
Netflix

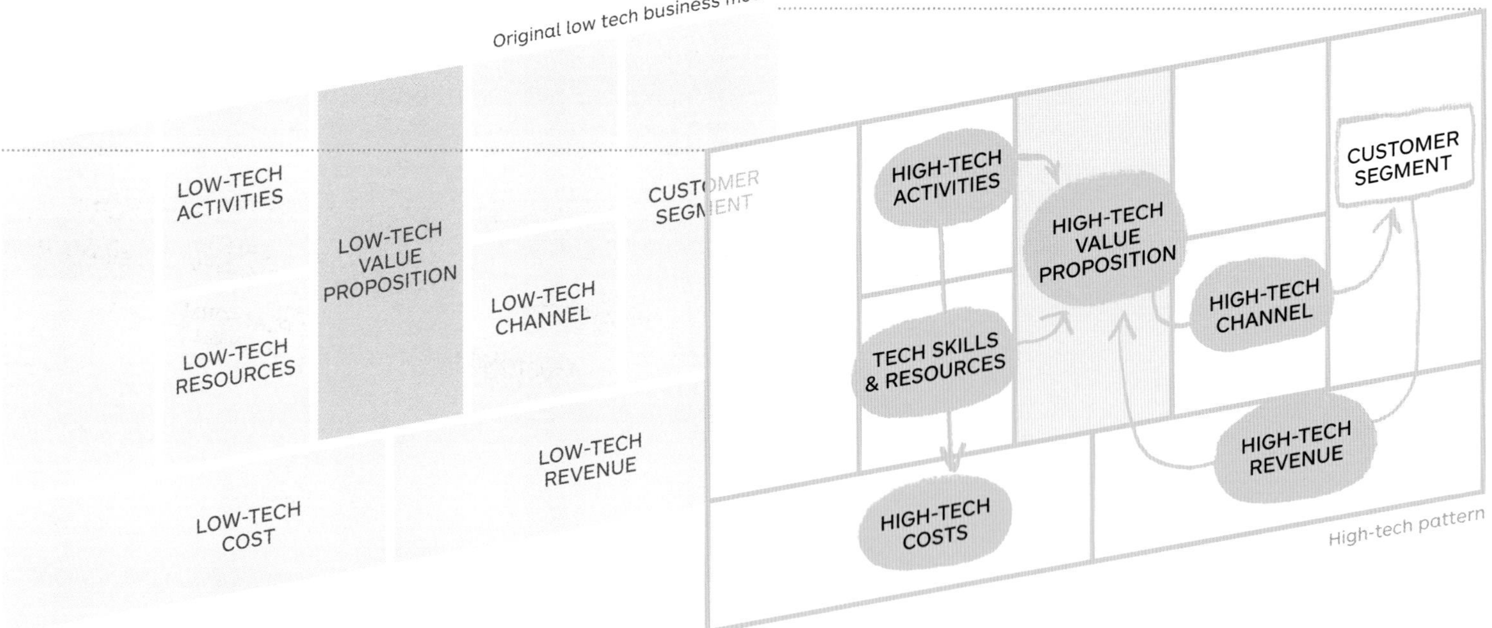

From Sales to Platform

is the shift from value-chain activities and selling products toward products that become a platform for third-party products and value-added services. Value increases for customers because they don't just purchase a product, but buy into a platform ecosystem. The value for third-party product and service providers is access to a customer base. Platforms are harder to disrupt than simple products because they create resource castles network effects (see p. 164).

STRATEGIC REFLECTION

How might we gain a competitive advantage by establishing ourselves as the platform connecting our customers with third-party products and service providers?

This will allow us to increase value for our customers and build an ecosystem of third-party product and service providers. Platform ecosystems are harder to replicate than copying products.

EXAMPLE
iPhone & App Store

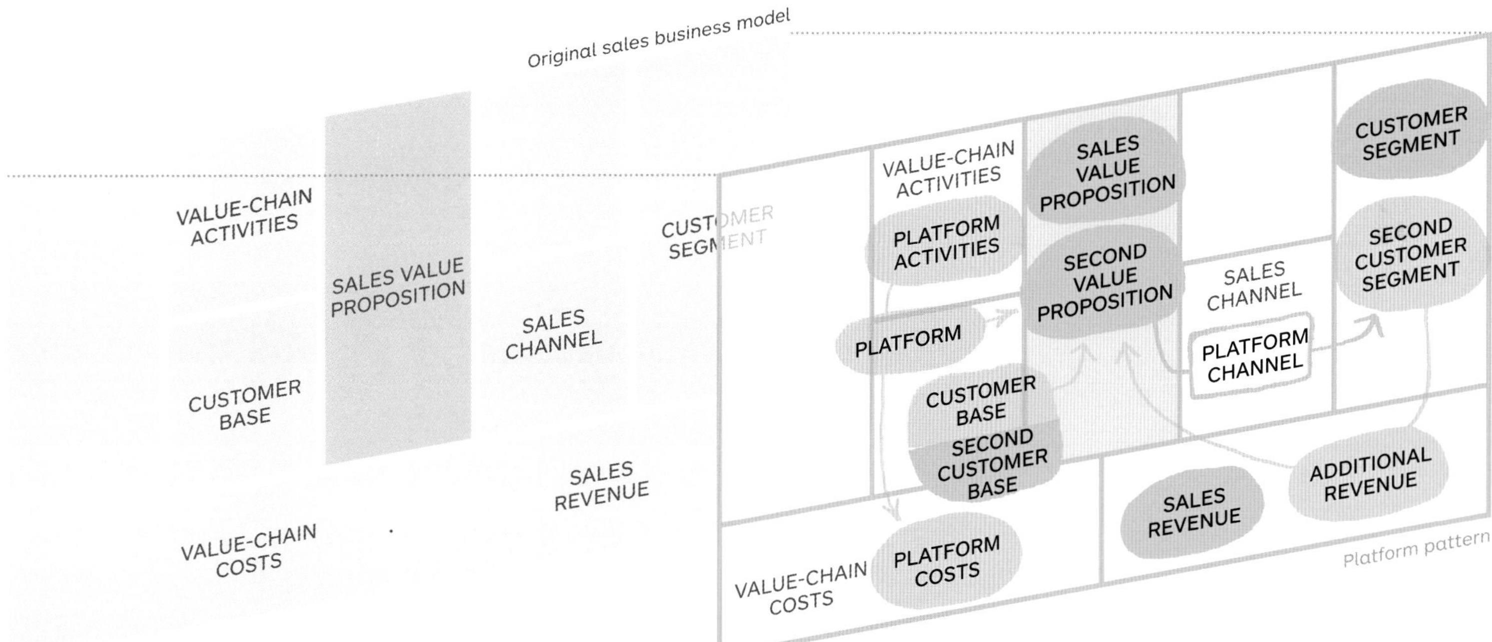

From Low Tech to High Tech
1998 ~~~ 2007

Netflix

Netflix shifts from a mail order DVD rental company to an online streaming platform in 2007 when Internet speeds and consumer devices align with Reed Hastings's vision of "movies on the Internet."

In 1998 Reed Hastings and Marc Randolph launched Netflix as an online DVD rental service. They believed it was the right product and service for the Internet at the time.

Yet from the start the founders had a vision of a video streaming platform. Netflix invested 1 to 2% of its revenue in downloading services, waiting patiently to transform its business model toward streaming with increasing Internet bandwidth.[3]

In 2007, Netflix successfully shifted from low tech to high tech, replacing physical DVDs with online streaming as its main source of revenue.

Revenues grew tenfold in the following decade, with physical DVD shipping no longer constraining scalability. By 2018, 96% of revenue came from streaming.

Netflix adapted its business model again in 2013 and began producing original content. In 2019, Netflix spent an estimated $15 billion on content.[4]

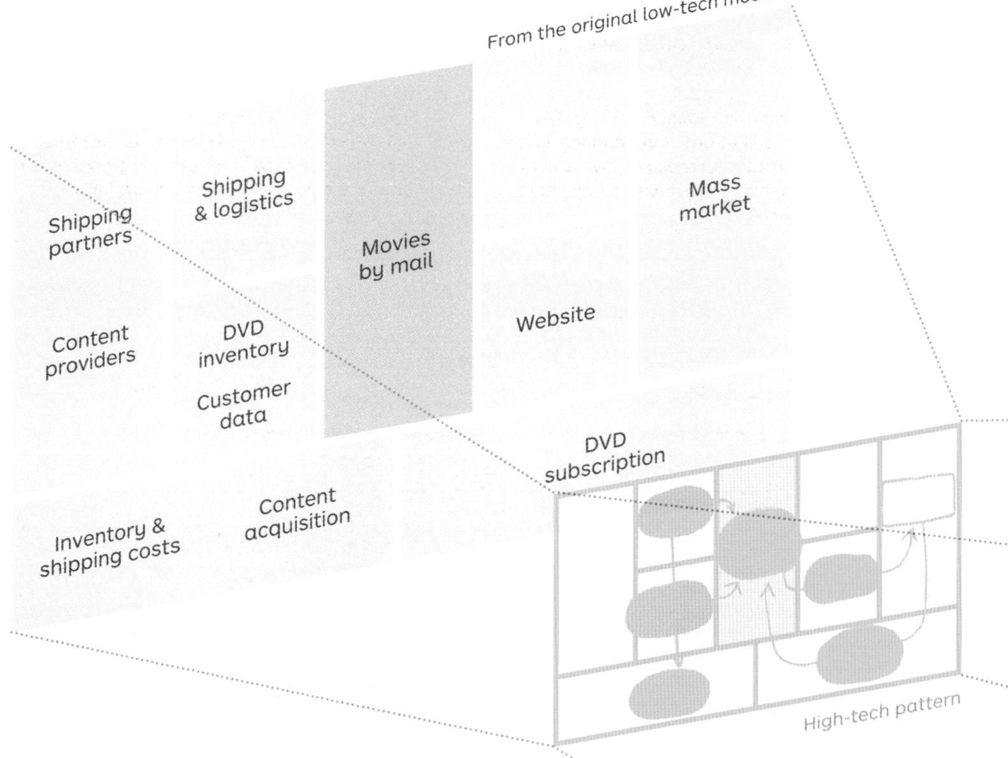

1 From Low-Tech to High-Tech Value Proposition

Netflix launches as an online DVD rental business in 1998, with the vision to move to streaming as soon as Internet speeds permit. In 2007 it makes that vision a reality and shifts to streaming content online.

2 From Low-Tech to High-Tech Activities

To deliver streaming Netflix executes a major shift in key activities. They move from labor-intensive activities such as shipping and logistics to tech activities such as streaming platform development and maintenance. Netflix also expands into licensing and producing content.

3 From Low-Tech to High-Tech Skills and Resources

Streaming results in major changes to key resources, with the streaming platform replacing the DVD inventory. Software and network engineering skills become central. Customer-viewing data and recommendation algorithms gain even more importance with the shift to streaming. Data drives content investment decisions and helps customers find relevant content.

4 From Low-Tech to High-Tech Costs

With the major shift in activities and resources Netflix's cost structure evolves from that of a logistics company to one of a software and platform company. Main costs are now platform development and maintenance. In the future Netflix will also increase its investments in content licensing and their own production.

5 From Low-Tech to High-Tech Revenues

Netflix experiments with several subscription plans. To boost growth in 2007 it lowers the price of its streaming plan to $9.99 per month (compared to its DVD subscription of $19.95 per month in 2004). While revenue per customer declines, the ease of access and global reach leads to high customer growth and subsequently greater revenues from its high-tech streaming value proposition.

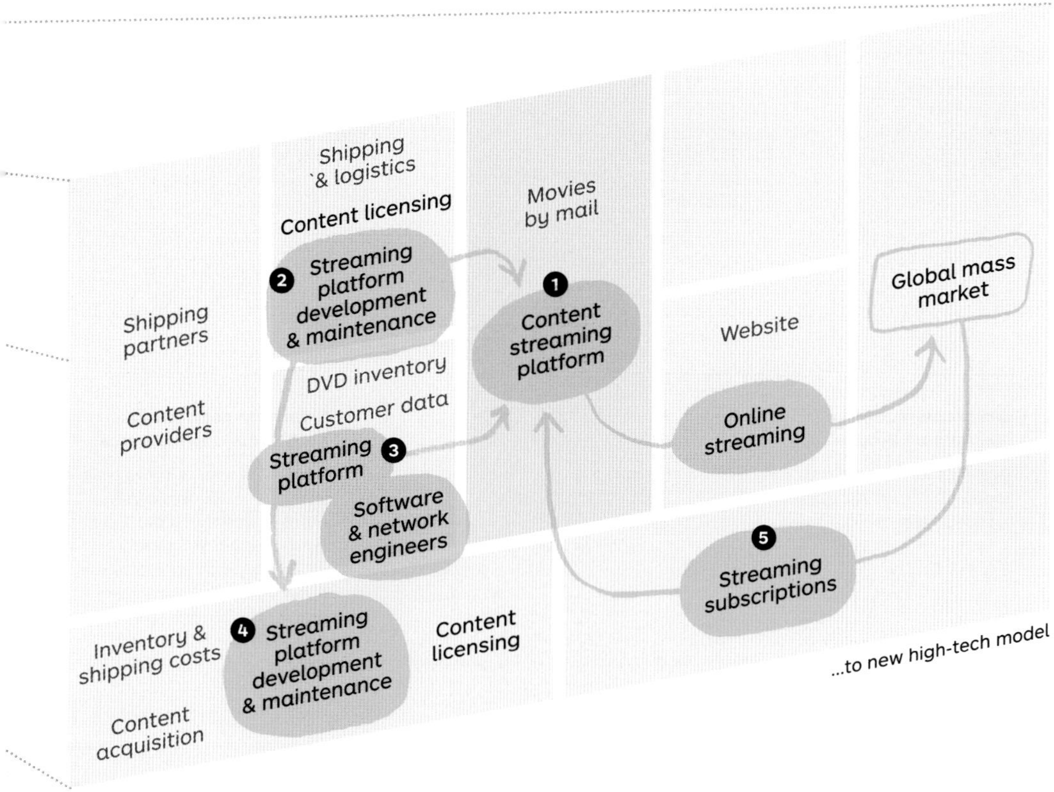

10%
of U.S. TV viewing

Netflix now accounts for 10% of U.S. TV viewing time. Netflix says it streams 100 million hours a day to TV screens in the United States.[5]

158
million

Paid subscribers globally as of September 2019.[6]

"DVDs will continue to generate big profits in the near future. Netflix has at least another decade of dominance ahead of it. But movies over the Internet are coming, and at some point it will become big business."

—REED HASTINGS IN 2005,
Netflix founder

From Sales to Platform

2007 ~~ 2008

The App Store

With the release of the App Store in 2008, Apple shifts its business model from selling hardware and music to a platform business connecting millions of app developers with iPhone users. This shift significantly increases customer value, creates a lock-in, and produces strong network effects.

Apple launched the iPhone in 2007 and the App Store, its platform for smartphone apps, in 2008.

Steve Jobs was initially hesitant to let third-party developers in the App Store but changed his mind as it ultimately fit into his vision of adding value to the iPhone. The App Store became a compelling, complementary value proposition to the iPhone. The two were promoted as one, with the memorable 2009 tagline: "There's an App for That."

The App Store enabled Apple to shift its business model from selling a phone to managing a platform. This platform became so powerful that in 2019, the U.S. Supreme Court allowed an antitrust lawsuit against Apple to proceed (based on the premise that Apple has an effective monopoly over the App Store).

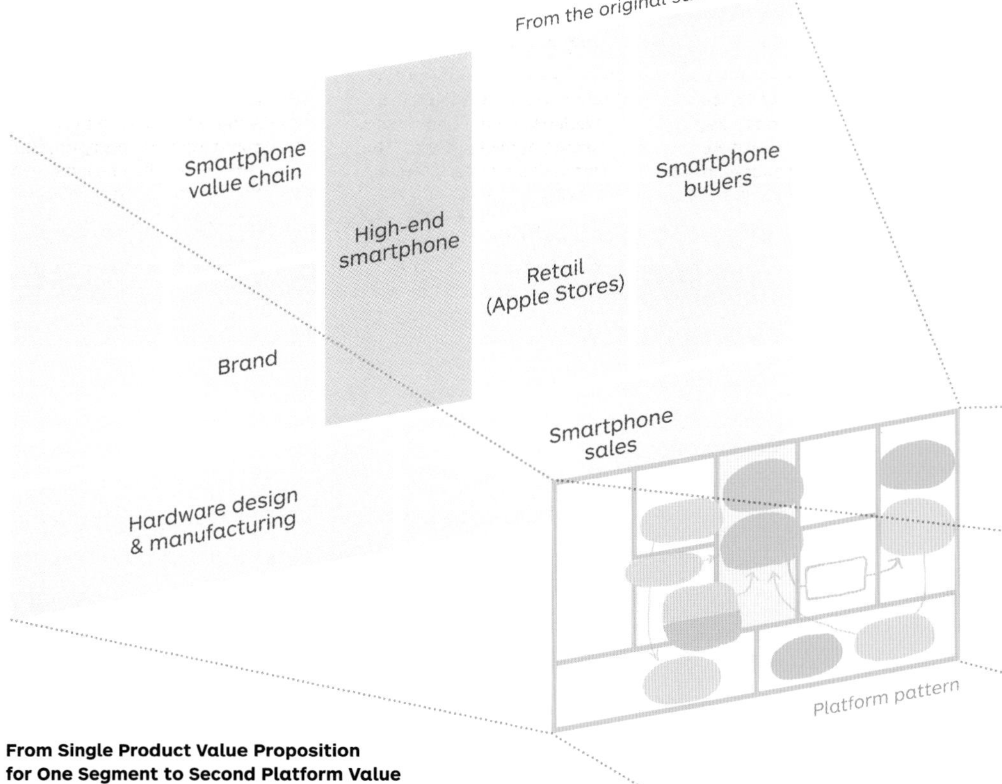

1 From Single Product Value Proposition for One Segment to Second Platform Value Proposition to Another Segment

One year after launching the iPhone, Apple releases the App Store, shifting from just selling phones to becoming a platform. This has two consequences:

1. The attractiveness of the iPhone grows with every additional game, utility, and entertainment app added to the App Store.
2. Apple's mass of iPhone users willing to pay for apps becomes an alluring value proposition to attract app developers.

Apple is the first mobile phone manufacturer to shift toward becoming a mobile-first platform that connects consumers with app developers on a large global scale.

2 From Sales Channel to Platform as a Channel

Apple also extends its channels with the shift from sales to platform. The App Store becomes a continuous platform channel that connects iPhone owners with app developers. Retail and Apple Stores where buyers get their phones is a much more transactional sales channel.

3 From Value Chain Activities to Platform Activities

Apple continues to manage value chain activities for its smartphones, yet adds key activities such as App Store development and maintenance to enable its platform business.

4 From Nonexistent to Strong Network Effects

The App Store becomes a significant part of Apple's business model and creates strong network effects. The more iPhone users, the more attractive the value proposition for app developers becomes. The more app developers, the more apps on the platform and, subsequently the more attractive the value proposition for iPhone buyers.

5 From Sales to Additional Revenue Stream

The App Store generates a new source of revenue for Apple—taking a 15 to 30% commission on every app and subscription purchased within the App Store. Later in Apple's history this recurring revenue helps Apple diversify away from a purely transactional, hardware sales model toward more service revenues.

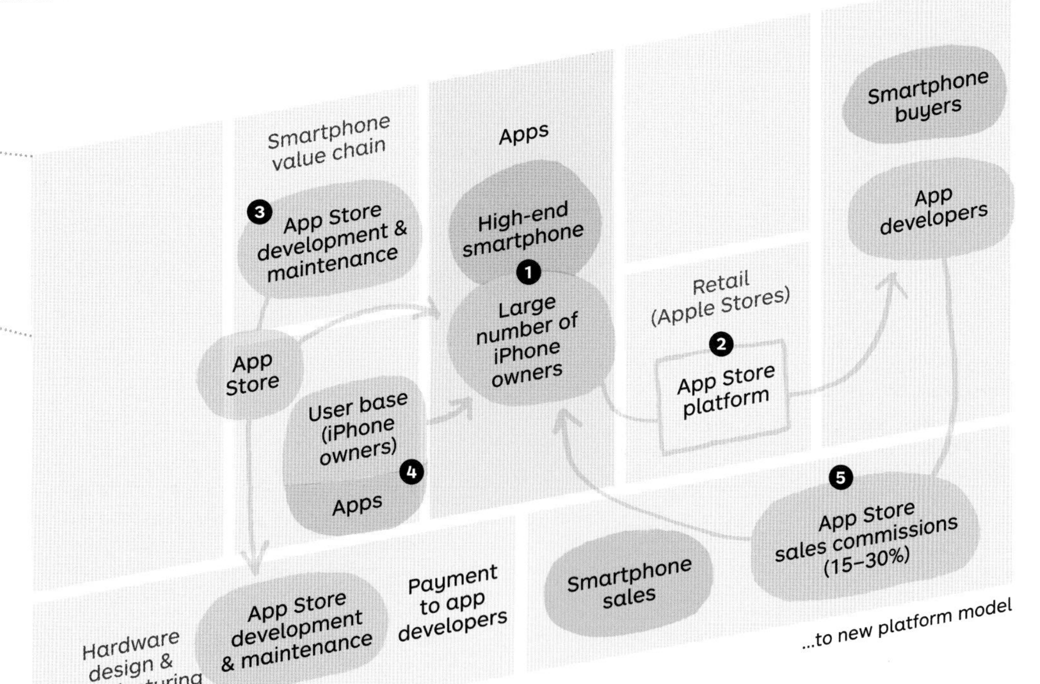

2 million

The App Store launched with 552 apps and has grown to 2 million with over 180 billion apps downloaded in the past decade.[7]

$120 billion

Amount Apple has paid developers since the App Store launched.[8]

Number of Available Apps in the Apple App Store[9]

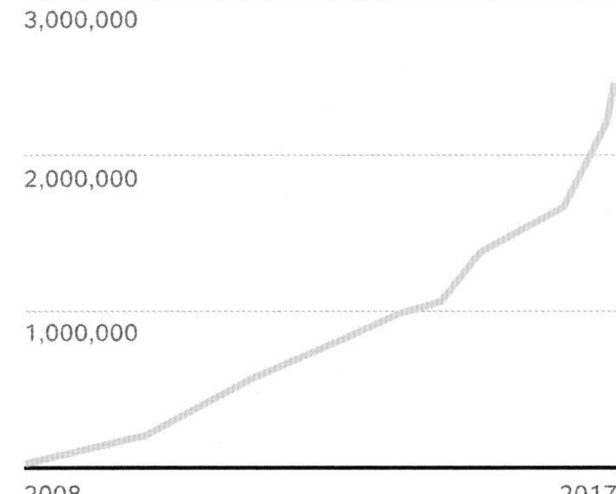

From High Tech to Low Tech

2003 ~~~ 2006

Nintendo Wii

In the early 2000s, Nintendo no longer has the means to compete on high-tech gaming consoles. In 2006, it turns a weakness into an opportunity and releases the Wii. The Wii features inferior technology but is an instant success with casual gamers.

In 2003, the profits of the Japanese game and console developer Nintendo fell by 38%. Several major game developers pulled their support for the GameCube, Nintendo's main console at the time. The company was in a "state of crisis." It had to react and decided to take a different approach.

Nintendo refocused on its core mission of play over power. It acknowledged that it could no longer compete in the race to build the most powerful console with the best graphics at the lowest cost. It sidestepped competition and released the Wii in 2006—a simplified console targeted at the mass market of casual gamers.

Nintendo sold five times more Wii than GameCube consoles. It regained market leadership for the next few years by shifting from high-tech to low-tech consoles with off-the-shelf components.[10]

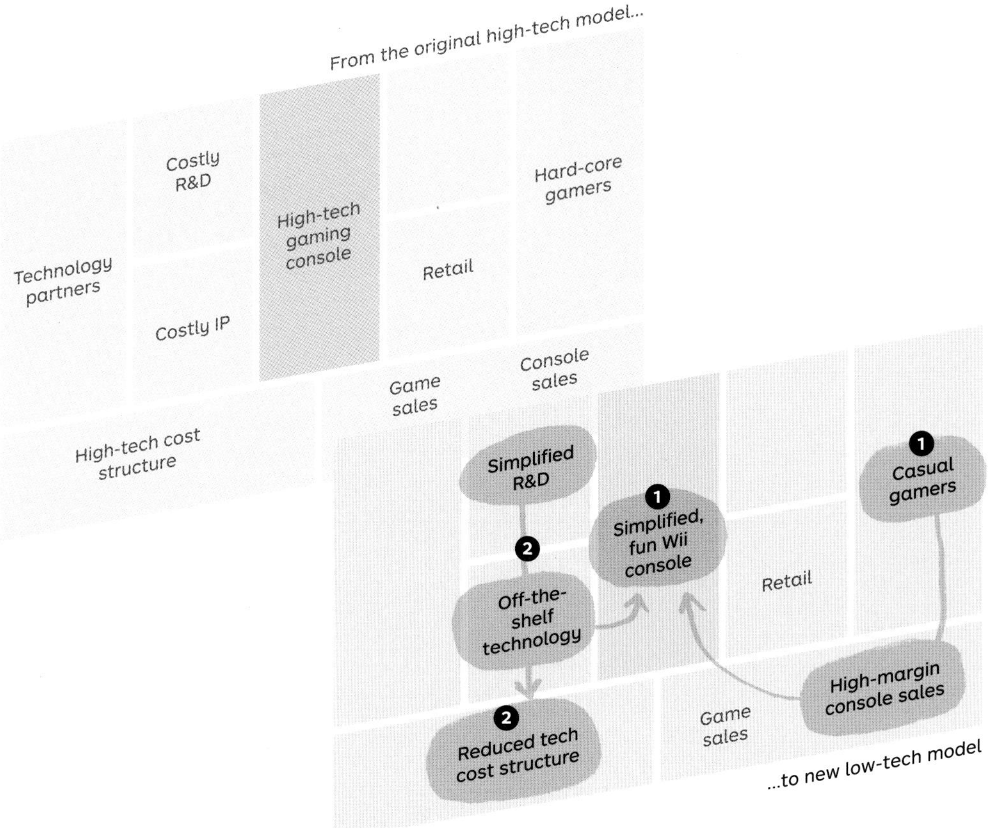

1 From High Tech for Traditional Customer Segment to Low Tech for Untapped Customer Segment

With the Wii, Nintendo decides to break the rules of competition in the game console market. It shifts from competing on technology performance for hardcore gamers to fun gameplay and motion control for casual gamers, all enabled by cheap, off-the-shelf technology. The Wii's main competitors at the time, the Xbox 360 from Microsoft and PS3 from Sony, have 20 times more graphic processing power and more than four times as much computing power. Yet the unique low-tech Wii resonates with the large and untapped market of casual gamers.

2 From High-Tech Cost Structure to Low-Tech Cost Structure

Nintendo shifts from costly high-tech activities and resources to lower-cost ones, because the Wii makes do with less processing power and lower quality graphics. Manufacturing the Wii is much simpler and cheaper because it uses off-the-shelf components. The significant changes in the cost structure allow Nintendo to make a profit on every Wii sold, as compared to Sony and Microsoft, who need to subsidize their consoles.

From Platform to Sales

2007 ~~~ 2009

Amazon Private Label

In 2009, Amazon expands from platform to sales by launching Amazon private labels. It copies third-party sellers who created successful businesses by sourcing products absent from Amazon's platform. Amazon sees this as an opportunity to create its own line of products.

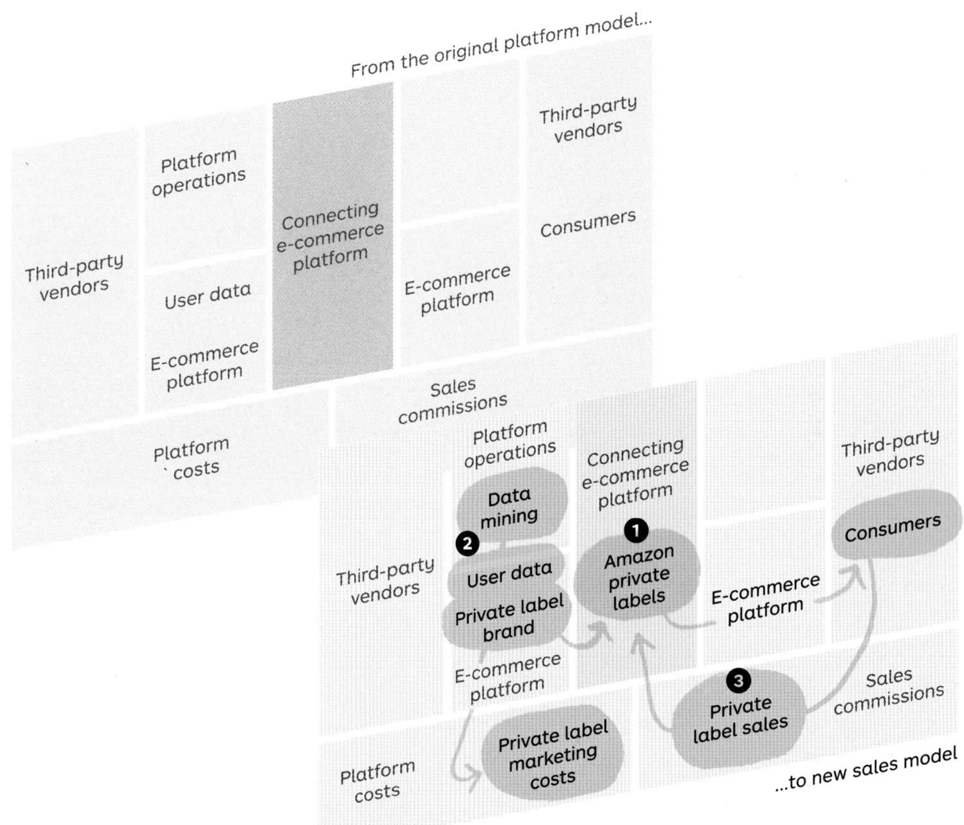

In 1999 Amazon launched its third-party seller marketplace and established itself as an incredibly successful e-commerce platform for other retailers. In 2007 Amazon began to use its platform to sell its own electronic devices (Kindle e-reader) and expanded to private label products under the AmazonBasics brand.

While many companies aim to shift from sales to platform, Amazon executed a reverse shift from platform to sales. With its private label business Amazon started to compete with third-party suppliers who are also customers of its e-commerce business.

Amazon continuously expanded its private label product catalog with a wide selection (from electronics to clothing and everyday accessories) and lower prices.

1 From Platform Value Proposition to Sales Value Proposition

With Amazon marketplace the company built the leading e-commerce platform for third-party products. In 2007 Amazon decides to shift towards also selling its own branded products. The Kindle e-reader is the first. In 2009 Amazon launches its private label business under the AmazonBasics name. It expands from selling charging cables and batteries to thousands of everyday items.

2 From Platform Activities to Sales-Focused Activities

Amazon uses the consumer data from its platform business to identify product candidates for its private label business. Amazon markets successful product candidates under the AmazonBasics brand. It purchases products in bulk from retailers already transacting on its platform, rebrands them and sells them as recommended products on its e-commerce platform.

3 From Platform Revenues to Sales Revenues

Amazon expands its revenue streams from transaction commissions to sales margins with the shift from platform to sales. Revenues from selling its own private label products are an attractive addition to a pure commission-based model.

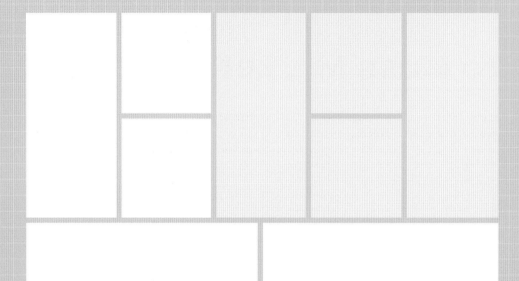

Frontstage Driven Shifts

A radical shift of who is targeted and how products and services are delivered

From Niche Market to Mass Market

is the shift from niche market player to mass market player. This often requires a simplification of the value proposition to cater to a larger market. The lower price that such a simplified value proposition commands is compensated by a larger volume of revenues from the mass market. This shift requires marketing activities, channels, and a brand that are tailored to the mass market.

STRATEGIC REFLECTION
How might we simplify our value proposition to break out of a niche market and cater to a mass market? How might we change marketing and brand to reach a mass market? How can we compensate for lower prices and increased marketing costs with more revenues from a larger mass market?

EXAMPLE
TED

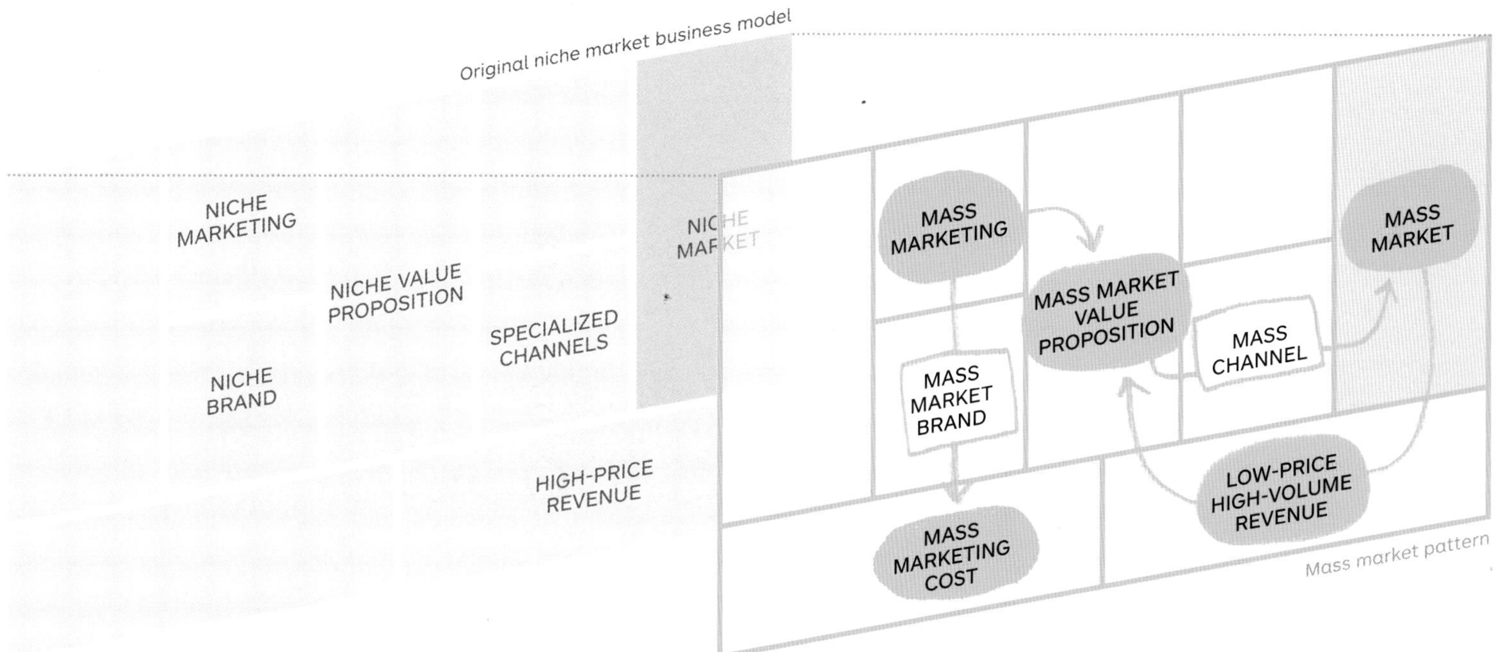

TED

TED puts six TED Talks online in 2006 and the success is overwhelming. TED transforms from an invite-only, niche conference to a mass, online destination for the intellectually curious.

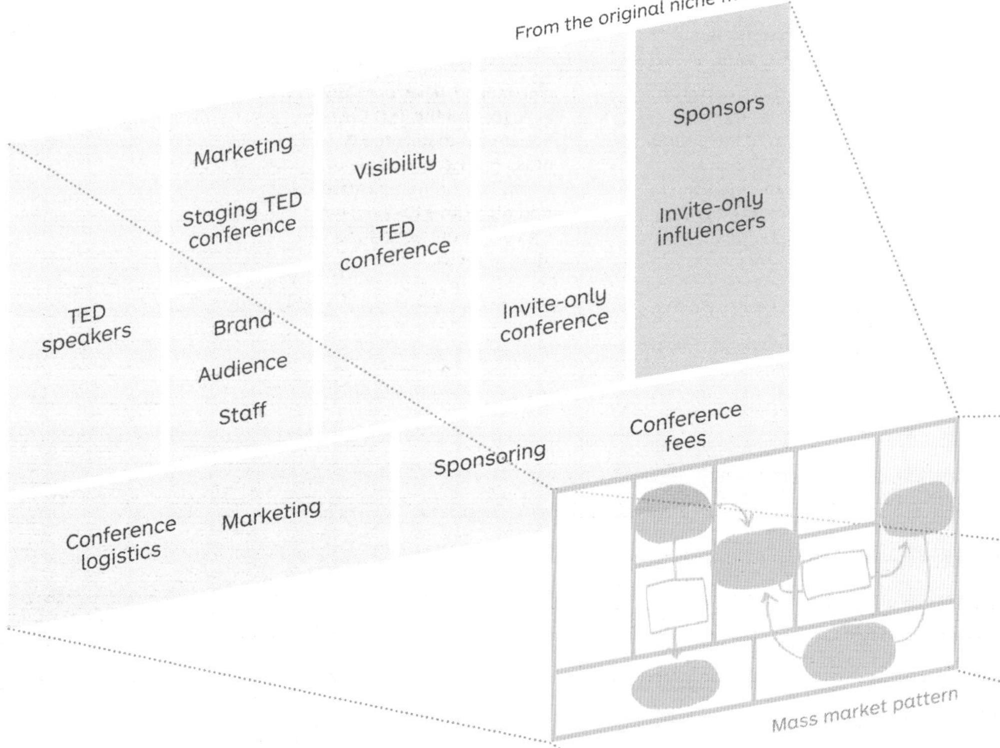

TED launched in 1984 as a conference for the intellectually curious on the topics of technology, entertainment, and design. The first conference in California lost money and the event wasn't held again until 1990. From then on, it became an annual event.

In 2001, a nonprofit acquired TED with a renewed commitment to seek "out the most interesting people on Earth and let them communicate their passion." It wasn't until six TED Talks were posted online (for free) in 2006 that TED became a mass market, viral sensation.

After one million views within three months TED relaunched its website to focus on videos. By 2012, TED Talks reached its one billionth view.[11]

TED continues to reinject profits from conferences and sponsored grants into its online platform, content development, and mass marketing activities. This way ideas shared in local TED conferences continue to be available to the masses via the recorded TED Talks.

1 From Niche to Mass Market

After the success of posting videos of a few talks online, TED decides to shift from an exclusive conference, once a year in California, to providing video content of all its talks online. TED shifts from locally impacting 800 people per year to reaching millions of people every day.

2 From Specialized Channels to Mass Channel

Historically TED used local channels to sell their invite-only tickets for their conference. With the success of TED Talks, TED develops a digital infrastructure to reach the masses. TED Talks are distributed globally through its website.

3 From Niche Activities to Mass Marketing

Historically TED's activities focused on the organization and sales of the yearly conference. TED evolves its activities to reach as many viewers as possible with its slogan "ideas worth spreading." It also expands its activities to world-class video production in order to capture and broadcast world-class content.

4 From Niche to Mass Brand

TED Talks have more than nine million views per day in 2018, and the TED brand has grown to become a mass market brand well-known to curious individuals and attractive to sponsors that are required to fund TED's growth.

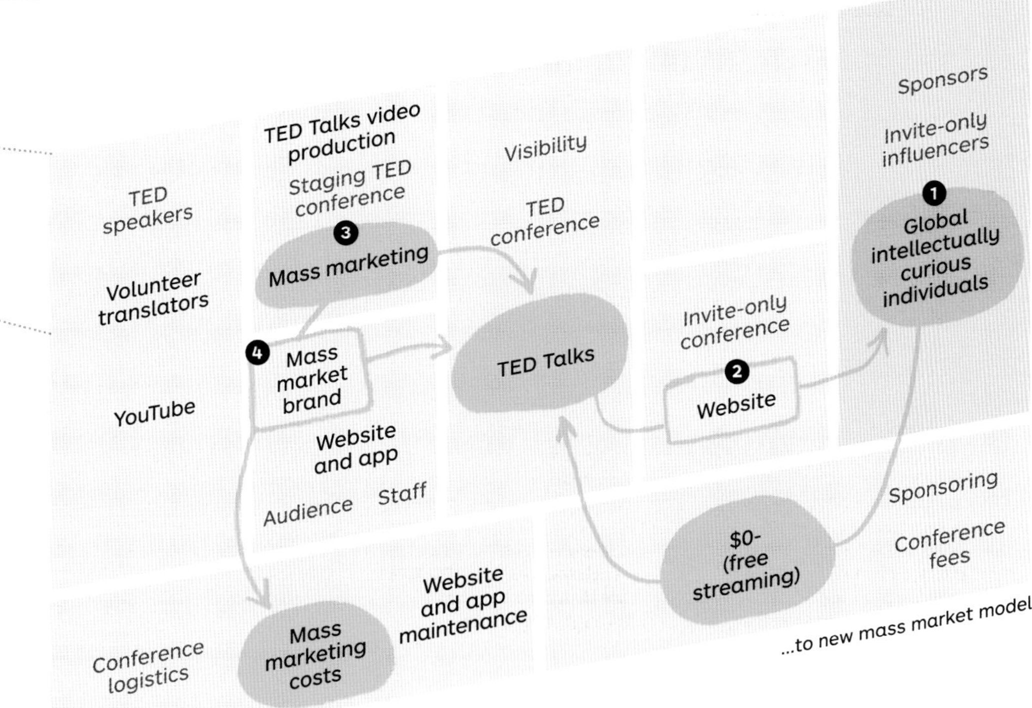

1
million views

The first six TED Talks posted online reached 1 million views within three months.[12]

3,200+
TED Talks online

As of December 2019, 3,200 TED talks are posted online for free.[13]

6,000

New video views per minute.[14]

"When we first put up a few of the talks as an experiment, we got such impassioned responses that we decided to flip the organization on its head and think of ourselves not so much as a conference but as 'ideas worth spreading,' building a big website around it. The conference is still the engine, but the website is the amplifier that takes the ideas to the world."

—CHRIS ANDERSON, MARCH 2012
Curator of TED

From B2B to B2(B2)C

is the shift from a B2B supplier that's invisible to the consumer toward a brand that matters to the consumer. This doesn't necessarily require a shift toward cutting out the middleman completely and going it alone. It's often a brand shift toward becoming more relevant to the consumer and includes increased consumer marketing and B2C brand development or extension.

STRATEGIC REFLECTION
How might we increase revenues by becoming more relevant to consumers if we are a "hidden" B2B supplier? How might we position ourselves to create value for consumers? How will that positioning make us more attractive to our B2B customer and incentivize them to make our brand visible in their product and/or service?

EXAMPLE
Intel Inside

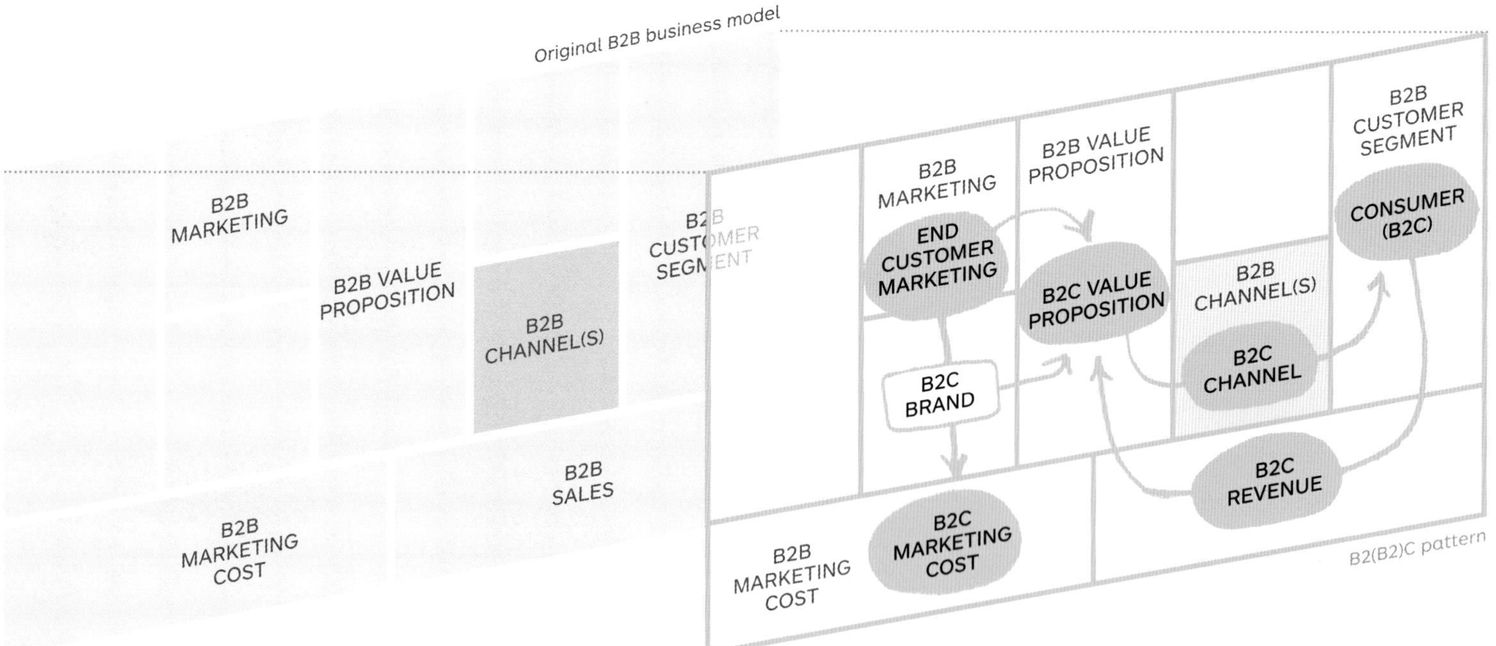

From Low Touch to High Touch

is the shift from standardized, low-touch value propositions toward customized, high-touch value propositions. This shift normally requires new human-based activities, which increase labor costs. However, high-touch value propositions command premium prices and lead to increased revenues.

STRATEGIC REFLECTION
How might we increase price and revenues by turning a standardized low-touch value proposition into a high-touch value proposition? How can we best maintain the scale benefits of standardization without incurring all of the scale limitations of a high-touch approach?

EXAMPLE
Apple Genius Bar

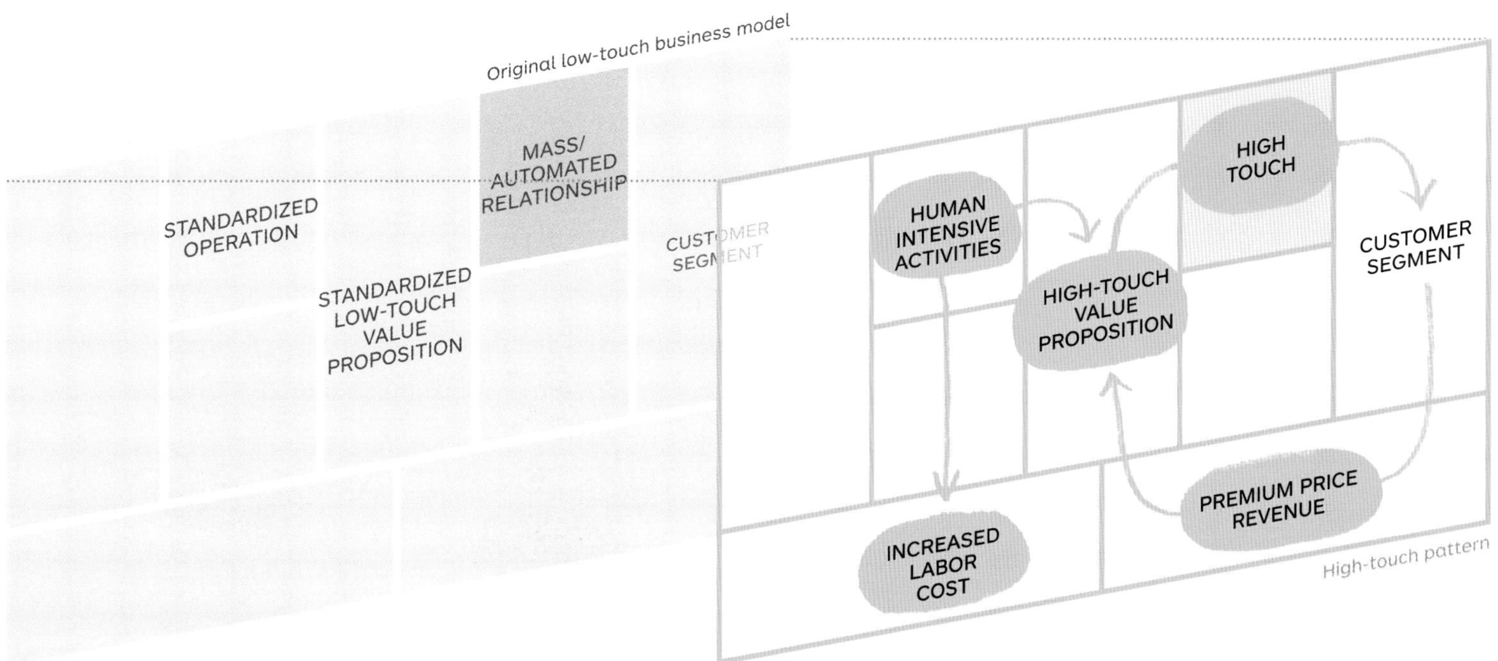

From B2B to B2(B2)C

1990 ~~~ 1991

Intel Inside

In the 1990s, PCs and the components within them are rapidly commoditizing. To respond to this threat, Intel launches the Intel Inside campaign to shift from a behind-the-scenes business-to-business microchip supplier to a trusted business-to-consumer brand.

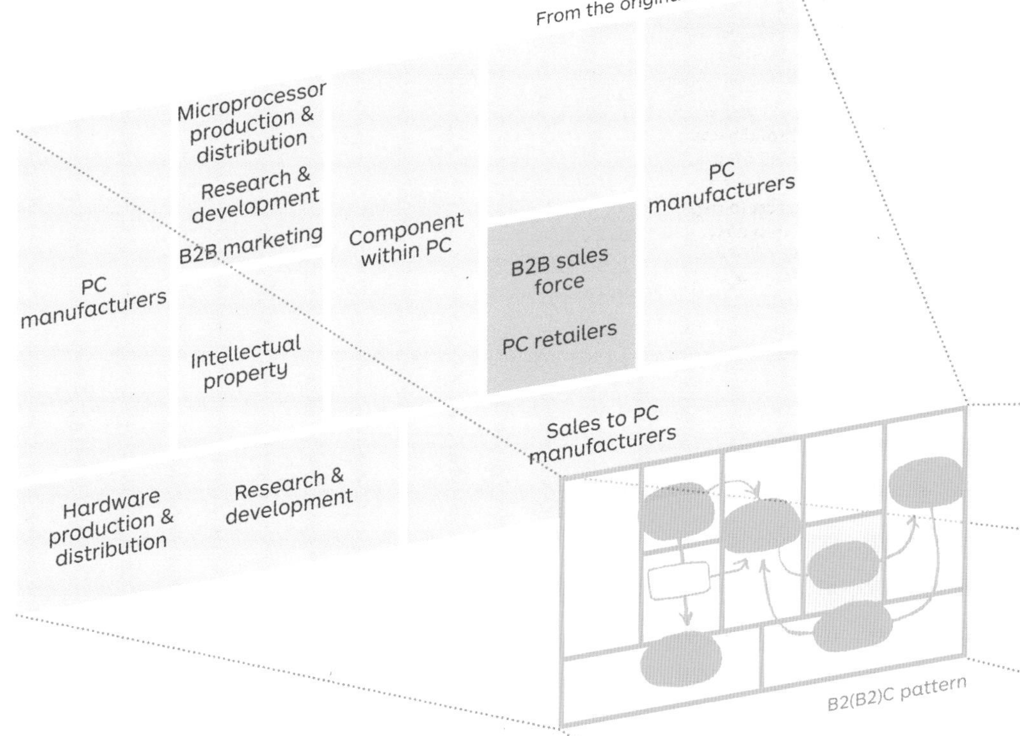

Intel created the Intel Inside marketing campaign in 1991 as a means to differentiate its microprocessors (and the PCs that contained them) from other, lower-quality PCs on the market. Previously, Intel had no direct relationship with the PC consumer—it was merely a producer of the component yet integral part of the PC, and Intel dealt only with the PC manufacturers.

Intel decided to split the cost of advertising with the PC manufacturers if they agreed to affix the Intel Inside logo and sticker on the PCs and their packaging.

The Intel Inside sticker became a "seal of approval"—consumers might not know what a processor did but they knew it meant quality, reliability, and performance.

Intel effectively transformed from an engineering company manufacturing a computer component to a consumer product company guaranteeing a level of performance.

1 From B2B to B2C Channel

In 1991, Intel launches the Intel Inside advertising campaign as a B2C channel to reach consumers directly. It drastically increases its visibility. Intel also convinces PC manufacturers to add the Intel Inside logo on their PCs, external packaging, and advertising in return for heavily contributing to marketing costs. Intel shifts from a behind-the-scenes B2B microchip supplier to a B2C brand with direct consumer access.

2 From B2B Marketing to End-Customer Marketing

Marketing mattered little when Intel was an engineering-driven B2B player. With the shift toward consumers, Intel needs to develop new end-customer marketing skills and a strong B2C brand. It succeeds and builds a consumer staple associated with quality, reliability, and performance.

3 From Less to More B2B Sales Thanks to B2C Brand as a Revenue Multiplier

The power of its newly gained B2C mass-market brand helps Intel differentiate itself from no-name microchip suppliers. PC manufacturers start to rely on Intel's trusted brand as a differentiator to charge higher premiums to the end customer. This leads to higher sales and revenues for PC manufacturers that multiply Intel's revenues from microprocessors.

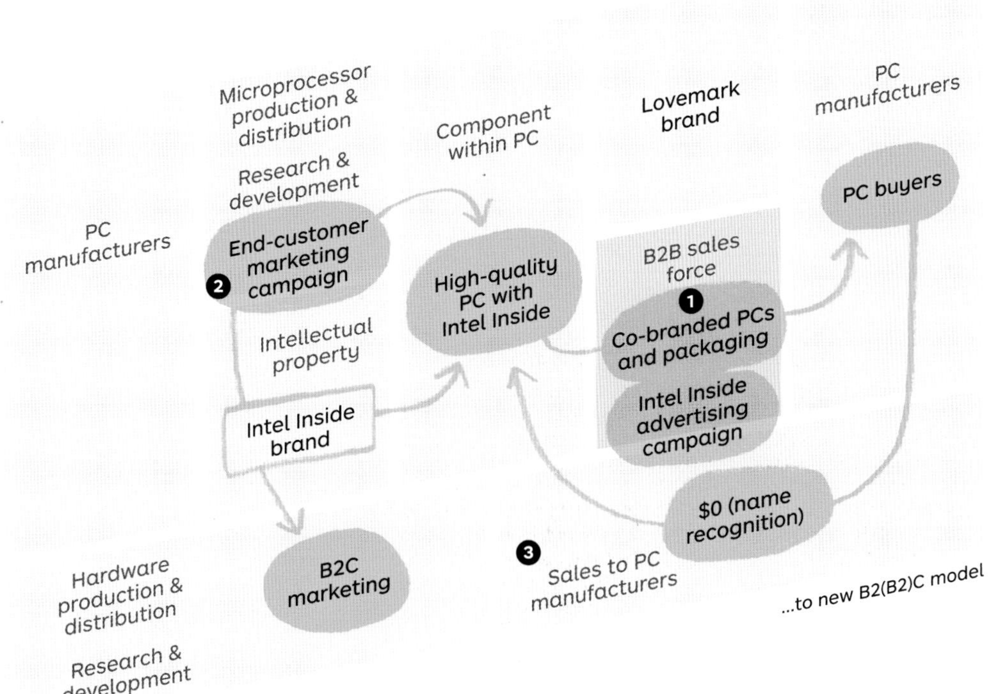

$110 million

Cost of advertising campaign over the first three years.[15]

#1

Market leader in semiconductor sales from 1992–2016 with 10 to 15% market share.[16]

3,000

In its first year (1991), the Intel Inside logo appeared on over 3,000 pages of its customers' (OEM) advertising.[17]

133 thousand

By 1993, 133 thousand PC advertisements were using the Intel Inside Logo and 1,400 OEMs had signed on to the program.[15]

$1 billion

Intel's net income topped $1 billion for the first time in 1992, following the Intel Inside campaign[18]

From Low Touch to High Touch
1976 ~~~ 2001

Apple Genius Bar

In 2001, Apple launches the Genius Bar as a key component of the Apple Store. They turn an undifferentiated and intimidating PC buying and support experience into a true, high-touch and high-value concierge-style service for customers.

Before Apple Stores, Apple used third-party retailers for both sales and technical support. This led to inconsistencies in customer experience both during and after sales.

In 2001, Apple launched the Apple Store with the Genius Bar embedded, as a key component of its retail strategy.

The Genius Bar provided personalized, friendly technical support, as well as product demos and training workshops. Geniuses used a high-touch, human-centred approach to make customers feel like true masters of their devices. The Genius Bar made going to the Apple Store and asking for support a lot less intimidating for customers.

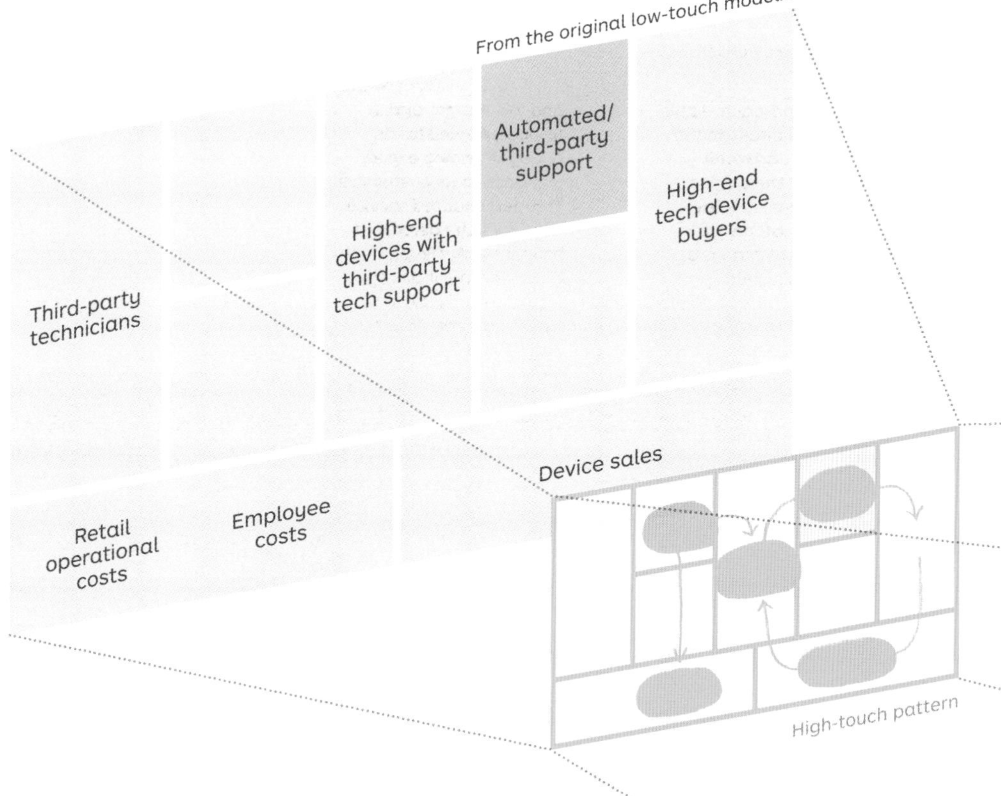

1 From Mass Automated to High-Touch Relationship

What happens when customers experience an issue with a device? They usually have to call a third-party call center, or go through a painful repair process via a partner (mass, undifferentiated approach). In 2001 Apple launches the Genius Bar, inside of its new Apple Stores, to control the entire customer experience over the lifetime of a product. If customers have an issue or even a question about their Apple devices, they can head to the Genius Bar in the nearest Apple Store.

2 From Standardized Operations to Human-Intensive Activities

Apple shifts from standardized, back office type support structure, often involving third parties, to new customer-facing activities. The Genius Bar provides face-to-face tech support, on-site repairs, as well as software training and workshops. To enable the shift, Apple trains and certifies a new breed of employees: the Geniuses. They are modeled after high-end hotel concierges who provide personalized services. They focus on building relationships, not upselling.

3 Increased Labor Cost

As a consequence of its high-touch approach, Apple accepts an increase in the cost of labor and retail operations of the Genius Bar. Apple considers the additional created value more important than the retail costs incurred.

4 Premium Price Revenue

In a sea of undifferentiated and low margin digital devices, Apple stands out by providing expert guidance to its customers. This personalized service reinforces the perceived benefits of Apple products and its brand. It ultimately helps justify Apple's premium prices and margins.

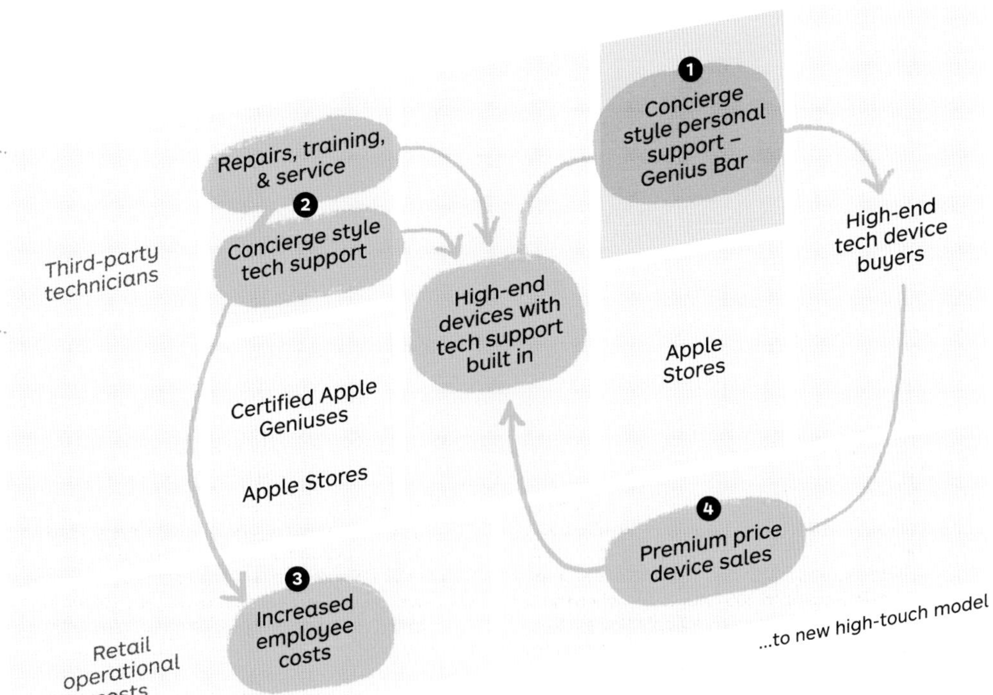

"I'm there to help the customer and their product have the best relationship they possibly can."

—LEAD GENIUS AT APPLE'S PALO ALTO STORE (2014)

50 thousand

Genius Bar appointments scheduled each day in 2014.[19]

Direct to Consumer Trend

Apple Stores

Apple launches it own retail stores in 2001 in order to control the entire customer experience. Previously, Apple had never sold through its own physical stores to consumers. It had always used third-party, retail locations. Apple Stores instantly become a hit with a very distinct experience from that of traditional computer retailers. Apple Stores are bright, open spaces. Customers come to engage with the devices and interact at the Genius bar. Training workshops and events turn Apple Stores into much more than a sales floor.

Nespresso Boutiques

Nespresso, a high-end coffee brand known for single-portioned coffee, opens its first boutique in 2000 in Paris as a concept store. At the time, Nespresso was already operating a successful e-commerce business, but needed a physical presence to cement Nespresso's position as a high-end brand. It steadily opened an increasing number of Nespresso boutiques to showcase the "ultimate coffee experience" to its customers and deliver on its brand promise. By the end of 2017, there are more than 700 Nespresso boutiques in prime locations in large cities around the globe.

Audemars Piguet

In 2013, Francois-Henry Bennahmias, CEO of Audemars Piguet (AP), the Swiss watch manufacturer, decides to move away entirely from third-party retailers. AP expects to remove all its multibrand retail partners completely by 2024. This radical shift helps AP regain control over the customer experience, customer data, and the customer relationship with the brand. The purchasing experience becomes highly personalized and uses more intimate locations than stores (its Lounges), like high-end apartments in major cities. In addition, cutting out the retail intermediary allows AP to capture the full margin on its retail sales.

Rise of Niche

Craft Beer

The craft beer movement has been on the rise over the last couple of decades—even forcing traditional incumbents to purchase or distribute craft beers.

For example, by the 1980s, beer in United States had become a mass-produced commodity with little or no character, tradition, or culture. Consumers started to turn to fuller-flavored beers created by small, regional brewers. As a result, industry heavyweights jumped into the market. AB Inbev (maker of Budweiser) purchased 10 formerly independent U.S. craft breweries between 2011–2017.

Co-Branded or Affinity Credit Cards

Credit cards used to mean Visa, Mastercard, or American Express. Today, the bank or financial lender is secondary to the retailer, offering benefits for card membership and usage. Retailers have issued their own cards since the 1980s but co-branding has hit new niche extremes: Starbucks, Uber, and Amazon Prime all offer Visa reward cards, for instance. Co-branded credit cards covered 41% of the U.S. consumer and small business credit card purchase value in 2017 and over $990 billion in purchase value in 2018 (Packaged Facts).

Exclusive Sneaker Drops

Nike and Adidas have taken niche to an entirely new level—limited, exclusive releases that drop on a weekly basis at specific times and exclusive retailers. The sneakers, which are produced in amounts ranging from the hundreds to hundred thousands, are targeted to sneakerheads looking for an exclusive fashion statement or a collectible (for online resale). Shoes that originally sell for $120 can balloon to over $4 thousand on the secondary market depending on rarity and prestige.

Backstage Driven Shifts

A radical shift of how value is created

From Dedicated Resources to Multi-Usage Resources

is the shift from using a resource for one value proposition toward using the same resource for a completely different value proposition—which targets a new customer. This leads to substantial synergies, while opening up an entirely new revenue stream.

STRATEGIC REFLECTION
How might we monetize one of our most important key resources with a new value proposition for a new customer segment? How might the synergies with our existing business allow us to disrupt that new market we are targeting?

EXAMPLE
Fujifilm

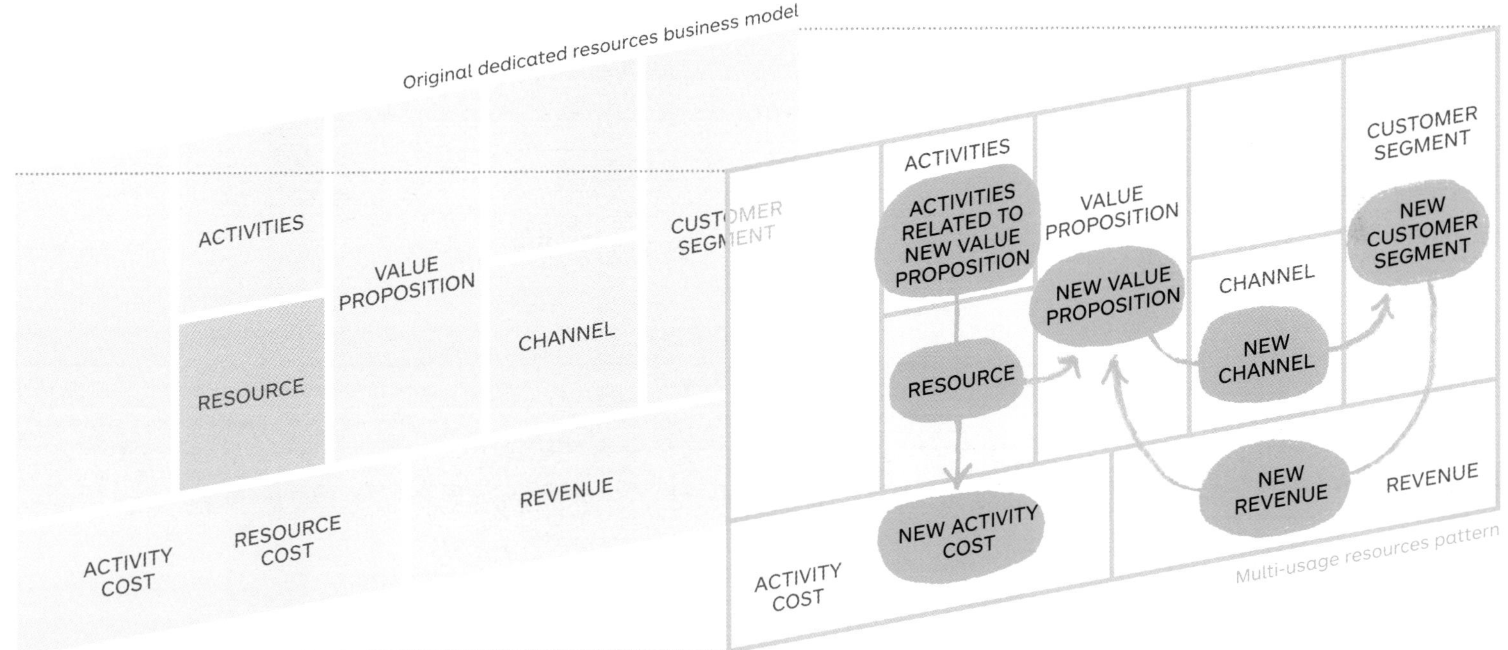

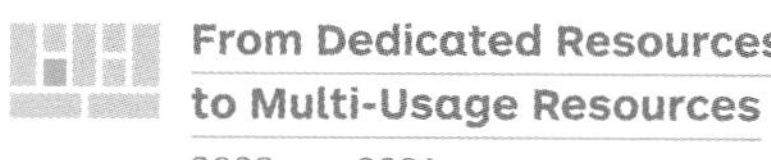

From Dedicated Resources to Multi-Usage Resources
2003 ~~~ 2006

Fujifilm

With the digitization of photography in the 2000s, Fujifilm realizes that it can no longer rely on continued revenue from analog film. Chairman Shigetaka Komori starts a period of transformation for Fujifilm with the VISION 75 plan. In 2006, Fujifilm puts its photographic film expertise to new use in cosmetics and launches Astalift skincare.

As part of the VISION 75 plan, Fujifilm created the Advanced Research Laboratories (R&D) to look for innovative uses of its technology in 2006. Fujifilm soon developed Astalift skincare and leveraged its brand name to market the new cosmetics line. By building a successful new business model around an existing key resource, Fujifilm was able to bounce back from the sharp decline of film, unlike its former competitor, Kodak.

This success became a launchpad to explore other businesses (e.g., functional materials, medical devices, etc.) and Fujifilm transformed into a diversified technology conglomerate. Fujifilm's Imaging Solutions Division accounted for 54% of the firm's revenue in 2001 versus just 15% in 2017.

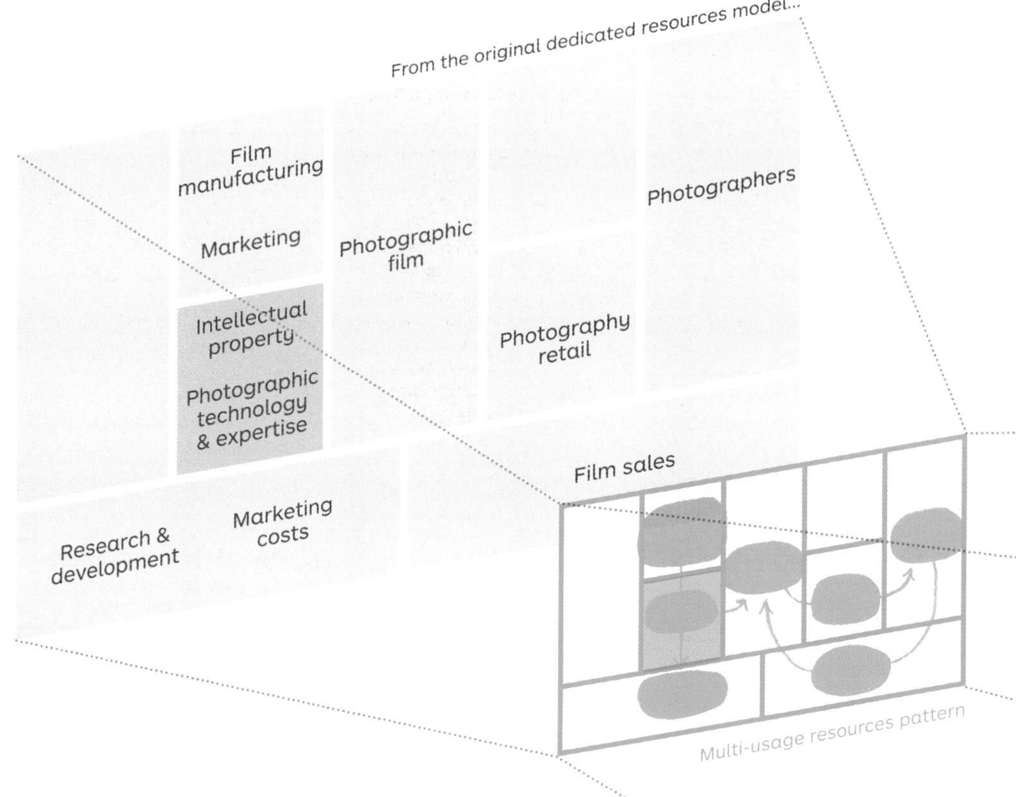

1 From Dedicated to Multi-Usage of a Key Resource

Fujifilm realizes that collagen is a major component of both film and skin, and that it can apply its photographic technology and expertise in film manufacturing to skincare production. Over the years, Fujifilm has developed 20,000 chemical compounds in its chemical library, originally for use with photographic film, and now applicable to pharmaceuticals and skincare.

2 From One Value Proposition to a New Value Proposition for a New Customer Segment

Fujifilm operates a radical shift from its original photographic film value proposition for photographers worldwide. It now targets Asian women with its Astalift, high-end skincare value proposition.

3 From Traditional Channel to New Channel

Photographic film and high-end skincare don't use the same retail channels, so Fujifilm opens up new retail channels dedicated to cosmetics for the Astalift business.

4 From Traditional Activities to New Activities and Costs Related to a New Value Proposition

Fujifilm creates the Advanced Research Laboratories to look for innovative uses of its photographic technology. It invests in the skincare business and backs up Astalift with a significant marketing campaign, as cosmetics require a strong brand. It then builds the skincare manufacturing and distribution infrastructure to support the new value proposition.

5 From Revenue to New Revenue

From its peak in 2001, demand for photographic film drops rapidly, almost disappearing in less than 10 years. To compensate for declining film revenues, Fujifilm creates a new revenue stream with high-end skincare and supplements that contribute to the growth of its healthcare division from 2006.

Film manufacturing
Marketing
Skincare manufacturing & marketing
1 Intellectual property
Cosmetics brand
1 Photographic technology & expertise
4
Photographic film
2 Skincare products (Astalift)
3 Cosmetics retail
Photography retail
Photographers
Asian cosmetic buyers
5 Skincare product sales
Film sales
Marketing costs
Research & development
Cosmetic manufacturing & marketing costs
...to new multi-usage resources model

2x

Astalift helps double Fujifilm's Healthcare business from ¥288 billion revenues in 2008 to ¥484 billion in 2018. Fujifilm's Astalift revenues are included in the healthcare division.[20,21]

20,000
Chemical compounds

Fujifilm had developed 20 thousand chemical compounds in its chemical library, originally all for use for photographic film, but now used for pharmaceuticals.[22]

Fujifilm vs. Kodak Revenue[23]
In millions USD

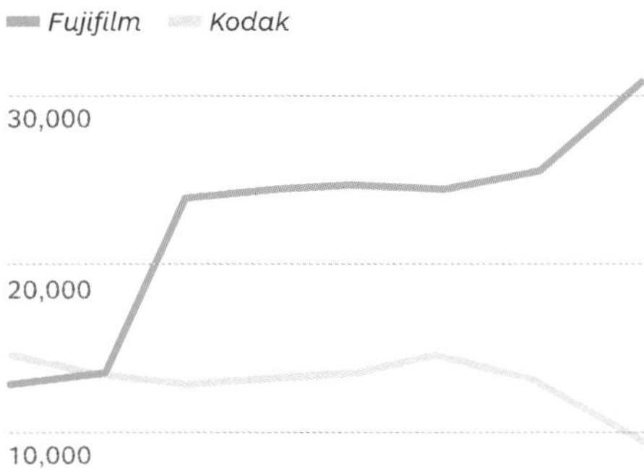

2000 2001 2002 2003 2004 2005 2006 2007

From Asset Heavy to Asset Light

is the shift from a business model based on high fixed costs and high capital expenditures toward an asset-light business with variable costs. This shift allows focusing on service provisioning and customer acquisition rather than building and maintaining assets. The freed-up capital and energy are invested in boosting growth and increasing revenues. In addition, third-party providers can often split the cost of building and maintaining assets between multiple clients. This leads to lower unit cost than if the company built and maintained the assets themselves.

STRATEGIC REFLECTION
How might we free up capital and energy from building and maintaining assets toward focusing on service provisioning and customer acquisition? How might that shift help us scale our customer base and increase revenues?

EXAMPLE
Bharti Airtel

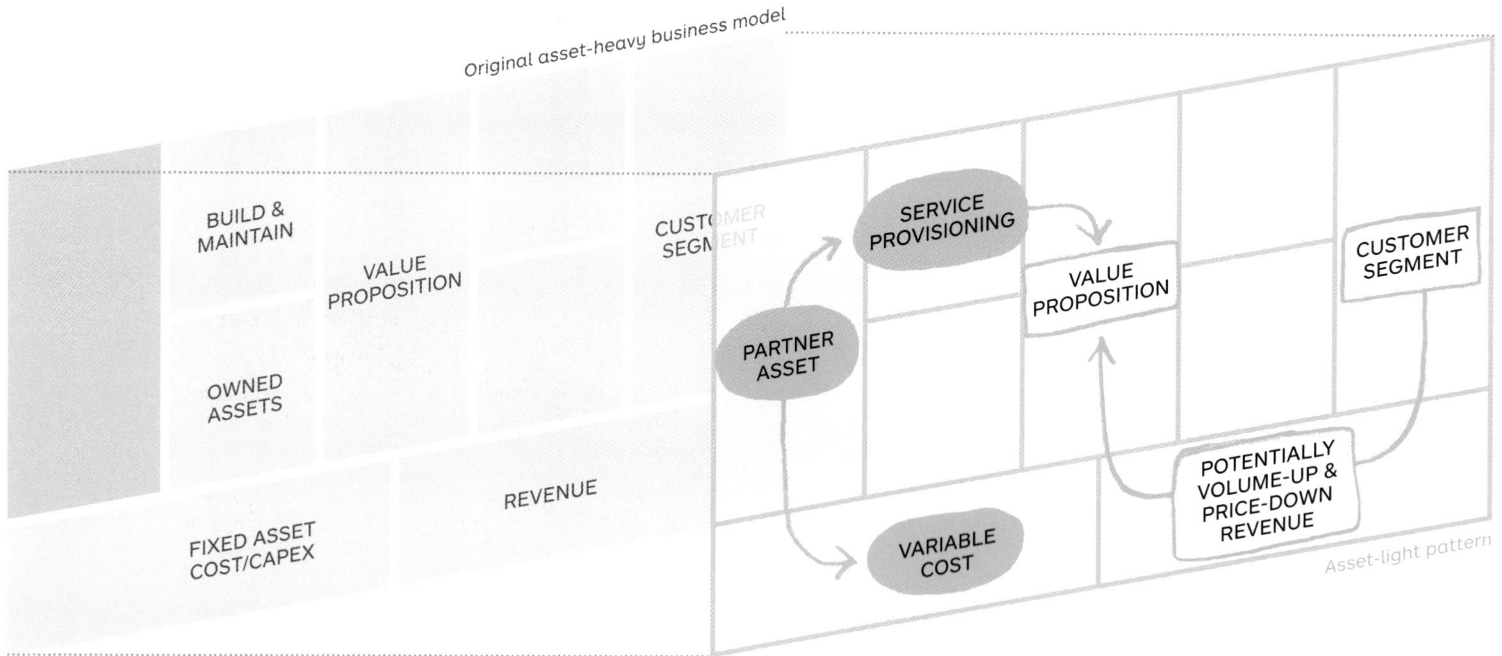

From Closed to Open (Innovation)

is the shift from a closed approach to developing new value propositions toward an open approach to developing new value propositions. This outside-in approach (to innovation) is based on external R&D and intellectual property (IP). A similar type of shift is from the tight protection of internal R&D and IP toward an inside-out approach of sharing R&D and IP with outside partners.

STRATEGIC REFLECTION

How might we make more usage of external R&D and IP (outside-in) or share internal R&D and IP with outside partners (inside-out)? Both should lead to a higher return on R&D through new revenues.

EXAMPLE
Microsoft

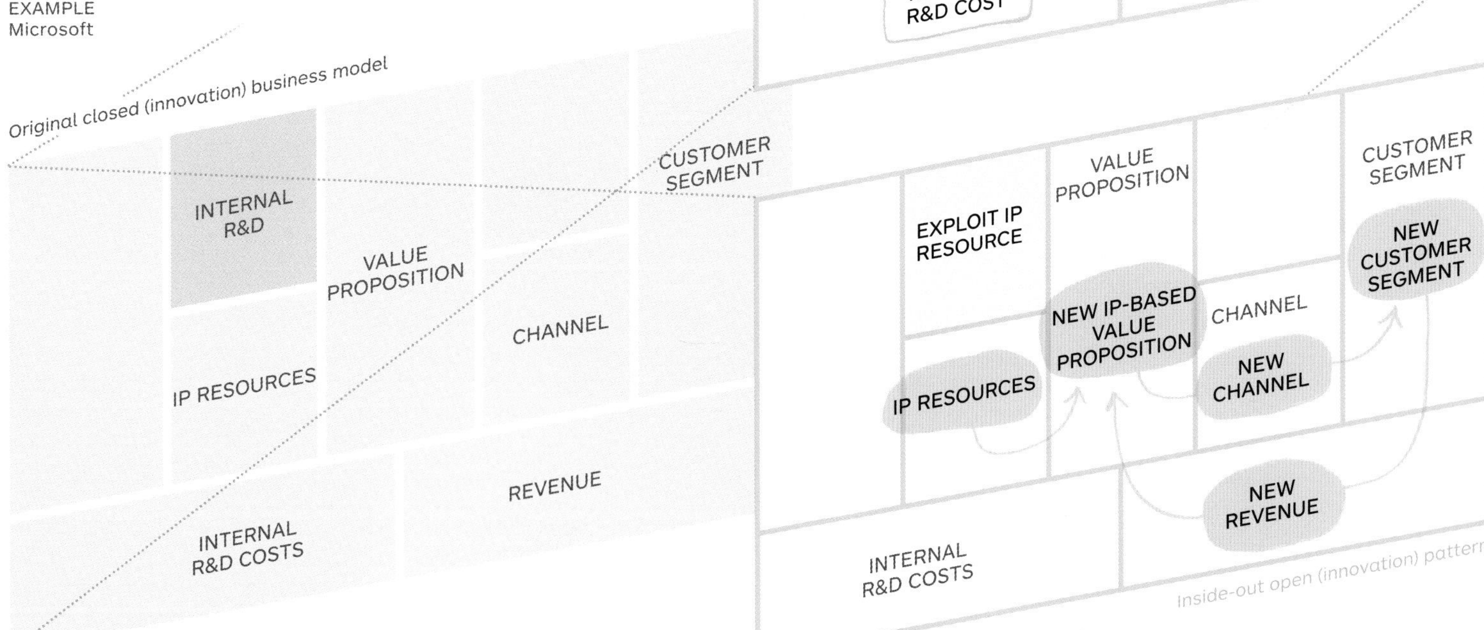

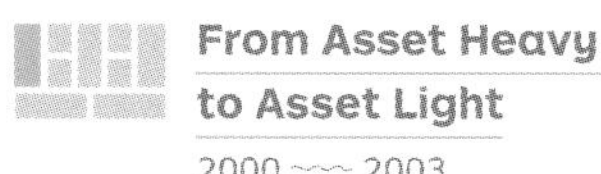

From Asset Heavy to Asset Light

2000 ~~~ 2003

Bharti Airtel

In the early 2000s, Airtel lacks the required capital to grow its telecom infrastructure. It decides to explore an unprecedented strategy in the telecom industry. Airtel outsources its entire network infrastructure and most of its operations to compete on service provisioning instead of infrastructure development.

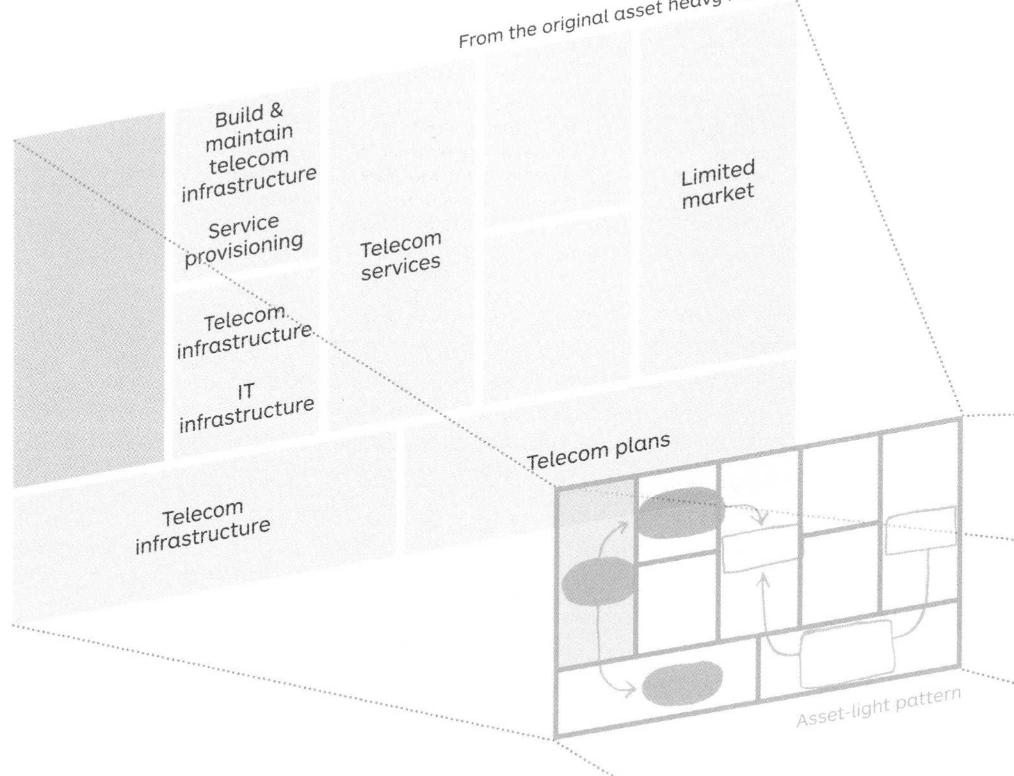

In the early 2000s, Bharti Airtel wanted to capture the lion's share of the Indian telecom market growth. However, it didn't have the capital to invest in the infrastructure required.

Instead of competing on infrastructure like everybody else, Airtel decided to get rid of this costly asset and compete on services.

In 2003, Airtel was the first major telecom company to outsource its infrastructure and most of its business operations to partners. Massive capital costs disappeared from their business model. This shift transformed capital expenditures into variable operating expenses based on customer usage. Airtel channeled savings from this shift back into price cuts and new value propositions that sustained the rapid growth of its subscriber base.

1 From Owned Key Assets to Partner Assets

In 2003–2004, Airtel makes the radical decision to outsource the operations and maintenance of the physical telecom infrastructure and most of its IT system in a multi-year deal with four global vendors. This is an unprecedented move for telecom operators who see their network as the main competitive advantage.

2 From Build and Maintain Activities to Service Provisioning Activities

Airtel reallocates the freed-up financial resources to expand sales, marketing, and customer service. Those activities enable faster customer growth and better service provisioning.

3 **From a Fixed to a Variable Cost Structure**

Airtel no longer has to spend on telecom equipment and own its infrastructure (fixed costs). Airtel negotiates a payment model with its partners that is based on usage and quality of service (variable costs).

4 **From Baseline Revenues to Lower Price, Higher Volume Revenues**

Airtel decides to pass on the savings from outsourcing its infrastructure to its customers by reducing the price of its telecom plans. With lower prices Airtel is able to achieve a much higher volume of sales and tap into the rapidly growing Indian telecom market. Because its growth is no longer constrained by its infrastructure, Airtel can quickly expand its customer base after the shift.

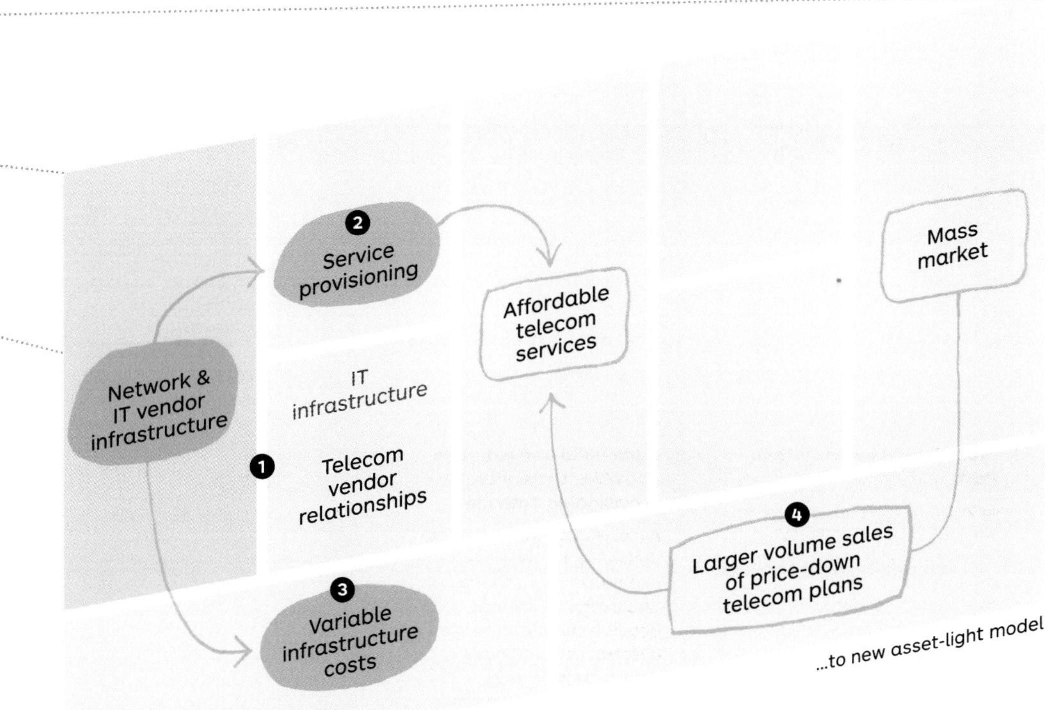

#3
in India

Third largest mobile operator in India in 2019.[24]

325
million

subscribers in India in 2019.[24]

27.5%
market share

of all Indian wireless subscriptions in 2019.[24]

120%
growth

120% compounded annual growth in sales revenues between 2003 and 2010 and growth in net profits of 282% per year.[25]

Microsoft

Enterprise users and developers no longer want to be tied to an operating system. To overcome this, Microsoft starts embracing open source. Microsoft shifts from calling open source a cancer in 2001 to joining its community in 2014.

In the Steve Ballmer era, Microsoft had been notoriously outspoken against open source. Patent litigation and overt threats against the theft of intellectual property were common. In 2012, Microsoft first experimented with open source with the creation of Microsoft Open Technologies in 2012.

In 2014, new CEO Satya Nadella radically sped up that shift toward an open approach. He moved Microsoft's focus away from proprietary Windows toward operating-system agnostic cloud solutions to satisfy enterprise users and developers.

To meet the needs of enterprise customers, Microsoft shifted from closed to open innovation. It no longer relied only on proprietary software development and opened up to the open source community. Microsoft made it easier for developers to work on its software and improved its Azure Cloud service offerings.

From the original closed (innovation) model...

Proprietary software development

Windows based offer

Enterprise users

Sales force

Windows IP

Developers

Patent litigation fees

Software development cost

Proprietary license fees

1

Enterprise cloud sales

Outside-in open (innovation) pattern

2

Inside-out open (innovation) pattern

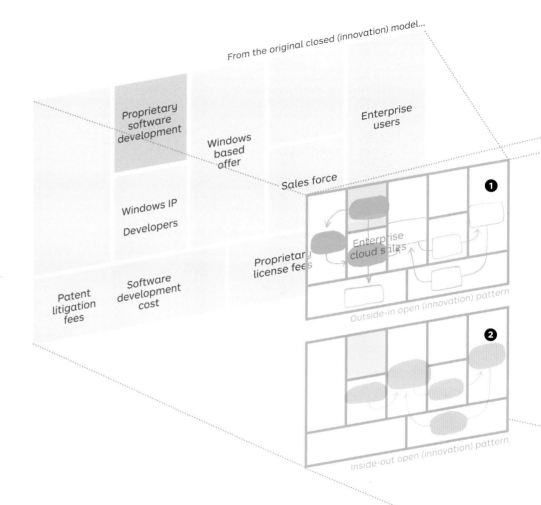

1 From Internal R&D to External R&D

Microsoft recognizes that to reach more enterprise users, it can no longer force its customers to use Windows. Closed software development (internal R&D) and the importance of Windows intellectual property become dated models. Under Satya Nadella's new leadership from 2014 on, Microsoft opens up to contributions from the open source community. It incorporates more and more open source code (external R&D) in its Azure cloud services to meet the needs of enterprise users.

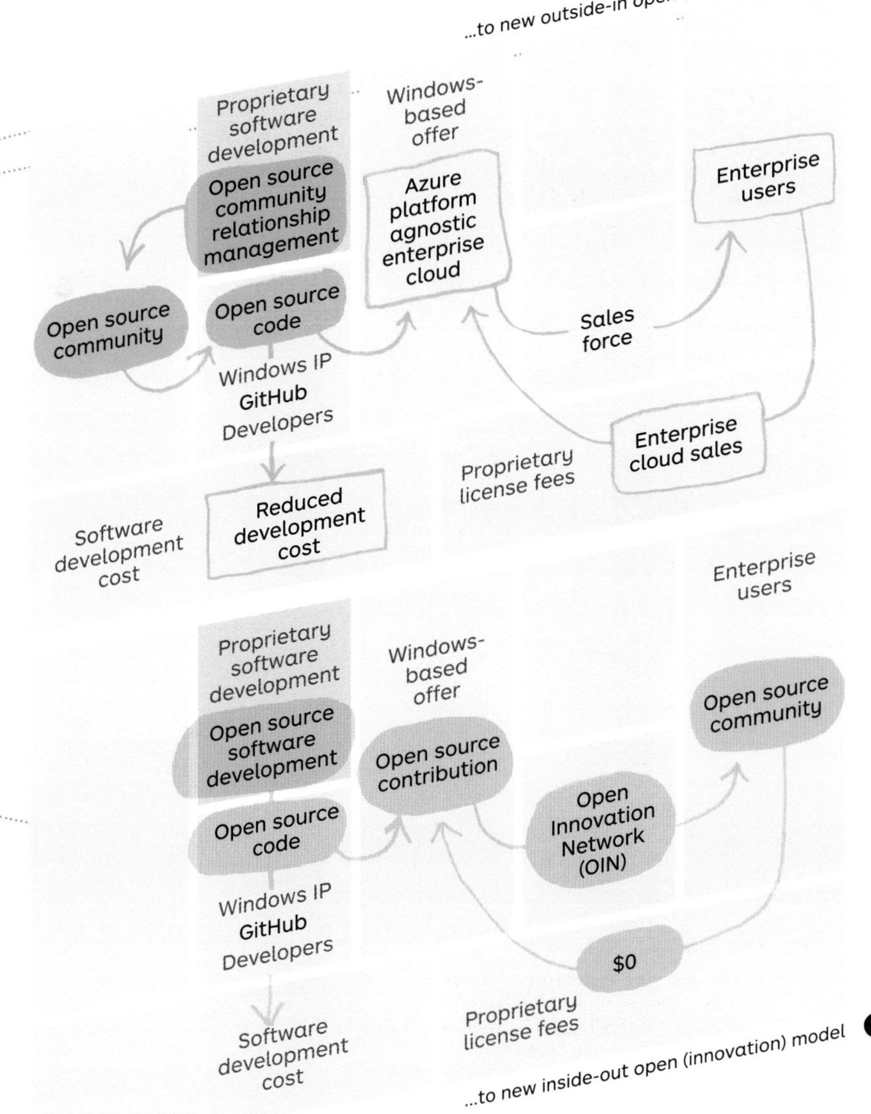

60
thousand patents

In 2018, Microsoft open sourced 60 thousand patents when it joined the OIN.[26]

$7.5
billion paid for GitHub

Microsoft purchases GitHub, the world's leading open software development platform in 2018.[27]

#1

Microsoft is the leading contributor to GitHub, with over 4,550 employees contributing in 2018.[28]

2 From Proprietary IP to New IP-Based Value Proposition

Microsoft joins the Linux Foundation in 2016. The Linux Foundation is an open technology consortium promoting open source development. In 2018 it also joins the Open Innovation Network (or OIN, a patent consortium). Microsoft opens over 60 thousand patents (proprietary IP) to the community upon membership to OIN.

In 2018, Microsoft purchases GitHub. GitHub is a platform for collaboration and software version control for the open source community. Microsoft soon becomes one of the largest contributors to the platform (new IP-based value proposition).

REVERSE

From Dedicated Resources to Multi-Usage Resources

2006 ~~~ 2019

Big Data Trends: 23andMe

Big data, the analysis of extremely large data sets, opens up many opportunities for new growth using the “from dedicated to multi-usage” pattern, as illustrated by 23andMe.

1 From Dedicated Usage: Genetic Testing

23andMe begins selling direct-to-consumer DNA testing kits in 2006. They offer both an ancestry report and a health analysis. 23andMe asks consumers buying their kits to opt into its research “to become part of something bigger.” On average 80% of users accept. With every new sale, 23andMe grows its database of users, DNA information, and self-reported behavioral data.

2 To Multi-Usage: Access to Database

23andMe knows its database will become a key resource for scientific research. 23andMe anonymizes the data and sells access to the database to researchers (in medical, government, and educational fields). In 2018, more than four million of 23andMe’s customers have agreed to let their DNA be used in research. The average 23andMe customer contributes to more than 230 studies.

3 To Multi-Usage: Drug Discovery

This wealth of data also enables 23andMe to enter the field of drug discovery. They explore this new field both on their own and through partnerships with leading pharmaceuticals companies. At the start of 2020, 23andMe, for the first time, has sold the rights to a new drug that it has developed using its customers’ data. This paves the way for substantial new revenue streams.

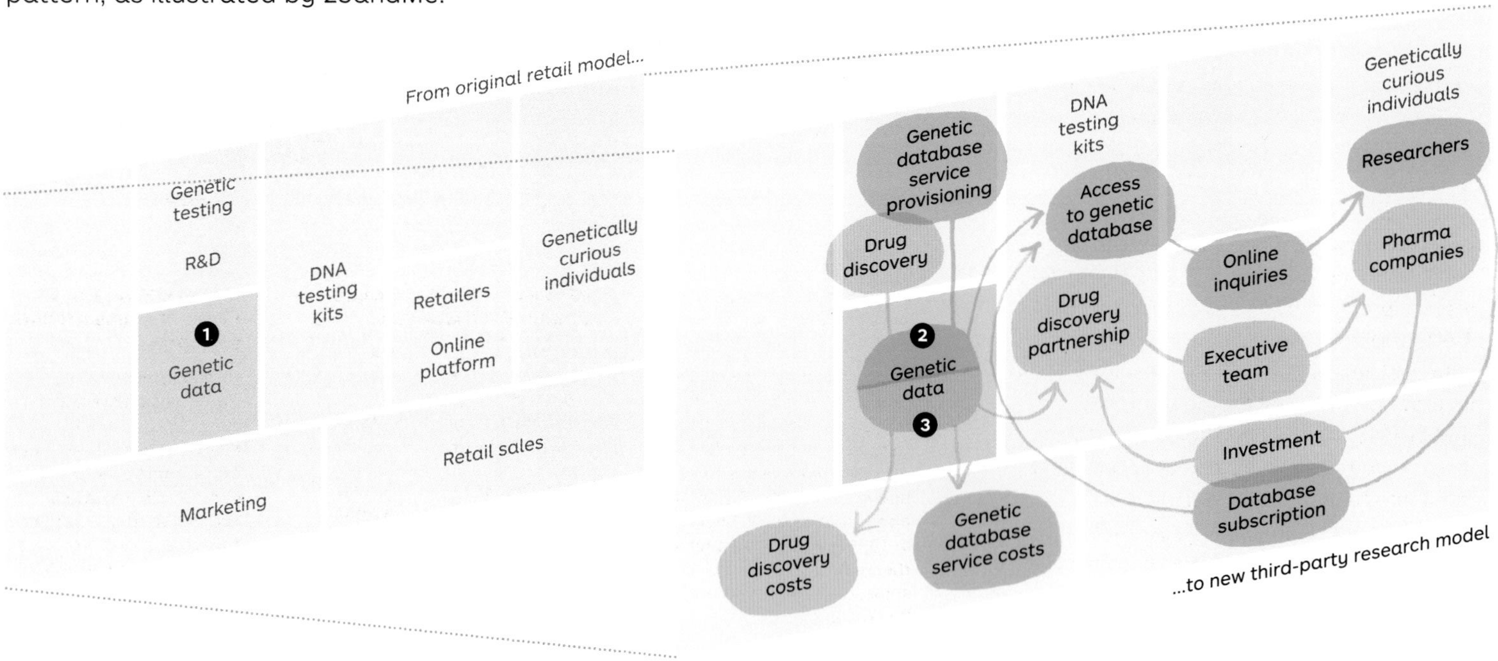

From original retail model...

Genetic testing

R&D

1 Genetic data

DNA testing kits

Retailers

Online platform

Genetically curious individuals

Marketing

Retail sales

Genetic database service provisioning

Drug discovery

2 Genetic data 3

DNA testing kits

Access to genetic database

Drug discovery partnership

Online inquiries

Executive team

Genetically curious individuals

Researchers

Pharma companies

Investment

Database subscription

Drug discovery costs

Genetic database service costs

...to new third-party research model

REVERSE

From Asset Light to Asset Heavy

1928 ~~~ 1955

Disney Parks & Resorts

In the 1930s, Disney founder Walt Disney dreams of giving families a magical experience both on screen and in real life. Following the success of his movies (light assets), he expands into theme parks in 1955 and resorts (heavy assets).

Walt Disney released his first Mickey Mouse cartoon in 1928. Four years later he began sketching his idea for a family-friendly amusement park. In 1955, Disneyland opened in California, and within its first 10 weeks, it attracted one million visitors. By 1960, that number would rise to five million visitors per year. Disney World followed in 1971, and both resorts opened hotels to support the tourists. In 1983, Disney opened its first international theme park in Tokyo, and in 1996 it launched the Disney Cruise Line. Disney's continual growth and investment into heavy assets has paid off. It built a profitable hospitality business next to its media empire. And Disney continues to be the most valuable media brand in the world. Another $24 billion is expected to be invested in theme parks through 2023.[29]

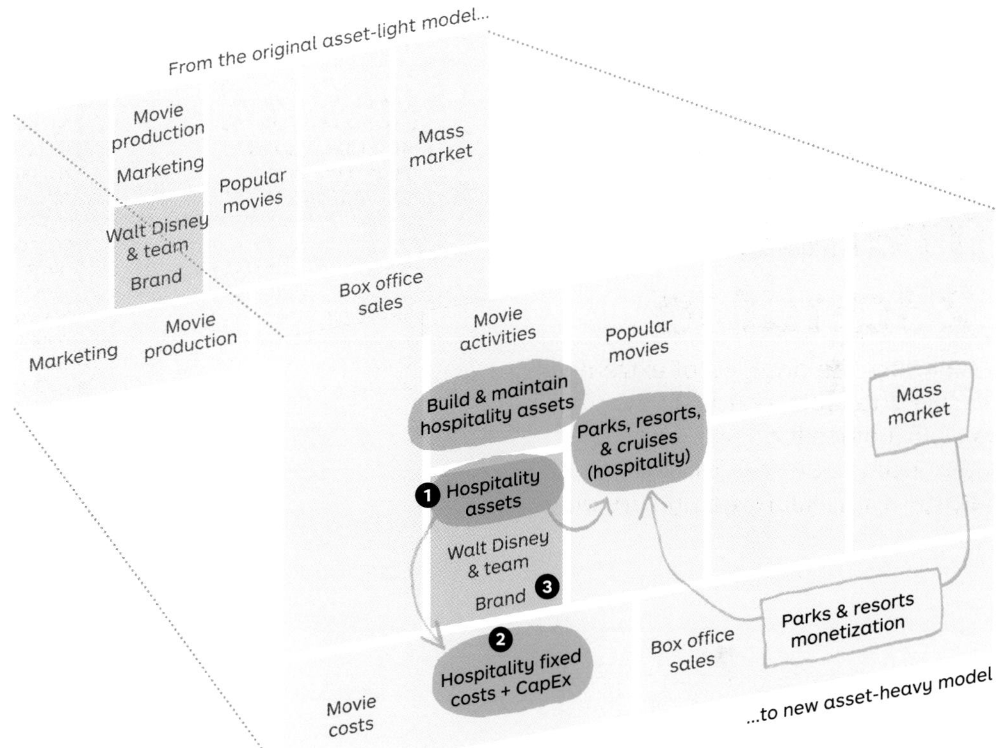

1 From Asset Light to Asset Heavy

Disney's movie business requires few assets beyond Walt Disney and his creative team. When Disney decides to shift to creating real world experiences, it accepts that it needs to invest in heavy hospitality assets. Disney opens its first park, Disneyland, in 1955 and adds another 11 theme parks, 51 resorts, 4 cruise ships, and 1 private island to its key resources.

2 From Asset-Light to Asset-Heavy Cost Structure

Movie	Park
Lady and the Tramp $38.1 million	Disneyland $162 million
The Jungle Book $30.6 million	Disney World $2.02 billion
The Little Mermaid $82 million	Disney Hollywood Studios $824 million

3 Asset Light and Asset Heavy Mutually Reinforce Each Other.

Disney uses its movie franchises and brand to market parks, resorts, cruises, and other products. At the same time, parks and resorts become a channel to reinforce the customer connection with the Disney brand.

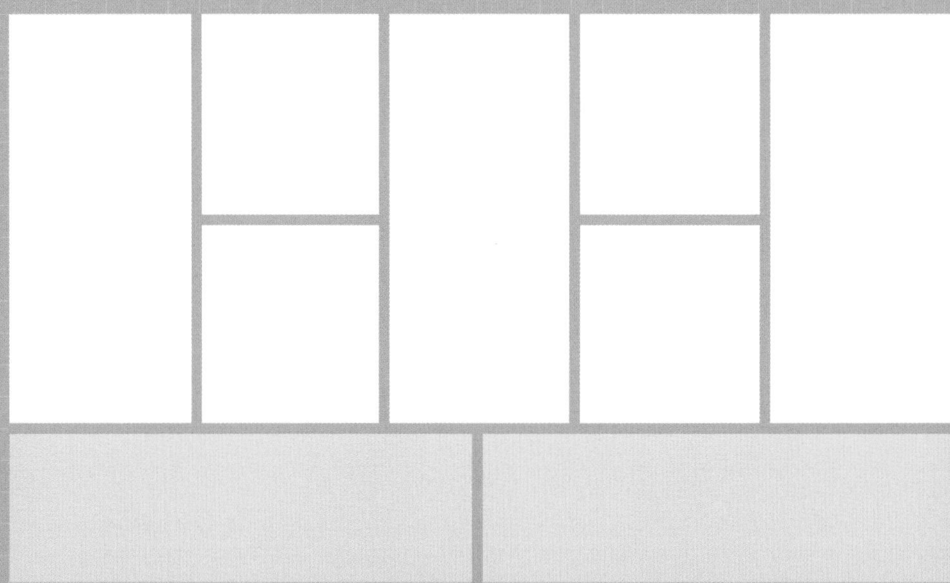

Profit Formula Driven Shifts

A radical change of how profits are made in terms of revenues and costs

From High Cost to Low Cost

is the shift toward a more efficient activity and resource configuration in order to substantially decrease the cost structure and offer price-conscious customers a low-price value proposition. This shift allows for the conquering of new customer segments that might have not had access to such a value proposition previously.

STRATEGIC REFLECTION
Which new, price-conscious customer segment might we conquer with a low-price value proposition? How might we reconfigure activities and resources to disrupt our cost structure and make that low price possible?

EXAMPLE
Dow Corning Xiameter

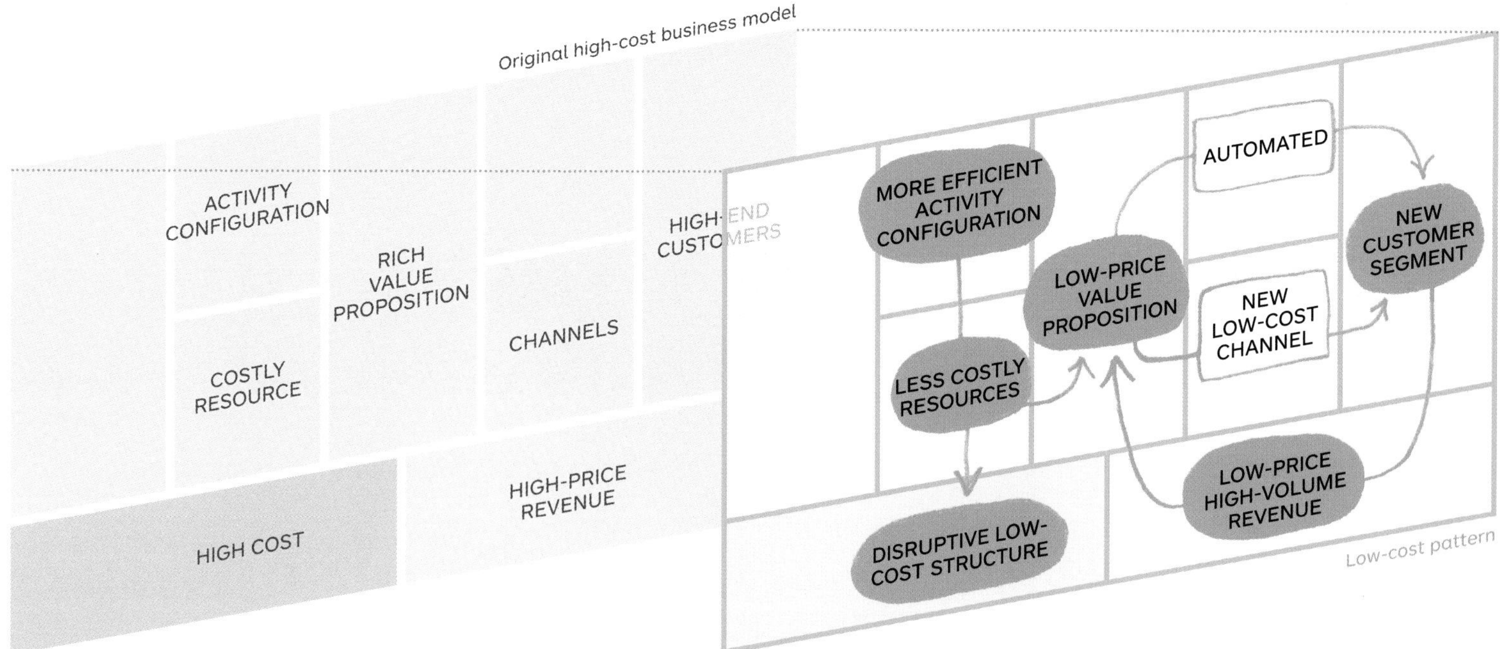

From High Cost to Low Cost

1990s ~~~ 2002

Dow Corning Xiameter

Silicone is becoming a commodity in the late 1990s, and Dow Corning's specialty silicone business is under threat. To respond, Dow Corning creates Xiameter in 2002, a no-frills standard silicone offering, sold online to price-sensitive manufacturers.

In the 1990s, silicone was becoming a commodity and Dow Corning could have given up the low end of the silicone market. Instead it took on the challenge of designing a business that could offer silicone at a 15% lower price point. This led to the launch of Xiameter in 2002: an online-only distribution platform for standard silicone products.

Dow Corning maintained its high-cost speciality silicone business alongside the low-cost Xiameter standard silicone business. Both business models successfully co-existed and helped the company overcome the threat of silicone commoditization.

Dow Corning was acquired by the Dow Chemical company in 2016.

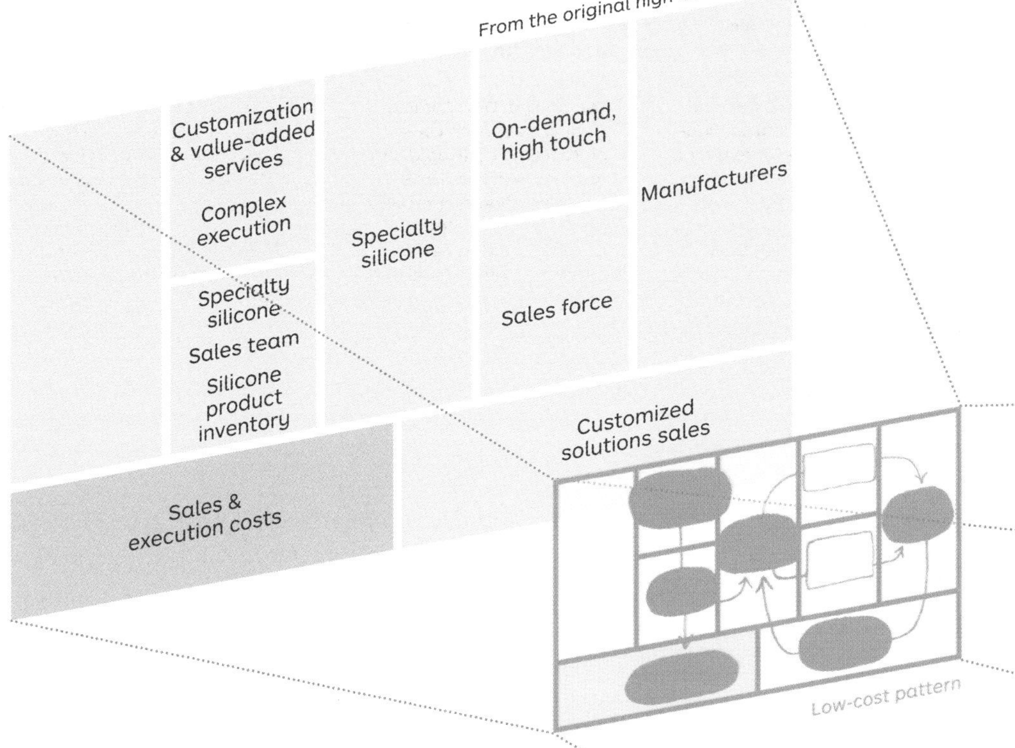

1 From High Cost to Disruptive Low-Cost Structure

Xiameter radically changes its cost structure from its Dow Corning parent. It achieves a disruptive low-cost structure thanks to less costly resources, less complex activities, and standardized sales.

2 From Costly to Less Costly Resources and Activities

Xiameter eliminates the most costly resources of Dow Corning's traditional business model. This includes the elimination of specialty silicone resources to reduce inventory and the elimination of a dedicated sales team. It also reduces the complexity of activities, such as customization of silicone products, value-added services, or specific contract terms. The new business model is designed for standardized sales and online execution.

3 From a Specialty Value Proposition to a Low-Price Value Proposition

The less costly resources and more efficient activity configuration allow Xiameter to offer a lower priced value proposition. It sells standard silicone online at a lower price point than Dow Corning. This value proposition attracts a new customer segment of price-sensitive manufacturers willing to forego specialty, high-touch sales activities in exchange for speed, convenience, and price.

4 From Traditional (Offline) Channels to New (Online) Channel

The original Dow Corning business depends completely on a dedicated sales team and has no online presence. Xiameter creates an e-commerce platform and introduces a new online channel to reach its customers.

5 From High-Price Revenues to Low-Price, High-Volume Revenues

Dow Corning sells its speciality silicone products at a high price. Xiameter aims for a 15% lower price. In exchange, customers have to purchase large-volume orders and agree to standard credit terms and lead times. Xiameter sales grow from 0 to 30% of Dow Corning total sales in less than 10 years.

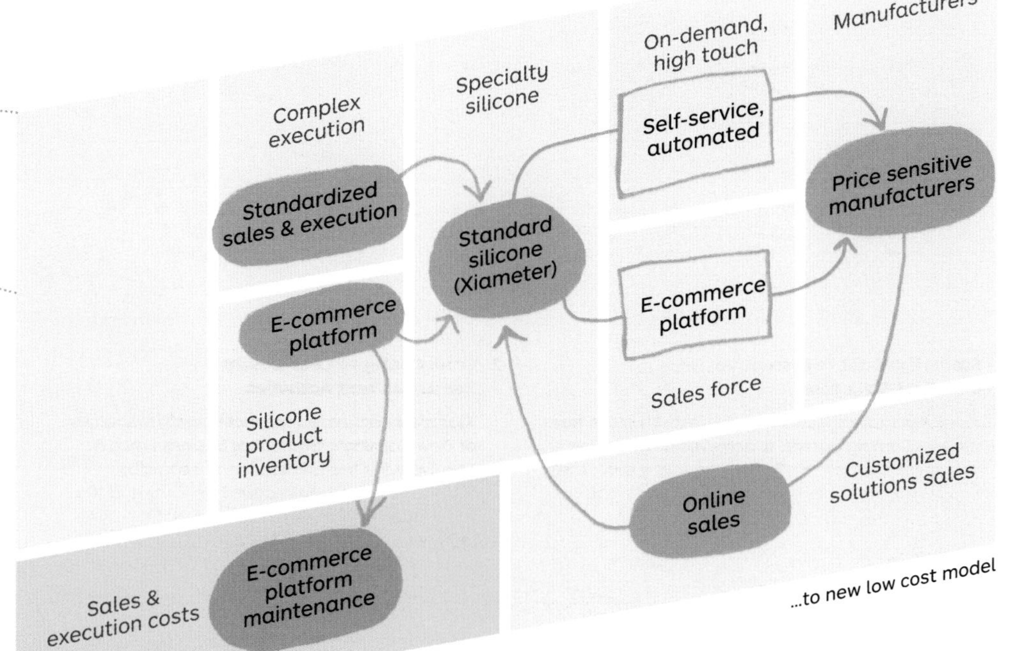

20% cheaper

price differential between Dow Corning and Xiameter.[30]

"Our two-brand strategy offers the choices and solutions that customers need to help them solve problems and seize opportunities."

—DONALD SHEETS

Chief financial officer and Americas area president, Dow Corning

0% to 30% online sales in less than 10 years

30% of Dow's sales were online in 2011 vs. 0% prior to the launch of Xiameter in 2002.[31]

13% sales growth

Peak in sales growth in 2006 and double digit growth every year since introduction in 2002.[32]

Adapted from Seizing the White Space, *by Mark W. Johnson*

From Transactional to Recurring Revenue

is the shift from having to sell again and again with continuous cost of sales toward acquiring customers/users once to then earn recurring revenues. This shift requires identifying a recurring customer job-to-be-done that you can address with a recurring value proposition. Because of the increased customer lifetime value from recurring revenues you can afford a higher upfront acquisition cost than in a transactional model. Advantages of recurring revenues include compound revenue growth and more revenue predictability.

STRATEGIC REFLECTION
Which recurring customer job-to-be-done might allow us to create a recurring value proposition with a long-term relationship and recurring revenues?

EXAMPLE
Adobe

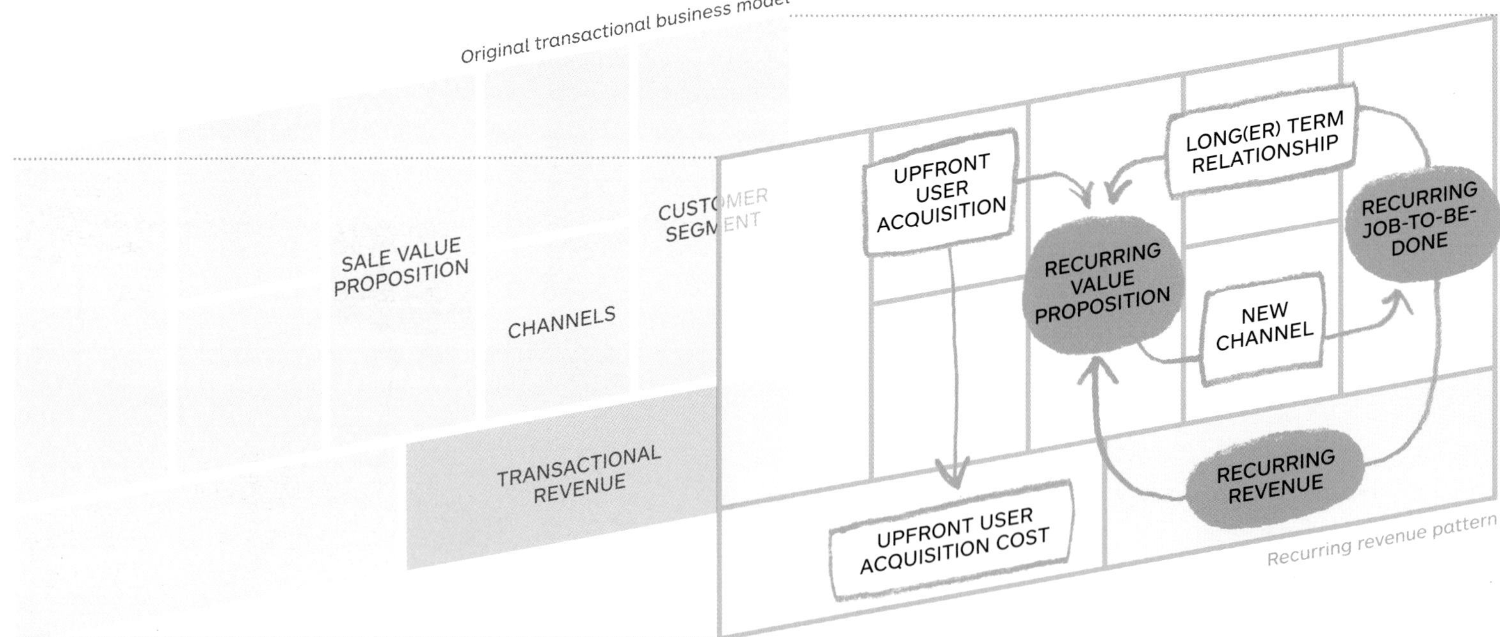

From Conventional to Contrarian

is the shift to significantly reduce costs and increase value at the same time. Contrarians eliminate the most costly resources, activities, and partners from their business model, even if that means limiting the value proposition. They compensate by focusing on features in the value proposition that a well-defined customer segment loves and is willing to pay for, but which are relatively cheap to provide.

STRATEGIC REFLECTION
Which of the most costly activities and resources might we eliminate or reduce, even if they create value for customers? How might we we replace that lost (expensive) value by augmenting our value proposition with cheap value creators that matter to customers most?

EXAMPLE
Apple iMac

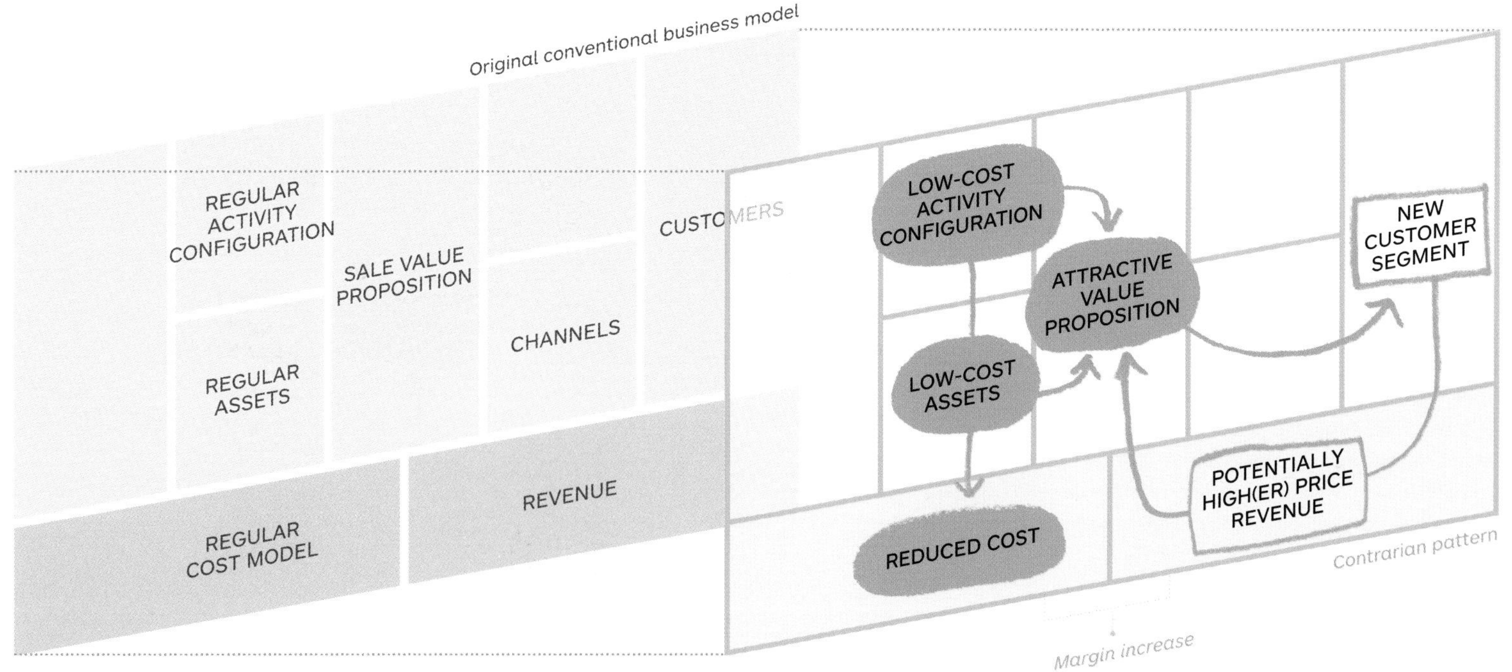

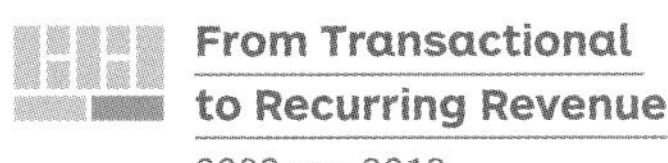

From Transactional to Recurring Revenue

2003 ~~~ 2012

Adobe

In the 2010s, software distribution over the Internet becomes possible and the software industry starts shifting toward software as a service (SaaS). Adobe seizes the opportunity early and switches from transactional sales of software to a cloud subscription service in 2012.

Adobe historically earned revenues from transactional sales of perpetual licenses to its software. Every few years it had to convince customers to upgrade to a new version.

In 2012, Adobe launched its Creative Cloud and joined a growing number of software providers selling software as a service (SaaS). Customers then received access to a full suite of products that were continuously upgraded and supported through the cloud.

In 2013, Adobe stopped selling its Creative Suite as a stand-alone, software product. Adobe's revenue dipped initially as it shifted from transactional to recurring revenues. But recurring revenues started to grow dramatically with the adoption of the Creative Cloud by the mass market.

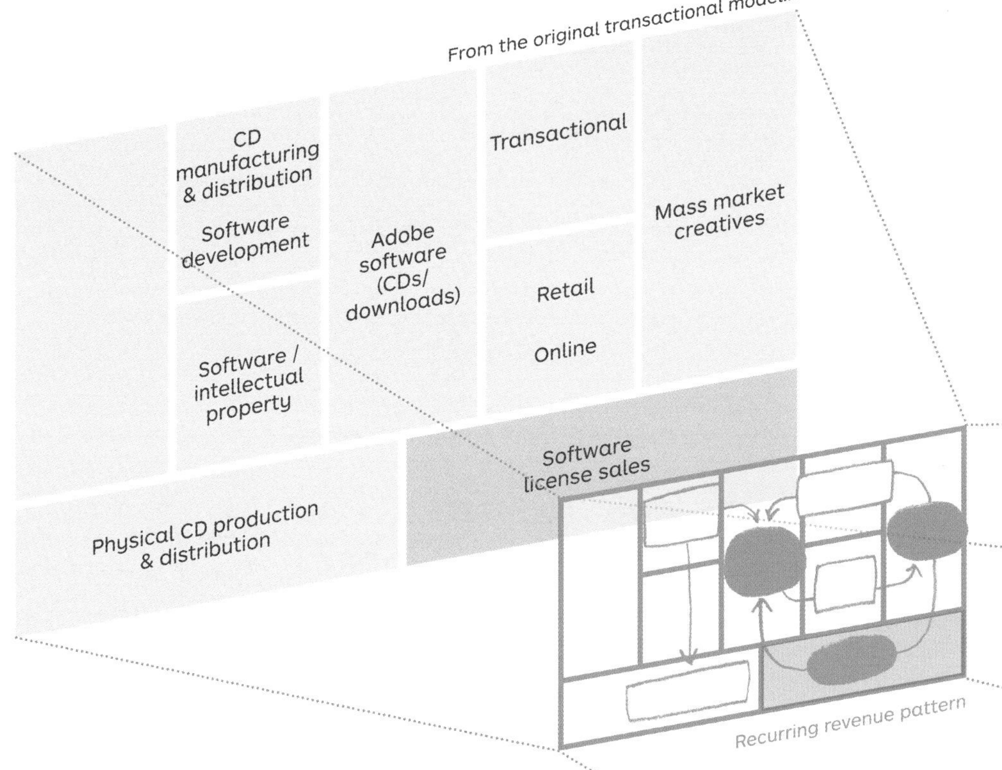

1 From Transactional to Recurring Revenues

Adobe decides to shift from offering perpetual software licenses to a monthly subscription service in 2012. At the time Adobe's complete Master Software Collection costs $2,500, versus a monthly $50 subscription for the entire Creative Cloud.

2 From Sales to Recurring Value Proposition

Prior to 2012, Adobe customers purchase a perpetual license that requires seasonal upgrades in order to get access to the latest software. Of course, customers want access to the best and latest software and features all the time, not once every few years. The shift to the Creative Cloud satisfies that recurring need with automatic updates, technical support, online storage, publishing capability, and file sharing.

3 From Transactional to Long-Term Relationship

The shift to the Creative Cloud effectively means transforming a transactional relationship with customers into a long-term one. Adobe invests heavily in creating an online user community. This leads to open discussions on the value and benefits of the new subscription model.

4 From Continuous Customer Acquisition Every Few Years to Important First-Time Customer Acquisition

Prior to 2012, Adobe bears the activity and cost of customer acquisition for every new software sale and every subsequent upgrade. With the shift from transactional to recurring revenue, Adobe invests in acquiring customers once, upfront, in order to collect subscription revenues over their lifetime.

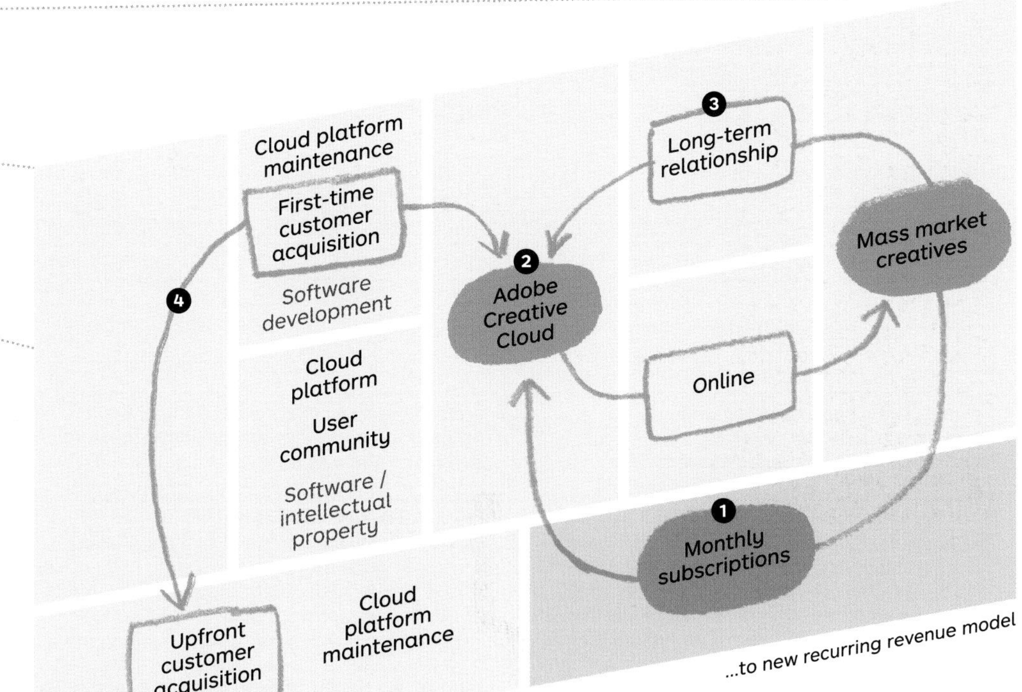

Adobe Net Profit Margin[33]

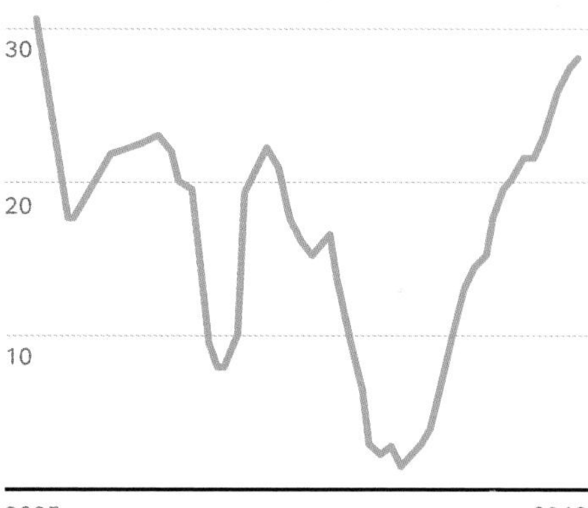

Adobe Revenues by Segment[34]
as a percentage of total revenues

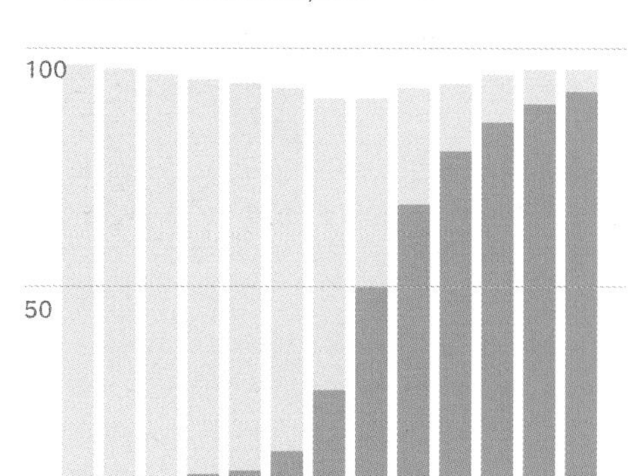

Apple iMac

In 1997, Steve Jobs returns to Apple, which is in a dire financial situation. Jobs significantly reduces operating costs, while focusing Apple's new desktop computer value proposition on exactly what design-sensitive consumers want with the iMac.

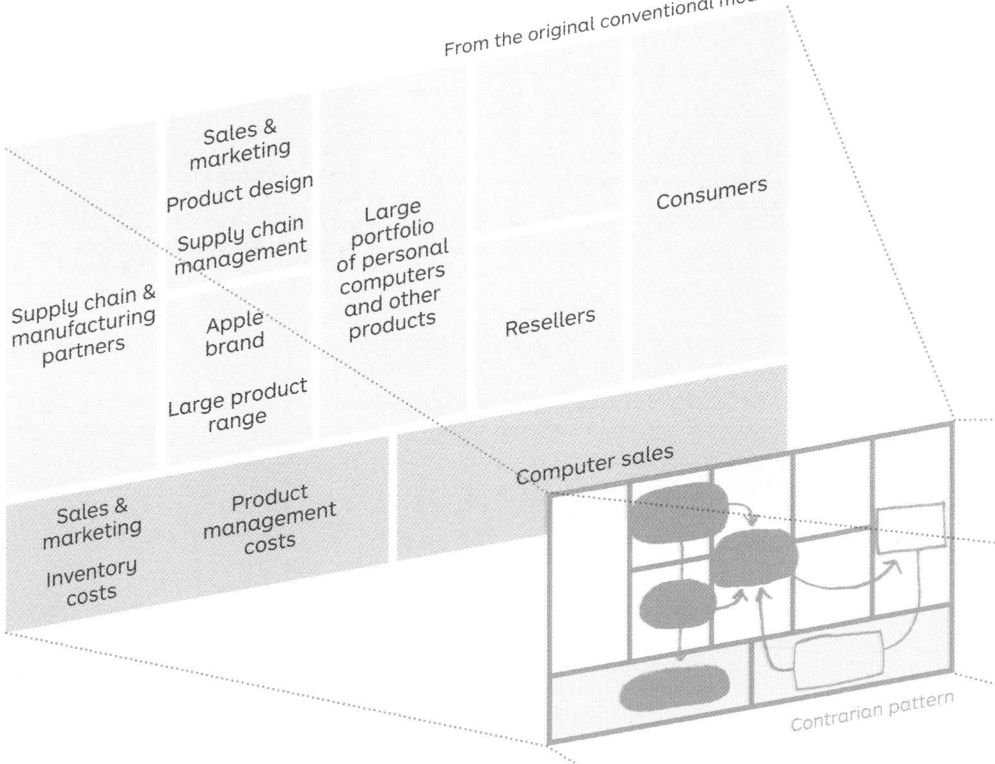

In late 1996 Apple acquired NeXT, the company launched by Apple founder Steve Jobs after resigning from Apple. Apple, which was close to bankruptcy, put Steve Jobs in charge to turn around the company. Jobs also acted swiftly on the product side and killed more than 70% of Apple's hardware and software portfolio to focus on very few projects. This decision resulted in the layoffs of over 3,000 employees, but allowed Apple to focus on reinventing the home computer. Newly appointed head of design Jonathan Ive was tasked with this reinvention. He designed the iconic iMac with its translucent Bondi blue casing. A year later Apple was back to profitable figures and the success of the iMac paved the way for future game-changing Apple products (iPod, iPhone, iPad). Its new operating system, Mac OS X, which was launched in 2001, also originated in the NeXT acquisition.

1 From Conventional Activities and Resources to Low-Cost Activity Configuration and Reduced Asset Costs

Apple shifts from costly and diversified activities and resources driven by an unnecessarily extensive product portfolio to a focused and trimmed cost structure. Steve Jobs eliminates product customizations for different resellers and reduces operating costs by killing 70% of Apple hardware and software developments. In parallel, Tim Cook leads the transformation of Apple's supply chain, which results in a significant reduction of inventory costs.

2 From Conventional to Attractive New Value Proposition for New Design-Sensitive Customer Segments and Apple Fans

Apple launches the iMac and breaks the beige or grey computer dogma in the PC market. The iMac is dramatically different from any previous computer: Apple increases both power and ease of use, especially to access the now popular Internet. Apple also creates a completely new aesthetic with the iMac's curvy, colorful design. Reasonably priced at $1,299, the iMac resonates immediately with a new segment of design-sensitive consumers.

3 From a Loss-Making to a High-Margin Business

Apple simplifies its product portfolio, ups its game in supply chain management, and focuses design efforts in the desktop computer for consumers segment on the new iMac. Within a year Apple returns to making profits.

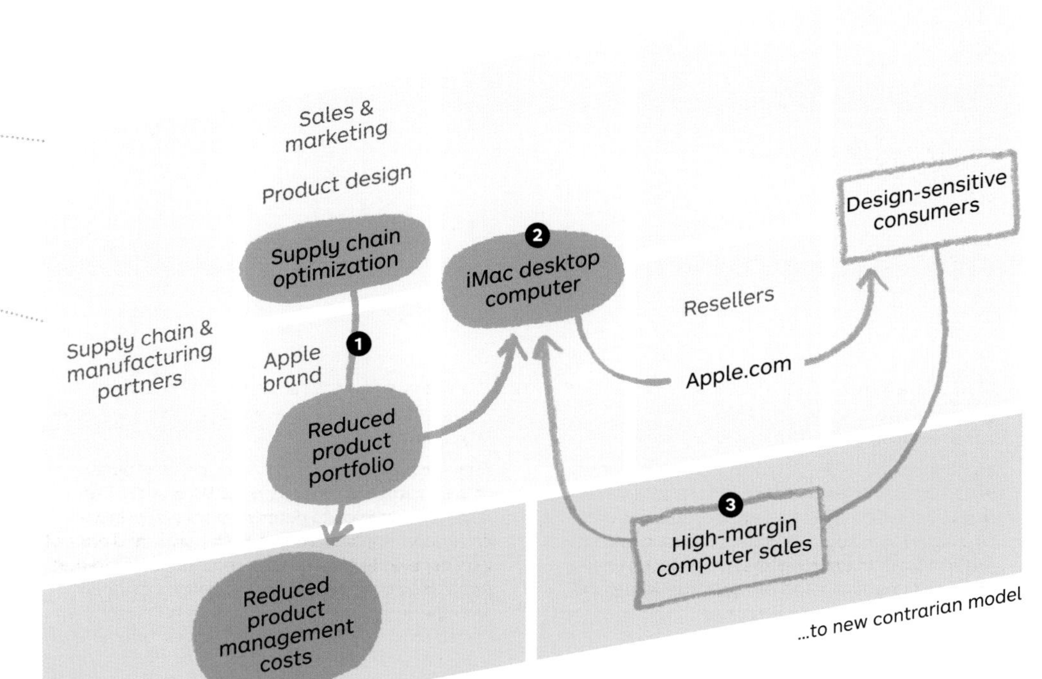

$309
million profit in 1998

vs.

$1,045
million loss in fiscal year 1997[35]

800,000
iMacs sold

within the first 140 days of release. An iMac was sold every 15 seconds.[36]

31 to 6
days, worth of supply held in inventory

In fiscal year 1997, Apple had $437 million tied up in inventory, or a full month's supply on the books. But by the close of fiscal year 1998, the company had slashed inventory levels by 80%, to just six days.[37]

Multiple Shift Patterns

2006 ~~~ 2017

Ørsted

In 2012, new CEO Henrik Poulsen leads the transformation of Ørsted from a fossil fuel energy producer and distributor to an exclusively green energy powerhouse. The shift comes after falling gas prices trigger a debt crisis.

Ørsted was established in the 1970s as DONG Energy, a Danish state-owned business that built coal-fired plants and offshore oil and gas rigs around Europe.

In 2009 DONG Energy decided to dramatically shift toward green energy. It announced targets to reduce the use of fossil fuels from 85% to 15% by 2040. This shift was supported by the Danish government, which started subsidizing renewable energy production.

In 2012, falling gas prices led to a debt crisis at DONG Energy and Henrik Poulsen was brought on as new CEO. Under his leadership, DONG Energy accelerated its shift to green energy. In 2019, it was the world's largest offshore wind farm developer.

In 2016, DONG Energy went public in a $15 billion IPO. In 2017, the company formally abandoned fossil fuels when it sold its oil and gas business and changed its name to Ørsted.[38]

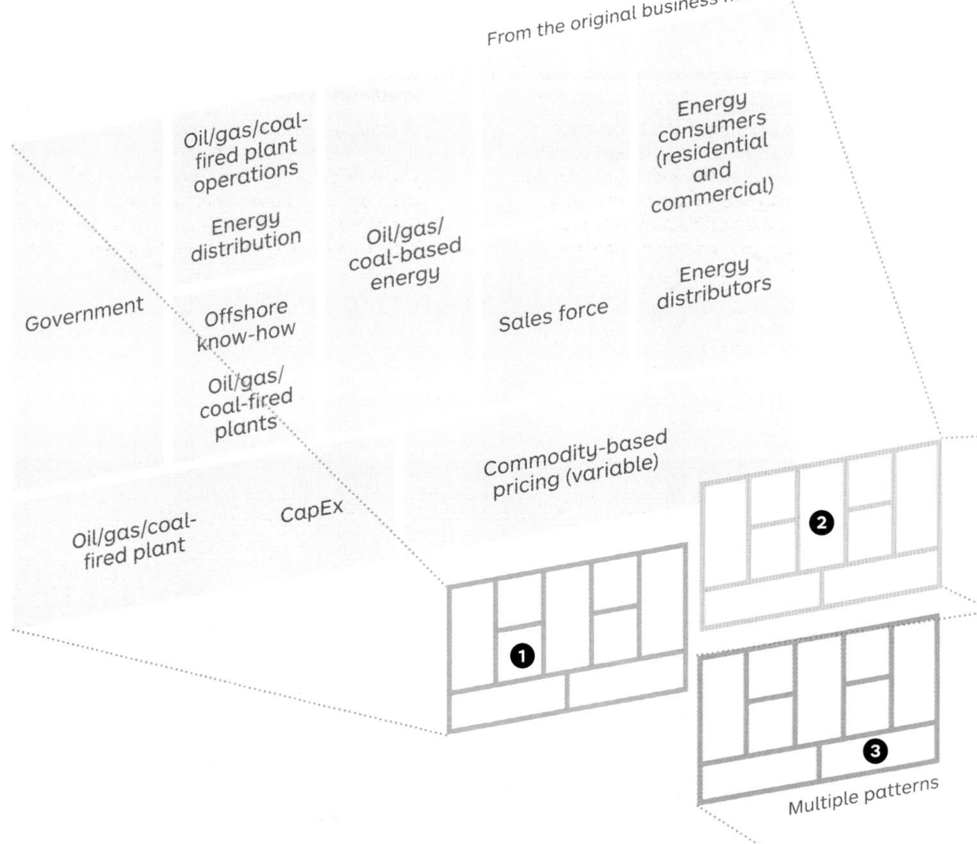

Ørsted's transformation toward becoming a sustainable business combines several shifts:

1 **From Dedicated to Multi-Usage of a Key Resource**

When Ørsted starts its transformation it applies its offshore know-how from years of North Sea drilling operations to building offshore wind farms. This facilitates the radical shift from its original focus on fossil fuel energy to the new focus on renewable energy.

2 From Low Tech to High Tech

Ørsted incurs significant investment costs to shift from its drilling operations to new high-tech green power plants. Government subsidies facilitate the transition. Meanwhile, oil and gas drilling in the North Sea becomes relatively expensive due to the basin's maturity, making Ørsted's transition to wind technology and wind farms operations highly relevant.

3 From Volatile Transactional Revenues to Predictable Recurring Revenues

Ørsted's traditional revenues from fossil fuels were highly volatile and prices depended on geo-political factors and fluctuating commodity prices. Ørsted's wind-based energy prices, however, are set at long-term, fixed prices due to government subsidies (and renewable certificates). In 2007, only 13% of Ørsted's production is based on fixed prices versus 81% in 2018.

Government
Energy distribution
Wind farm production and operations
Wind turbine manufacturers
Offshore know-how
1
Wind farms
2
Renewable energy (wind farms)
Value-based relationship (sustainability)
Sales force
Energy consumers (residential and commercial)
Energy distributors
Reduced cost due to government subsidies
Wind farm operations
CapEx
Fixed pricing for renewable energy
3
Higher prices (green energy premium)
...to new business model

75%

of energy produced from renewables

Green share of generation increased from 64% to 75% in 2018.[39]

81%

reduction in CO_2 emissions

Reduced carbon emissions from 18 million tons in 2006 to 3.4 million tons in 2018.[39]

87%

of capital invested in renewables. In 2007, 16% of total capital employed was invested in renewables. In 2018, the share of renewables had increased to 87%.[39]

From Product to Recurring Service
1990s ~~~ 1999

Rolls-Royce

Rolls-Royce launches TotalCare© in the late 1990s. It is the first jet engine manufacturer to shift from selling an engine (product) to selling care for every stage of the product lifecycle (service).

Rolls-Royce's civil aerospace business recognized in the 1990s that its business model was misaligned with its airline and business aviation customers: in order to generate a new sale, Rolls-Royce engines had to break or malfunction.

In 1999, American Airlines asked Rolls-Royce to deliver not only a large engine order but also all after-sales services related to repair, maintenance, transportation, and peripheral supplies. TotalCare service was born out of this initial request.

TotalCare transferred the risk of managing a jet engine over its lifetime from the customer to Rolls-Royce. TotalCare realigned Rolls-Royce's incentives with those of its customers with a recurring revenue model where Rolls-Royce gets paid by the flying hour of its jet engine.

With TotalCare, Rolls-Royce has shifted from a product to a recurring service business model. Its jet engines are sold at a loss and Rolls-Royce recoups losses with the service contract over time.

14.3 million charged hours

14.3 million large engine invoiced flying hours in 2018.[40]

90% of fleet covered

90% of the 2018 Rolls-Royce widebody fleet is covered by TotalCare service agreements.[40]

From Niche to Mass Market
2013 ~~~ 2016

The Washington Post

Jeff Bezos purchases the *Washington Post* in 2013 in order to transform the niche local newspaper into a national, digital, mass-media powerhouse.

In 2103, Jeff Bezos purchased the *Washington Post* (*The Post*) for $250 million. *The Post* was struggling to survive as a print publication, hyper-focused on Washington politics. Bezos used his Internet expertise to transform the newspaper into a global, digital media company focused on a mass market, leveraging the free distribution of the Internet.

The Post kept the integrity of its editorial, investigative journalism while also making a broad outreach to additional readers. It installed a paywall to increase its subscriber revenues and it created a platform for aggregating news across platforms, reaching more journalists and more readers.

1.7 million digital subscriptions

From 484,000 print subscribers and 28,000 digital subscriptions in 2012 to over 1.7 million digital subscriptions in 2019.[41,42]

87 million unique visitors

in March 2019 with an increase of 84% in three years (vs. 28 million in 2010, 41 million in 2012).[43]

From B2B to B2(B2)C

1976 ~~~ 1989

GORE-TEX

In 1989, W.L. Gore launches the "guaranteed to keep you dry" promise on products using its Gore-Tex fabrics. That allows Gore to shift from a behind-the-scenes B2B fabric manufacturer to a trusted B2C brand.

Gore-Tex was developed by W.L. Gore in 1969 as the world's first waterproof and breathable fabric. The company received its first commercial Gore-Tex order in 1976 to develop rainwear and tents for an outdoor company.

In 1989, Gore-Tex introduced the Guaranteed to Keep You Dry \ promise on its waterproof products, which included a lifetime product warranty. W.L. Gore, which doesn't manufacture the final product, convinced clothing and outdoor brands to market this guarantee with hang tags on the garments using its fabrics. This gave consumers an extra sense of quality and peace of mind and made Gore-Tex a ubiquitous brand by piggybacking established clothing manufacturers.

"It is one thing for a company to guarantee what it makes. It is quite another for it to guarantee what others make. But that is exactly what they do."

—THE GORE-TEX PROMISE

Although Gore didn't manufacture the end garments, the supplier extended its promise to consumers. If consumers weren't "completely satisfied" with their garment, Gore would take care of it. Gore used its logo and its Gore-Tex label to show end consumers that their garments could be trusted regardless of the manufacturer.

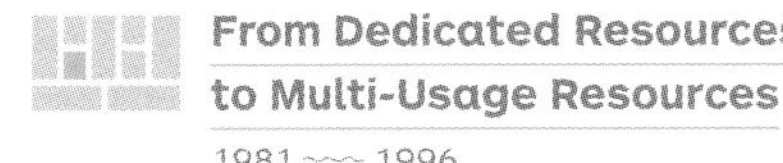

From Dedicated Resources to Multi-Usage Resources

1981 ~~~ 1996

Delta Airlines

In 1996 Delta Airlines puts its SkyMiles to new use and resells them to American Express for their loyalty program.

Delta Airlines created its SkyMIles frequent flier program in 1981. SkyMiles were a key resource in Delta's air travel business model—to rewarding its loyal customers.

In 1996, Delta Airlines realized it could reuse that key resource for another value proposition. It started selling SkyMiles to a new customer, American Express (AmEx) who would distribute these SkyMiles to their own customers, AmEx credit card holders.

This partnership allowed AmEx to target high-end travelers interested in earning SkyMiles with their credit card spending and allowed Delta to find another usage for its SkyMiles.

35%

of Delta's income ($3.4 billion of value) came from selling miles to American Express in 2018.[44]

2x

Delta expects its benefit from the relationship to double to nearly $7 billion by 2023.[45]

Questions for Leaders

Value Proposition Shifts

Shift	How might we...
From → To **Product** ↔ **Service**	...shift to a business business model built around a recurring service that provides predictable and recurring revenues?
To ← From	...add scalable products to our services to increase the share of wallet and lifetime value of each customer and boost overall revenues?
From → To **Low Tech** ↔ **High Tech**	...leverage technology activities or resources to transform our value proposition, radically modify our cost structure, or dramatically extend our reach?
To ← From	...leverage low-tech activities or resources to provide value to customers that they really appreciate, but that doesn't cost much to provide or that technology can't offer?
From → To **Platform** ↔ **Sales**	...turn a product or service into a valuable platform that connects users with third-party product and service providers and vice-versa?
To ← From	...add our own scalable products and services to our platform to increase the lifetime value of each customer and boost overall revenues?

Frontstage Driven Shifts

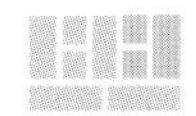

Shift	How might we...
From → To **Niche Market** ↔ **Mass Market**	...modify our value proposition, adapt our marketing and branding, and extend our reach to shift from a niche market to a mass market?
To ← From	...create niche value propositions for a series of niche segments with specific needs? How would that affect our marketing and branding and distribution strategy?
From → To **B2B** ↔ **B2C**	...become relevant and visible to our end customers, the consumers? How would we have to modify our value proposition to our direct customers (B2B) and consumers (B2C) to make that happen?
To ← From	...use our B2C customer experience and relationships, infrastructure, resources, activities, and expertise, to create value for B2B customers and even competitors?
From → To **High Touch** ↔ **Low Touch**	...create a high-touch experience, improve our value proposition, and increase price and revenues, while maintaining the advantages of standardization and scale?
To ← From	...create or maintain customer value, while shifting from a high-touch to a low-touch experience? Which aspects of high touch do customers not value as much as the price of providing them?

Backstage Driven Shifts

Shift	How might we...
From Dedicated Resources → To Multi-Usage Resources	...monetize one of our key resources to create a new value proposition for a completely new customer segment? How might our key resources enable us to provide a better value proposition than competitors?
From Multi-Usage Resources → To Dedicated Resources	...trim our business model by refocusing resources used to serve several value propositions and dedicate them to one only? How might that help us improve our profit formula?
From Asset Heavy → To Asset Light	...free up capital and energy from building and maintaining assets toward focusing on client-related activities? How might we better put that available capital to use and improve our profit formula?
From Asset Light → To Asset Heavy	...leverage our light assets like IP and brand to invest in heavy assets? How might that help us create a competitive advantage, make us difficult to copy, or create barriers to market entry?
From Closed → To Open	... leverage the strengths of our business model to use external R&D, IP, and resources (outside-in) or share internal R&D, IP, and resources with outside partners (inside-out)? How might that lead to a higher return on R&D or capital invested?
From Open → To Closed	...create a competitive advantage by internalizing R&D, IP, resources, and activities? How might that create cost, knowledge, or profit efficiencies? How might we stop sharing R&D, IP, resources, and activities with outside partners?

Profit Formula Driven Shifts

Shift	How might we...
From High Cost → To Low Cost	...create value for price-conscious customer segments? How might we reconfigure activities and resources to disrupt our cost structure and make that low price possible?
From Low Cost → To High Cost	...create value for price-insensitive customer segments? How might we leverage our resources and activities to create a high-value, high-price value proposition?
From Transactional Revenue → To Recurring Revenue	...focus on recurring customer jobs-to-be-done in order to create a recurring value proposition with a long-term relationship and recurring revenues?
From Recurring Revenue → To Transactional Revenue	...add transactional revenues to our recurring revenues in order to improve customer share of wallet and boost our overall revenues?
From Conventional → To Contrarian	...eliminate or reduce costly activities and resources, even if they create value for customers? How might we replace that lost value with less costly value creators that matter most to customers?
From Contrarian → To Conventional	...add costly resources and activities to our business model to substantially increase value, price, and luxury feel? Or, conversely, how might we strip our business model to shift to a pure low-cost model?

Invincible Companies Transcend Industry Boundaries

Tencent social networks, online gaming, online advertising, content production, financial services, software, music...

Apple smartphones, personal computers, tablets, wearables, software, music, movies, health, photography, personal productivity, credit cards, mobile payments...

Ping An banking, insurance, healthcare, auto services, real estate, smart cities...

Amazon retail, logistics, electronics, streaming, IT infrastructure, publishing, e-commerce infrastructure, online advertising, SMB loans...

You...

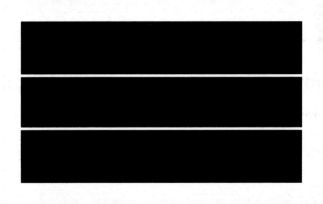

Design Your Culture

To build an Invincible Company you need to create, manage, and harmonize two completely antagonistic cultures under one roof—and they both have an important role to play. You need to explore and exploit simultaneously.

Explore

Your exploration culture cultivates the creation, discovery, validation, and acceleration of completely new ideas that are foreign to an organization.

Exploit

Your exploitation culture cherishes the management, systematic improvement, and growth of existing businesses.

Cultivate Explore and Exploit Under One Roof

Invincible Companies design, manage, and maintain both a strong Explore and a strong Exploit culture. They cherish operational excellence, planning, and constant improvements when managing the present. Yet, they know they can't cost cut themselves into the future. They simultaneously embrace risk, experimentation, failure, and adaptation when exploring ideas for the coming years and decades. However successful today, they don't rest on their laurels; they already work on tomorrow.

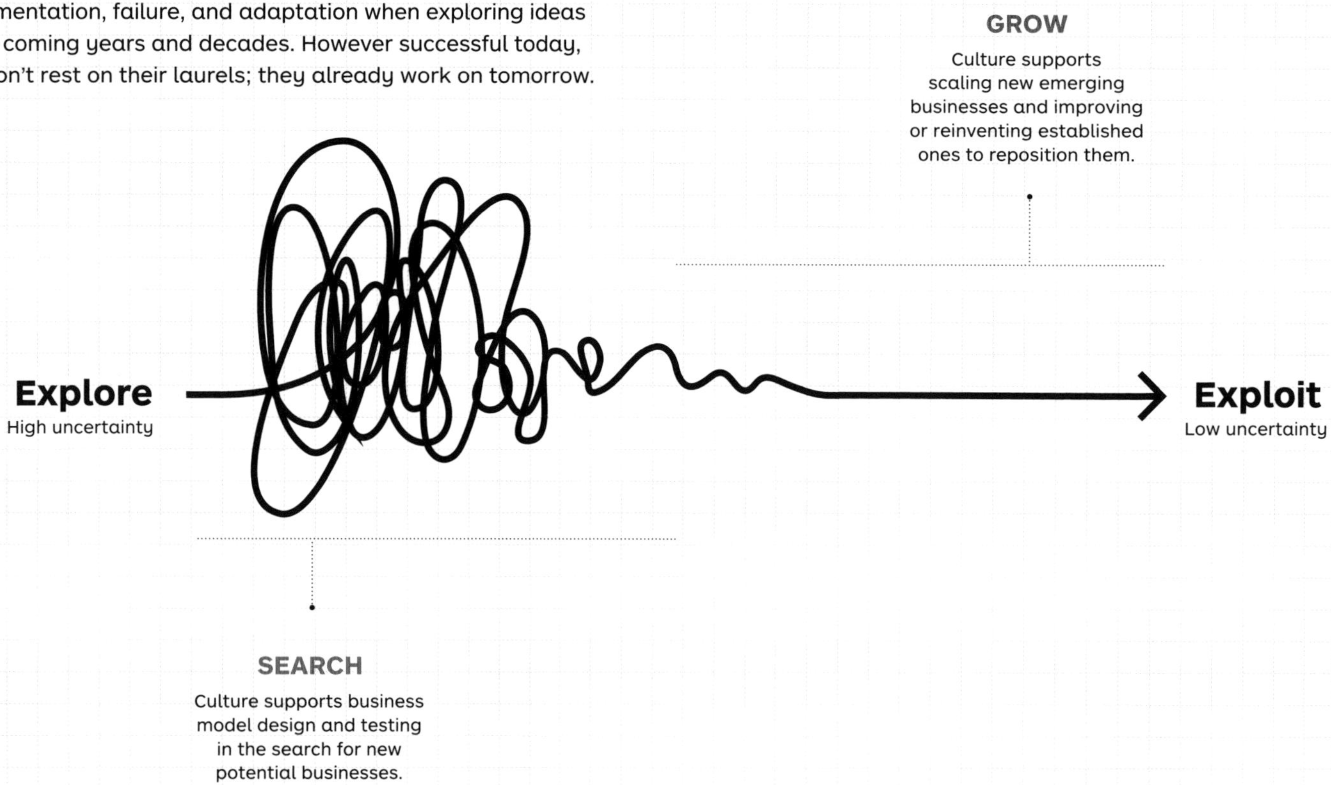

GROW

Culture supports scaling new emerging businesses and improving or reinventing established ones to reposition them.

Explore
High uncertainty

Exploit
Low uncertainty

SEARCH

Culture supports business model design and testing in the search for new potential businesses.

Explore	⟷	Exploit
We admit that we don't know and adopt a beginner's mindset. We search for a solution and accept that not all projects will succeed.	**What's the mindset?**	We rely on our experience and adopt our expert's mindset. We plan and execute and believe failure is not an option.
We embrace risk and uncertainty. We manage them by experimenting, learning, and adapting. We make many small bets to find winners.	**How do we deal with risk and uncertainty?**	We shun risk and uncertainty. We minimize them by planning, executing, and managing. We make few and well-calculated bets on winners.
We work iteratively and make rough prototypes.	**How do we work?**	We work sequentially with high fidelity.
Failure is an inevitable side product of exploration. We embrace, manage, and learn from failure and minimize the cost of it by making many small bets.	**What's our attitude toward failure?**	Failure is unacceptable. We avoid and punish it. It can be avoided through careful planning and sound execution.
We define hypotheses to make risk explicit. Then we measure the reduction of risk of a new idea.	**How do we measure progress and success?**	We define milestones to make progress steps explicit. We measure whether we are on time and on budget.
We reward people for trying, learning, and reducing the risk of new ideas.	**What do we reward people for?**	We reward people for planning, executing, and staying on time and on budget.
We move fast on reversible decisions and test them as quickly and cheaply as possible to produce real-world evidence.	**What's our attitude toward speed of decision-making?**	We take time to carefully analyze, think through, and plan irreversible decisions with large sunk costs.
We make small bets when risk and uncertainty are high. We increase our investments based on the strength of the evidence.	**How do we invest?**	We take time to plan a project and release funds based on reaching milestones.
We value the ability to deal with ambiguity, to move fast and adapt, and to test ideas and reduce their risk.	**What do we value?**	We value rigor, the ability to plan and execute, the skill to design processes, and reliable delivery.

How It Fits Together

Your corporate identity defines who you want to be and sets the context for everything else. It allows you to specify the guidance that will shape your entire portfolio. Your portfolio is a reflection of who you are in terms of businesses you own (Exploit), and who you are trying to become in terms of businesses you are exploring (Explore).

In order to smoothly manage this type of dual portfolio you need to put in place a so-called ambidextrous culture that is world-class at both exploration and exploitation. This entire chapter describes how to achieve that by eliminating blockers and implementing enablers that will facilitate your cultural transformation.

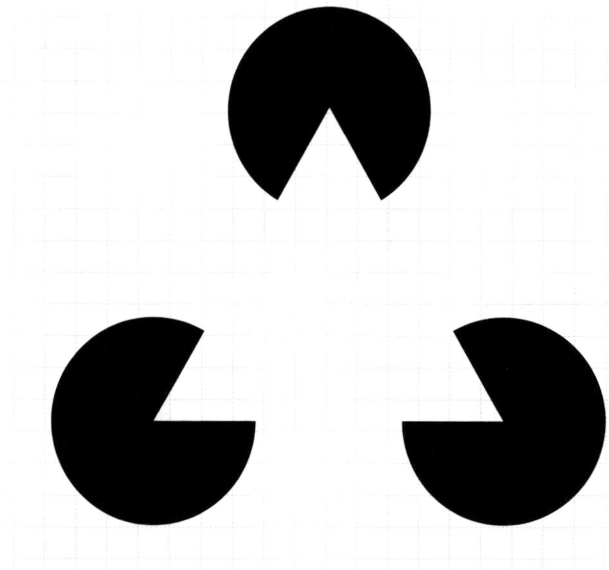

Corporate Identity

WHO WE ARE

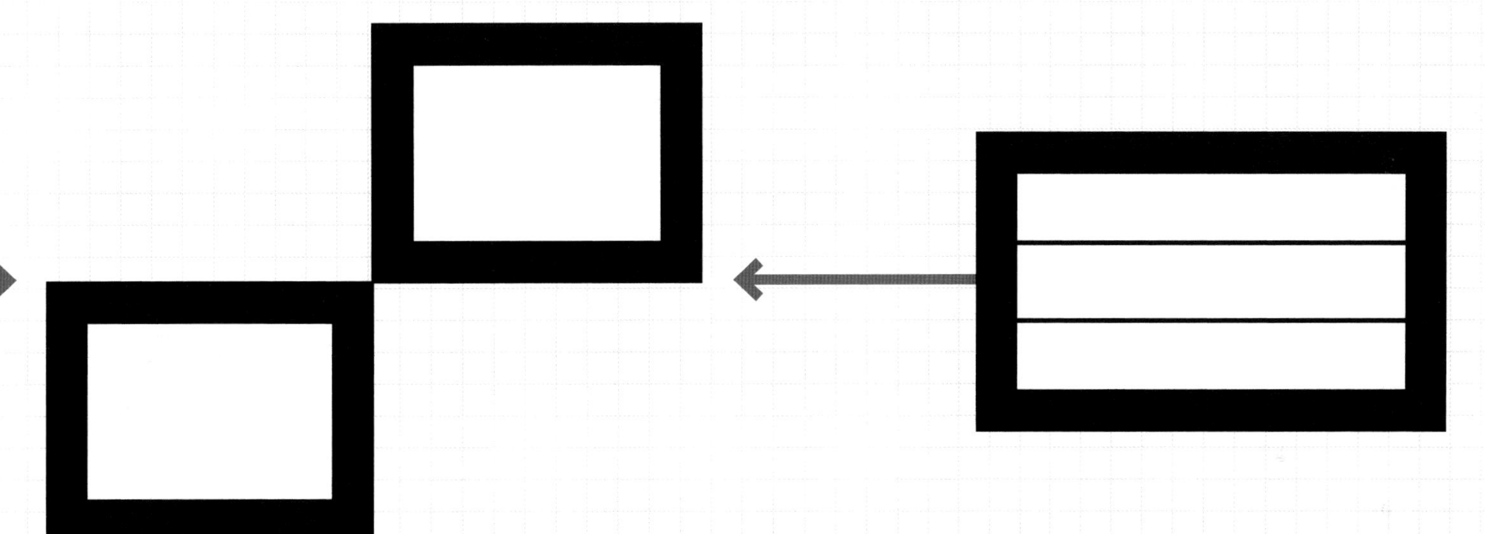

Portfolio Map

WHAT WE'RE DOING

Culture Map

HOW WE'LL DO IT

293

Every company has a corporate culture.

Yet, too many companies let culture just happen. Invincible Companies actively understand, design, and manage culture. They create world-class innovation and execution cultures that live in harmony. In this section we outline how you can map corporate culture and what it takes to create a world-class innovation culture.

What are our desired outcomes?
What behaviors will allow us to achieve our desired outcomes?
What enables and blocks us from our goals?

The Culture Map

Together with Dave Gray, Strategyzer developed the Culture Map as a tool to design better-performing companies. The Culture Map is a practical, simple, and visual tool to understand, design, test, and manage the corporate culture you want to bring to fruition in your organization. In this book we use the Culture Map to map and design an innovation culture.

DAVE GRAY

Author and entrepreneur

"If you want to understand culture, you need to map it."

Outcomes

The concrete positive or negative consequences resulting from people's behavior.

Behaviors

How do individual and teams act or conduct themselves within the company? What do they do or say? How do they interact? What patterns do you notice?

Enablers/Blockers

The levers that lead to positive or negative behaviors inside your company. These could be formal policies, processes, and reward systems, or informal rituals and actions that influence people's behaviors and, ultimately, influence a company's outcomes.

The Culture Map Beta

A Change Management Tool

Designed for: | Designed by: | Date: | Iteration:

Outcomes

Behaviors

Enablers/Blockers

DAVE GRAY:
davegrayinfo.com

Strategyzer
strategyzer.com

LEADERS DON'T CREATE GROWTH

LEADERS CREATE CONDITIONS FOR GROWTH

Cultivate corporate culture like a garden.

You can't mechanistically design a corporate culture like you'd — for example — design a car. An organization is a social system that is infinitely more complex than a car. That doesn't mean you shouldn't design the aspects of your organization that are under your control. We really like Dave Gray's analogy of designing culture like you'd design and cultivate a garden.

The **outcomes** in your culture are the fruits. These are the things you want your culture to achieve, or what you want to "harvest" from your garden.

The **behaviors** are the heart of your culture. They're the positive or negative actions people perform every day that will result in a good or bad harvest.

The **enablers and blockers** are the elements that allow your garden to flourish or not. Some are under your control, like sufficient water or fertilizer. You need to take care of the soil, seeds, and the young plants for your garden to flourish. Other elements, like the weather, are not under your control and you can only prepare your garden to minimize the damage or maximize the positive impact.

Culture Map

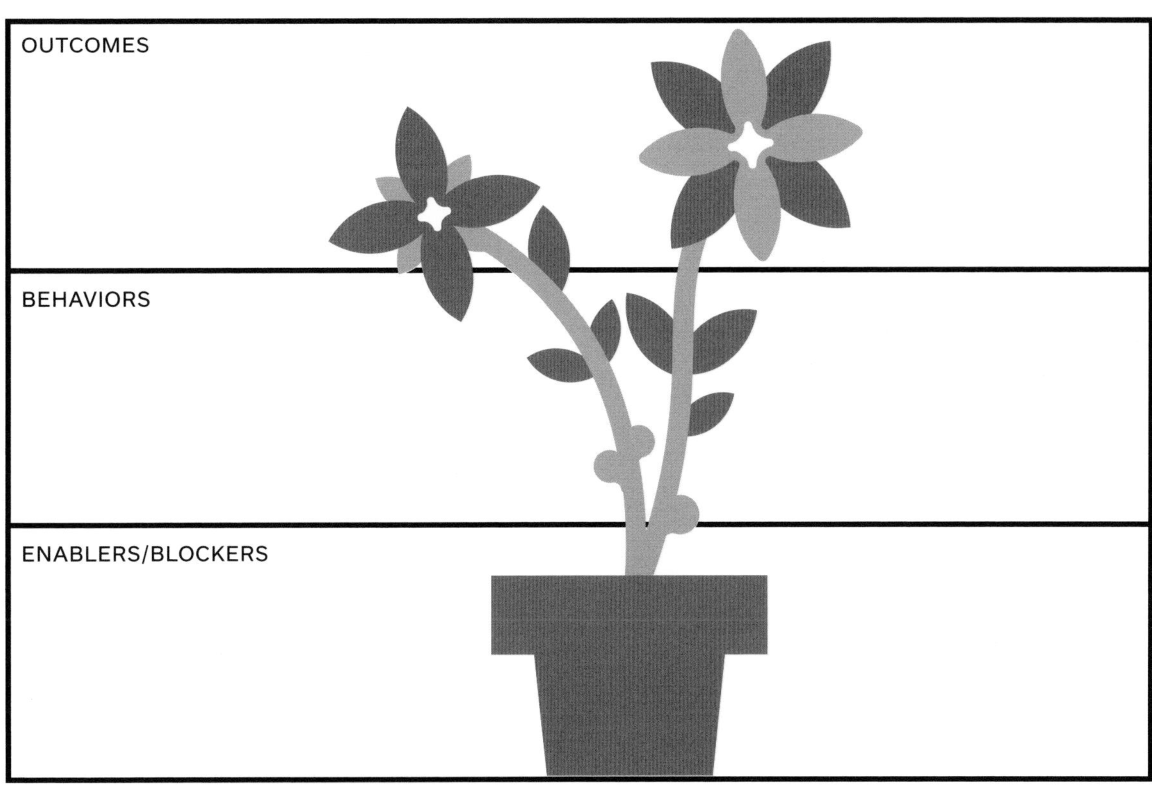

Amazon's Innovation Culture

Amazon's stellar growth and constant reinvention aren't magic, they're ingrained in the company culture. Read Jeff Bezos's letters to shareholders to understand how Amazon built a company culture that constantly pioneers in new spaces.

"We want to be a large company that's also an invention machine [...] with the speed of movement, nimbleness, and risk-acceptance mentality normally associated with entrepreneurial start-ups."

JEFF BEZOS

Amazon founder & CEO

amazon.com

1997 LETTER TO SHAREHOLDERS
(Reprinted from the 1997 Annual Report)

To our shareholders:

Amazon.com passed many milestones in 1997: by year-end, we had served more than 1.5 million customers, yielding 838% revenue growth to $147.8 million, and extended our market leadership despite aggressive competitive entry.

But this is Day 1 for the Internet and, if we execute well, for Amazon.com. Today, online commerce saves customers money and precious time. Tomorrow, through personalization, online commerce will accelerate the very process of discovery. Amazon.com uses the Internet to create real value for its customers and, by doing so, hopes to create an enduring franchise, even in established and large markets.

We have a window of opportunity as larger players marshal the resources to pursue the online opportunity and as customers, new to purchasing online, are receptive to forming new relationships. The competitive landscape has continued to evolve at a fast pace. Many large players have moved online with credible offerings and have devoted substantial energy and resources to building awareness, traffic, and sales. Our goal is to move quickly to solidify and extend our current position while we begin to pursue the online commerce opportunities in other areas. We see substantial opportunity in the large markets we are targeting. This strategy is not without risk: it requires serious investment and crisp execution against established franchise leaders.

It's All About the Long Term

We believe that a fundamental measure of our success will be the shareholder value we create over the *long term*. This value will be a direct result of our ability to extend and solidify our current market leadership position. The stronger our market leadership, the more powerful our economic model. Market leadership can translate directly to higher revenue, higher profitability, greater capital velocity, and correspondingly stronger returns on invested capital.

Our decisions have consistently reflected this focus. We first measure ourselves in terms of the metrics most indicative of our market leadership: customer and revenue growth, the degree to which our customers continue to purchase from us on a repeat basis, and the strength of our brand. We have invested and will continue to invest aggressively to expand and leverage our customer base, brand, and infrastructure as we move to establish an enduring franchise.

Because of our emphasis on the long term, we may make decisions and weigh tradeoffs differently than some companies. Accordingly, we want to share with you our fundamental management and decision-making approach so that you, our shareholders, may confirm that it is consistent with your investment philosophy:

- We will continue to focus relentlessly on our customers.
- We will continue to make investment decisions in light of long-term market leadership considerations rather than short-term profitability considerations or short-term Wall Street reactions.
- We will continue to measure our programs and the effectiveness of our investments analytically, to jettison those that do not provide acceptable returns, and to step up our investment in those that work best. We will continue to learn from both our successes and our failures.
- We will make bold rather than timid investment decisions where we see a sufficient probability of gaining market leadership advantages. Some of these investments will pay off, others will not, and we will have learned another valuable lesson in either case.
- When forced to choose between optimizing the appearance of our GAAP accounting and maximizing the present value of future cash flows, we'll take the cash flows.
- We will share our strategic thought processes with you when we make bold choices (to the extent competitive pressures allow), so that you may evaluate for yourselves whether we are making rational long-term leadership investments.
- We will work hard to spend wisely and maintain our lean culture. We understand the importance of continually reinforcing a cost-conscious culture, particularly in a business incurring net losses.
- We will balance our focus on growth with emphasis on long-term profitability and capital management. At this stage, we choose to prioritize growth because we believe that scale is central to achieving the potential of our business model.
- We will continue to focus on hiring and retaining versatile and talented employees, and continue to weight their compensation to stock options rather than cash. We know our success will be largely affected by our ability to attract and retain a motivated employee base, each of whom must think like, and therefore must actually be, an owner.

We aren't so bold as to claim that the above is the "right" investment philosophy, but it's ours, and we would be remiss if we weren't clear in the approach we have taken and will continue to take.

With this foundation, we would like to turn to a review of our business focus, our progress in 1997, and our outlook for the future.

Obsess Over Customers

From the beginning, our focus has been on offering our customers compelling value. We realized that the Web was, and still is, the World Wide Wait. Therefore, we set out to offer customers something they simply could not get any other way, and began serving them with books. We brought them much more selection than was possible in a physical store (our store would now occupy 6 football fields), and presented it in a useful, easy-to-search, and easy-to-browse format in a store open 365 days a year, 24 hours a day. We maintained a dogged focus on improving the shopping experience, and in 1997 substantially enhanced our store. We now offer customers gift certificates, 1-Click℠ shopping, and vastly more reviews, content, browsing options, and recommendation features. We dramatically lowered prices, further increasing customer value. Word of mouth remains the most powerful customer acquisition tool we have, and we are grateful for the trust our customers have placed in us. Repeat purchases and word of mouth have combined to make Amazon.com the market leader in online bookselling.

By many measures, Amazon.com came a long way in 1997:

- Sales grew from $15.7 million in 1996 to $147.8 million – an 838% increase.
- Cumulative customer accounts grew from 180,000 to 1,510,000 – a 738% increase.
- The percentage of orders from repeat customers grew from over 46% in the fourth quarter of 1996 to over 58% in the same period in 1997.
- In terms of audience reach, per Media Metrix, our Web site went from a rank of 90th to within the top 20.
- We established long-term relationships with many important strategic partners, including America Online, Yahoo!, Excite, Netscape, GeoCities, AltaVista, @Home, and Prodigy.

Amazon

Each Culture Map is based on an analysis of Jeff Bezos's letters to shareholders between 1997 and 2018. We captured the main outcomes, behaviors, enablers, and blockers related to innovation that Bezos mentions in his letters and visualized them in a Culture Map.

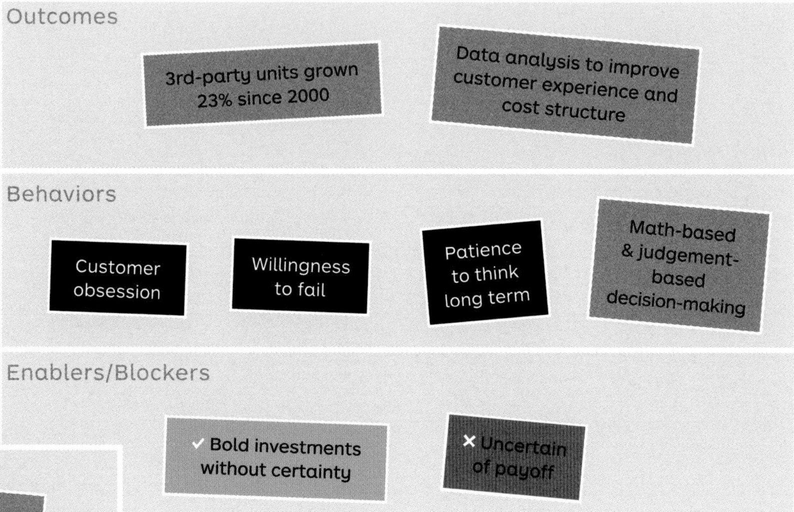

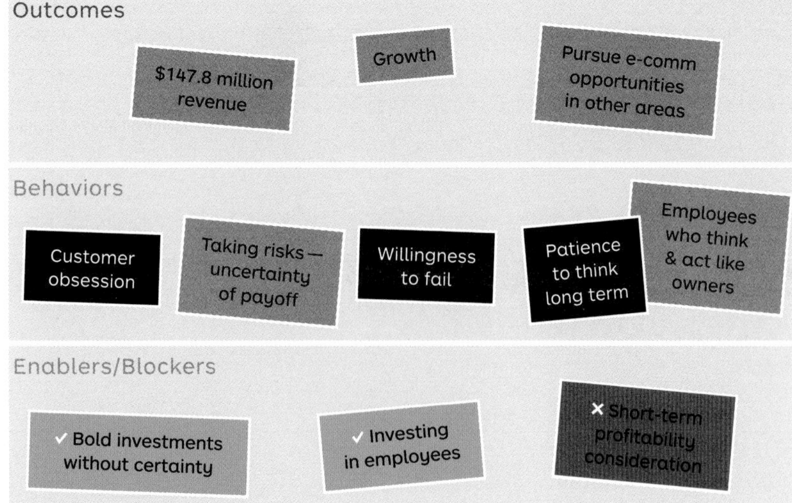

The foundation of Amazon's corporate culture was laid out in Bezos's 1997 letter to shareholders in the first annual report. The pillars of this culture (customer obsession, willingness to fail, patience to think long term) remain fundamentally unchanged and a copy of the 1997 letter has been attached to every subsequent annual report. We analyzed the annual shareholder letters for you to visualize and highlight the consistency of its innovation culture and show the progression of results and outcomes.

2018

Outcomes

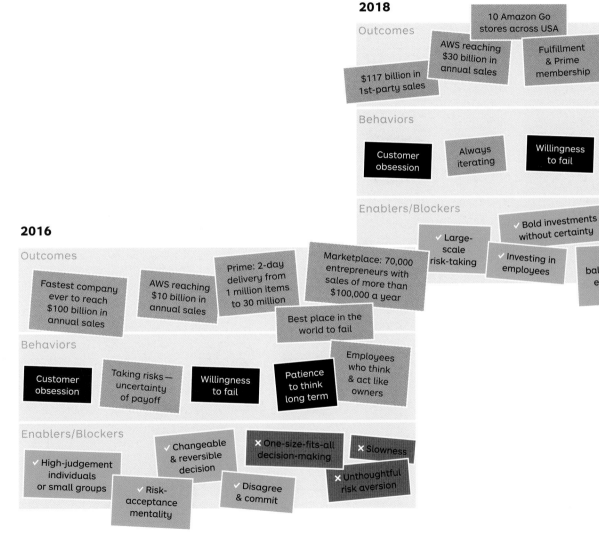

- 10 Amazon Go stores across USA
- 100 million Alexa-enabled devices sold
- AWS reaching $30 billion in annual sales
- Fulfillment & Prime membership
- $117 billion in 1st-party sales
- 3rd-party sales now 58% of total sales—$169 billion

Behaviors

- Customer obsession
- Always iterating
- Willingness to fail
- Patience to think long term
- Employees who think & act like owners

Enablers/Blockers

- ✓ Large-scale risk-taking
- ✓ Bold investments without certainty
- ✕ Uncertainty of payoff
- ✓ Investing in employees
- ✓ Finding balance between exploring and efficiency
- ✕ Unthoughtful risk aversion

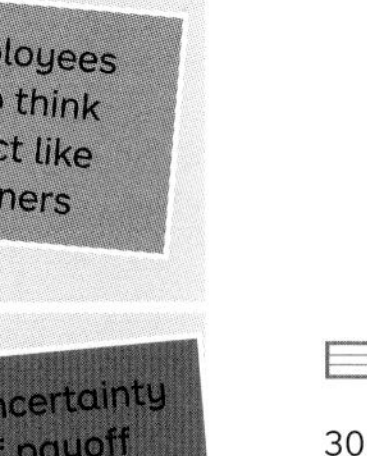

2016

Outcomes

- Fastest company ever to reach $100 billion in annual sales
- AWS reaching $10 billion in annual sales
- Prime: 2-day delivery from 1 million items to 30 million
- Marketplace: 70,000 entrepreneurs with sales of more than $100,000 a year
- Best place in the world to fail

Behaviors

- Customer obsession
- Taking risks—uncertainty of payoff
- Willingness to fail
- Patience to think long term
- Employees who think & act like owners

Enablers/Blockers

- ✓ High-judgement individuals or small groups
- ✓ Changeable & reversible decision
- ✕ One-size-fits-all decision-making
- ✕ Slowness
- ✓ Risk-acceptance mentality
- ✓ Disagree & commit
- ✕ Unthoughtful risk aversion

Applying the Culture Map

From existing culture to desired culture. Of course it's up to you to decide if your session should start top down by tackling outcomes and then the associated behaviors, enablers, and blockers. Practice shows that starting with behaviors is an easy place to get going.

Current State Innovation Culture

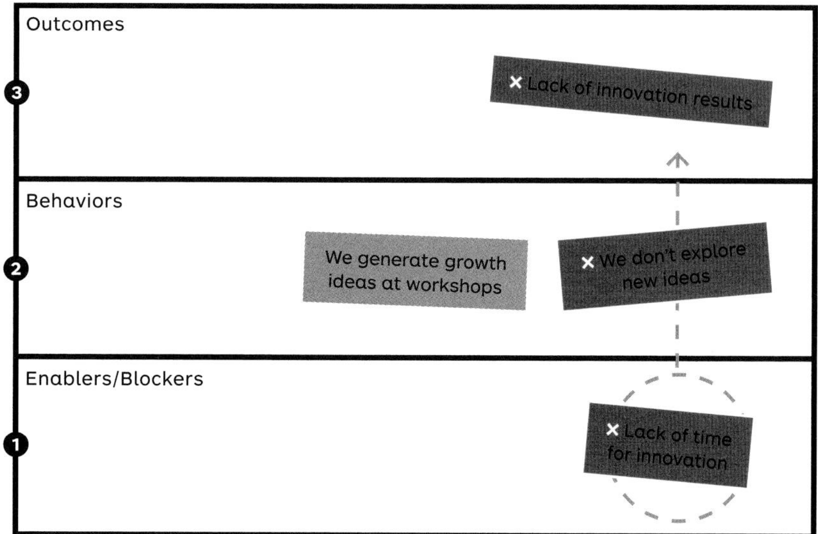
Outcomes
3
× Lack of innovation results
Behaviors
2
We generate growth ideas at workshops
× We don't explore new ideas
Enablers/Blockers
1
× Lack of time for innovation

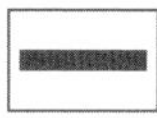

1. Start with Mapping Behaviors

There can be a tendency to describe behaviors in an abstract way, like "We don't innovate." Make sure you use specific examples and get into the habit of mapping behavior based on evidence, not opinion. For example, "Last year we conducted two workshops to develop new growth ideas, but nobody made time to explore them after we left the workshop." Make sure you capture positive and negative behaviors alike. Behave like an anthropologist who neutrally captures what's going on in your team or organization.

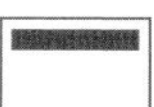

2. Capture Resulting Outcomes

Now continue with capturing the positive and negative outcomes resulting from the behaviors you just mapped out. Ask which behaviors you missed, if new outcomes arise that are not related to the already mapped behaviors. Again, remain neutral and make sure you capture both the positive and the negative.

3. Identify Enablers and Blockers

Now that you've captured behaviors and outcomes ask yourself what led to them. Ask "What are the enablers that made good or bad behaviors possible?" and "What are the blockers that prevented good or bad behaviors to emerge?" Make sure you identify formal enablers and blockers, like processes and incentive systems, and informal ones, like meeting rituals or lack of knowledge. Take note that behaviors, such as those of leaders, can also be enablers and blockers.

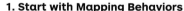

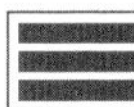

4. Design Your Desired Culture

When you've completed the Culture Map of your existing culture it's time to dream up your desired state. Design the desired outcomes, the required behaviors, and the enablers and blockers that will make that culture possible.

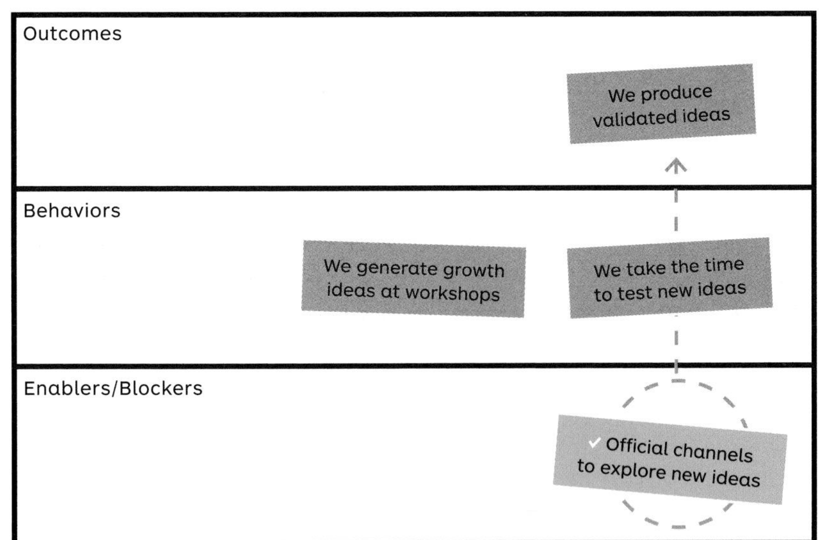

Desired Innovation Culture
Outcomes
We produce validated ideas
Behaviors
We generate growth ideas at workshops
We take the time to test new ideas
Enablers/Blockers
Official channels to explore new ideas
4

Tips & Tricks

Create a Safe Space
Designing an innovation culture without the buy-in of leadership is likely to fail. Make sure leaders are genuinely interested in creating an innovation culture. Show leadership the current state Culture Map to get them interested.

Blockers and Enablers Only
Consider working on the blockers and enablers only. First identify the blockers holding you back from innovating. Then brainstorm which enablers could boost innovation and how blockers could be eliminated. Categorize ideas into buckets of what can be done immediately, within a month, quarter, or year, or what's practically impossible to achieve.

Display Desired Culture
Prominently display the culture you want to establish. Place the map in a space where everyone can see it and is reminded of the tasks ahead. Put it up in meeting rooms so decisions can be made inline with the information on your Culture Map.

Invincible Companies build a strong exploration and exploitation culture under the same roof. In this book we mainly outline how to build a strong exploration culture, since most companies already have a pretty strong exploitation culture. We believe there are three main levers that you can work on to create an exploration culture.

Designing an Exploration Culture

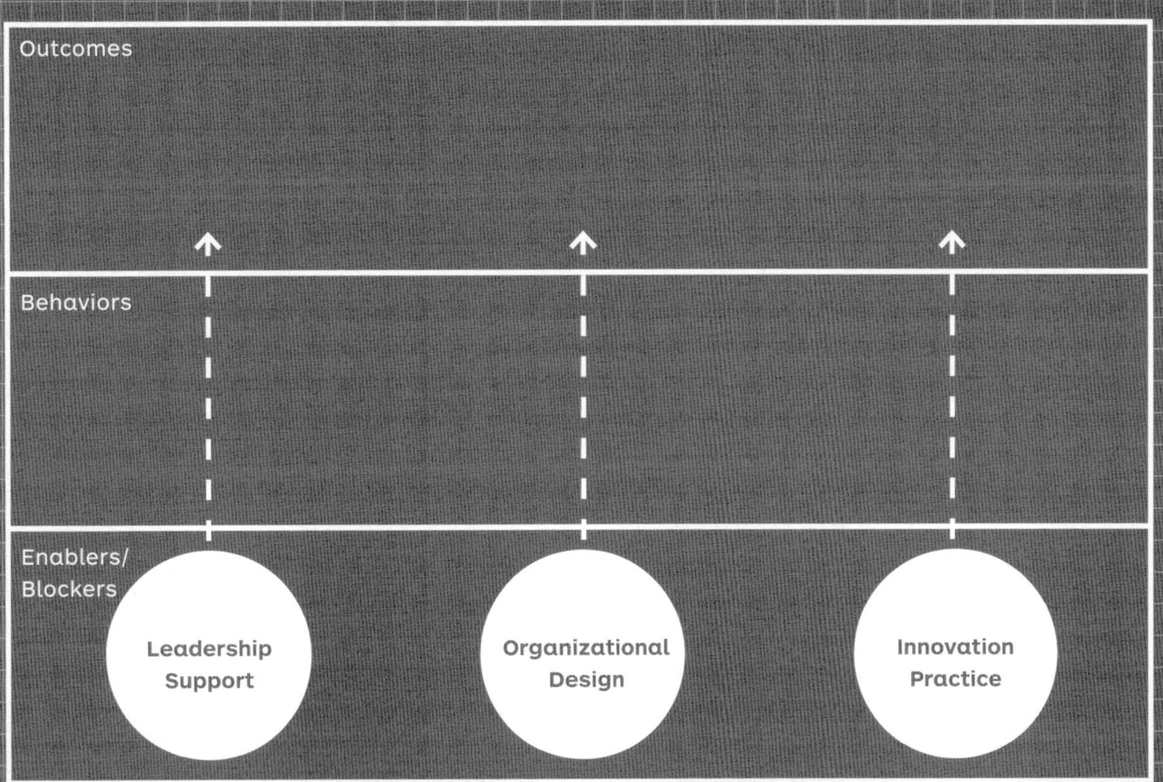
Outcomes
Behaviors
Enablers/
Blockers
Leadership
Support
Organizational
Design
Innovation
Practice

Innovation Behaviors and Outcomes

Invincible Companies design great enablers and eliminate the blockers in each one of these three areas: leadership support, organizational design, and innovaton practice. This leads to the following innovation behaviors that you can observe:

✓ Leadership Behavior

Leaders understand how innovation works and they invest a substantial amount of their time into innovation. They provide clear strategic guidance for innovation projects and they regularly review a company-wide Exploit and Explore portfolio. They are eager to explore new growth opportunities and they understand how the related risk is managed.

✓ Organizational Behavior

In organizations with an exploration culture, nobody gets fired for experimenting with new growth opportunities that fit the strategy. You find innovation on the agenda of the most important meetings and people choose innovation as a career path. Innovators understand the constraints of leaders and managers of the exisitng business and they, in return, do their best to help innovators. Exploration and execution form a true partnership to manage the present and explore the future.

✓ Innovation Team Behavior

Innovators pursue ideas based on evidence from experiments, not their opinions or their boss's opinions. Risk and uncertainty of ideas are systematically measured and projects start with cheap and quick experiments. Experiment time and costs increase with increasing evidence and decreasing uncertainty. People accumulate skills over years of practice and learn and grow from failures in any project.

Culture Map: Innovation Culture Blockers

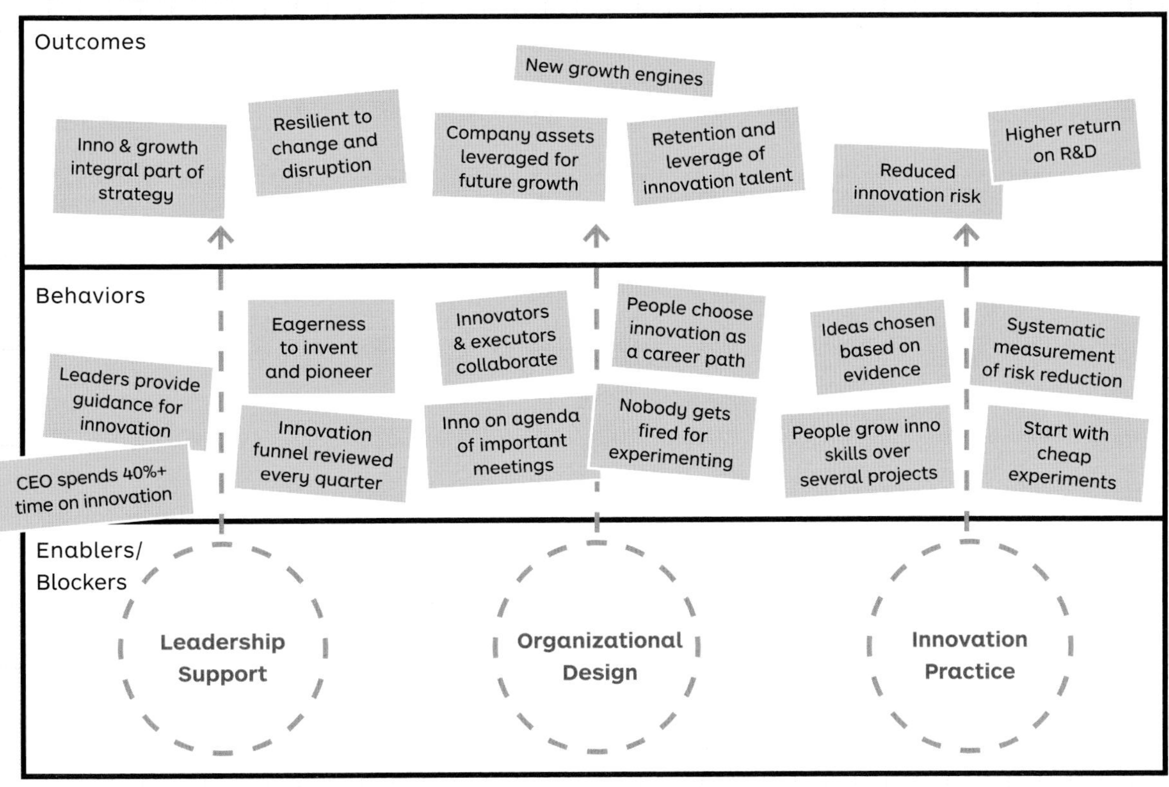
Outcomes
New growth engines
Inno & growth integral part of strategy
Resilient to change and disruption
Company assets leveraged for future growth
Retention and leverage of innovation talent
Reduced innovation risk
Higher return on R&D
Behaviors
Leaders provide guidance for innovation
CEO spends 40%+ time on innovation
Eagerness to invent and pioneer
Innovation funnel reviewed every quarter
Innovators & executors collaborate
Inno on agenda of important meetings
People choose innovation as a career path
Nobody gets fired for experimenting
Ideas chosen based on evidence
People grow inno skills over several projects
Systematic measurement of risk reduction
Start with cheap experiments
Enablers/ Blockers
Leadership Support
Organizational Design
Innovation Practice

Innovation Culture Blockers

In companies that lack innovation you can find at least some of the following innovation show stoppers:

× Leadership Support

Leaders focus predominantly on quarterly results and see innovation as a black box. There is no explicit innovation strategy, nor overall long-term innovation portfolio management. The management is locked into the current business model and exploring new directions is not part of the regular leadership discussion.

× Organizational Design

The reward system is geared toward managing and improving the existing business model. Failure is not an option, which is mandatory for world-class operations management, but lethal for experimenting with new ideas. Innovation teams have little autonomy and are slowed down by operational processes, and it's difficult for them to access customers and resources to experiment (e.g. brand, prototyping resources, other expertise).

× Innovation Practice

Innovation is a profession in itself, just like finance, marketing, or operations. You don't get good at it overnight, but with experience over time. Not having a substantial team with innovation as their sole job description will prevent an organization from developing a world-class innovation practice. Just like finance, sales, or operations, innovation needs its own processes, key performance indicators (KPIs), and culture.

Culture Map: Innovation Culture Blockers

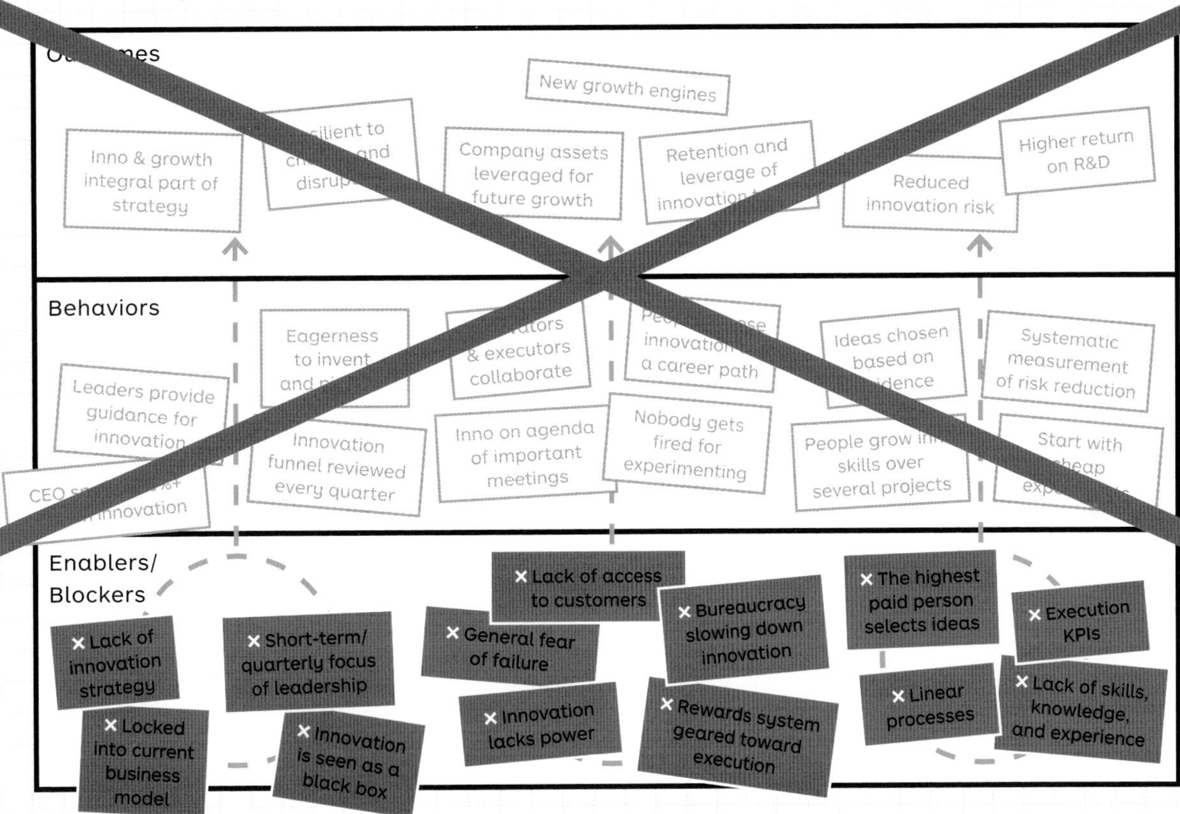

New growth engines
Inno & growth integral part of strategy
Company assets leveraged for future growth
Reduced innovation risk
Higher return on R&D
Behaviors
Leaders provide guidance for innovation
Innovation funnel reviewed every quarter
Inno on agenda of important meetings
Nobody gets fired for experimenting
Systematic measurement of risk reduction
Enablers/ Blockers
Lack of innovation strategy
Locked into current business model
Short-term/ quarterly focus of leadership
Innovation is seen as a black box
Lack of access to customers
General fear of failure
Innovation lacks power
Bureaucracy slowing down innovation
Rewards system geared toward execution
The highest paid person selects ideas
Linear processes
Execution KPIs
Lack of skills, knowledge, and experience

Innovation Culture Assessment

In the previous sections we showed you how Invincible Companies behave and how most companies still block innovation. Now let us show you how you can assess your innovation culture readiness with a scorecard we co-developed with Tendayi Viki, author of *The Corporate Startup*. Then we will help you reflect on how you can move toward becoming an Invincible Company by putting the right enablers in place.

To build an Invincible Company there are three main categories with three enablers each that you need to work on:

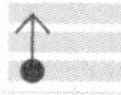

Leadership Support

- **Strategic Guidance:** a clear and explicitly communicated innovation strategy that is an important part of the overall strategy. It defines where to play, what's in, and what's out.
- **Resource Allocation:** an institutionalized allocation of resources available for innovation, which differs from the R&D budget. It includes a budget, time, and everything required to test business ideas.
- **Portfolio Management:** the exploration of the whole innovation spectrum from efficiency innovations, to sustaining innovations, to radical growth innovations with new business models. This includes a broad innovation funnel.

Organizational Design

- **Legitimacy and Power:** the status that growth and innovation and teams working on that topic have within the organization.
- **Bridge to the Core:** the access that growth and innovation has to resources and skills from the core business and the partnership that existing businesses build with innovation teams.
- **Rewards and Incentives**: a dedicated reward system that differs from management and operations and is tailored for experimentation around growth and innovation.

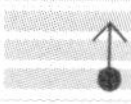

Innovation Practice

- **Innovation Tools:** the application and mastery of state-of-the art innovation concepts and tools that are practiced across leading organizations.
- **Process Management:** dedicated innovation processes and metrics that measure the reduction of risk and uncertainty from idea to scalable business.
- **Skills Development:** the existence of world-class innovation skills and experience across your organization, from professional innovation teams to existing business units.

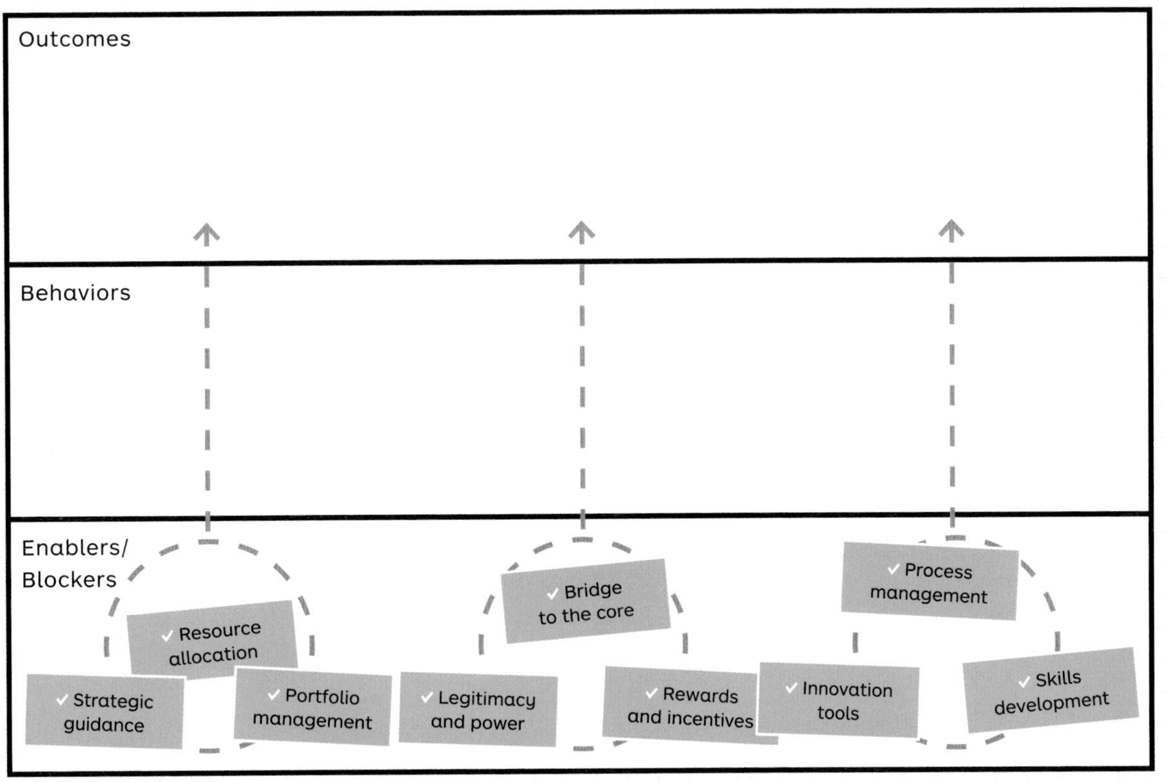
Outcomes
Behaviors
Enablers/
Blockers
✓ Resource allocation
✓ Strategic guidance
✓ Portfolio management
✓ Bridge to the core
✓ Legitimacy and power
✓ Rewards and incentives
✓ Process management
✓ Innovation tools
✓ Skills development

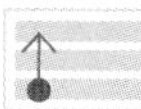

Leadership Support

Strategic Guidance

In companies with clear strategic innovation guidance, leadership communicates the strategy at important meetings at least once a quarter. The innovation guidance is completely aligned with the overall strategy and is widely understood across the organization. Good examples of clear guidance are Amazon and Ping An.

Resource Allocation

In Invincible Companies resources for innovation are institutionalized and leaders commit an important proportion of their time to innovation. Resources include:

- Leadership Time: In companies that innovate the CEO or a co-CEO invests 50% to 100% of his or her time to innovation. A great example is Bracken Darrell, CEO of Logitech or Ping An's co-CEO Jessica Tan.
- Innovation Funds: Money that is invested in internal and external innovation teams that start with small bets and get follow-up investments based on evidence. These funds differ from R&D investments.
- Innovation Core Team: A team of professional and experienced innovators who lead projects or coach project teams across an organization.
- Time: One of the scarcest resources in organizations is time. Systematically testing and de-risking ideas requires a substantial time investment from project teams.
- Prototyping Resources: Innovation teams run experiments and need access to resources for physical or digital prototypes, graphic design, videographers, and so on.
- Access to Customers, Brand, and Skills: Innovation teams need access to resources controlled by the core business. Testing requires access to customers, the use of the company brand, and often other skills and resources of the core business.

Portfolio Management

In Invincible Companies leadership is eager to pioneer. Leaders invest in a large innovation pipeline of small bets of which the best get follow-up investments. The portfolio covers the whole range of exploration, from efficiency innovation to breakthrough growth innovation.

Culture Map: Innovation Culture Enablers

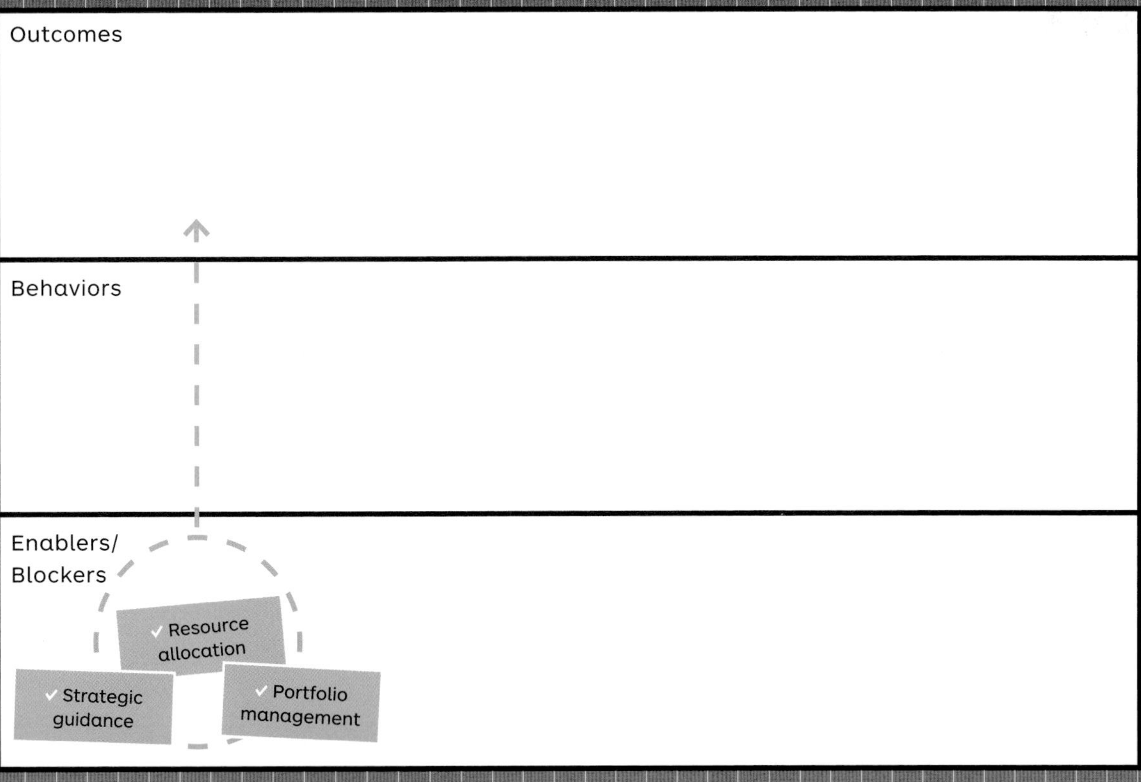

- ☐ Give your company a score from 1 to 5 for each area.
- ☐ Define which area you'd like to improve over the next 12 and 36 months.
- ☐ Eliminate the blockers and implement the enablers that will help you achieve your improvement goals.

Score Your Leadership Support

	BEGINNER *We have little to no experience with this topic*	*We have some experience*	INTERMEDIATE *We regularly work this way, but not systematically*	*We frequently work this way*	WORLD CLASS *Our practice is used as a case study for others to learn from*
Strategic Guidance	1 Leadership does not provide explicit strategic guidance for innovation	2	3 There is some strategic guidance for innovation but not everybody in the company knows it	4	5 Leadership provides strategic innovation guidance at important meetings and everybody knows it
Resource Allocation	1 Resources for innovation are bootstrapped or on an ad-hoc project basis	2	3 Resources for innovation are available, but they are not substantial and not protected	4	5 Resources for innovation are institutionalized and leaders commit at least 40% of their time to innovation
Portfolio Management	1 Leadership is mainly focused on improving the core business	2	3 We make some investments to explore the future and new business models, but it's not systematic	4	5 Leadership is eager to pioneer and invests in a large innovation pipeline of small bets of which the best get follow-up investments

Culture Map: Innovation Culture Enablers

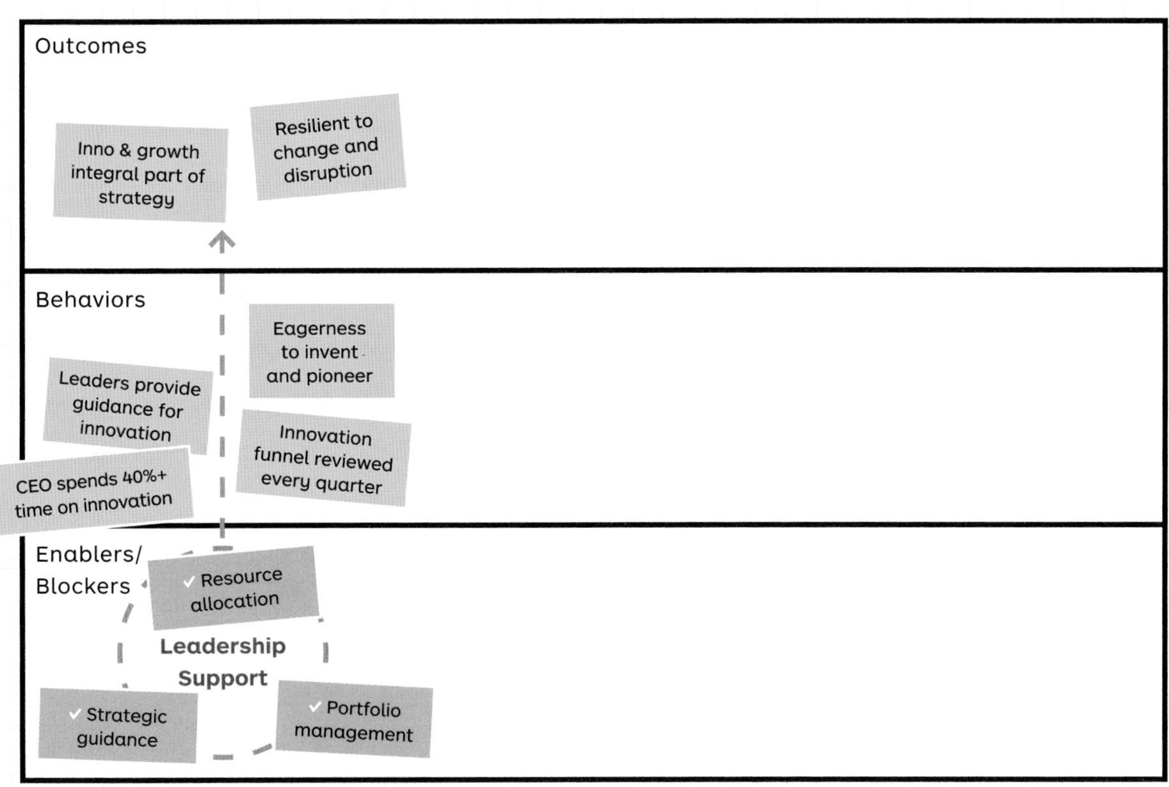

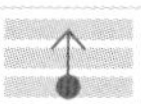

Organizational Design

Legitimacy and Power

Invincible Companies like Amazon or Ping An give innovation power and legitimacy. To have an impact, innovation needs to feature in the organizational chart and at the very top. Either the CEO, a co-CEO, or somebody reporting directly to the board needs to be responsible for growth and innovation and spend serious bandwidth, time, and energy on it. Talking about it at the top level is not enough.

Unfortunately, innovation still lacks legitimacy and power in most organizations. We see a lot of heads of innovation who are two to three levels down in the org chart. They are the sub-department of a leader who is the sub-department of another leader — guess how much impact that creates.

When growth and innovation lack power and legitimacy that sends a very strong signal to the company and often leads to severe consequences with long-term impact:

1. Innovation is not prestigious and it's not seen as a priority, so everybody puts it at the bottom of their to-do list.
2. People avoid exploring new ideas, because they fear taking risks and damaging their careers.
3. Promising innovation projects remain vulnerable and get killed by the antibodies in the organization, because innovation is not perceived as crucial. Few of them get scaled, because the short-term agenda prevails.
4. Your best talent doesn't choose innovation as a career path and either leaves to go to the competition or to start-ups.

Bridge to the Core

In Invincible Companies, Explore and Exploit operate as equal partners that live in harmony. There are clear policies that help innovation teams and the core business collaborate. Innovators get easy access to valuable resources from the core.

When there is no clear bridge to the core, innovation teams have only limited, conflicting, or no access to customers, resources, and skills of the core business. In the worst case, innovation projects are blocked from getting access to what they need to explore and test ideas. They basically have to operate like a start-up in chains: with the same limited resources as start-ups, but without the impetus. We therefore advocate for a so-called Chief Internal Ambassador and a supporting team who explicitly manage the relationship between Exploit and Explore on behalf of the CEO or the board (p. 322).

Rewards and Incentives

In our advisory work we often hear that the drive to innovate is intrinsic to innovators and entrepreneurs. Now imagine an innovator who gets punished every time he/she tries something out that was not in the plan. Or imagine an innovator who repeatedly creates new multimillion-dollar businesses for an organization and gets rewarded with promotions and pay raises. Will they perform to the very best of their innovation talent? Will they stay at your organization?

We argue that a dual strategy to rewards and incentives works best. First and foremost, eliminate all the downsides that prevent innovators from innovating in your organization. Once you've achieved that, develop a reward system for innovation.

Culture Map: Innovation Culture Enablers

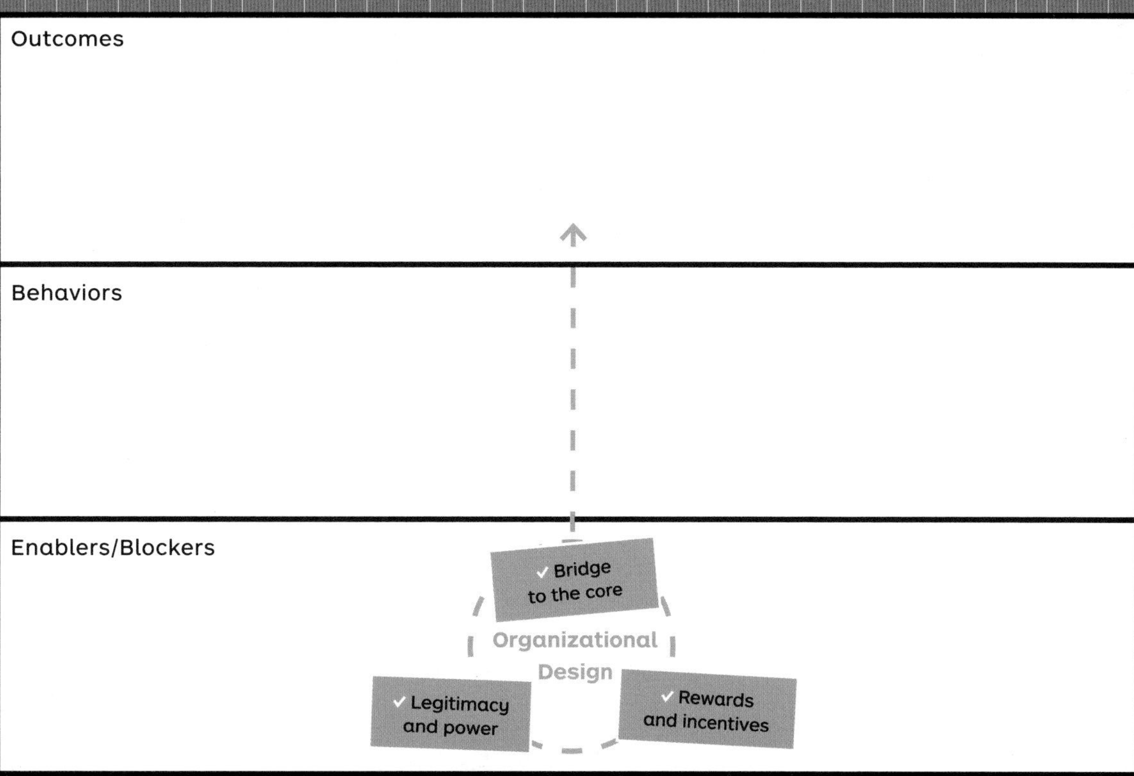

Legitimacy, Power, and Bridge to the Core

CEOs and the traditional leadership staff are generally excellent at growing and running a company within a known business model. But they often fall short at the task of innovating future growth engines. To create and manage new growth, companies need a Chief Entrepreneur with a dedicated staff. This new team is responsible for creating the future of the company while traditional executives take care of the existing business. Of course, they need to operate in harmony.

Chief Entrepreneur: The Chief Entrepreneur is responsible for managing a portfolio of entrepreneurs who experiment with new business models and value propositions. This is someone with a track record and passion for taking calculated risks to create new growth. The Chief Entrepreneur needs to be as powerful as the CEO. In fact, in some organizations like Amazon, the CEO is the Chief Entrepreneur. In others, there is a co-CEO who focuses on the future, like Jessica Tan at Ping An.

Chief Portfolio Manager: The Chief Portfolio Manager makes sure the company looks at a range of opportunities and business models that generate future growth. Some of those opportunities will be risky, some less so. Some will have a potential return, while others will have a guaranteed return. It is the Chief Portfolio Manager's job to establish and manage a portfolio that positions the company for the future.

Chief Venture Capitalist: The Chief Venture Capitalist (VC) allocates budgets and manages financing rounds for internal and external teams. A project won't get full funding right away, but it receives money in instalments. The Chief VC provides angel investments to fund early, cheap experiments. When those experiments succeed and produce evidence, the VC invests more. The Chief VC mirrors the role of the CFO in an established business. The CFO allocates budgets to the existing business, while the Chief VC allocates money to the discovery of a future business.

Chief Risk Officer: Some of the experiments a team will conduct may be detrimental to the brand and could carry legal liabilities. Legal can be a big constraint to experimentation in a company. The Chief Risk Officer is there to enable teams. The CRO helps entrepreneurs understand how to run experiments without putting the company at risk.

Chief Internal Ambassador: The Chief Internal Ambassador (CIA) is a trusted person with clout who knows everything going on on both sides of the company. The CIA and her team know all of the resources, activities, and patents that exist in the execution arm of the organization, and also have the trust of the powerful people that manage them. The CIA makes sure the Chief Entrepreneur and his team benefit from the strengths of the existing company by negotiating access to elements like clients, the salesforce, the brand, the supply chain, and other skills and knowledge. The CIA establishes and maintains a partnership between existing businesses and innovation. We've seen most success when this person is at the summit of their career and has nothing else to prove nor any political games to play to advance their career.

Entrepreneurs: The Entrepreneurs are internal and external people who build the businesses, with each one responsible for a particular project as its leader. This role is a lot stronger than your regular product or project manager: these are real entrepreneurs with clear incentives and a stake in the projects.

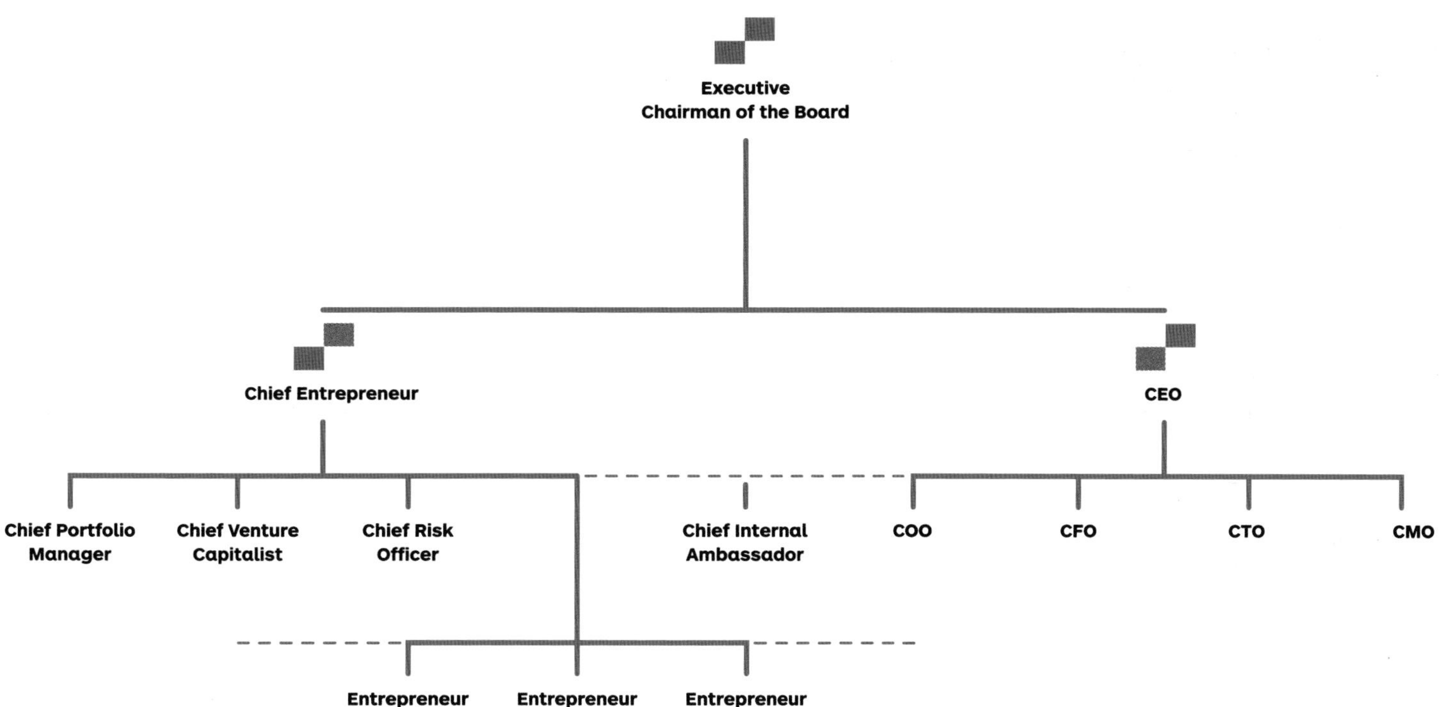
Executive
Chairman of the Board
Chief Entrepreneur
CEO
Chief Portfolio
Manager
Chief Venture
Capitalist
Chief Risk
Officer
Chief Internal
Ambassador
COO
CFO
CTO
CMO
Entrepreneur
Entrepreneur
Entrepreneur

Chief Entrepreneur Head Hunting

Fortune 50 company seeks a Chief Entrepreneur who will build the future. The Chief Entrepreneur will be responsible for managing a portfolio of entrepreneurs experimenting with new business models and value propositions. The candidate is someone with a passion for taking calculated risks. This is not a CTO role or a role that reports to the CEO. The Chief Entrepreneur is an executive as powerful as the CEO, with clear leadership over radical innovation within the company.

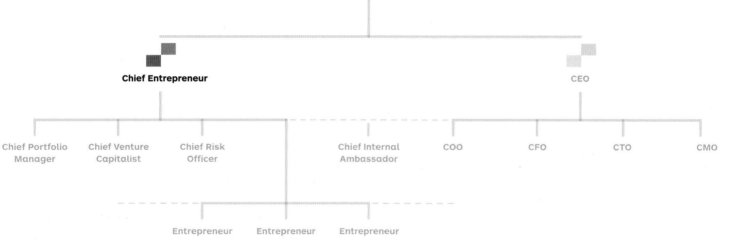

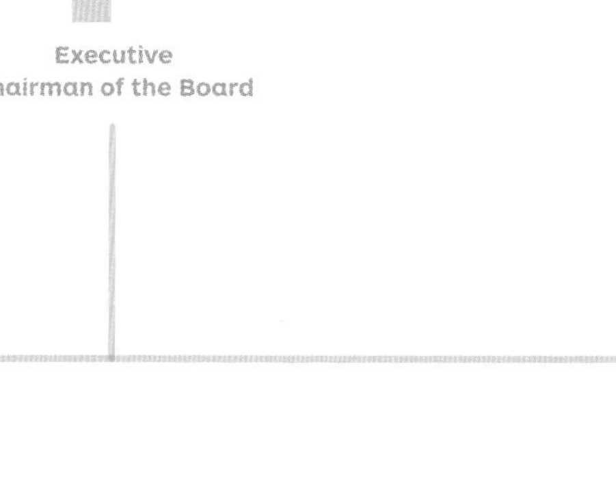

We are looking for an individual who...

- **Is passionate about building businesses.**
  You produce growth engines with calculated bets, not "wild-ass gambles."
- **Believes anything is possible.**
  You persevere. You have the charm, charisma, enthusiasm, work ethic, and marketing mind to encourage and drive your teams to think anything is possible.
- **Has built a $1 billion+ business from nothing.**
  You're especially valuable if you've met these figures in a large corporation.
- **Is comfortable with uncertainty.**
  You don't fear failure. You see failure as an opportunity to learn and iterate toward a solution.
- **Is tremendously diplomatic.**
  You address conflict head-on with one focus in mind: secure the money and resources you need to test your ideas.

Sound like you?
OK, now let's consider your day-to-day tasks.

The Chief Entrepreneur's Responsibilities

- ☐ Build the future for the company. We cannot stress this enough. The Chief Entrepreneur is responsible for developing new business models and value propositions for the company's future growth.
- ☐ Guide and support your own team of entrepreneurs. You've been here before and you have knowledge to share. Your team will be searching for and validating business models and value propositions around opportunities for growth. This means managing entrepreneurs who can navigate trends and market behaviors.
- ☐ Design and maintain a space for invention. You are responsible for creating the habitat for your team to experiment, fail, and learn. This is an additional culture where ideas can be thoroughly tested. You must defend the culture, processes, incentives, and metrics that are born in this space.
- ☐ Introduce innovation metrics. You must develop a new process that measures whether you're making progress in building new businesses. How are your experiments helping your team to learn, reduce uncertainty and risk, and move forward?
- ☐ Establish and nurture a partnership with the CEO. You will have to work with the CEO to ensure resources and assets are available to validate or invalidate your ideas. You will be responsible for building a partnership to discuss progress and share new ideas. Communication will be key to this partnership because the CEO is the person who can help finance your future experiments. You will also recognize the importance of handing over a validated business model that demonstrates opportunities to scale.
- ☐ Report your progress directly to the Executive Chairman of the Board of Directors. You do not work for the CEO, or alongside the CTO, CIO, and CFO. These roles are mandated to keep the existing business in good shape. If the CE reported to the CEO, then the CEO could veto potential ideas in order to reserve resources and safeguard the company against failure.

Where Does Innovation Live?

Sometimes leaders say that everybody needs to be an innovator. That is true and silly at the same time. There are different types of innovation that require different skills, processes, and mindsets.

We distinguish between three types of innovation, heavily leaning on the work of Harvard professor Clayton Christensen. We distinguish between efficiency innovation, sustaining innovation, and transformative innovation, which often happens to be disruptive.

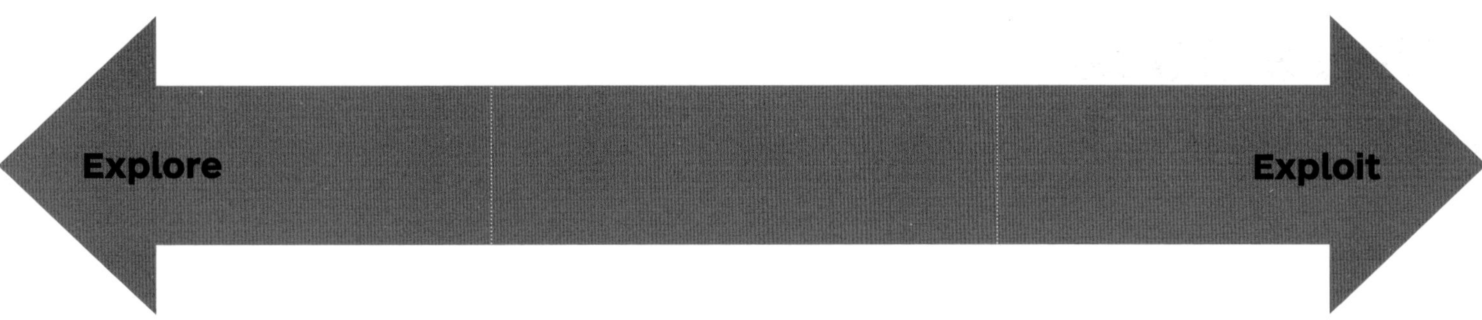

Transformative

This type of innovation is the most radical and includes substantially new business models that a company is not familiar with. It may—but doesn't necessarily—include the cannibalization of the established business model. Transformative innovation has the largest long-term growth potential and helps position the company for the future. It requires the most advanced testing and requires the exploration of a broad portfolio of projects, because of high uncertainty.

Financial impact *Substantial in the long term*

Protection from disruption *Very strong*

Home *Outside the core established businesses to ensure survival*

Protagonists *Professional innovators with support from the core business for specific skills and resources*

Uncertainty *Maximum—because it explores uncharted territory*

Testing *Desirability, viability, feasibility, and adaptability*

Sustaining

With sustaining innovation you improve and expand your proven business model. Here uncertainty is higher because it may involve new market segments, new value propositions, or new channels. As a consequence you may also have to master new activities and resources. This type of innovation also includes business model shifts and can have a substantial impact on the longevity of a company's business model.

Financial impact *Potentially substantial—rarely immediate*

Protection from disruption *Limited*

Home *Inside the core established businesses, potentially outside*

Protagonists *Staff from the core businesses with support from professional innovators*

Uncertainty *Medium—because innovations build on top of the proven business model*

Testing *Desirability, viability, feasibility, and adaptability depending on the nature of the innovation*

Efficiency

This type of innovation is all about improving how smoothly your existing business models run. Uncertainty is relatively low, since it's about improving your proven business model. However, efficiency innovation may involve highly sophisticated technology innovations with high feasibility risk. Efficiency innovation may also include desirability risk, as when you create digital tools for internal stakeholders, like sales, customer support, marketing, finance, or operations. The immediate financial impact of efficiency innovations can be very high, for example, in the form of expanded margins.

Financial impact *From small to extremely large—often immediate*

Protection from disruption *None*

Home *Inside the core established businesses*

Protagonists *Staff from the core businesses*

Uncertainty *Low*

Testing *Mainly feasibility, some internal desirability, potentially cost savings or revenue impact*

ORGANIZATIONAL DESIGN

Rewards and Incentives

Kill Blockers

In many organizations going into innovation equals career suicide. It doesn't have to be that way. On this page we outline how to remove the downside for people when they innovate in your organization. In discussion with fellow innovation expert Scott Anthony, from Innosight, we realized that this will already go a long way to boost innovation activities, even before putting in place formal rewards.

Eliminate the Downside

Blockers	Don't…	Provide…
Barriers to Starting	…make it difficult, in the form of bureaucracy or other hurdles, for innovators to try out new ideas.	…easy access and small time or financial budgets for anybody who wants to start testing an idea. Provide follow-up funding for ideas that show traction.
Business Plan/Cases	…force innovators to write detailed business plans that make ideas look good in spreadsheets, but will mask the true risk of new ideas.	…process guidelines to test ideas and measure the reduction of risk and uncertainty. Judge evidence from testing, rather than good-looking ideas in PowerPoint presentations.
Execution-Focused KPIs	…reward innovators for execution only, because it will prevent them from experimenting and reducing innovation risk.	…KPIs specifically designed for innovators who experiment with new ideas. These must differ from KPIs for people who execute projects and must deliver on time and on budget.
Lack of Autonomy	…ask innovation teams to ask for approval for every experiment and every decision to adapt their idea, which reduces speed and adaptability.	…autonomy to test ideas, find evidence, and adapt ideas as long as they don't put the organization at risk.
Lack of Access	…make it difficult for innovators to access the resources they need to try out new ideas (customers, brand, prototyping, leadership support, etc.).	…infrastructure and support to help innovators rapidly, cheaply, and painlessly test ideas with appropriate experiments.
Lack of Skills	…confuse managerial and innovation/entrepreneurial skills. It's a whole different ball game to explore and adapt new ideas.	…innovation and entrepreneurship training. Avoid using good managers to explore new ideas without equipping them with the right skills and mindset to test new ideas.
Career Risk	…make failure from experimenting with new ideas a career-limiting move.	…visibility and promotions for people who have tried out new ideas throughout their career, even if those experiments failed.

Create Enablers

Focus on the upside, once you've eliminated the downside. Design a reward system that incentivizes people to innovate. Make sure you don't just award successful outcomes, because many, many failed experiments allow you to detect the outliers that will succeed big. Reward good innovation behavior just as much as outcomes. Results will follow naturally. Finally, make sure you focus on impact, which is a crucial reward to attract and retain the best innovation talent.

Reward the Upside

Reward	Find Creative Ways to...	Incentives
Behavior *Make Innovation Sexy*	...make innovation just as prestigious at your organization as managing large teams and huge budgets. Promote people not just for their management merits, but for their courage to try out new ideas, even if they fail. Reward innovation, not just innovation outcomes. Reward the entire portfolio of innovation projects, not just the few big winners.	• Career promotions • Prestigious innovation rewards (for behavior, not just outcomes) • Company-wide visibility and recognition • Visibility with top management • Access to new exciting projects • Rewards at every stage of the innovation funnel, even for failure
Outcomes *Entrepreneurial Participation*	...allow innovators to participate in the financial upside of new ideas. Do so through internal mechanisms or through corporate venture capital. Allow people or teams to explore their ideas outside the organization with the option to invest and potentially buy back the venture.	• Financial stake in an idea • Success-dependent bonuses (e.g., number of new products or services sold; revenue, margin, or profit thresholds; etc.) • Start-up capital or investments to explore an idea externally
Impact *Change the World*	...attract outside innovation talent with an appealing company mission. Show world-class innovators how joining your organization will allow them to make a difference in the universe and have a real impact on society. Highlight what makes your company more attractive than creating or joining a start-up or competitor.	• Work for a company that stands for something • Make a difference (societal impact) • Access to resources a start-up or competitors don't have (e.g., infrastructure, brand, IP, market reach, etc.)

- ☐ Give your company a score from 1 to 5 for each area.
- ☐ Define which area you'd like to improve over the next 12 and 36 months.
- ☐ Eliminate the blockers and implement the enablers that will help you achieve your improvement goals.

Score Your Organizational Design

	BEGINNER *We have little to no experience with this topic*	*We have some experience*	INTERMEDIATE *We regularly work this way, but not systematically*	*We frequently work this way*	WORLD CLASS *Our practice is used as a case study for others to learn from*
Legitimacy and Power	1 Innovation projects are skunk work and outside official channels	2	3 Innovation is officially in the org chart, but lacks power and influence	4	5 Innovation is at the very top of the org chart and has power and influence
Bridge to the Core	1 Innovation teams have limited or no access to customers, resources, and skills of the core business	2	3 The core business and innovation teams collaborate, but there are conflicts	4	5 There are clear policies that help innovation teams and the core business collaborate as equal partners
Rewards and Incentives	1 Innovation does not have a dedicated incentive system that differs from the core business	2	3 We have some incentives in place to encourage innovation and reward it differently from execution	4	5 Innovation has a dedicated incentive system that rewards experimentation and new value creation

Culture Map: Innovation Culture Enablers

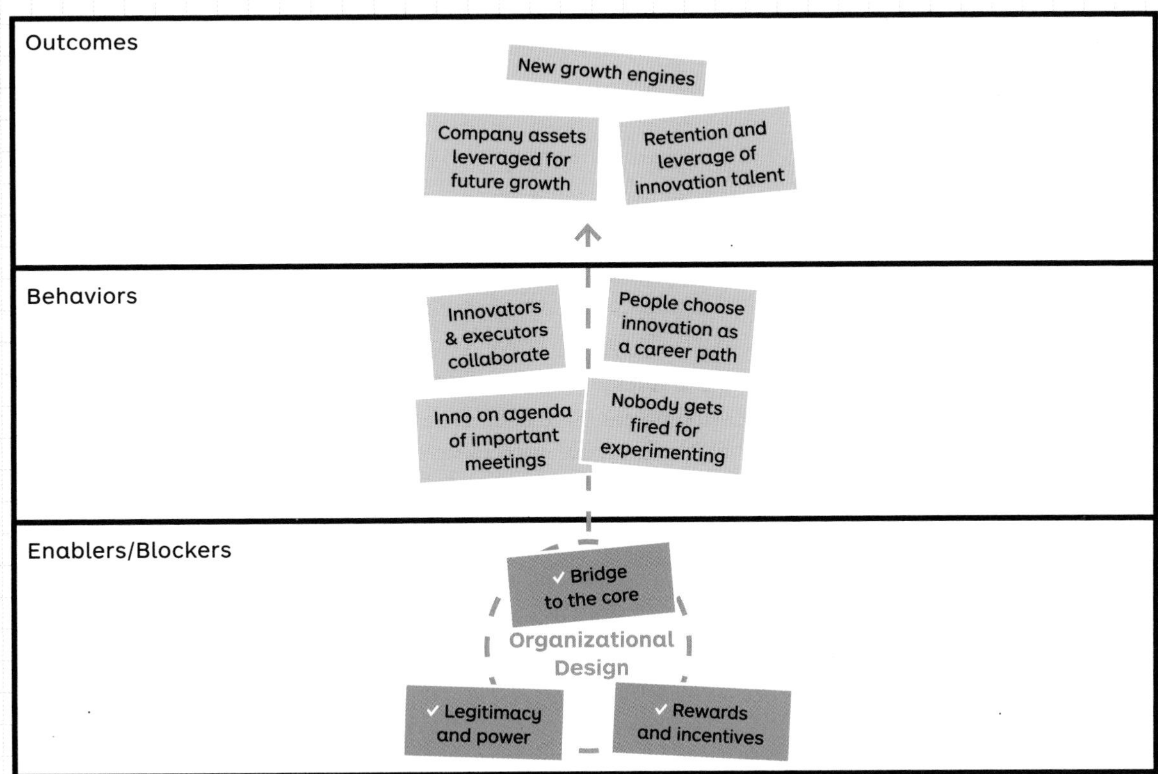

Outcomes
New growth engines
Company assets leveraged for future growth
Retention and leverage of innovation talent
Behaviors
Innovators & executors collaborate
People choose innovation as a career path
Inno on agenda of important meetings
Nobody gets fired for experimenting
Enablers/Blockers
✓ Bridge to the core
Organizational Design
✓ Legitimacy and power
✓ Rewards and incentives

Innovation Practice

Innovation Tools

Innovation professionals need to master a set of dedicated tools, just like a surgeon commands a set of surgical tools. We believe the quality of the innovation toolset you use has a substantial impact on the quality of your growth and transformation work. Tools are not neutral. They heavily influence the quality of your results. That's why it's incredibly important to carefully select the tools you use and learn how to apply them correctly.

Process Management

Invincible companies have dedicated processes and decision-making that are both optimized for innovation. They measure the systematic and effective reduction of risk in new ideas, rather than on-time and on-budget delivery, which are typical execution KPIs. We discussed the innovation process and innovation metrics intensely in Chapter 2: Manage.

Skills Development

Managing the existing and inventing the new are two fundamentally different professions. Innovators are typically comfortable with high uncertainty and radical pivots to adapt to the reality of new market insights. Invincible companies systematically develop world-class innovation talent with extensive innovation experience across the organization.

Culture Map: Innovation Culture Enablers

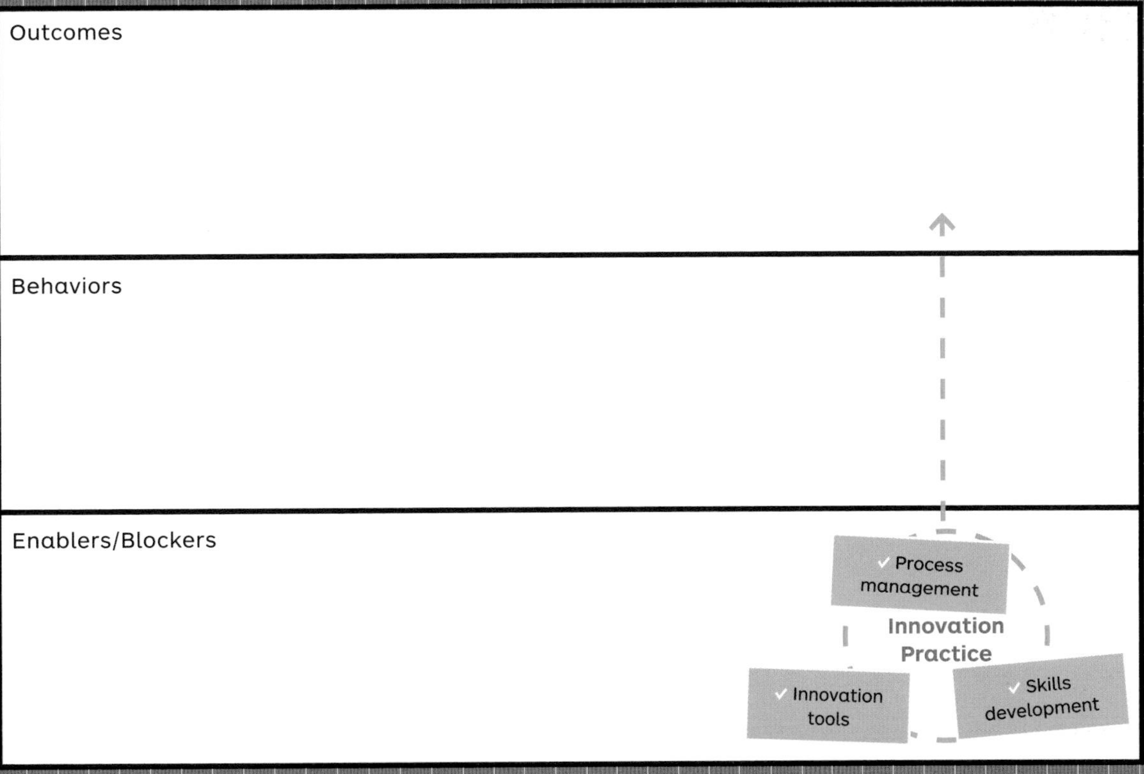

333

Innovation Tools and Process

Mastering the tools of innovation radically facilitates the search for new growth engines. We suggest a toolbox of integrated tools to shape, test, and grow ideas in your organization.

Corporate Identity Triangle

A strategic management framework to make your corporate identity explicit in order to define your portfolio guidance.

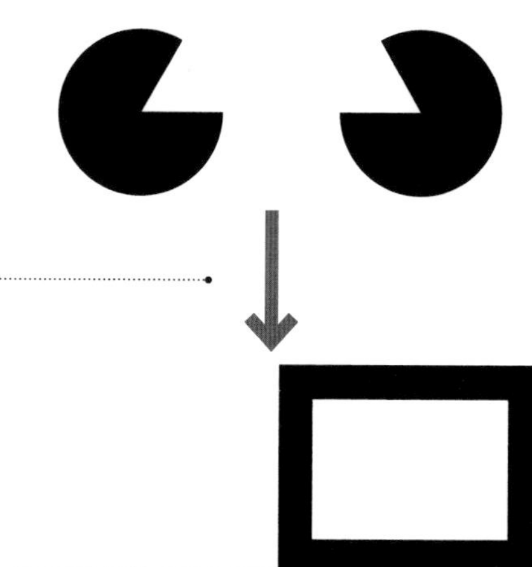

Portfolio Guidance
The guidelines that define what types of innovations you want to pursue. They make explicit what is "in" and what is "out".

Portfolio Map

An analytical strategy tool to simultaneously visualize, analyze, and manage the business models you are improving and growing and future business models you are searching for and testing.

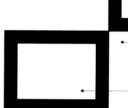

The Team Alignment Map
A project management tool to keep teams aligned over the course of an (innovation) project journey.

The Culture Map

A strategic management tool to help assess, design, implement, and transform a company's (innovation) culture.

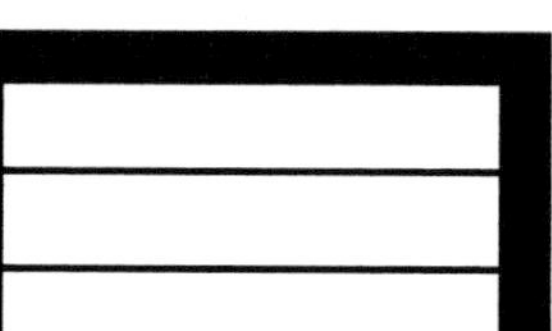

Business Design

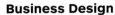

Business Environment Map
A foresight and scanning tool to map the environment in which you conduct business. It captures the trends that might disrupt your organization or represent new opportunities for growth and transformation.

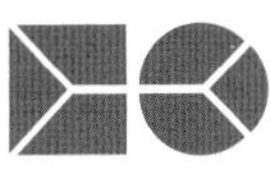

Business Model Canvas
A strategic management tool to make explicit how you create, deliver, and capture value. Used to improve existing business models or invent new ones. Serves as the foundation to identify hypotheses to test new business ideas.

Value Proposition Canvas
A product management tool to make explicit how you create value for customers. Used to assess and improve existing value propositions or to invent new ones. Serves as the foundation to identify customer and product/service hypotheses.

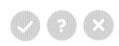

Testing

Strategyzer Innovation Metrics
A metrics system to measure the reduction of risk and uncertainty of new business ideas, visualize progress from idea to validated business case, and evaluate the disruption risk of a company's business portfolio.

Assumptions Map
A tactical tool to identify the hypotheses you need to test first.

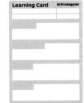

Test Card
A tactical tool to design sound business experiments to test your business hypotheses.

Learning Card
A tactical tool to capture insights from your business experiments and define decisions and actions.

Skills Development

Among the many skills required in entrepreneurship and innovation there are three learnable ones that are crucial on your journey from big idea to real business:

1. Business Design (Different From Managing a Business):
The ability to shape and constantly adapt value propositions and business models to develop the most promising ones.

Master the value proposition canvas (VPC):
- Design value propositions that attract customers.
- Design value propositions that customers are willing to pay for.

Master the business model canvas (BMC):
- Design business models that are profitable and scalable.
- Design business models that are protectable.

2. Testing (and Learning):
The ability to break down big ideas into hypotheses you test in order to reduce the risk of pursuing ideas that won't work.

- Identify the most important hypotheses.
- Design and run experiments to support or refute your hypotheses.
- Detect patterns in the evidence.

3. Lead and Execute:
The ability to inspire a team and overcome the biggest obstacles.

- Lead and coordinate your team from idea to real business.
- Make sure every team member is always focused on what can best advance the team from idea to scalable business.
- Lead in the face of adversity and motivate the team to overcome the inevitable obstacles on the innovation journey.

☐ **Skills Evolution from Idea to Business**
Over the course of a project journey the skills required by leadership and the team substantially change. Here are some of the key differences from discovery to execution and scaling.

	Discovery	Validation	Acceleration	Execution and Scaling
Key Evidence	• Market size • Opportunity size $ • Customer jobs, pains, and gains • Problem/solution fit • Willingness to pay (basic evidence)	• Value proposition • Willingness to pay and pricing (strong evidence) • Feasibility (basic evidence)	• Product/market fit • Feasibility (strong evidence) • Acquisition and retention • Profitability	• Revenue (or user) growth
Key Questions	Is there an opportunity?	Can we create value in this market?	How can we best create demand and grow?	How can we scale our organization to satisfy demand?
Team size	1–3	3–8	8+	Unlimited
Key leadership skills	• Envision and motivate • Question fundamental assumptions • Pattern recognition • Pivot • Business model	• Envision and motivate • Pattern recognition • Pivot • Business model	• Envision and motivate • Lead domain matter experts • Business model	• Motivate and engage • Scale • Hire • Manage
Team skills	• Resourceful • Testing • Extreme adaptability • Perseverance	• Testing • Prototyping • Perseverance	• Domain matter expertise and building • Marketing • Perseverance	• Leadership, execution, and scaling • Deep domain matter expertise • Hiring • Functional expertise (marketing, finance, legal, etc.)

Entrepreneurial Leadership and Team

We believe that the most successful project teams in Invincible Companies are not led by project managers who manage several projects in parallel. They are led by people who see themselves as entrepreneurs. They are all in to bring an idea to fruition and behave like entrepreneurs even if they are actually employees on a company's payroll. Based on research from entrepreneurial performance labs we believe successful innovators and entrepreneurs and their teams have the following traits.

Innovators and entrepreneurs who lead teams and ventures are often...

Able to Create Reality Distortion Fields

- Gifted and captivating communicators who are able to mobilize resources and talent for their cause.
- Know what direction they want people to go and make stakeholders and team members believe the impossible.
- Create a compelling sense of "pull" to lead the team on a journey of discovery, validation, acceleration, and scaling.

Relentless and Resilient

- Yearn to overcome the status quo to improve things.
- Are action-biased, don't get stuck in analysis paralysis, and persevere in the face of adversity. They persistently work to overcome obstacles and are not easily derailed by setbacks.
- Display a crazy work ethic and set high standards for themselves and others, yet maintain mental and physical reserves necessary to deal with challenges.

Deeply Curious

- Some of their best ideas come from cross-fertilization of different domains and markets.
- Are incredibly agile intellectually (Jeff Bezos: from books to Amazon Web Services; Steve Jobs: from computers to music players to mobile phones; Elon Musk: from payment software to electric cars to rockets).

Independent

- Are willing or inclined to operate on their own with minimal support from others.
- Are comfortable standing apart from the herd.
- Prefer to control their environment and are likely to be dissatisfied working for someone else.

We believe great founding teams should display the following characteristics to complement the entrepreneurial leader. They are:

Inventive

- Generate ideas and explore new possibilities.
- Discern useful patterns from large amounts of information and are emergent learners, adapting through experience and experimentation.
- Easily navigate big-picture strategic questions and nitty-gritty experiments or domain matter expertise.

Risk Tolerant

- Break big ideas down into smaller testable hypotheses to test with business experiments.
- Feel comfortable making decisions with incomplete or contradicting information and skillfully deal with ambiguity and complexity.
- Are fearless and scared simultaneously, yet can distinguish between internal feelings of anxiety and more objective measures of actual risk.

Market Oriented

- See the market and financial potential of an opportunity, technology, or market need and turn that into concrete value propositions and business models.
- Constantly adapt business model and value propositions based on feedback from the field and evidence from experiments.
- Are opportunistic and pivot toward the most interesting direction.

Pragmatic and (Ideally) Experienced

- Understand which actions and decisions will substantially move the needle.
- Bring and apply valuable experience from previous innovation and entrepreneurship journeys.
- Have a strong 'no nonsense' radar.

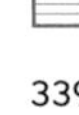

Library of Congress, Prints and Photographs Division, NYWT&S Collection, [LC-USZ62-123247]

At the peak of her career, one of the wealthiest women in the world.

ELIZABETH ARDEN
Founded Elizabeth Arden Inc. in 1910

"Daniel Ek, CEO and Co-founder of Spotify" Stuart Isett/Fortune Brainstorm TECH/CC BY 2.0

Spotify has forever changed how consumers interact with music.

DANIEL EK
Founder of music streaming service Spotify

"Beech, Olive Ann" by San Diego Air and Space Museum Archive

Dubbed "The First Lady of Aviation" for being the first woman to lead a major aircraft company.

OLIVE ANN BEECH
Co-founder of Beech Aircraft Corporation

Jack Ma World Economic Forum/Ben Hider/ CC BY 2.0

Ranked 21st in the World's Most Powerful People of 2019 list by Forbes magazine.

JACK MA
Co-founder of Alibaba Group

"TechCrunch Disrupt SF 2017 - Day 2" by Techcrunch/CC BY 2.0

23andMe's DNA-testing kit was Time's 2008 Invention of the Year.

ANNE WOJKICKI
Co-founder of 23andme

"A photo of rock climber Yvon Chouinard." by Tom Frost/CC BY 2.0

One of the original pioneers of "do good to do well" business movement.

YVON CHOUINARD
Founder of sports apparel brand Patagonia

"Africa Progress Panel" by Rodger Bosch for APP/CC BY 2.0

Ranked 33nd in Fortune *magazine's World's Greatest Leaders list for 2017.*

STRIVE MASIYIWA

Founder of media and tech company Econet Wireless

"Yang Lan" by World Economic Forum from Cologny, Switzerland/CC BY 2.0

One of China's most powerful women in media and ranked 100 on the100 Most Powerful Women List of 2013 by Forbes.

YANG LAN

Co-founder of Sun Media Group

Considered "Japan's Thomas Edison," Kiichiro converted the family loom business into automobile manufacturing.

KIICHIRO TOYODA

Founder of Toyota Motor Corporation

"Jacqueline Novogratz" by Acumen/CC BY 2.0

Uses entrepreneurial approaches to address global poverty.

JACQUELINE NOVOGRATZ

Founder of Acumen Fund

"Mexican businessman Carlos Slim Helú." by José Cruz/ABr/CC BY 3.0

Ranked 8th in the list of World's Billionaires by Forbes *and considered the richest person in Latin America in 2019.*

CARLOS SLIM

Founder of Grupo Carsó conglomerate

"HTC Chairwoman, Cher Wang, shows off new mobile phone mother board" by Robert Scoble/CC BY 2.0

Ranked 46th Most Powerful Woman in the World 2013 by Forbes.

CHER WANG

Co-founder of HTC Corporation

☐ Give your company a score from 1 to 5 for each area.

☐ Define which area you'd like to improve over the next 12 and 36 months.

☐ Eliminate the blockers and implement the enablers that will help you achieve your improvement goals.

Score Your Innovation Practice

	BEGINNER *We have little to no experience with this topic*	*We have some experience*	INTERMEDIATE *We regularly work this way, but not systematically*	*We frequently work this way*	WORLD CLASS *Our practice is used as a case study for others to learn from*
Innovation Tools	1 We do not use business model, lean startup, or design thinking tools for innovation	2	3 Business model, lean startup, or design thinking tools are used in pockets of the organization	4	5 Business model, lean startup, or design thinking tools are widely adopted and mastered
Process Management	1 Our processes are linear and require detailed business plans with financial projections	2	3 We occasionally use iterative processes and systematic business experiments to test business ideas	4	5 Our processes are optimized for innovation and we systematically measure the reduction of risk in new ideas
Innovation Skills	1 We don't hire for innovation skills and experience and don't develop them	2	3 We occasionally hire experienced innovation talent and train some specialized staff in innovation	4	5 We hire and develop world-class innovation talent with extensive experience across the organization

Culture Map: Innovation Culture Enablers

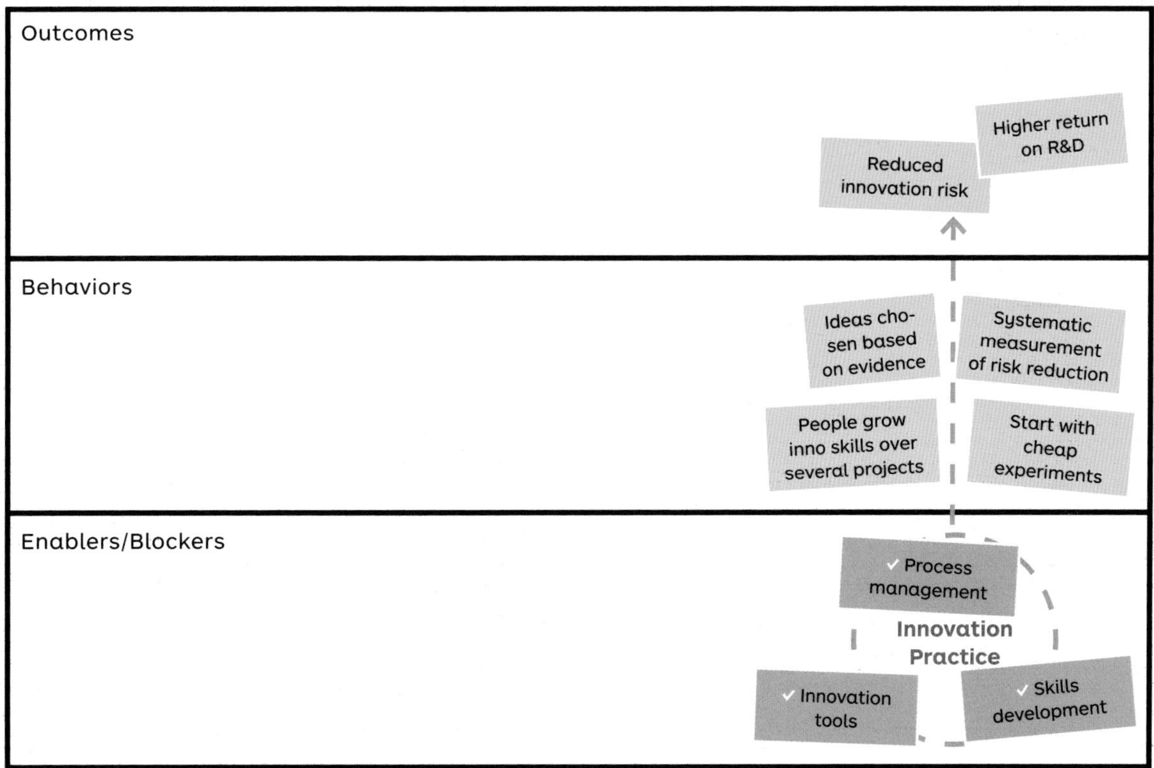

Innovation Culture Readiness

How ready are you to become an invincible company?

- ☐ Give your company a score from 1 to 5 for each area.
- ☐ Define which area you'd like to improve over the next 12 and 36 months.
- ☐ Eliminate the blockers and implement the enablers that will help you achieve your improvement goals.

Leadership Support	Strategic Guidance
	Resource Allocation
	Portfolio Management
Organizational Design	Legitimacy and Power
	Bridge to the Core
	Rewards and Incentives
Innovation Practice	Innovation Tools
	Process Management
	Innovation Skills

BEGINNER *We have little to no experience with this topic*	*We have some experience*	INTERMEDIATE *We regularly work this way, but not systematically*	*We frequently work this way*	WORLD CLASS *Our practice is used as a case study for others to learn from*
1 Leadership does not provide explicit strategic guidance for innovation	2	3 There is some strategic guidance for innovation but not everybody in the company knows it	4	5 Leadership provides strategic innovation guidance at important meetings and everybody knows it
1 Resources for innovation are bootstrapped or on an ad-hoc project basis	2	3 Resources for innovation are available, but they are not substantial and not protected	4	5 Resources for innovation are institutionalized and leaders commit at least 50% of their time to innovation
1 Leadership is mainly focused on improving the core business	2	3 We make some investments to explore the future and new business models, but it's not systematic	4	5 Leadership is eager to pioneer and invests in a large innovation pipeline of small bets of which the best get follow-up investments
1 Innovation projects are skunk work and outside official channels	2	3 Innovation is officially in the org chart, but lacks power and influence	4	5 Innovation is at the very top of the org chart and has power and influence
1 Innovation teams have limited or no access to customers, resources, and skills of the core business	2	3 The core business and innovation teams collaborate, but there are conflicts	4	5 There are clear policies that help innovation teams and the core business collaborate as equal partners
1 Innovation does not have a dedicated incentive system that differs from the core business	2	3 We have some incentives in place to encourage innovation and reward it differently from execution	4	5 Innovation has a dedicated incentive system that rewards experimentation and new value creation
1 We do not use business model, lean startup, or design thinking tools for innovation	2	3 Business model, lean startup, or design thinking tools are used in pockets of the organization	4	5 Business model, lean startup, or design thinking tools are widely adopted and mastered
1 Our processes are linear and require detailed business plans with financial projections	2	3 We occasionally use iterative processes and systematic business experiments to test business ideas	4	5 Our processes are optimized for innovation and we systematically measure the reduction of risk in new ideas
1 We don't hire for innovation skills and experience and don't develop them	2	3 We occasionally hire experienced innovation talent and train some specialized staff in innovation	4	5 We hire and develop world-class innovation talent with extensive experience across the organization

Afterword

Glossary

Adaptability Risk
The risk that a business won't be able to adapt to the competitive environment; technology, regulatory, social, or market trends; or that the macro environment is not favorable (lacking infrastructure, recession, etc.).

Business Design
Process to shape and reshape a business idea to turn it into the best possible business model and value proposition. Early iterations are based on intuition and starting point (product idea, technology, market opportunity, etc.). Subsequent iterations are based on evidence and insights from the testing.

Business Model
Rationale of how an organization creates, delivers, and captures value.

Business Model Canvas
Strategic management tool to describe how an organization creates, delivers, and captures value, initially presented in the book *Business Model Generation.*

Business Model Pattern
A repeatable configuration of different business model building blocks to strengthen an organization's overall business model. Helps new ventures develop a competitive advantage beyond technology, product, service, or price. Helps established companies shift from an outdated to more competitive business model. A single business model can incorporate several patterns.

Business Model Portfolio
The collection of existing business models a company exploits and the new business models it explores in order to avoid disruption and ensure longevity.

Business Model Shift
Describes an organization's transformation from a declining or expired business model to a more competitive one.

Business R&D
Activities a company undertakes to spot, create, test, de-risk, and invest in a portfolio of novel business opportunities. To improve existing business(es) and explore new ones. The heart of business R&D is the art and science of shaping value propositions and business models and testing risks. Complements traditional technology and product R&D, which mainly focus on feasibility.

Culture Map
Strategic management tool to understand, design, test, and manage the corporate culture you want to bring to fruition in your organization.

Death and Disruption Risk
The risk that a business is going to die or get disrupted. Risk is high when a business is either emerging and still vulnerable, or when a business is under threat of disruption from technology, competition, regulatory changes, or other trends. Risk decreases with the moats protecting your business.

Desirability Risk
The risk that the market a business is targeting is too small, that too few customers want the value proposition, or that the company can't reach, acquire, and retain targeted customers.

Evidence
Data generated from an experiment or collected in the field. Proves or disproves a (business) hypothesis, customer insight, or belief about a value proposition, business model, strategy, or the environment.

Expected Return
How lucrative a business idea could be for a company if it turned out to be successful.

Experiment
A procedure to validate or invalidate a value proposition or business model hypothesis that produces evidence. Used to reduce risk and uncertainty of a business idea.

Exploit Portfolio
Your portfolio of existing businesses, value propositions, products and services, all mapped out in terms of return and death and disruption risk.

Explore Portfolio
Your portfolio of innovation projects, new business models, new value propositions, new products and services, all mapped out in terms of expected return and innovation risk.

Feasibility Risk
The risk that a business can't manage, scale, or get access to key resources (technology, IP, brand, etc.), key activities, or key partners.

Grow
Activity of keeping your existing business models on a growth trajectory. Includes scaling emerging business models, renovating declining ones, and protecting successful ones. You ensure growth by improving returns and minimizing disruption risk.

Guidance
Context for portfolio management. Helps with resource allocation and portfolio actions. Provides explicit boundaries to understand what to focus on and what not to focus on, where to invest and where to divest, and what to explore and what not to explore.

Hypothesis
An assumption that your value proposition, business model, or strategy builds on. What you need to learn about to understand if your business idea might work. Relates to the desirability, feasibility, viability, or adaptability of a business idea.

Innovation Funnel
Mechanism to explore and test a constant stream of business ideas and innovation projects. The front of the funnel contains many ideas that you gradually reduce based on evidence from testing and then invest in the remaining projects with metered funding.

(Strategyzer) Innovation Metrics
A set of tools to measure the reduction of the risk and uncertainty of new business ideas before you invest big and scale.

Innovation Risk
The risk that a (convincing) business idea is going to fail. Risk is high when there is little evidence beyond slides and spreadsheets to support the success chances of an idea. Risk decreases with the amount of evidence that supports the desirability, feasibility, viability, and adaptability of a business idea.

Metered Funding
Funding practice, coming from the venture capital industry, where you incrementally increase investments in projects that produce evidence from testing and shelve those that don't.

Pivot
The decision to make a significant change to one or more elements of your business model and value proposition.

Portfolio Actions
The actions you perform in your EXPLORE portfolio (ideate, invest, persevere, pivot, retire, spinout, transfer) and your EXPLOIT portfolio (acquire, partner, invest, improve, merge, divest, dismantle).

Portfolio Map
A strategic management tool to simultaneously visualize, analyze, and manage the business models you are improving and growing and the future business models you are searching for and testing.

Return
How lucrative a business area is for a company.

Search
Search for new ideas, value propositions, and business models to ensure the future of your company. Involves maximizing expected returns and minimizing innovation risk.

Team Map
A visual tool created by Stefano Mastrogiacomo to boost alignment among team members for more effective meetings and conversations.

Test
Process of identifying and testing the most critical hypotheses underlying a business idea to make informed business design and investment decisions.

Types of Innovation
We distinguish between three different types of innovation heavily, borrowing from Harvard professor Clayton Christensen: efficiency, sustaining, and transformative innovation.

Viability Risk
The risk that a business can't generate successful revenue streams, that customers are unwilling to pay (enough), or that the costs are too high to make a sustainable profit.

Notes

TOOL

1. "The Bosch Group at a Glance," https://www.bosch.com/company/our-figures/.
2. Nestle, "Acquisitions and Disposals," https://www.nestle.com/investors/overview/mergers-and-acquisitions.
3. "Nestlé Closes the Sale of Nestlé Skin Health," October 02, 2019, https://www.nestle.com/media/pressreleases/allpressreleases/nestle-closes-sale-nestle-skin-health.
4. "The Gore Story," https://www.gore.com/about/the-gore-story.

MANAGE

1. Charles Arthur, "Amazon Writes Off $170M on Unsold Fire Phones," The Guardian, October 24, 2014. https://www.theguardian.com/technology/2014/oct/24/amazon-unsold-fire-phones.
2. "Ping An Tops Global Insurance Brands for the Third Consecutive Year," PR Newswire Asia, May 30, 2018, https://www.asiaone.com/business/ping-ranks-third-among-global-financial-services-companies-2018-brandztm-top-100-most.
3. Shu-Ching Jean Chen, "Chinese Giant Ping An Looks Beyond Insurance to a Fintech Future," June 2018, https://www.forbes.com/sites/shuchingjeanchen/2018/06/06/chinese-giant-ping-an-looks-beyond-insurance-to-a-fintech-future/.
4. Ping An 2019 Interim Report.
5. Ericson Chan, "FinTech, If It Doesn't Kill You, Makes You Stronger," April 13, 2018, https://www.youtube.com/watch?v=UixV7NNSgVI.
6. "Ping An to Employ Micro-Expression Technology to Deter Scammers," November 1, 2018, https://www.chinaknowledge.com/News/DetailNews/81721/Ping-An-to-employ-micro-expression-technology-to-deter-scammers.
7. Shu-Ching Jean Chen, "Chinese Giant Ping An Looks Beyond."
8. "Ping An Powering Ahead with World-Leading Fintech and Healthtech," PR News Asia, November 07, 2018, https://www.prnewswire.com/news-releases/ping-an-powering-ahead-with-world-leading-fintech-and-healthtech-300745534.html.
9. Ping An Annual Report 2018.
10. Kane Wu, "Ping An-Backed Lufax Raises $1.3 Billion at Lower Valuation: Sources," December 3, 2018, https://www.reuters.com/article/us-lufax-fundraising/ping-an-backed-lufax-raises-13-billion-at-lower-valuation-sources-idUSKBN1O20HG.
11. Laura He, "Ping An Good Doctor Prices US$1.12 Billion IPO at Top End Amid Retail Frenzy," April 27, 2018, https://www.scmp.com/business/companies/article/2143745/ping-good-doctor-prices-us112-billion-ipo-top-end-amid-retail.
12. Autohome Annual Report 2018.
13. "Autohome Inc. Announces Transaction between Shareholders and Board Change," February 22, 2017, https://www.globenewswire.com/news-release/2017/02/22/926600/0/en/Autohome-Inc-Announces-Transaction-Between-Shareholders-and-Board-Change.html.

14. Michael O'Dwyer, "China In-Depth: Digital Insurance Ecosystems," https://www.the-digital-insurer.com/china-in-depth-ecosystems-in-china/.
15. "Ping An to Buy Autohome Stake from Telstra for $1.6 Billion," April 15, 2016, https://www.bloomberg.com/news/articles/2016-04-15/ping-an-to-buy-stake-in-autohome-from-telstra-for-1-6-billion.
16. Tendayi Viki, "Innovation Versus R&D Spending," May 20, 2019, https://www.strategyzer.com/blog/innovation-versus-rd-spending.
17. Barry Jaruzelski, Robert Chwalik, and Brad Goehle, "What the Top Innovators Get Right," October 30, 2018, https://www.strategy-business.com/feature/What-the-Top-Innovators-Get-Right?gko=e7cf9.
18. Chris Wray, "Sony 2018-19 Financial Year Results – Most Profitable Year Ever," April 27, 2019, https://wccftech.com/sony-2018-19-financial-year-results/.
19. Steven J. Vaughan-Nichols, "What Does Microsoft Joining the Open Invention Network Mean for You?," October 11, 2018, https://www.zdnet.com/article/what-does-microsoft-joining-the-open-invention-network-mean-for-you/.
20. Surur, "Microsoft Finally Reveals How Many HoloLens Units Have Been Sold," April 25, 2018, https://mspoweruser.com/microsoft-finally-reveals-how-many-hololens-units-have-been-sold/.
21. Heather Kelly, "Microsoft's New $3,500 HoloLens 2 Headset Means Business," February 25, 2019, https://edition.cnn.com/2019/02/24/tech/microsoft-hololens-2/index.html.
22. Allison Linn, "Microsoft's Project Oxford Helps Developers Build More Intelligent Apps," May 1, 2015, https://blogs.microsoft.com/ai/microsofts-project-oxford-helps-developers-build-more-intelligent-apps/.
23. "Microsoft to Acquire GitHub for $7.5 Billion," June 4, 2018, https://news.microsoft.com/2018/06/04/microsoft-to-acquire-github-for-7-5-billion/.
24. Alex Hern and Jana Kasperkevic, "LinkedIn Bought by Microsoft for $26.2BN in Cash," June 13, 2016, London and New York, https://www.theguardian.com/technology/2016/jun/13/linkedin-bought-by-microsoft-for-262bn-in-cash.
25. "Microsoft Google Amazon Cloud Acquisitions," https://app.cbinsights.com/login?status=session&goto=https%3A%2F%2Fapp.cbinsights.com%2Fresearch%2Fmicrosoft-google-amazon-cloud-acquisitions-expert-intelligence%2F.
26. Tom Warren, "Microsoft Wasted at Least $8 Billion on Its Failed Nokia Experiment," May 25, 2016, https://www.theverge.com/2016/5/25/11766540/microsoft-nokia-acquisition-costs.
27. Paul Thurrott, "To Grow, Microsoft Must Deemphasize Windows," February 04, 2014, https://www.itprotoday.com/compute-engines/grow-microsoft-must-deemphasize-windows.
28. Daniel B. Kline, "What Declining PC Sales Mean for Microsoft," May 9, 2016, https://www.fool.com/investing/general/2016/05/09/what-declining-pc-sales-mean-for-microsoft.aspx.
29. Tom Krazit, "Azure Revenue Remains a Mystery, but Cloud Services Continue to Drive Microsoft Forward," April 24, 2019, https://www.geekwire.com/2019/azure-revenue-remains-mystery-cloud-services-continue-drive-microsoft-forward/.
30. Tom Warren, "Microsoft and Amazon Release Preview of Cortana and Alexa Integration," August 15, 2018, https://www.theverge.com/2018/8/15/17691920/microsoft-amazon-alexa-cortana-integration-preview-features.
31. "Unilever's Purpose-Led Brands Outperform," November 6, 2019, https://www.unilever.com/news/press-releases/2019/unilevers-purpose-led-brands-outperform.html.
32. "Unilever Tightens Belt with Slim-Fast Sale," *The Telegraph*, January 20, 2020 https://www.telegraph.co.uk/finance/newsbysector/retailandconsumer/10960347/Unilever-tightens-belt-with-Slim-Fast-sale.html.

33. Unilever, "Acquisitions and Disposals," https://www.unilever.com/investor-relations/understanding-unilever/acquisitions-and-disposals/.
34. Milly Vincent, "Marmite, Pot Noodles and Magnums Face Being Sold by Unilever If They Can't Prove They Make 'Meaningful' Impact on the Planet," July 27 2019, https://www.dailymail.co.uk/news/article-7291997/Marmite-favourites-like-Pot-Noodles-Magnums-face-sold-Unilever.html.
35. Lance Whitney, "Logitech Confesses to 'Gigantic' Mistake with Google TV, November 11, 2011, https://www.cnet.com/news/logitech-confesses-to-gigantic-mistake-with-google-tv/.
36. Logitech Annual Report 2019.
37. Logitech, "Acquisitions," https://www.crunchbase.com/organization/logitech/acquisitions/acquisitions_list#section-acquisitions.
38. "Lifesize Splits from Logitech," January 14, 2016, https://www.lifesize.com/en/company/news/in-the-news/2016/20160114-comms-business-lifesize-splits-from-logitech.
39. Anton Shilov, "Logitech Formally Exits OEM Mouse Market," January 22, 2016, https://www.anandtech.com/show/9984/logitech-exits-oem-mouse-market.
40. "Inside the Storm Ep 2: Fujifilm," Channel News Asia, February 1, 2017, https://www.channelnewsasia.com/news/video-on-demand/inside-the-storm-s2/fujifilm-7824486.
41. Fjuifilm Annual Report 2019.
42. "Medium Term Management Plan VISION 75 (2008)," April 28, 2008, https://www.fujifilmholdings.com/en/pdf/investors/ff_vision75_2008_001.pdf.

INVENT

1. Jessica Caldwell, "Drive by Numbers – Tesla Model S Is the Vehicle of Choice in Many of America's Wealthiest Zip Codes," October 31, 2013, Edmunds.com.
2. Blue Ocean Strategy.
3. Fred Lambert, "Tesla Is Accelerating Supercharger Deployment, 10 More V3 Stations Confirmed," September 25, 2019, https://electrek.co/2019/09/25/tesla-accelerating-supercharger-deployment-v3-stations-confirmed/.
4. Alex Hern, "Tesla Motors Receives $10BN in Model 3 Pre-Orders in Just Two Days," April 4, 2016, *The Guardian*, https://www.theguardian.com/technology/2016/apr/04/tesla-motors-sells-10bn-model-3-two-days.
5. "Global Top 20 November 2019," December 27, 2019, http://ev-sales.blogspot.com/2019/12/global-top-20-november-2019.html.
6. Kevin P. Donovan, "Mobile Money, More Freedom? The Impact of M-PESA's Network Power on Development as Freedom," University of Cape Town, *International Journal of Communication* 6 (2012): 2647–2669.
7. "The Mobile Money Revolution: M-Pesa," Ben & Alex, June 15, 2018, https://medium.com/@benandalex/the-mobile-money-revolution-m-pesa-f3fc8f86dbc9.
8. Rob Matheson, "Study: Mobile-Money Services Lift Kenyans Out of Poverty," MIT News Office, December 8, 2016, https://news.mit.edu/2016/mobile-money-kenyans-out-poverty-1208.
9. "M-Pesa Users Outside Kenya Hit 13.4 Million," *Business Daily*, January 29, 2019, https://www.businessdailyafrica.com/corporate/companies/M-Pesa-users-outside-Kenya-hit-13-4-million/4003102-4956208-16s8a9/index.html.
10. World Bank, "What Kenya's Mobile Money Success Could Mean for the Arab World," October 3, 2018, https://www.worldbank.org/en/news/feature/2018/10/03/what-kenya-s-mobile-money-success-could-mean-for-the-arab-world.
11. Leo Van Hove and Antoine Dubus, "M-PESA and Financial Inclusion in Kenya: Of Paying Comes Saving?," MDPI, January 22, 2019.
12. "What Is M-Pesa?," https://www.vodafone.com/what-we-do/services/m-pesa.
13. "Mobile Currency in Kenya: the M-Pesa," CPI, March 21, 2016, https://www.centreforpublicimpact.org/case-study/m-currency-in-kenya/.

14. Sears Archives, http://www.searsarchives.com/history/history1890s.htm.
15. John Murray Brown and Arash Massoudi, "Unilever Buys Dollar Shave Club for $1BN," Financial Times, July 20 2016, https://www.ft.com/content/bd07237e-4e45-11e6-8172-e39ecd3b86fc.
16. Youtube – Dollar Shave Club, https://www.youtube.com/watch?v=ZUG9qYTJMsI.
17. Barbara Booth, "What Happens When a Business Built on Simplicity Gets Complicated? Dollar Shave Club's Founder Michael Dubin Found Out," CNBC, March 24, 2019, https://www.cnbc.com/2019/03/23/dollar-shaves-dubin-admits-a-business-built-on-simplicity-can-get-complicated.html.
18. Kat Eschner, "The Story of Brownie Wise, the Ingenious Marketer behind the Tupperware Party," Smithsonian.com, April 10, 2018, https://www.smithsonianmag.com/smithsonian-institution/story-brownie-wise-ingenious-marketer-behind-tupperware-party-180968658/.
19. Bob Kealing, *Life of the Party: The Remarkable Story of How Brownie Wise Built, and Lost …*, (New York: Crown/Archetype, 2008).
20. Dory Owens, "Tupperware Takes Its Parties into the Workplace," July 12, 1987, https://www.washingtonpost.com/archive/business/1987/07/12/tupperware-takes-its-parties-into-the-work-place/1cc29d20-49ff-4d63-94b4-32f46cbca15b/.
21. Kat Eschner, "The Story of Brownie Wise," https://www.smithsonianmag.com/smithsonian-institution/story-brownie-wise-ingenious-marketer-behind-tupperware-party-180968658/.
22. Avil Beckford, "Earl Tupper, Business Leader, Invented Tupperware, Air-Tight Plastic Containers," February 15, 2013, https://theinvisiblementor.com/earl-tupper-business-leader-invented-tupperware-air-tight-plastic-containers/.
23. Natura & Co. 2018 report, https://naturaeco.com/report_2018_en.pdf.
24. Microsoft Windows history, updated November 16, 2019 by Computer Hope, https://www.computerhope.com/history/windows.htm.
25. Amy Stevenson, "Windows History: Windows 3.0 Takes Off," January 25, 2018, https://community.windows.com/en-us/stories/story-of-windows3.
26. Emil Protalinski, "OEMs Pay Microsoft about $50 for Each Copy of Windows," September 17, 2009, https://arstechnica.com/information-technology/2009/09/microsoft-oems-pay-about-50-for-each-copy-of-windows/.
27. James Gleick, "Making Microsoft Safe for Capitalism," November 5, 1995, https://www.nytimes.com/1995/11/05/magazine/making-microsoft-safe-for-capitalism.html.
28. "Microsoft Revenue by Year – Fiscal 1990–2019," https://dazeinfo.com/2019/11/11/microsoft-revenue-worldwide-by-year-graphfarm/.
29. Jacob Kastrenakes, "The Halo Franchise Has Made More Than $5 Billion, November 4, 2015, https://www.theverge.com/2015/11/4/9668876/halo-franchise-5-billion-guardians-launch-sales.
30. "Police Urge Google to Turn Off 'stalking' Feature on Mobile App for Drivers," Associated Press, Washington, January 27, 2015, https://www.theguardian.com/technology/2015/jan/26/police-pressure-google-turn-off-waze-app-feature.
31. TechCrunch, "Waze." (No data available for 2014–2016.)
32. Aaron Pressman and Adam Lashinsky, "Why Waze Doesn't Share Traffic Data with Google Maps – Data Sheet," October 11, 2019, https://fortune.com/2019/10/11/waze-google-maps-how-it-works/.
33. Kristen Hall-Geisler, "Waze and Esri Make App-to-Infrastructure Possible," AEDT, October 12, 2016, https://techcrunch.com/2016/10/11/waze-and-ezri-make-app-to-infrastructure-possible/.
34. Zhou Xin, Ed., "DiDi Completes 7.43 Bln Rides in 2017," Xinhua, January 8, 2008, http://www.xinhuanet.com/english/2018-01/08/c_136880236.htm.
35. "Didi Now Serves 550M Users 30M Rides per Day, Growing against Meituan Challenges," June 7, 2018, https://kr-asia

.com/didi-now-serves-550m-users-30m-rides-per-day-growing-against-meituan-challenges.

36. Jane Zhang, "Didi by the Numbers: Ride-Hailing Firm Covered More Miles in 2018 Than 5 Earth-to-Neptune Round-Trips," January 23, 2019, https://www.scmp.com/tech/start-ups/article/2181542/didi-numbers-ride-hailing-firm-covered-more-miles-2018-5-earth.
37. Chloe Sorvino, "Inside Billionaire James Dyson's Reinvention Factory: From Vacuums to Hair Dryers and Now Batteries," September 13, 2016, https://www.forbes.com/sites/chloesorvino/2016/08/24/james-dyson-exclusive-top-secret-reinvention-factory/.
38. Michael Pooler and Peggy Hollinger, "Dyson's Perfectionists Invent a Future beyond Vacuum Cleaners, February 8, 2017, https://www.ft.com/content/2041b5b2-ec75-11e6-ba01-119a44939bb6.
39. Sophie Chapman, "Dyson Reaches Record Profits in 2017, Hitting £801MN," March 02, 2018, https://www.manufacturingglobal.com/leadership/dyson-reaches-record-profits-2017-hitting-ps801mn.
40. Brian Dolan, *Wedgwood: The First Tycoon* (New York : Viking, 2004).
41. "Model T," *Encyclopaedia Britannica*, December 5, 2019, https://www.britannica.com/technology/Model-T.
42. "Henry Ford with Ten-Millionth Ford Model T and 1896 Quadricycle, 1924," https://www.thehenryford.org/collections-and-research/digital-collections/artifact/276378/.
43. "100 Years of the Moving Assembly Line," https://corporate.ford.com/articles/history/100-years-moving-assembly-line.html.
44. "Ford's Assembly Line Starts Rolling," November 13, 2009, https://www.history.com/this-day-in-history/fords-assembly-line-starts-rolling.
45. "Ford's Assembly Line Turns 100: How It Changed Manufacturing and Society," *New York Daily News*, October 7, 2013, https://www.nydailynews.com/autos/ford-assembly-line-turns-100-changed-society-article-1.1478331.
46. Mary Hanbury, "We Went Inside One of the Sprawling Factories Where Zara Makes Its Clothes. Here's How the World's Biggest Fashion Retailer Gets It Done," October 29, 2018, https://www.businessinsider.com.au/how-zara-makes-its-clothes-2018-10?r=US&IR=T.
47. Seth Stevenson, "Polka Dots Are In? Polka Dots It Is!," June 21, 2012, https://slate.com/culture/2012/06/zaras-fast-fashion-how-the-company-gets-new-styles-to-stores-so-quickly.html.
48. Dell Inc. history, http://www.fundinguniverse.com/company-histories/dell-inc-history/.
49. Liam O'Connell, "Annual Revenue of IKEA worldwide from 2001 to 2019," October 15, 2019, https://www.statista.com/statistics/264433/annual-sales-of-ikea-worldwide/.
50. Liam O'Connell, "Number of Visits to IKEA Stores Worldwide from 2010 to 2019," October 15, 2019, https://www.statista.com/statistics/241828/number-of-visits-to-ikea-stores-worldwide/.
51. "Why Is IKEA So Successful?," July 12, 2018, https://furnitureblog.simplicitysofas.com/blog/why-is-ikea-so-successful/.
52. Jan-Benedict Steenkamp, Global Brand Strategy: World-Wise Marketing in the Age of Branding (New York: Springer 2017).
53. "Quantity of Furniture U.S. Homeowners Bought from IKEA in the Last Decade 2016, Statista Research Department, September 3, 2019, https://www.statista.com/statistics/618639/quantity-of-furniture-us-homeowners-bought-from-ikea-in-the-last-decade/.
54. IBM Newsroom, "IBM Closes Landmark Acquisition of Red Hat for $34 Billion; Defines Open, Hybrid Cloud Future, Armonk, NY and Raleigh, NC, July 9, 2019, https://newsroom.ibm.com/2019-07-09-IBM-Closes-Landmark-Acquisition-of-Red-Hat-for-34-Billion-Defines-Open-Hybrid-Cloud-Future.
55. Gary Sims, "ARM's Rise from a Small Acorn to a World Leader," May 19, 2014, https://www.androidauthority

.com/arms-rise-small-acorn-world-leader-376606/.
56. Kristin Bent, "ARM Snags 95 Percent of Smartphone Market, Eyes New Areas for Growth," July 16, 2012, https://www.crn.com/news/components-peripherals/240003811/arm-snags-95-percent-of-smartphone-market-eyes-new-areas-for-growth.htm.
57. Arash Massoudi, James Fontanella-Khan, and Richard Waters, "SoftBank to Acquire UK's ARM Holdings for £24.3BN," July 19 2016, https://www.ft.com/content/235b1af4-4c7f-11e6-8172-e39ecd3b86fc.
58. "Dan Swinhoe,"UK Government Gives £36 Million to ARM to Develop Secure Chips," October 24 2019, https://www.csoonline.com/article/3447856/uk-government-gives-36-million-to-arm-to-develop-secure-chips.html.
59. ARM Annual Report and Accounts 2009, http://www.annualreports.com/HostedData/AnnualReportArchive/a/LSE_ARM_2009.pdf.
60. ARM Annual Report and Accounts 2018.
61. Jenna Goudreau, "Disney Princess Tops List of the 20 Best-Selling Entertainment Products," https://www.forbes.com/sites/jennagoudreau/2012/09/17/disney-princess-tops-list-of-the-20-best-selling-entertainment-products/.
62. Victoria Sherrow, *Encyclopedia of Hair: A Cultural History* (Westport, CT: Greenwood Publishing Group, 2006).
63. Martha Matilda Harper, National Women's Hall of Fame, https://www.womenofthehall.org/inductee/martha-matilda-harper/.
64. "Martha Matilda Harper: Servant Girl to Beauty Entrepreneur," https://racingnelliebly.com/strange_times/servant-girl-beauty-entrepreneur/.
65. Jaimie Seaton, "Martha Matilda Harper, The Greatest Business Woman You've Never Heard Of," January 11, 2017, https://www.atlasobscura.com/articles/martha-matilda-harper-the-greatest-businesswoman-youve-never-heard-of.
66. "National Economic Impact of Franchising," International Franchise Association, https://franchiseeconomy.com/.
67. Clive Thompson, "How the Photocopier Changed the Way We Worked—and Played," March 2015, https://www.smithsonianmag.com/history/duplication-nation-3D-printing-rise-180954332/.
68. "Xerox Introduces the First Photocopier," November 28, 2019, https://www.encyclopedia.com/science/encyclopedias-almanacs-transcripts-and-maps/xerox-introduces-first-photocopier.
69. Daniel Gross, "Betting the Company: Joseph Wilson and the Xerox 914 from Forbes Greatest Business Stories of All Time," https://www.stephenhicks.org/wp-content/uploads/2012/01/forbes-xerox.pdf.
70. Alex Hutchinson, *Big Ideas: 100 Modern Inventions That Have Transformed Our World* (New York: Sterling Publishing, 2009).
71. "Xerox 914 Plain Paper Copier," National Museum of American History, https://americanhistory.si.edu/collections/search/object/nmah_1085916.
72. "The Story of Xerography," https://www.xerox.com/downloads/usa/en/s/Storyofxerography.pdf.
73. Louis Columbus, "The State of the Subscription Economy, 2018," Forbes, https://www.forbes.com/sites/louiscolumbus/2018/03/04/the-state-of-the-subscription-economy-2018/.
74. "Activating Brave," Intrabrand, https://www.interbrand.com/best-brands/best-global-brands/2018/articles/activating-brave/.
75. James Cowling, "Kodak: From Brownie and Roll Film to Digital Disaster," BBC News, January 20, 2012, https://www.bbc.com/news/business-16627167.
76. John McDonough and Karen Egolf, *The Advertising Age Encyclopedia of Advertising,* (Chicago, IL: Fitzroy Dearborn Publishers, 2002).
77. Jason Farago, "Our 'Kodak Moments' – and Creativity – Are Gone," August 23, 2013, https://www.theguardian.com/commentisfree/2013/aug/23/photography-photography.

78. David Usborne, “The Moment It All Went Wrong for Kodak,” January 20, 2012, https://www.independent.co.uk/news/business/analysis-and-features/the-moment-it-all-went-wrong-for-kodak-6292212.html.
79. Jorn Lyseggen, *Outside Insight: Navigating a World Drowning in Data* (London: Penguin, 2016).
80. Mansoor Iqbal, “Spotify Usage and Revenue Statistics (2019),” May 10, 2019, https://www.businessofapps.com/data/spotify-statistics/.
81. Becky Peterson, “Spotify Has Spent $10 Billion on Music Royalties since Its Creation and It’s a Big Part of Why It’s Bleeding Money,” March 1, 2018, https://www.businessinsider.com.au/spotify-has-spent-10-billion-on-music-licensing-and-revenue-since-it-started-2018-2?r=US&IR=T.
82. Monica Mercuri, “Spotify Reports First Quarterly Operating Profit, Reaches 96 Million Paid Subscribers,” https://www.forbes.com/sites/monicamercuri/2019/02/06/spotify-reports-first-quarterly-operating-profit-reaches-96-million-paid-subscribers/.
83. “Spotify Technology S.A. Announces Financial Results for Second Quarter 2019,” July 31, 2019, https://investors.spotify.com/financials/press-release-details/2019/Spotify-Technology-SA-Announces-Financial-Results-for-Second-Quarter-2019/default.aspx.
84. Mark Mulligan, “Spotify Q4 2018: Solid Growth with a Hint of Profitability but Longer Term Questions,” February 14, 2019, https://www.midiaresearch.com/blog/spotify-q4-2018-solid-growth-with-a-hint-of-profitability-but-longer-term-questions/.
85. Paul Sawers, “Spotify Grows Users 30% in Q3 2019, Premium Subscribers Reach 113 Million,” October 28, 2019, https://venturebeat.com/2019/10/28/spotify-grows-users-30-in-q3-2019-premium-subscribers-reach-113-million/.
86. Ariel, “Spotify Was Downloaded on 25 Million iPhones in the U.S. in 2018,” October 23, 2018, https://blog.appfigures.com/pandora-chases-spotify-but-spotify-charges-ahead/.
87. Keith Caulfield, “2019 U.S. On-Demand Audio Streams Surpass Half-Trillion, Ariana Grande’s ‘Thank U, Next’ First Album to Reach 2 Billion Streams This Year,” September 21, 2019, https://www.billboard.com/articles/business/chart-beat/8530681/2019-on-demand-audio-streams-surpass-half-trillion-ariana-grande.
88. Kayleigh Vanandelmdy, “Case Study: How Spotify Achieves Astonishing 46% Conversion Rate from Free to Paid,” October 08, 2019, https://growthhackers.com/articles/case-study-how-spotify-achieves-astonishing-46-conversion-rate-from-free-to-paid.
89. “Fortnite Phenomenon Turns a Game Developer into a Billionaire,” July 24, 2018, https://adage.com/article/media/fortnite-phenomenon-turns-game-developer-into-a-billionaire/314357.
90. Catherine New, “How Much Are People Making from the Sharing Economy?,” June 13, 2017, https://www.earnest.com/blog/sharing-economy-income-data/.
91. Airbnb Newsroom Fast Facts, https://news.airbnb.com/fast-facts/.
92. S. Lock, “Share of Leisure and Business Travelers using Airbnb in the United States and Europe from 2015 to 2018,” January 16, 2019, https://www.statista.com/statistics/795675/travelers-using-airbnb/.
93. Zack Quaintance, “A First in 2018: American Consumers Spent More on Airbnb Than on Hilton,” April 13, 2019, https://tophotel.news/a-first-in-2018-american-consumers-spent-more-on-airbnb-than-on-hilton/.
94. Parmy Olson, “Exclusive: The Rags-To-Riches Tale of How Jan Koum Built WhatsApp into Facebook’s New $19 Billion Baby,” February 19, 2014, forbes.com/sites/parmyolson/2014/02/19/exclusive-inside-story-how-jan-koum-built-whatsapp-into-facebooks-new-19-billion-baby/.

95. Ryan Bushey, "Texting App WhatsApp Now Has 400 Million People Using It Every Month," December 20, 2013, https://www.businessinsider.com.au/whatsapp-400-million-users-2013-12?r=US&IR=T.
96. Dominic Rushe, "WhatsApp: Facebook Acquires Messaging Service in $19BN Deal," February 20, 2014, https://www.theguardian.com/technology/2014/feb/19/facebook-buys-whatsapp-16bn-deal.
97. Diane Dragan, "10 Outrageous Markups You'd Never Guess You Were Paying," rd.com/advice/saving-money/10-outrageous-markups-youd-never-guess-you-were-paying/.
98. Mansoor Iqbal, "WhatsApp Revenue and Usage Statistics (2019)," February 19, 2019, https://www.businessofapps.com/data/whatsapp-statistics/.
99. "Mobile messaging volumes in the U.S. from 2004 to 2014," https://www.statista.com/statistics/215776/mobile-messaging-volumes-in-the-us/.
100. Charles Arthur, "App Messaging Damages Mobile Networks' Text Revenues," April 29, 2013, https://www.theguardian.com/technology/2013/apr/29/app-messaging-damages-mobile-text-revenues.
101. Citizen M Hotel Bankside London, https://archello.com/project/citizen-m-hotel-bankside-london.
102. Matylda Krzykowski, "CitizenM by Concrete," November 7, 2008, dezeen.com/2008/11/07/citizenm-by-concrete/.
103. W. Chan Kim and Renée Mauborgne, "How CitizenM Created New Market Space in the Hotel Industry," https://www.blueoceanstrategy.com/blog/citizenm-hotels-a-blue-ocean-chain-in-a-red-ocean-industry/.
104. "Hotels That Arrive Prebuilt: How CitizenM Manufactures Its Buildings," December 15, 2017, https://www.wired.co.uk/article/hotels-that-arrive-prebuilt.
105. "CitizenM Celebrates Yet Another Year of Affordable Luxury," https://www.citizenm.com/news/citizenm-celebrates-yet-another-year-of-affordable.
106. "A Million New iPhones Sold in the First Weekend," Reuters, July 15, 2008, https://www.nytimes.com/2008/07/15/technology/15apple.html.
107. Matthew Jones, "iPhone History: Every Generation in Timeline Order," September 14, 2014, https://historycooperative.org/the-history-of-the-iphone/.
108. Bill of Materials from Techinsights; Apple Product Announcements.
109. Chuck Jones, "Apple's iPhone: Why Care about Units When It Captures All the Profits," https://www.forbes.com/sites/chuckjones/2015/11/16/apples-iphone-why-care-about-units-when-it-captures-all-the-profits/.
110. J. Clement, "Number of Apps Available in Leading App Stores 2019," October 9, 2019, https://www.statista.com/statistics/276623/number-of-apps-available-in-leading-app-stores/.
111. Sam Costello, "How Many iPhones Have Been Sold Worldwide?," December 27, 2019, https://www.lifewire.com/how-many-iphones-have-been-sold-1999500.
112. How citizenM Created New Market Space in the Hotel Industry By W. Chan Kim & Renée Mauborgne https://www.blueoceanstrategy.com/blog/citizenm-hotels-a-blue-ocean-chain-in-a-red-ocean-industry/
113. CitizenM by Concrete Matylda Krzykowski | 7 November 2008 https://www.dezeen.com/2008/11/07/citizenm-by-concrete/ \h https://www.dezeen.com/2008/11/07/citizenm-by-concrete/
114. Innovation Management: Effective Strategy and Implementation By Keith Goffin, Rick Mitchell 2017 Palgrave
115. OneConnect moves up in the 2019 IDC Financial Insights FinTech Rankings Top 100 list October 11, 2019 https://finance.yahoo.com/news/oneconnect-moves-2019-idc-financial-130700278.html

116. Ping An Fintech Vehicle OneConnect Plans to List in New York by as Soon as September: Domestic Reports China Banking News http://www.chinabankingnews.com/2019/06/18/ping-ans-fintech-vehicle-oneconnect-plans-to-list-in-new-york-by-september-domestic-reports/
117. finleap connect partners with OneConnect to bring superior technology to Europe Aug 26, 2019, https://www.prnewswire.com/news-releases/finleap-connect-partners-with-oneconnect-to-bring-superior-technology-to-europe-300906797.html
118. Why banks can't delay upgrading core legacy banking platforms https://www.ey.com/en_gl/people/keith-pogson \h Keith Pogson 18 Jun 2019 https://www.ey.com/en_gl/banking-capital-markets/why-banks-can-t-delay-upgrading-core-legacy-banking-platforms
119. Ping An Accelerates Digital Transformation in Indonesia's Finance Industry 21 February 2019 https://www.bloomberg.com/press-releases/2019-02-20/ping-an-accelerates-digital-transformation-in-indonesia-s-finance-industry
120. An Overview of Pingan's OneConnect Will Huyler, May 20 2019 https://www.kapronasia.com/asia-banking-research-category/an-overview-of-pingan-s-oneconnect.html

IMPROVE

1. Ramon Casadesus-Masanell, Oliver Gassmann ,and Roman Sauer, "Hilti Fleet Management (A): Turning a Successful Business Model on Its Head," September 2018, https://www.hbs.edu/faculty/Pages/item.aspx?num=52550.
2. Dr. Christoph Loos, CEO of Hilti, correspondence.
3. Michelle Castillo, "Reed Hastings' Story about the Founding of Netflix Has Changed Several Times," May 23, 2017, https://www.cnbc.com/2017/05/23/netflix-ceo-reed-hastings-on-how-the-company-was-born.html.
4. Todd Spangler, "Netflix Spent $12 Billion on Content in 2018. Analysts Expect That to Grow to $15 Billion This Year," January 18, 2019, https://variety.com/2019/digital/news/netflix-content-spending-2019-15-billion-1203112090/.
5. Lauren Feiner, "Netflix Says It Has 10% of All TV Time in the US and Discloses Some Colossal Numbers for Its Shows," January 17, 2019, https://www.cnbc.com/2019/01/17/netflix-how-many-people-watch-bird-box.html.
6. Amy Watson, "Number of Netflix Paid Streaming Subscribers Worldwide 2011–2019," October 18, 2019, https://www.statista.com/statistics/250934/quarterly-number-of-netflix-streaming-subscribers-worldwide/.
7. J. Clement, "Number of Available Apps in the Apple App Store 2008–2017," September 12, 2018, https://www.statista.com/statistics/263795/number-of-available-apps-in-the-apple-app-store/.
8. Alex Guyot, "A Decade on the App Store: From Day One Through Today," July 11, 2018, https://www.macstories.net/news/a-decade-on-the-app-store-from-day-one-through-today/.
9. Mike Wuerthele, "Apple Has Paid Out $120 Billion to Developers since 2008," January 28, 2019, https://www.macstories.net/news/a-decade-on-the-app-store-from-day-one-through-today/.
10. Dedicated Video Games Sales Units, September 30, 2019, https://www.nintendo.co.jp/ir/en/finance/hard_soft/.
11. "TED Reaches Its Billionth Vdeo View!," November 13, 2012, https://blog.ted.com/ted-reaches-its-billionth-video-view/.
12. "History of TED," https://www.ted.com/about/our-organization/history-of-ted.
13. "TED," https://www.ted.com/talks.
14. "TED Opens Annual Conference in Vancouver as Media Platform Sees Record Global Audience Growth," April 10, 2018, https://blog.ted.com/ted-opens-annual-conference-in-vancouver-as-media-platform-sees-record-global-audience-growth/.
15. Intel Annual Report 1993, https://www.intel.com/content/www/us/en/history/history-1993-annual-report.html.

16. "Worldwide Semiconductor Revenue Grew 2.6 Percent in 2016," Stamford, CT, May 15, 2017, https://www.gartner.com/en/newsroom/press-releases/2017-05-15-worldwide-semiconductor-revenue-grew-2-percent-in-2016-according-to-final-results-by-gartner.
17. Intel Annual report 1991, https://www.intel.com/content/www/us/en/history/history-1991-annual-report.html.
18. Intel Corporation History, http://www.fundinguniverse.com/company-histories/intel-corporation-history/.
19. Jim Dalrymple, "Apple Stores See 300 Million Visitors in FY 2012, 50,000 Genius Bar Visits a Day," August 20, 2012, https://www.loopinsight.com/2012/08/20/apple-stores-see-300-million-visitors-in-2012-50000-genius-bar-visits-a-day/.
20. Fujifilm Annual report 2006.
21. Fujifilm Annual Report 2019.
22. "Inside the Storm Ep 2: Fujifilm," Channel News Asia, February 1, 2017, https://www.channelnewsasia.com/news/video-on-demand/inside-the-storm-s2/fujifilm-7824486.
23. Jake Nielson, "Story of Kodak: How They Could Have Saved the Business," August 22, 2014, https://www.ignitionframework.com/story-of-kodak/.
24. Telecom Regulatory Authority of India, New Delhi, December 30, 2019, https://main.trai.gov.in/sites/default/files/PR_No.128of2019.pdf.
25. Vijay Govindarajan, "Telecom's Competitive Solution: Outsourcing?," May 08, 2012, https://hbr.org/2012/05/telecoms-competitive-solution-outsourcing.
26. Steven J. Vaughan-Nichols, "What Does Microsoft Joining the Open Invention Network Mean for You?," October 11, 2018, https://www.zdnet.com/article/what-does-microsoft-joining-the-open-invention-network-mean-for-you/.
27. "Microsoft to Acquire GitHub for $7.5 Billion," June 4, 2018, https://news.microsoft.com/2018/06/04/microsoft-to-acquire-github-for-7-5-billion/.
28. "Microsoft Is the Largest Single Corporate Contributor to Open Source on Github," https://ballardchalmers.com/2018/05/07/microsoft-largest-single-corporate-contributor-open-source-github/.
29. Brooks Barnes, "Disney Is Spending More on Theme Parks Than It Did on Pixar, Marvel and Lucasfilm Combined," November 16, 2018, https://www.nytimes.com/interactive/2018/11/16/business/media/disney-invests-billions-in-theme-parks.html.
30. Linda Rosencrance, "Dow Corning Launches Business Unit, Xiameter," March 14, 2002, https://www.computerworld.com/article/2587477/dow-corning-launches-business-unit--xiameter.html.
31. Bruce Meyer, "Xiameter Business a Web Success Story," August 23, 2011, https://www.rubbernews.com/article/20110823/NEWS/308239996/xiameter-business-a-web-success-story.
32. "Two-Brand Strategy Spells Success for Dow Corning," Noria Corporation, https://www.reliableplant.com/Read/5144/two-br-strategy-spells-success-for-dow-corning.
33. "Adobe Profit Margin 2006–2019," https://www.macrotrends.net/stocks/charts/ADBE/adobe/profit-margins.
34. Itu Rathore, "Adobe Quarterly Subscription Revenue by Segment," November 7, 2019, https://dazeinfo.com/2019/11/07/adobe-quarterly-subscription-revenue-by-segment-graphfarm/.
35. John Markoff, "Company Reports; Apple's First Annual Profit Since 1995," October 15, 1998, https://www.nytimes.com/1998/10/15/business/company-reports-apple-s-first-annual-profit-since-1995.html.
36. "Apple Announces That 800,000 iMacs Sold/ 45% of Buyers New to Mac," January 6, 1999, https://www.macobserver.com/news/99/january/990106/800000imacs.html.
37. Doug Bartholomew, "What's Really Driving Apple's Recovery?," March 16, 1999, https://www.industryweek.com/leadership/companies-executives/article/21960994/whats-really-driving-apples-recovery.

38. "The Transformation 20: The Top Global Companies Leading Strategic Transformations," September 2019, https://www.innosight.com/insight/the-transformation-20/.
39. Ørsted ESG Performance Report 2018, https://orsted.com/-/media/Annual_2018/Orsted_ESG_performance_report_2018.ashx?la=en&hash=315A4E48E0AD794B64B9A-C56EE7ED2F1.
40. 2018 Annual Report Rolls-Royce Holdings PLC.
41. Amy Mitchell, Mark Jurkowitz, and Emily Guskin, "The Washington Post: By the Numbers," August 7, 2013, https://www.journalism.org/2013/08/07/the-washington-post-by-the-numbers/.
42. Joshua Benton, "The L.A. Times' Disappointing Digital Numbers Show the Game's Not Just about Drawing in Subscribers – It's about Keeping Them," July 31, 2019, https://www.niemanlab.org/2019/07/the-l-a-times-disappointing-digital-numbers-show-the-games-not-just-about-drawing-in-subscribers-its-about-keeping-them/.
43. "The Washington Post Records 86.6 Million Unique Visitors in March 2019," April 18, 2019, https://www.washingtonpost.com/pr/2019/04/17/washington-post-records-million-unique-visitors-march/.
44. Matthew Kazin, "Delta's American Express Credit Card Helps Boost Airline's Bottom Line," https://www.foxbusiness.com/markets/deltas-american-express-credit-card-helps-boost-airlines-bottom-line.
45. "American Express and Delta Renew Industry-Leading Partnership, Lay Foundation to Continue Innovating Customer Benefits," https://news.delta.com/american-express-and-delta-renew-industry-leading-partnership-lay-foundation-continue-innovating.

Image Credits

TOOL

Bosch–Courtesy of Bosch
Gore–Courtesy of Gore

MANAGE

Amazon–Courtesy of Amazon

Ping An–Courtesy of Ping An
Sony Startup Accelerator Program–Courtesy of Sony
Microsoft–Courtesy of Microsoft
Unilever–Courtesy of Unilever
Logitech–Courtesy of Logitech
Fujifilm–Courtesy of Fujifilm

INVENT

Tesla–Courtesy of Tesla

Tesla–"2018 Tesla Model S 75D Taken in A464, Priorslee Road, Shifnal" by Vauxford / CC BY 4.0, https://commons.wikimedia.org/wiki/File:2018_Tesla_Model_S_75D.jpg

Toyota Prius–"Toyota Prius" by SPanishCoches / CC BY 2.0, https://www.flickr.com/photos/39302751@N06/6790397898

Smart Electric–"Smart Electric Drive" by John Karakatsanis / CC BY 2.0, https://www.flickr.com/photos/johnkarakatsanis/14408896673/in/photostream/

Dollar Shave Club–Dollar Shave Club youtube, https://www.youtube.com/watch?v=ZUG9qYTJMsI

Tupperware–Serious Partying, Tupperware Ad. Courtesy of the Smithsonian, National Museum of American History, https://americanhistory.si.edu/object-project/refrigerators/tupperware

Ikea–"Shopping at IKEA: backyard patio tiles" by osseous / CC BY 2.0, https://www.flickr.com/photos/10787737@N02/46561611371

Harper–(ca. 1914) Rear view of woman, possibly Martha Matilda Harper, with hair reaching down near her ankles., ca. 1914. [Photograph] Retrieved from the Library of Congress, https://www.loc.gov/item/2002698518/.

Xerox– Xerox 914 Plain Paper Copier. Courtesy of the Smithsonian, National Museum of American History, https://americanhistory.si.edu/collections/search/object/nmah_1085916

Kodak Brownie–"the Basic Brownie Camera" by Alan Levine / CC0 1.0, https://en.wikipedia.org/wiki/Brownie_(camera)#/media/File:2014-365-233_The_Basic_Brownie_Camera_(14809795240).jpg

Kodak Film–"Eastman Kodak Non Curling 116 Film by" by Thistle33 is licensed underCC BY-SA 4.0, https://commons.wikimedia.org/wiki/File:Kodak_NonCurling_1925.jpg#/media/File:Kodak_NonCurling_1925.jpg

Airbnb–Photo by Matthew T Rader on Unsplash, https://unsplash.com/photos/9ZaqDVDdMwg

citizenM–(a) Courtesy of citizenM (b) "citizenM" by Jumilla / CC BY 2.0, https://flic.kr/p/aSSQUe (c) Courtesy of citizenM

IMPROVE

Hilti–Courtesy of Hilti

Apple Genius Bar–"Genius Bar" by renatomitra / CC BY-SA 2.0, https://www.flickr.com/photos/33029569@N00/3554552146/

Direct to Consumer Trend

Apple Stores: "1373" by ptwo / CC BY 2.0, https://search.creativecommons.org/photos/45d908ee-a3d2-4ce4-85b9-babae4603d4a

Nespresso Boutique: Photo by Ayach Art on Pexels, https://www.pexels.com/photo/coffee-market-room-shop-453098/

Audemars Piguet: "Place de la Fusterie: magasin Audemars Piguet" by MHM55 / CC BY 4.0, https://commons.wikimedia.org/wiki/File:Place_de_la_Fusterie-03.jpg

Rise of Niche

Craft Beer: "Craft Beer Booze Brew Alcohol Celebrate Refreshment" / CC0 1.0, https://www.rawpixel.com/image/33597/premium-photo-image-beer-bar-alcohol

Co-branded credit card: "Amazon Prime Rewards Card" by Ajay Suresh / CC BY 2.0, https://commons.wikimedia.org/wiki/File:Amazon_Prime_Rewards_Card_(32861518627).jpg

Limited edition sneakers: Photo by Florian Olivo on Unsplash, https://unsplash.com/photos/5d4EhqeV0Og

Apple iMac–"Apple iMac G3 computer." by Musee Bolo / CC BY 2.0 France, https://upload.wikimedia.org/wikipedia/commons/2/22/IMac-IMG_7042.jpg

Orsted–Photo by Nicholas Doherty on Unsplash, https://unsplash.com/photos/pONBhDyOFoM

CULTURE

The Culture Map–Courtesy of David Gray

Amazon Innovation Culture–Courtesy of Amazon

Entrepreneurial Leadership and Team:

Elizabeth Arden–Library of Congress, Prints and Photographs Division, NYWT&S Collection, [LC-USZ62-123247] http://hdl.loc.gov/loc.pnp/cph.3c23247

Jack Ma–Jack Ma attends the 20th Anniversary Schwab Foundation Gala Dinner on September 23, 2018 in New York, NY USA. Copyright by World Economic Forum / Ben Hider / CC BY 2.0, https://commons.wikimedia.org/wiki/File:20th_Anniversary_Schwab_Foundation_Gala_Dinner_(44887783681).jpg

Anne Wojcicki–"TechCrunch Disrupt SF 2017 - Day 2" by Techcrunch / CC BY 2.0, https://www.flickr.com/photos/52522100@N07/36938473750/

Yvon Chouinard–"A photo of rock climber Yvon Chouinard." by Tom Frost / CC BY 2.0, https://commons.wikimedia.org/wiki/File:Yvon_Chouinard_by_Tom_Frost.jpg

Daniel Elk–Daniel Ek, CEO and Co-founder of Spotify, is interviewed by Andy Serwer of Fortune Magazine at Fortune Brainstorm TECH at the Aspen Institute Campus. Photograph by Stuart Isett/Fortune Brainstorm TECH / CC BY 2.0, https://commons.wikimedia.org/wiki/File:Fortune_Brainstorm_TECH_2011_(5961801428).jpg

Strive Masiyiwa–"Africa Progress Panel" by Rodger Bosch for APP / CC BY 2.0, https://www.flickr.com/photos/africaprogresspanel/8738568324/in/photostream/

Olive Ann Beech–"Beech, Olive Ann" by San Diego Air and Space Museum Archive, https://commons.wikimedia.org/wiki/File:Beech,_Olive_Ann.jpg

Cher Wang–"HTC Chairwoman, Cher Wang, shows off new mobile phone mother board" by Robert Scoble / CC BY 2.0, https://www.flickr.com/photos/scobleizer/2215637255

Carlos Slim–"Mexican businessman Carlos Slim Helú." by José Cruz/ABr / CC BY 3.0, https://commons.wikimedia.org/wiki/File:Carlos_Slim_Hel%C3%BA.jpg

Yang Lan–"Yang Lan" by World Economic Forum from Cologny, Switzerland / CC BY 2.0, https://zh.m.wikipedia.org/wiki/File:Yang_Lan_-_Annual_Meeting_of_the_New_Champions_2012.jpg

Kiichiro Toyoda–"Kiichiro Toyoda was an engineer in Japan.", https://de.m.wikipedia.org/wiki/Datei:Kiichiro_Toyoda.jpg

Jacqueline Novogratz–"Jacqueline Novogratz" by Acumen / CC BY 2.0, https://www.flickr.com/photos/acumenfund/38439020321/in/photostream/

Index

D

Q

R

S

T

Acknowledgments

This book would have been impossible to create without the love and support of our families, the Strategyzer team, the thinkers who inspired us, the practitioners who get things done, and everybody who gave us feedback.

We want to thank the core team who contributed to the book content and design, namely Lauren Cantor, Matt Woodward, and Erin McPhee.

A special thanks goes to all the thinkers and authors who inspired us, who we built upon, and many of whom gave us feedback. We'd like to particularly thank Dave Gray, Steve Blank, Rita McGrath, Roger Martin, Henry Chesbrough, Luis Felipe Cisneros Martinez, Scott Anthony, Bill Fischer, Saul Kaplan, and Marshall Goldsmith.

Several business and innovation leaders have taken time out of their agenda to contribute directly to case studies, namely Amy Calhoun, Bracken Darrell, Christoph Loos, Dave Liss, François-Henry Bennahmias, Uwe Kirschner, and Shinji Odashima.

The entire Strategyzer team has helped make this book possible and many projects had to take a step back to get this book done. The Strategyzer Advisory Team has put a particular effort into testing parts of the book. We thank Tendayi Viki, Shamira Miller, Paris Thomas, Greg Bernarda, Christian Doll, and Michael Wilkens.

We also thank the general community of Strategyzer coaches and innovation practitioners who helped test content, namely, Caroline Baumgart, Pete Cohen, Tim Daniel, Josie Gibson, John Hibble, and Nick Rakis.

We'd like to thank the executives who took time out of their agenda to test book content, namely, Sally Bateman, Vincent Besnard, Thierry Bonetto, Baudouin Corman, Carol Corzo, Eglantine Etiemble, Jay Jayamaran, Andrew Jenkin, Kate Koch, Tim Regan, Michel de Rovira, and Henning Trill.

Last but not least, we'd like to thank the entire Wiley team that has published all the books in the Strategyzer series, in particular, Richard Narramore, who took us on with *Business Model Generation*.

AUTHOR

Alex Osterwalder

Founder, Speaker, Business Thinker

Alex is a leading author, entrepreneur and in-demand speaker whose work has changed the way established companies do business and how new ventures get started. Ranked No. 4 of the top 50 management thinkers worldwide Alex also holds the Thinkers50 Strategy Award. Together with Yves Pigneur he invented the Business Model Canvas, Value Proposition Canvas, and Business Portfolio Map—practical tools that are trusted by millions of business practitioners.

@AlexOsterwalder
strategyzer.com/blog

COAUTHOR

Yves Pigneur

Professor, Business Thinker

Yves has been a professor at the University of Lausanne since 1984, and has held visiting professorships at Georgia State University, University of British Columbia, National University of Singapore, and HEC Montreal. Together with Alex Osterwalder, he invented the Business Model Canvas and co-authored the international bestselling books *Business Model Generation* and *Value Proposition Design*. Yves and Alex are ranked No. 4 among the Thinkers50's Most Influential Management Thinkers in the world and hold the Thinkers50 Strategy Award.

COAUTHOR

Fred Etiemble

Executive Advisor, Implementer

Fred is an executive advisor on strategy and innovation. He works with courageous leaders on how to develop an innovation culture, explore new growth engines, and transform their businesses. He has been working with or in large organizations for more than 20 years and knows their challenges from the inside. Fred co-creates tools and methodologies for strategy and innovation with other business thinkers and facilitates regular trainings on how to use them in Europe and Asia. Fred has been an associate at Strategyzer since 2017.

fredericetiemble.com

COAUTHOR

Alan Smith

Founder, Explorer, Designer

Alan uses his curiousity and creativity to ask questions and turn the answers into simple, visual, practical tools. He believes that the right tools give people confidence to aim high and build big meaningful things.

He cofounded Strategyzer with Alex Osterwalder, where he works with an inspired team to build great products. Strategyzer's books, tools, and services are used by leading companies around the world.

strategyzer.com

DESIGNER

Chris White

Designer, Art Director

Chris is a multidisciplinary designer who lives in Toronto. He has spent his time working on a number of business publications in various roles, most recently as Assistant Art Director at *The Globe and Mail,* focusing on presentation design for both print and online stories.

This is the first book he has collaborated on with the Stategyzer team.

DESIGNER

Trish Papadakos

Designer, Photographer, Creator

Trish holds a Master's in Design from Central St. Martins in London and a Bachelor's of Design from the York Sheridan Joint Program in Toronto.

She has taught design at her alma mater, worked with award-winning agencies, launched several businesses, and is collaborating for the fifth time with Strategyzer.

@trishpapadakos

CONTENT LEAD

Lucy Luo

Advisor, Problem Solver

Lucy is an innovation advisor to organizations large and small, helping them ideate and launch new products to seek breakthrough growth. She enjoys working with multinationals to build out and implement their innovation strategies as well as early-stage start-ups across Europe and Asia.

Lucy has a passion for addressing social and sustainability challenges through the use of innovation toolkits and has worked with a number of not-for-profit and social enterprise organizations such as the United Nations, the Atlantic Council, and World Economic Forum Global Shapers.

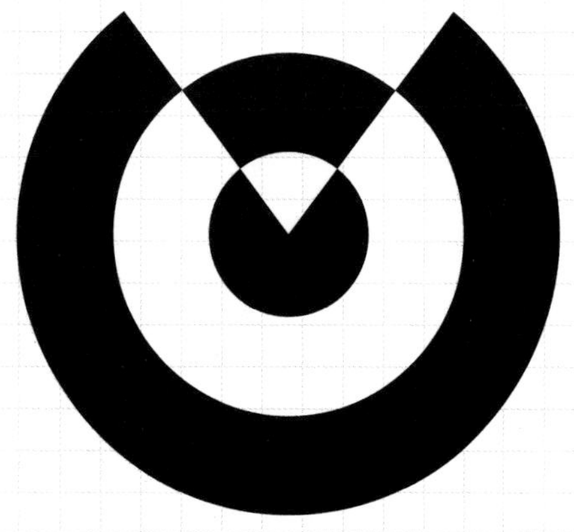

Strategyzer uses the best of technology and coaching to support your transformation and growth challenges.

Discover what we can do for you at Strategyzer.com

TRANSFORMATION

Create Change

Build skills at scale with the Strategyzer Cloud Academy course library and online coaching.

Mastering value propositions, mastering business models, mastering business testing, mastering culture, and mastering team alignment.

GROWTH

Create Growth

Systematize and scale your growth efforts, innovation culture, and business portfolio.

Innovation culture readiness assessment, growth strategy, growth funnel design and implementation, innovation management, coaching, and innovation metrics.